A
MAN
OF
IRON

The
Turbulent Life
and Improbable
Presidency *of*
GROVER
CLEVELAND

TROY SENIK

THRESHOLD EDITIONS
New York   London   Toronto   Sydney   New Delhi

Threshold Editions
An Imprint of Simon & Schuster, Inc.
1230 Avenue of the Americas
New York, NY 10020

First Threshold Editions hardcover edition September 2022

THRESHOLD EDITIONS and colophon are trademarks of Simon & Schuster, Inc.

For information about special discounts for bulk purchases, please contact Simon & Schuster Special Sales at 1-866-506-1949 or business@simonandschuster.com.

The Simon & Schuster Speakers Bureau can bring authors to your live event. For more information, or to book an event, contact the Simon & Schuster Speakers Bureau at 1-866-248-3049 or visit our website at www.simonspeakers.com.

Interior design by Davina Mock-Maniscalco

Manufactured in China

10 9 8 7 6 5 4 3 2 1

Library of Congress Cataloging-in-Publication Data

Names: Senik, Troy, author.
Title: A man of iron : the turbulent life and improbable presidency of Grover Cleveland / Troy Senik.
Other titles: Turbulent life and improbable presidency of Grover Cleveland
Description: First Threshold Editions hardcover edition. | New York : Threshold Editions, 2022. | Includes bibliographical references. |
Summary: "A long-overdue biography of Grover Cleveland, the honest, principled, plain-spoken, and incorruptible twenty-second and twenty-fourth president whose country has largely forgotten him"—Provided by publisher.
Identifiers: LCCN 2021041779 (print) | LCCN 2021041780 (ebook) | ISBN 9781982140748 (hardcover) | ISBN 9781982140779 (trade paperback) | ISBN 9781982140786 (ebook)
Subjects: LCSH: Cleveland, Grover, 1837-1908. | Presidents—United States—Biography.
Classification: LCC E697 .S46 2022 (print) | LCC E697 (ebook) | DDC 973.8/5092 [B]—dc23
LC record available at https://lccn.loc.gov/2021041779
LC ebook record available at https://lccn.loc.gov/2021041780

ISBN 978-1-9821-4074-8
ISBN 978-1-9821-4078-6 (ebook)

For Nan and Bampa,
who planted an acorn with faith that it would become an oak

"Watch well, then, this high office, the most precious possession of American citizenship. Demand for it the most complete devotion on the part of him to whose custody it may be entrusted, and protect it not less vigilantly against unworthy assaults from without."

—Grover Cleveland, on the presidency,
July 13, 1887,
Clinton, New York

CONTENTS

———◆◆◆———

Lewis F. Allen: Grover Cleveland's uncle and a leading citizen of Buffalo. Cleveland lived with Allen when he first relocated to the city, and Allen furnished him with introductions to the Buffalo legal community.

Edgar Apgar: New York's deputy treasurer and self-appointed talent scout for the Democratic Party. Apgar took notice of Cleveland's abilities during the latter's stint as mayor of Buffalo and was instrumental in his political rise.

George H. Ball: The Buffalo minister who first publicized the scandal regarding Cleveland's relationship with Maria Halpin, a revelation that became central to the 1884 presidential campaign.

Lyman K. Bass: Cleveland's friend and political rival from his early years in Buffalo. Bass defeated Cleveland in the 1865 election for district attorney of Erie County, at a time when the two men were roommates. Bass would later become one of Cleveland's law partners before serving two terms in the House of Representatives.

Thomas Bayard: The aristocratic Delaware senator who was one of Cleveland's rivals for the 1884 Democratic presidential nomination. He served as Cleveland's secretary of state in his first term and his ambassador to the United Kingdom in his second term.

Wilson "Shan" Bissell: Perhaps Cleveland's closest friend, the pair were law partners in Buffalo. Bissell would serve as Cleveland's postmaster general for part of his second term.

James G. Blaine: One of the leading Republican politicians of the late nineteenth century, Blaine served as Speaker of the House, U.S. senator, and secretary of state under Presidents Garfield and Benjamin Harrison. He was the Republican presidential nominee facing Cleveland in the mud-slinging presidential election of 1884.

Edward S. Bragg: A former brigadier general in the Union Army and Wisconsin congressman, his passionate speech in support of Cleveland at the 1884 Democratic convention marked the moment at which party enthusiasm for Cleveland reached a tipping point.

William Jennings Bryan: The Nebraska representative who became the most prominent figure among pro-silver Democrats during Cleveland's second term. He went on to be the Democratic Party's presidential nominee in 1896, 1900, and 1908, losing all three contests and earning Cleveland's enmity for his populist stances.

Samuel Burchard: The Presbyterian minister whose infamous "Rum, Romanism, and Rebellion" speech at a Blaine event in the dying days of the 1884 presidential campaign was blamed for turning public opinion against the Republican presidential nominee.

Benjamin Butler: The former Massachusetts governor and political chameleon who mounted an 1884 presidential campaign on the Greenback Party ticket. Butler's campaign was funded in part by Jay Gould in an attempt to keep Cleveland out of the White House.

Roscoe Conkling: The former New York senator and leading figure in the pro-patronage Stalwart movement who intervened in the state's Republican gubernatorial nomination process in 1882 and later withheld support from his nemesis Blaine in the 1884 presidential contest.

George Cortelyou: Cleveland's clerk during the second term of his presidency, hired despite the fact that he was a Republican. Cortelyou subsequently served in Theodore Roosevelt's cabinet and Cleveland entertained the idea of supporting him in the 1908 presidential election.

Richard Croker: "Honest John" Kelly's successor as Grand Sachem of New York's Tammany Hall political machine. Croker was instrumental in brokering a truce between Cleveland and the machine prior to the former's 1892 reelection to the presidency.

Eugene Debs: The labor leader who formed the American Railway Union and stood at the center of the Pullman Strike. Debs would be jailed for his role in the dispute and would later run for president repeatedly on the Socialist Party ticket.

E. J. Edwards: The New York correspondent of the *Philadelphia Press*, he managed to break the story of Cleveland's secret cancer surgery but was met with widespread ridicule and incredulity until the tale was verified by one of Cleveland's surgeons nearly twenty-five years later.

William C. Endicott: The former Massachusetts Supreme Court judge who served as Cleveland's secretary of war during his first term. It was Endicott who facilitated Cleveland's controversial (and later rescinded) decision to return Civil War battle flags to members of the regiments who fought under them.

Oscar Folsom: One of Cleveland's closest friends and one of his law partners in Buffalo. Upon Folsom's accidental death in 1875, Cleveland was given legal responsibility for his widow and young daughter, Frances, the latter of whom became Cleveland's wife a little over a decade later.

Augustus Garland: The Arkansas senator and former Confederate whose appointment as Cleveland's first-term attorney general was one of the president's gestures toward sectional reconciliation. Garland was Cleveland's main intermediary in the fight with the Senate over the Tenure of Office Act.

Richard Watson Gilder: The editor of *The Century Magazine* who became one of Cleveland's closest friends in his later years. Gilder later wrote a book containing previously unreported vignettes from Cleveland's personal life.

Jay Gould: The New York robber baron whom Cleveland spared, despite their political differences, with his gubernatorial veto of a bill that would have limited fares on Gould's elevated New York City railway.

Thomas Grady: A New York state legislator whose hot temper and close ties to Tammany Hall made him a perennial antagonist of Cleveland's.

Walter Q. Gresham: The federal appellate judge who was considered as an alternative to Benjamin Harrison for the 1888 Republican presidential nomination. He went on to serve as Cleveland's secretary of state in the second term before dying in office in 1895.

Maria Halpin: The widow with whom Cleveland carried on a romantic relationship in the years before his political ascent. Tales of the child that supposedly resulted from the relationship—and the rough treatment of both mother and son—dogged Cleveland during the 1884 presidential contest.

Benjamin Harrison: Cleveland's opponent in both the 1888 and 1892 presidential campaigns, Harrison's four years in the White House represented a sharp departure from many of the signature policies of Cleveland's first term.

Thomas Hendricks: Cleveland's first-term vice president, he had previously served as Samuel Tilden's running mate in the 1876 presidential contest. He died in office less than a year into Cleveland's term.

David B. Hill: Cleveland's lieutenant governor in New York, he would succeed him as governor and later become a U.S. senator. Hill grew into one of Cleveland's main political foes and was widely regarded as a potential presidential nominee for Democrats in 1892 before his overt ambition turned voters against him.

W. W. Keen: The renowned surgeon who took the lead on Cleveland's secret cancer surgery performed at sea. A written account of the procedure he produced years later provides most of the existing detail about the ordeal.

"Honest John" Kelly: The Grand Sachem of Tammany Hall, he was Cleveland's foremost political adversary during his governorship and his first run for the presidency. Laid low by illness, he died during Cleveland's first term in the White House.

Lucius Quintus Cincinnatus Lamar: A former Mississippi senator, he served as Cleveland's first term secretary of the interior, where he oversaw attempts to thwart the exploitation of Native Americans and western land. He left the role when Cleveland appointed him to the Supreme Court.

Daniel Lamont: Cleveland's indispensable political aide since his days as governor of New York, he served as secretary of war during the president's second term and remained one of his closest confidants.

Daniel Manning: Cleveland's political mentor, he played an essential role in his gubernatorial campaign and his first run for the presidency. He was Cleveland's first secretary of the Treasury before illness forced him from office and shortly thereafter claimed his life.

William McKinley: The Republican Ohio representative whose advocacy for a protective tariff put him at loggerheads with Cleveland over the issue. In 1896, he was elected as Cleveland's successor as president, an outcome the incumbent preferred to seeing William Jennings Bryan crowned the victor.

Richard Olney: The Massachusetts railroad lawyer who served, by turns, as attorney general and secretary of state during Cleveland's second term. Olney's truculent demeanor inflamed both the Pullman Strike and the diplomatic impasse with Britain over Venezuela.

George F. Parker: A Cleveland staffer whose organizational work laid the groundwork for the president's successful 1892 campaign. He later wrote a biography of Cleveland with the president's blessing.

John Sherman: The Republican Ohio senator and brother of General William Tecumseh Sherman who was one of the leading figures in the fight over silver coinage.

John L. Stevens: The U.S. minister to the Hawaiian Kingdom in the administration of Benjamin Harrison. His support for the overthrow of Queen Liliuokalani laid the predicate for the American attempts to annex the islands that Cleveland combatted during his second term.

Adlai E. Stevenson: A former Illinois congressman and assistant postmaster general in Cleveland's first term, he served as vice president during Cleveland's second term. A critic of Cleveland's views on silver, he was selected as running mate to bridge the ideological divides within the party for the 1892 presidential election.

John St. John: The former Kansas governor whose 1884 presidential candidacy on the Prohibition Party ticket played a key role in siphoning off Republican votes and handing the presidency to Cleveland.

Allen Thurman: The Ohio senator who was one of Cleveland's rivals for the 1884 presidential nomination. He was Cleveland's running mate and primary surrogate in the failed 1888 campaign, a race in which his advanced age led to clear strains on his health.

Samuel J. Tilden: The Democratic Party's presidential nominee in the 1876 campaign, his potential candidacy in 1884 was regarded as one of the foremost barriers to a Cleveland run. When he stood down, Cleveland was the natural second choice for his reform-minded supporters.

James B. Weaver: The former Iowa congressman whose 1892 campaign as the People's Party's presidential candidate earned him 22 electoral votes and foreshadowed the growing power of the populist movement.

William C. Whitney: Cleveland's first-term secretary of the Navy, he emerged as one of the most effective executives in the administration. He displayed a similar acumen in 1892, when he successfully managed the campaign that returned Cleveland to the White House.

William L. Wilson: The West Virginia representative who carried Cleveland's tariff reform bill in the second term and released the inflammatory letter in which the president denounced his fellow Democrats for abandoning their principles. After losing his seat in Congress, he served as postmaster general during Cleveland's final years in office.

Woodrow Wilson: The future commander in chief who worked alongside Cleveland at Princeton, where the former was the university's president and the latter was a member of the board of trustees. Though Wilson's scholarly work praised Cleveland's time in office, he would subsequently embrace a progressivism at odds with Cleveland's simple, conservative convictions.

A Man of Iron

H. L. Mencken could be a real pain in the ass. Through nearly a half century as one of America's leading social critics, he spared no figure of any public import, least of all presidents. When Franklin D. Roosevelt died, Mencken's remembrance of the thirty-second president included the phrase "He had every quality that morons esteem in their heroes."[1] He characterized Woodrow Wilson as a "pedagogue gone mashugga"* (*sic*).[2] Warren G. Harding was derided as "simply a third-rate political wheel horse with the face of a moving-picture actor, the intelligence of a respectable agricultural implement dealer, and the imagination of a lodge joiner."[3]

It is thus a matter of some note that Mencken, twenty-five years after the death of Grover Cleveland, opened a column about the former president this way: "We have had more brilliant Presidents than Cleveland, and one or two who were considerably more profound, but we have never had one, at least since Washington, whose fundamental character was solider [*sic*] and more admirable . . . [he] came into office his own man and he went without yielding any of that character for an instant."[4]

That praise, however, sounds discordant to modern ears. There's an implicit consensus in American life that we know who our great presi-

---

*"Meshugga" is a Yiddish word for "crazy."

dents are. We chisel them onto Mount Rushmore, slap them onto currency, and invoke their names as secular saints. Membership in that club is hard to come by, and commanders in chief who fail to make the cut are, especially with the passage of time, regarded as little more than historical detritus. When was the last time you heard the names of Zachary Taylor or Rutherford B. Hayes as anything other than *Jeopardy!* clues?

How then ought we to navigate the mention of Grover Cleveland in the same breath as George Washington, especially from a source so notoriously hard to please? The easiest explanation is that Mencken lacked adequate perspective; that this tribute is one of those superannuated embarrassments, like the (often repeated, but apocryphal) story of the patent commissioner who declared in the late 1800s that there was nothing left to invent.[5] This book, however, operates from a different assumption: Mencken was right and the rest of us are wrong.

To be sure, this volume does not claim that Grover Cleveland had one of America's greatest presidencies; but it does claim that, despite his many shortcomings, he was one of our greatest *presidents*. If that claim strikes you as paradoxical, then perhaps you have succumbed to the pathological way we've come to think about the office.

The presidents whose greatness is a matter of widespread assent were nearly all elevated to that pantheon by crisis. George Washington had to hold a young nation together and breathe life into the presidency on the fly. Abraham Lincoln prevented the dissolution of the republic, prosecuted a civil war, and ended slavery. Franklin Roosevelt navigated the Great Depression and World War II. We can, and should, be grateful that those men were there to meet those moments. But we also ought to be grateful that we don't need heroism on that scale very often. Most opportunities for presidential "greatness," after all, are also moments of extraordinary national hardship. In government, as in life, intermittent challenges on that scale can be character-forming. Persistent ones, however, would be debilitating.

If our definition of greatness is, by its very nature, exceptional—that is, contingent on circumstances that rarely arise—then it's worth asking how we should define presidential success in less dramatic times. Historians of the presidency tend to render judgment according to factors such as how much legislation a president successfully shepherds through Congress; how he performs as a foreign policy leader; and whether his presidency is possessed of an all-encompassing "vision." That approach, however, suffers from a crippling defect: it presumes we can judge all presidents by the standards of modern inhabitants of the office. Prior to the expansionist impulses of Theodore Roosevelt, Woodrow Wilson, and Franklin Roosevelt, the presidency, especially in peacetime, was widely understood to be a far more constrained office than it is today.

Judge them by volume or quality of legislation passed? That standard is difficult to apply to a world where the chief executive often stood apart from the work of Congress, his main contribution either a signature or a veto at the end of the legislative process. Indeed, even as late as William Howard Taft's tenure (1909–13) one can witness the president of the United States arguing that even *exerting political pressure* on Congress would be exceeding the constitutional limits of his office.[6] To be sure, earlier eras had their activists—no one would accuse Andrew Jackson, for example, of passivity—but they were the exception rather than the rule up through the end of the nineteenth century.

Judge them by foreign policy leadership? The America of the 1800s was not the world-bestriding colossus that dominated the twentieth century. Yes, there were occasional foreign wars, some consequential acts of diplomacy, and an ever-growing role in Latin America following the enunciation of the Monroe Doctrine. But for a nineteenth-century president it also wasn't unheard-of to have your signature foreign policy accomplishment be a treaty on fishing rights. Not exactly the kind of work that secures you a monument on the National Mall.

Judge them by the sweep of their "vision"? The concept would have been alien to many of our early presidents, men whose inaugural addresses often took the form of generalized observations about the country, tended to be overstuffed with stagy self-deprecation, and occasionally made explicit the executive's obligation to defer to Congress. While the presidency has always carried profound responsibilities, the notion of the chief executive as gnostic priest, imbued with the power to lead the nation to a future he's uniquely capable of seeing, finds little sanction in the constitutional design of the office. Indeed, Article II of the Constitution—the section of the document outlining the powers of the executive branch—is notable primarily for the modesty of the powers conveyed, especially on domestic matters. The mandate that the president "take care that the laws be faithfully executed" is hardly a "seers wanted" sign hanging in front of the White House.

So let us stipulate that Cleveland's greatness was not of the variety that sends sculptors racing for their marble (perhaps to the benefit of the nation's quarries, given that Cleveland topped out at 275 pounds). He was not a master strategist like Lincoln, a frenzied crusader like Theodore Roosevelt, or a philosopher-king like Thomas Jefferson. In fact, in every sense but the literal one, Grover Cleveland was not a larger-than-life figure. He was, in many ways, ordinary. And that was where his greatness resided.

Grover Cleveland didn't look like a president. He looked like a foundry foreman. With his hulking, oxlike physique, his walrus mustache, and his thinning hairline he probably seemed right at home in the German saloons he frequented during his decades in Buffalo. It's a difficult visage, however, to picture pacing the halls of the White House.

Grover Cleveland didn't sound like a president. While the decidedly masculine profile he cut seems suggestive of a booming, basso profundo voice, he actually spoke in a high, nasal tone that often took visitors by surprise.[7] And his utterly workmanlike rhetoric often plodded rather than soared. During a first-term speaking tour through the South and West, he literally lifted his speeches almost verbatim from encyclopedia entries on whichever town he was visiting.[8]

Grover Cleveland didn't have the pedigree of a president. He was the fifth of nine children, born in New Jersey and then shuttled around New York State to whichever locations were demanded by the vocation of his father, a Presbyterian minister. By the time he was sixteen, his father was dead and the welfare of the family, never possessed of means in the first place, rested largely on his shoulders. He would forgo college and work a string of odd jobs before settling in Buffalo and learning the law with a prominent local firm, living modestly in boardinghouses while much of the proceeds from his practice flowed back to his widowed mother and unmarried sisters.

Most remarkably, Grover Cleveland didn't have the ambition of a president. Imbued with a judicial temperament, his aspirations likely stopped at the New York bench.[9] Yet he was repeatedly summoned to run for office by others who saw in his reputation for honesty, integrity, and fearlessness the makings of a statesman. What followed was one of the most improbable journeys in American political history. At the age of forty-four, the only elected office Grover Cleveland had ever held was sheriff of Erie County, New York—a role he had relinquished nearly a decade earlier, returning to a rather uneventful life as a workaholic bachelor lawyer. In the next four years, he would become, in rapid succession, the mayor of Buffalo, the governor of New York, and the twenty-second president of the United States. Four years later, he would win the popular vote but nevertheless lose the presidency. And in another four, he'd become the first—and, to date, only—president to be returned to office after having been previously turned out.

What made that rise all the more remarkable was how at odds it was with the political trends of the day. Cleveland was the only Democrat elected president between James Buchanan in 1856 and Woodrow Wilson in 1912, an era as long as that separating the presidencies of John F. Kennedy and Donald Trump. And at a time when Democratic Party politics was still heavily influenced by New York's infamous Tammany Hall political machine, Cleveland ran—and governed—in opposition to corruption in all its forms, Democrat or Republican. As Edward S. Bragg remarked during a nominating speech for Cleveland at the 1884 Democratic convention, "we love him for the enemies he has made."

Grover Cleveland was precisely the kind of self-made, scrupulously honest man that Americans often say they want as their president. We had him for eight years. And, somehow, we forgot him.

Why the amnesia? One obvious factor is the era Cleveland inhabited. Ask the average American what happened in the years between Reconstruction and the presidency of Theodore Roosevelt and he's likely to stare at his shoes. More lettered types might mutter something about robber barons and cramped factory floors. But during his two stints in the White House, Cleveland had to contend with the largest economic depression the nation had seen up to that time; a coup in which American business interests overthrew the Hawaiian monarchy and attempted to have the island kingdom annexed by the United States; a massive labor strike that shut down much of the nation's rail traffic and led to rioting, industrial sabotage, and murder; a sweeping—and ultimately failed—attempt to rethink the country's relationship with Native Americans; a huge, party-splitting battle over whether Democrats should embrace economic populism; and an international crisis in which there were rumblings of war with Britain over the United Kingdom's ambitions in Venezuela. If this was a quotidian era, someone forgot to tell Grover Cleveland.

The abundance of story lines was not limited to official business. Cleveland came to office having endured a sex scandal during the 1884 presidential campaign, when he was accused of having fathered a child out of wedlock during his years as a Buffalo bachelor and subsequently having the mother institutionalized. His first term would be punctuated by a wedding (the only time a president has tied the knot in the White House) to the twenty-one-year-old daughter of his deceased law partner—a woman who had once been his ward. His second term included a secret cancer surgery, performed at sea under unthinkable conditions and concealed from the public for nearly a quarter century thereafter. We've had presidents known for moral probity and presidents known for tongue-wagging tabloid fodder. Grover Cleveland may be the only one who's given us both.

Another source of Cleveland's obscurity is the way he approached his office. Short of presiding over a moment of national tribulation, the best way for a president to endear himself to historians is to aggressively exercise his power to reshape the nation, often testing constitutional boundaries in the process. Grover Cleveland was both temperamentally and ideologically ill-suited for such aggrandizements. Even during his second term, when he adopted a considerably more aggressive leadership style, he always regarded his powers as circumscribed. He would be the final Democratic president to embrace the classical liberal principles of the party's founder, Thomas Jefferson. Cleveland believed in a narrow interpretation of the Constitution, a limited role for the federal government, and a light touch on economic affairs. To casual observers, such an approach is often mistaken for do-nothing passivity, a criticism that has been leveled at Cleveland with some regularity. That epithet, however, represents a fundamental misunderstanding of his presidency.

In fact, Cleveland arguably belongs to a presidential category of one: the reactive activist. True, his conception of presidential power was often negative in nature. He defined his role not as "leading" the American people but serving as their bulwark. But that was not a prescription for inertia. Indeed, Cleveland operated as a kind of ombudsman in chief. Over the course of his two terms, this led to an astonishing 584 vetoes, more than any other president save Franklin Roosevelt (who got to 635—in twelve years).[10] In his first term alone, Cleveland vetoed more bills than all twenty-one of his predecessors combined. Even during a two-year span of his second term when his own party controlled both houses of Congress, Cleveland still rejected eighty-one pieces of legislation.[11]

As a result, Grover Cleveland has become a minor icon for modern-day libertarians (and sympathetic conservatives). That interpretation has much to recommend it. Cleveland's faction of the Democratic Party was associated with laissez-faire capitalism, federalism, the gold standard, and anti-imperialism. *Mutatis mutandis*, they looked more like the modern right than the modern left. But as with most intergenerational comparisons in American politics, the analogy elides important distinctions. Cleveland, for instance, was the first president to put an American industry under federal regulation, with the Interstate Commerce Act giving Washington oversight of the railroads.[12] He also fretted over income inequality and signed the law allowing the federal incorporation of trade unions. It's an oversimplification to imagine that his convictions graft neatly enough onto contemporary politics to make him any partisan's dashboard saint.

In fact, the sense of ideological affinity that has kept Grover Cleveland's memory alive in certain minor precincts of modern America is, at best, a mixed blessing. It is preferable, of course, to having him entirely forgotten. But the defining features of Cleveland's greatness— a virulent opposition to corruption in all its forms; the willingness to follow principle regardless of the political consequences; the conviction, as he famously put it, that "a public office is a public trust"—have nothing sectarian about them. One does not have to share his politics to admire his character.

And indeed, even in his own day, plenty of people *did not* share Grover Cleveland's politics, a fact that would become only too apparent by the end of his presidency. As we inventory the reasons for his anonymity, one cannot overlook the fact that Cleveland's second term, marred by economic depression and labor unrest, precipitated (or at least accelerated) an historic realignment in American politics—*away* from his party. Democratic congressional losses in the 1894 midterms, the last of Cleveland's presidency, were so severe that future Speaker of the House Champ Clark referred to it as "the greatest slaughter of innocents since the days of King Herod."[13] The party would lose 125 seats in the House of Representatives alone, the largest such defeat in American history. The aftershocks were enduring. After Cleveland left the White House, Republicans won seven of the next nine presidential elections and Democrats abandoned his classical liberalism, which would go into hibernation before being rediscovered by the GOP later in the twentieth century.

Losses on that scale constitute a serious black mark on Cleveland the politician (though it is excessive to blame him for the shortcomings of future Democratic presidential candidates, only one of whom— Alton B. Parker in 1904—was an ideological kinsman). In a democracy it is idle to praise the virtues of a statesman who can't persuade the public. But we should not judge him entirely by that failure, either. The voters turned against him, after all, for standing firm on the same beliefs he held when they elected him—sound money, freer trade, and limited government interference in the economy. In some sense it was a testimony to his integrity: even at a moment of maximum political peril, Grover Cleveland's principles were not open for bidding. As Mencken remembered, "When enemies had at him they quickly found that his weight was the least of their difficulties; what really sent them sprawling was the fact that his whole huge carcass seemed to be made of iron. There was no give in him, no bounce, no softness. He sailed through American history like a steel ship loaded with monoliths of granite."

In over 230 years of the American presidency there's never been another figure quite like him: thoroughly unimpressed by the pretensions of politics, unwilling to jettison his core beliefs even when expediency or prudence may have counseled otherwise, unmoved by hate or scorn as long as he believed he was keeping faith with his principles.

ONE

He Did Not Shine

There is a perennial temptation to read the greatness of distinguished men backward into their youth; to imagine that, if one just knows where to look, their early lives will provide evidence that the fully formed person was there in microcosm all along. This mythmaking is especially prevalent with presidents: the (false) story of George Washington chopping down the cherry tree; a teenaged Andrew Jackson refusing to shine the boots of the British soldier who held him prisoner; a young Abraham Lincoln splitting rails by day and spending evenings educating himself by candlelight. The defining vignette for the young Grover Cleveland? Getting locked in an office.

On the very first day of his apprenticeship at the storied Buffalo law firm of Rogers, Bowen, & Rogers, nineteen-year-old Grover Cleveland, tucked in a corner with a copy of Blackstone's *Commentaries,* noticed that the office had gone quiet. Looking up from his book, he discovered an eminently reasonable explanation: the place was empty. So unremarkable was the new hire—at least that's how he interpreted it—that by the time midday had rolled around, everyone in the office had forgotten he existed. The lawyers headed out for lunch, locked the place up, and left the future president of the United States trapped inside.*

---

*Some versions of the story—perhaps too pat to be taken literally—have the young Cleveland consoling himself with "Someday I will be better remembered."

This was not an aberration in the life of the young Cleveland. The thin records that exist of his early years contain no hint that anyone saw him as destiny's child. Most accounts from those who knew him during his upbringing either emphasize his puritan virtues—self-discipline, a relentless work ethic, moral uprightness—or the playful side of the boy who enjoyed fishing (the subject of the only book he'd ever write) and practical jokes. No one, however, pegged him as a leader of men— or even an especially gifted figure. In the recollection of his sister Margaret, he was "a lad of rather unusual good sense, who did not yield to impulses—he considered well, and was resourceful—but as a student Grover did not shine. The wonderful powers of application and concentrations which afterwards distinguished his mental efforts were not conspicuous in his boyhood."[1]

That boyhood began on March 18, 1837, two weeks to the day that Andrew Jackson had been succeeded by Martin Van Buren, the first New York Democrat to serve as president. It's doubtful that the Reverend Richard F. Cleveland and his wife, the former Ann Neal, ever entertained any idea that their new son would be the second—not least because he wasn't yet a New Yorker.

Stephen Grover Cleveland was born in Caldwell, New Jersey, where his father was the pastor of the First Presbyterian Church. Despite the fact that the church dated back to the days of the Constitutional Convention, Richard, who had assumed the job only three years before Grover's birth, was just the second pastor in its history, his predecessor having tended to the flock since 1787. As if nearly a half century of service to his congregation wasn't legacy enough, that clergyman, Stephen Grover, would also wind up the namesake of an American president. The tribute, of course, would be diminished, as Cleveland—like Grant before him and Wilson, Coolidge, and Eisenhower* after—sloughed off his christening in favor of a more distinctive middle name. The only vestige

---

*Though the thirty-fourth president is often referred to as Dwight David Eisenhower, his birth name was David Dwight.

of his original appellation would come from the friends who referred to him as "Big Steve" (a slightly insensitive sobriquet, but gentler than the most frequently employed alternative: "Uncle Jumbo").

Grover's New Jersey birth—and his eventual failure to become a man of the cloth—marked him as an anomaly in the family tree. The Cleveland line had first come to the New World in 1635, when a Moses "Cleaveland" made the journey from the English town of Ipswich to Massachusetts.[2] In the two centuries that passed between Moses's first breath of North American air and Grover's, there were two constants in the Cleveland line: New England and the church. The Clevelands were generally to be found in Connecticut and Massachusetts, and usually behind a pulpit. As George Frederick Parker, who acted as a kind of authorized biographer for the president, noted in 1909, "As in a Puritan society it generally required only about two generations, from the beginning, to start the development of the ministerial habit, so it was in the Cleveland family. Since that time no generation has passed without one or more of the name in the ministry of some of the Protestant churches—generally Congregational or Presbyterian."[3]*[4]

Despite the modest circumstances of Grover's own upbringing, the family line was not without distinction. The president's great-great-grandfather, Aaron Cleveland, established the first Presbyterian church in Canada and died beneath the roof of his friend Benjamin Franklin, who penned his obituary in the *Pennsylvania Gazette*.[5] Aaron's son—who, exhibiting the lack of imagination that was a hallmark of Cleveland nomenclature, was also named Aaron—was a member of the Connecticut legislature and authored the state's first bill calling for the abolition of slavery. Prior to Grover, the most famous individual to bear the surname was General Moses Cleaveland, the founder and namesake of the Ohio metropolis and a distant cousin of the president. But even

---

*This trend continues to this day. The president's grandson, Thomas G. Cleveland, who died during the writing of this book, was an Episcopal priest who spent most of his life in Massachusetts and New Hampshire.

the eponymous outpost in the Midwest was, in truth, a New England project: when the city of Cleveland was established in 1796, northeastern Ohio was being settled as part of Connecticut's "Western Reserve."* And indeed, Moses Cleaveland went back to Connecticut after the city's founding—and never returned.

The tradition of New England ministers ran right up through the president's father, Richard Falley Cleveland. Born and raised in Connecticut, Richard would complete his undergraduate studies at Yale in 1824 and take courses at Princeton's theological seminary in 1827–28. To support himself in the period between, he worked for a time as a tutor at a private school in Baltimore, where he was studying theology under the tutelage of a local minister and fellow Yale alumnus. It was there that Richard Cleveland met and courted Ann Neal, the woman who would become his wife and the president's mother.

The marriage was in some regards an improbable one. Unlike the quintessentially Yankee Richard, Ann's father was a Protestant immigrant from Ireland and her mother was a German Quaker from Pennsylvania. Abner Neal, the president's maternal grandfather, was a successful publisher and bookseller, meaning Ann had grown up accustomed to a life of means and not a little luxury. Richard's intended field, the ministry, was a road to neither. But Ann's devotion proved stronger to Richard than to her economic station.

In 1829, the twenty-five-year-old Richard and the twenty-three-year-old Ann were married. The blending of their disparate lifestyles, however, was not immediately seamless. A month after the wedding, when the couple settled in Windham, Connecticut, the site of Richard's first church, Ann came to town sporting the accoutrements of a southern woman of means: gaudy jewelry, revealing (by the standards of the day) dresses, and a (free) black servant. After some gentle but unambiguous nudging from the congregation, the servant was sent away and the

---

*A designation that still survives in the less-than-euphonious name of Cleveland's Case Western Reserve University.

new Mrs. Cleveland adopted the somewhat less garish (not to say dowdy) aesthetic expected of a New England parsoness.

The Clevelands were not to be long for Connecticut, however. The peripatetic nature of Richard's work would see him break the family's long-standing ties to New England in short order. Three years after arriving in Windham, they left for a pulpit in Portsmouth, Virginia, a location chosen partly (and ominously) because, even in his twenties, Richard was already seeking a climate that would be less taxing upon his brittle health.[6] From there, a recommendation from one of his former professors at Princeton landed Richard the job in Caldwell—roughly fifteen miles from Newark, but, given the transportation constraints of the day, almost entirely disconnected from it—where Stephen Grover became the fifth of what were eventually nine children.

There's a limit, of course, to what can be gleaned about Grover Cleveland from this audit of his lineage, but the family history does point toward at least two important insights about the man who eventually became president.

The first is that Cleveland—despite spending virtually all of his non–White House years in New York or New Jersey—was, by temperament as well as heritage, best understood as a New Englander. The president himself playfully suggested as much when he told a meeting of the New England Society of Brooklyn in 1891, "From the time the first immigrant of my name landed in Massachusetts, down to the day of my advent, all the Clevelands from whom I claim descent were born in New England. The fact that I first saw the light in the state of New Jersey I have never regarded as working a forfeiture of any right I may have derived from my New England lineage."[7] While we need to apply the appropriate discount to a politician playing to the crowd, there was more truth in the statement than he may have realized. Cleveland— much like a later president to whom he deserves comparison, Calvin Coolidge—was firmly in the Yankee tradition: self-denying, laconic, and industrious to the point of self-flagellation. Indeed, the earliest work traceable to his hand—an essay the nine-year-old Grover penned as a student at New York's Fayetteville Academy—displayed a precocious respect for self-discipline that would have done his Puritan ancestors proud:

> Time is divided into seconds—minutes, hours, days, weeks, months, years, and centuries. If we expect to become great and good men and be respected and esteemed by our friends, we must improve our time when we are young. George Washington improved his time when he was a boy, and he was not sorry when he was at the head of a large army fighting for his country. A great many of our great men were poor and had small means of obtaining an education, but by improving their time when they were young and in school, they obtained their high standing. Jackson was a poor boy, but he was placed in school and by improving his time he found himself a president of the United States, guiding and directing a powerful nation. If we wish to become great and useful in the world, we must improve our time in school.

It is entirely possible, of course, that the young Cleveland was simply (and adroitly) parroting the homilies of his instructors. But even if that's the case, what began as regurgitation eventually became assimilation.

It didn't hurt matters any that a similar kind of austerity pervaded the private life of the Cleveland family. As the son of a minister, Grover dutifully kept a severe sabbath, with all toys and playthings put away by sundown Saturday, not to reemerge until the next evening. In the intervening twenty-four hours there would be two long church services, Sunday school, and a prayer meeting. And, with the exception of Sunday dinner, all time not spent in official church gatherings was to be spent in personal religious devotion and study.[8] And while Sundays were different in degree than the rest of the week, they were not different in kind. Indeed, the family conducted their own worship every night.[9]

There's no evidence to suggest he sought to defy this regimen, and the resulting ethos of self-discipline stayed with the future president for the rest of his life. Nor did he bear any particular marks of repression. Indeed, Cleveland's reminiscences of his childhood were just as likely to include memories of pranks—unlatching the neighbors' gates or conspiring with his brother Will to loudly ring the town bell in the middle of the night—as they were to focus on the quasi-monastic aspects of his youth.

Cleveland's later life, however, does reveal one significant deviation from this conditioning. Though he never called attention to the fact, he spent most of his adult life at arm's length from organized religion. Once he moved to Buffalo at the age of eighteen, he rarely attended church services (though he conveniently became more devout when returning home to visit his mother). Despite his unfulfilled dreams of receiving a college education, he declined a family friend's offer to put him through school if he was willing to follow his father's footsteps into the ministry. Even his decision decades later to hold his marriage ceremony in the White House was made partially because the president did not belong to a church in Washington.

This pattern has led at least one biographer to brand Cleveland a deist, though there is little evidence to suggest such a diagnosis.[10] In his later years in particular, Cleveland expressed religious sentiments with some frequency, though usually in private and rarely in sectarian terms. If it was not quite as rigid a faith as he was raised in, it nevertheless seemed a heartfelt one.

The second insight we can glean is that despite a somewhat distinguished pedigree there was nothing especially privileged about Grover Cleveland's upbringing. Though Richard Cleveland went to Yale and Princeton, in that era and that region of the county such was par for the course for an aspiring clergyman (indeed, both schools had been founded for the education of ministers). Whatever the fruits of his attendance, he did not gain the skeleton key to America's elite precincts that we associate with modern matriculants. Indeed, from the day that

Richard Cleveland left Princeton he would spend the rest of his life in small, isolated towns living off the relatively meager wages associated with his pulpit. For most of Grover's childhood his father supported a family of eleven on a salary of $600 a year (in 1837, the year of Grover's birth, that was the equivalent of about $18,500 in 2019 dollars). There were professional perks that lessened the burden—the family would live, as was the custom, in a parsonage provided by the church, for example. But Grover Cleveland went to work at the age of fourteen, couldn't afford to go to college, and was largely responsible for the financial support of his family by the time he was sixteen years old. The academic credentials of his father—who was resting six feet beneath the upstate New York soil before Grover reached the age of majority—weren't putting any food on the table.

The combination of Richard Cleveland's vocation, financial struggles, and ill health would make Grover's childhood into something of an odyssey. By the time he was three, the family had left Caldwell, relocating more than 225 miles to Fayetteville, in upstate New York, where Richard would be tasked with growing a congregation on what was essentially a frontier. Located ten miles from Syracuse, Fayetteville was one of many upstate communities expanding near the recently completed Erie Canal, which had galvanized the American economy—and the Empire State's in particular—by creating a water passage from the Atlantic Ocean to the Great Lakes. Planted only a mile from the canal, Fayetteville was intimately tied up with the waterway, not least because it depended on passing barges to take limestone, the town's biggest economic asset, to market.

One of the mechanisms by which this commerce was accomplished was sending children canal-side to flag down passing vessels that would pick up the local product, a task that would earn the errand boys a modest finder's fee. The process soon came to be dominated by a group of local boys who jealously elbowed out the competition, establishing a de facto monopoly on the process. The cartel began to crack, however, when a young Grover Cleveland started showing up at 4 a.m. to get a jump on the competition. For the historian, it feels like a moment rich in metaphor. *We must improve our time when we are young.* And so he had.

Given the meager resources at the Cleveland family's disposal, work would be a constant of the future president's life from a young age. They were odd and unglamorous jobs, and could even be dangerous: one that required him to operate a corn-cutting machine resulted in the loss of a fingertip. Whatever modest contributions he was able to make to the family budget, however, would prove insufficient. With nine children—including four boys all destined for college educations—Richard Cleveland was quickly realizing that, no matter how frugal the family's conduct, his salary would be insufficient for their support.

As a result, he would move the family again in 1851, heading thirty-five miles east to Clinton, near Utica. This time, however, Richard would not have a congregation of his own. He had taken the role of district secretary with the Central New York Agency of the American Home Missionary Society, an organization dedicated to starting up new churches and shepherding their path to independence. It would prove to be the most influential position he ever held, as well as the most lucrative. At $1,000 a year (a little more than $30,000 per annum in 2019), he'd be better able to support his family. And given that Clinton was also the home of Hamilton College, the Cleveland boys would be able to attend university and still be home for summer.

The idea that Clinton would solve many of the family's problems, unfortunately, proved to be ephemeral. While the Clevelands' financial pressures had abated, they certainly hadn't disappeared. As a result, Grover's time in the town would be short-lived. Less than a year into the family's residence, financial necessity compelled him to return alone to Fayetteville, where he been offered a position as a clerk in a local general store, with room, board, and a $50 annual salary that would climb to $100 in his second year.

Though Cleveland would later romanticize his time in retail as his first great tutorial in human nature, the reality of the situation was spartan. He'd be up every morning at five (in the winter months he'd sleep in ... until five thirty) to prepare the store for the day's business—building a fire, setting up inventory, cleaning the premises—and then spend the workday tending to customers and running errands. At night, he retired to a room above the store that he shared with another worker, furnished with no more that simple cord beds and essentially unheated save for the ambient warmth from a pipe running down into the store itself. As if merciless upstate New York winters didn't make that experience grueling enough, he also had to take his morning constitutional in the predawn air of a nearby horse trough. Even for a man as legendarily hardy as Grover Cleveland, it's no surprise that he didn't make it far into that second year before returning to his family.

The circumstances that drew him back to Clinton were, initially, happy ones. His oldest sister, Anna, was to be married in March 1853, her intended a minister and a graduate of Hamilton College. Grover, on the cusp of his sixteenth birthday, chose to stay in town in preparation for his own matriculation at Hamilton in the fall. Little did he know that he was about to experience the first iteration of what would become a lifelong trend: for Grover Cleveland, things rarely went according to plan.

Richard Cleveland had been diagnosed with a gastric ulcer, an ailment that would've been torture enough in the relatively sedentary life of a local pastor. In his capacity at the Missionary Society, however, he was frequently on the road, the travel made all the more grueling by the wretched conditions of the roads he traversed and the inclement weather often encountered along the way. His physician counseling a less demanding line of work, in September 1853 the family relocated seventeen miles north to Holland Patent, where Richard returned to the pulpit.

On Sunday, September 19, he delivered his first sermon to the new congregation. It would also be his last. Within a few days, his ailment—now a full-blown case of acute peritonitis—had progressed to the point that he was ordered to bed rest. Ever dutiful, Grover monitored his father and took on many of Richard's responsibilities. On the morning of October 1, that meant accompanying his sister Mary Allen, the next of the Cleveland girls headed to the altar, into Utica to help choose a wedding dress. Before they left the house, Grover checked in to find his father sleeping. A few hours later, while waiting for his sister in a carriage outside the dress shop, he received the fateful news in a brutally impersonal fashion: a newsboy on the street was announcing to passersby that the Reverend Richard Cleveland was dead at the age of forty-nine.

TWO

Buffalo Gals

With Richard Cleveland's death, the family was thrown into chaos. His wife's widowhood should have been cushioned by a sizable inheritance from her wealthy parents in Baltimore, but the money had been almost entirely squandered by a trustee.[1] Neighbors and members of the church offered to help in the wake of Richard's demise, but Ann, in a trademark act of Cleveland independence, was too proud to accept any assistance. Her one concession was to remain in the parsonage provided by the church, ensuring that widowhood wasn't followed immediately by homelessness (her son Fred would eventually purchase the house for her[2]). The family had little capacity to absorb the economic blow.

Any hopes Grover Cleveland had for a college education had died with his father. His mother and his four younger siblings were now without support. The lion's share of the responsibility for their welfare fell on the sixteen-year-old Grover and his older brother William, both able to be quickly deployed into the labor force. The improvised solution to the family's financial straits involved Grover making the biggest move of his already nomadic life—250 miles southeast, to Manhattan. It was there that he joined William, who'd arrived shortly before his younger brother, as an instructor at the New York Institute for the Blind, where he would spend the next year teaching English, math, and geography while William taught philosophy, chemistry, physics, and history. Despite the institution's anodyne name, the "school" operated more like an asylum. Blind children from throughout the state were sent to the campus* for both education and boarding, the latter of which translated in practice to warehousing. The students were largely kept at a remove from the outside world, residing in austere quarters and subject to regular and (by Grover's lights) excessive discipline.

The head from which this particular fish was rotting was an authoritarian headmaster with the implausibly Dickensian name of T. Colden Cooper. His reign—compounded, no doubt, by Grover's penury and the lingering sting of his father's loss—left the future president, by all accounts, miserable. But with his mother's subsistence on the line, he largely stifled his discontent . . . for a time.†

After a year a depressed Cleveland had had enough. With the vast majority of his earnings being funneled back home, the excitements available to a footloose bachelor in New York City eluded him. What little hope he had owed to the fact that he was still young enough to imagine his circumstances impermanent. When the school year ended, he took his leave and returned to Holland Patent.

Undercapitalized, undereducated, and at loose ends, Cleveland could have easily wound up adrift had it not been for an overdue bit of providence. Word had reached Ingham Townsend, the wealthy brother-in-law of the man whose general store Cleveland had tended in Fayetteville, that this young man with a sterling reputation was casting about for prospects. Townsend, an elder in his church, made Cleveland an offer: he'd pay for Grover's long-desired college education if he'd commit himself to following his father's path into the ministry.

That Grover Cleveland was in such desperate need of a gift horse at that particular moment makes it all the more remarkable that he looked it in the mouth. Drawing on the same reserves of pride and stubborn-

---

*During the time that Cleveland served on the institute's faculty it occupied the entire block between Eighth Avenue and Ninth Avenue and West Thirty-Third Street and West Thirty-Fourth Street, catty-corner to what is now Madison Square Garden.
†One of Cleveland's colleagues at the institute was Fanny Crosby, later to become one of the most successful and prolific hymnists of the nineteenth century. The two remained friends for life.

ness displayed by his newly widowed mother, he refused the offer. Perhaps he thought it immoral to use the pulpit as a means to an education when he didn't feel God's calling. Perhaps he still felt too much pressure to provide for his family. Or perhaps the religious constraints of his childhood had gotten to him more than he ever let on. Regardless, the firmness that would define him as an adult was already beginning to make itself known. And while he was never going to be a man of the cloth, he had resolved that he was going to be *something*—and whatever it was would require resources. Upon declining Townsend's offer, he asked instead for a twenty-five-dollar loan that would help finance his relocation to a new, more promising city. Townsend—whose generosity was all the more remarkable given that he mostly knew Grover by reputation—provided the amount and told the dutiful boy to consider it a gift.

Like many young men of the era, Grover believed that the wind of opportunity primarily blew to the west. Even in those early hours of the country, the East was already developing an establishment of sorts, where the right bloodlines and the right credentials—two resources he was short on—tended to have an influence beyond what one might expect in a pure meritocracy. And while he was not suited to the rough-and-tumble of the *true* West—he was hardy, but not Theodore-Roosevelt-sabbatical-on-a-North-Dakota-ranch-hardy—there was plenty of opportunity to be found in the burgeoning cites of the Midwest.

It was a reasonable calculation, so far as it went, but Grover Cleveland was also a boy of seventeen and prone to the correspondent deficiencies of mind. As such, he had settled on Cleveland, Ohio, as his ultimate destination . . . in part because he shared a name with the city. It would be a trip of nearly four hundred miles from his mother's home in Holland Patent. But the hardship of the journey would be mitigated by the fact that he could stop roughly halfway in Buffalo, home to one of his paternal aunts, and, more consequentially, to her husband: Lewis F. Allen.

Allen was one of Buffalo's leading civic figures. He had made a fortune starting insurance companies in the early days of Buffalo's growth and compounded it with real estate investments, allowing him to win election to the state legislature and purchase an impressive home originally built for Peter Porter, who briefly served as secretary of war for President John Quincy Adams.* Allen, a committed Whig and later Republican, would use the home to host the likes of Henry Clay; Daniel Webster; Winfield Scott, hero general of the Mexican War (and the 1852 Whig candidate for president); fellow Whig Millard Fillmore, the first Buffalonian to make it to the White House; and William Seward, the New York governor and senator who would go on to become Abraham Lincoln's secretary of state.

It was to that home in Buffalo's Black Rock neighborhood that Grover paid a visit as he made his journey west. Fond of his nephew—and appropriately alarmed by the imprecision of his plans for life in Ohio—Allen suggested to him that Buffalo, where he would at least have the foundation of family, would be a more suitable landing spot.

Allen, whose wealth had allowed him to spend much of his time on a passion for raising cattle and sheep, was at the time involved in intensive work on the type of eccentric passion project that only a high net worth can sanitize: compiling the *Shorthorn Herd Book*, a sprawling work of . . . cattle genealogy. He suggested that Grover could earn his keep by assisting in the drafting. In exchange the young man would get a place in the family home and the eventual prospect of introductions around town, with the ultimate goal of getting him installed in one of the city's elite law firms. (While a handful of law schools existed by the mid-nineteenth century, the vast majority of lawyers at the time entered the profession by "reading law"—that is, apprenticing with those already established in the field.) Restless though he was, the offer was too good for Cleveland to turn down. Perhaps he thought his time in Buffalo would merely be a way station on the way to bigger and better things.

---

*Porter, who commanded American forces on the Niagara frontier during the War of 1812, had built the residence to overlook the former site of Fort Erie, where he had seen combat during the conflict. Long regarded as Buffalo's oldest mansion, the home was torn down in 1911.

And in a way it was. He'd remain in the city for the next twenty-seven years, only departing when election to the New York governorship compelled a relocation to Albany.

The importance of Allen to Grover Cleveland's development into a figure of historical significance can't be overstated, though its effects did not play out in quite the way one might assume. Allen was a politico, but as an influential Whig and later Republican he didn't share his nephew's politics. Yet while he was not directly responsible for Grover's political rise, he was essential to placing him on the path that enabled it.

Whatever the virtues of Grover's deceased father—and the records we have from his contemporaries are overwhelmingly positive, as were the president's own recollections—Richard Cleveland was not known for his ambition. No one was more sensitive to that fact than the high-achieving Allen, who judged that his brother-in-law "could never take advantage of his opportunities for advancement."[3]

Allen would not treat Grover as a charity case, but he would not let his promise go similarly unfulfilled. And indeed, it was his uncle's connections that got the young Grover his first real job: an apprenticeship at the prestigious Buffalo firm of Rogers, Bowen, & Rogers, where he would stay on even after passing the bar, eventually rising to the role of chief clerk.

Having an influential Sherpa like Allen certainly helped grease the skids for Grover, but it also helped matters that Buffalo was a town seemingly tailored for his ascent. If an ambitious kid was going to make a name for himself from practically nothing, a city that had likewise emerged ex nihilo was an ideal place to do it. When Grover arrived, Buffalo was in the midst of one of the most aggressive civic growth spurts in American history. In 1830, five years after the opening of the Erie Canal—and two years prior to the city's actual incorporation—Buffalo's population stood at 8,668. By 1860, around the time the twenty-three-year-old Grover was admitted to the bar, the population had grown to more than 81,000, making it one of the ten largest cities in the nation. That number would nearly double by the time he became mayor in 1882, reaching more than 155,000.

The canal was at the core of the city's success, making it a thoroughfare for shipping and trade. The year that Cleveland arrived in town, 1855, marked the apex of that trend, with more than 33,000 commercial shipments traversing the waterway.[4] As major cities grew up on Great Lakes waterfronts—Chicago not least among them—Buffalo's direct water access helped it grow in tandem. The influx of new residents—and, even more so, the steady supply of transients that inevitably characterizes a port city—meant that Cleveland's Buffalo was a rough-and-tumble place. Accounts of the era note that police officers would only travel down some streets in pairs—and then, only during daylight hours. Prostitution was so widespread that it even inspired a song that became a part of the American canon. To modern ears, the lyrics "Buffalo gals, won't you come out tonight," ring quaint; in their original context, they were decidedly less so.

Not all of the tumult was of an illicit quality. As the city's initial wave of New England settlers began to be diluted by immigrants (primarily German and Irish, nonnatives would eventually make up approximately 60 percent of Buffalo's population[5]) the culture began to change in at least two ways that were propitious for the young Grover Cleveland. The first was the immigrants' attraction to Cleveland's Democratic Party, which displayed less hostility to foreigners than the then-regnant Whigs. The second was the changes wrought to the city's culinary landscape. The Germans in particular brought with them a cuisine heavy on beer and sausages, both of which would become staples of the Cleveland diet. The earliest surviving picture of Cleveland—in which the bearded, follically intact Grover looks, if not svelte, at least reasonably proportioned—gives credence to the reports that he gained roughly one hundred pounds (in presidential terms, the equivalent of swallowing James Madison whole) during his time in Buffalo.

Mid-century Buffalo was not pure hedonism, however. By the time

Grover came to town, the city's proximity to Canada had made it the penultimate stop on one line of the Underground Railroad. Nearby, Harriet Tubman had taken escaped slaves north across a wooden suspension bridge close to Niagara Falls on multiple occasions. In the 1830s, a slave couple from Tennessee fled into Ontario with their six-week-old baby, only to be kidnapped by slave hunters dispatched by their erstwhile owner. When the couple was brought back stateside, a contingent of about fifty of Buffalo's free blacks set them free and then fought their way back to the Canadian border through two hours of armed conflict with a local posse assembled by the slaveholder.[6]

Given that current in the city's culture, it's disappointing that we have little record of Grover Cleveland's thoughts on slavery and the events that were soon to precipitate a civil war. For most of the 1850s the White House was controlled by his fellow northern Democrats, New Hampshire's Franklin Pierce and Pennsylvania's James Buchanan. The de facto position of both men was that, whatever the evils of slavery, the abolitionists' potential to destabilize a fragile status quo was the greater menace. Grover had grown up hearing a similar diagnosis from his father.[7]

But what did the future president himself believe? We know that Cleveland was repulsed by the flamboyance and egotism of John Frémont, who in 1856 became the first Republican nominee for president. (That same arrogance would get Frémont cashiered from his generalship in the Union army a few years later, when he defied orders from President Lincoln.) But we also know that Cleveland didn't look at the war through a purely partisan lens. He was an ardent supporter of unionism and an admirer of Abraham Lincoln, even defending the sixteenth president's suspension of habeas corpus at a time when many of his fellow Democrats were enraged by it. ("It seems to me," Cleveland thundered, "that the government has a right in time of war to resort to every possible method in order to protect itself."[8])

His convictions about the war, however, did not lead to his service in it. Two of Cleveland's older brothers donned Union uniforms in the course of the conflict: Cecil served in the west under Ulysses S. Grant; Fred was in the Army of the Potomac. Whether Grover desired to be on a battlefield is unknown, though it seems improbable; his love for the masculine thrills of hunting and fishing never seemed to translate to a lust for martial glory, and there are no records to suggest otherwise. But there was a practical consideration as well: with two brothers on the battlefield and another living off the crumbs of a Long Island ministry, Grover had become the sole source of financial support for his mother and younger sisters.

That posed a dilemma when, in 1863, Cleveland's number was pulled on the first day of the draft in Buffalo.[9] The law provided an out, however: draftees were allowed to forgo service if they paid $300 (approximately $6,250 in 2019 funds) or furnished a substitute.

Mindful of the stress on the family, Fred offered to reenlist in his place, prompting his brother to reply with a characteristically terse "Fred has done enough." Instead, Grover paid $150 to a Polish sailor named George Benninsky to serve in his place. Though Cleveland's political opponents would later claim that Benninsky suffered unspeakable horrors in the course of the war, the reality was that he never saw major combat and spent most of the conflict as a hospital orderly after suffering a back injury.[10] Even the real story, however, probably wouldn't have prevented the allegations that Cleveland was an unpatriotic elite who bought his way out of the war. Perhaps he *was* derelict in not answering the call (though the practice was relatively common). But "elite" was a stretch. Grover Cleveland, though recently installed as assistant district attorney of Erie County, had to get a loan to pay Benninsky. After all, he had a family to support.

THREE

The Hangman

The crucifix hit the ground.[1] How was the son of a minister ever going to forget that? Just a moment earlier it had been clasped in the hands of John Gaffney as he addressed his wife and children, and the priests nearby tried to calm him down. He continued to grasp it until a moment—and only a moment—after Grover Cleveland executed him.

A decade had passed since Grover Cleveland's name was called in the draft. And while he had never been forced to take a life for the United States of America, he was now taking one—on Valentine's Day, no less—on behalf of Erie County, New York. That was part of the job—the least savory, as far as he was concerned—when you were the sheriff.

The road he traveled to the gallows was rambling, if not quite as rocky as Gaffney's. His first serious foray into public life had been the aforementioned appointment as assistant district attorney for the county, beginning in 1863. The man to whom he served as deputy, Cyrenius Torrance, lived in Gowanda, approximately thirty miles away from Buffalo, and the combination of the distance and his failing health meant that Grover had the top job in all but name.

Cleveland had come to the attention of Torrance and other members of the city's legal community through his stint at Rogers, Bowen, & Rogers, a firm prominent enough in the city that even its chief clerk gained notoriety as word of what one colleague called his "indomitable industry, unpretentious courage, and unswerving honesty" spread.[2] His habit of volunteering for menial tasks on behalf of the party, as well as a brief stint as a ward supervisor, had also put him on the radar of local party elders, who, their ranks swelled by conservatives made homeless by the implosion of the Whig Party, were on the lookout for talent.

If your plan was to treat your office as a sinecure and delegate most major responsibilities to a second in command, you couldn't find a better deputy than the young Grover Cleveland. Twenty-five years old and single, Grover thrived in the role thanks to a work ethic that in a later era would have gotten him medicated. He would draw up virtually all of the indictments himself, personally prosecute at least half of the cases—at a rate of up to four per day—and return to the office after dinner to prepare for the following day's work. His normal work hours: 8 a.m. to 3 a.m. Given that his sole respite—and the only area in his life where his penchant for self-control seemed to fail him—was food and drink, it's no surprise that this was the period in which he began to expansively gain weight, a war of attrition he would spend decades losing.

While the assistant DA position offered Grover newfound prominence, his annual earnings fell by roughly half when he accepted the position, and his disposable income more so given his ongoing support of the family (his younger sister Susan wouldn't learn until years later that Grover had cut his finances to the bone to provide her the college education he had been denied).[3] He was also accumulating debt. Cleveland owed Torrance for the money to compensate his draft replacement and he wouldn't have the funds to repay Ingham Townsend for the loan that got him to Buffalo until 1867, a dozen years after he made the journey.*

Why *choose* austerity at a time when money was already so dear? It's likely that Grover had by this point resolved on a career in government, and a position of this stature, especially for someone so young, was too alluring to pass up. Perhaps he even believed he'd simply lily-pad to positions of increasing significance and compensation. Given

---

*Though Townsend had intended the money as a gift, the future president insisted on repayment.

the uneven trajectory of his life up to that point, however, he should've known better.

In 1865, Cleveland was nominated to succeed Torrance as Erie County's district attorney. The *Buffalo Courier*, the city's Democratic newspaper, enthused that the young nominee's "character is above reproach. He will be supported by hundreds of Republicans on those grounds."[4] That statement would prove true in just about every election in which Cleveland was ever on the ballot . . . except for 1865. While Cleveland performed well within Buffalo's city limits, the margins captured by his opponent, Lyman K. Bass, in the outlying regions were too significant to overcome. Grover took his leave and wished the new DA well. On that last front, he didn't have much choice: Bass was also his roommate.

After losing the election, he opened a law partnership with Isaac K. Vanderpoel, a Democrat who had been New York's state treasurer in the late 1850s. The collaboration augured well for Grover; a previous partner of Vanderpoel's, Frederick P. Stevens, had gone on to serve as mayor of Buffalo. It was also the start of a pattern in Cleveland's legal practice: he'd inevitably join up with some prominent politico, usually with impeccable connections and a healthy dose of charisma, and toil diligently, capably, and largely unnoticed in the background. Grover was, by constitution, a workhorse. He was also smart enough to make sure that he was always yoked to a show horse.

The partnership, however, would prove short-lived, as Vanderpoel returned to public life in 1869 as a Buffalo police magistrate. In need of partners once more, Cleveland converted the firm into a trio. Into the political operator slot previously occupied by Vanderpoel slipped A. P. Laning, who had served in both houses of the New York legislature and was an influential member of the state party. While the association with Laning kept Grover in the orbit of the Empire State's Democratic elite, it would be the other new partner, Oscar Folsom, who would permanently alter the course of his life.

Cleveland was responsible, honorable, and, to outward appearances, a bit staid. Folsom was impulsive, rakish, and charismatic. While Grover would spend sleepless nights poring over his legal briefs, Oscar was more likely to be found gambling or carriage racing (and, not infrequently, gambling *on* carriage racing). One such incident gained particular notoriety when a panicked Folsom showed up at Buffalo's Sandpit Hotel in search of his six-year-old daughter, Frances. He had deposited her there earlier in the evening, concerned that the extra weight of a young girl in the carriage was placing him at a competitive disadvantage as he raced his friend John C. Level through the streets of Buffalo. As the night went on, Folsom and Level commemorated each lap with a round of cocktails at another hotel near the end of their course. Only upon retiring for the evening did Folsom remember that he had left his daughter elsewhere in the city—though where he couldn't immediately call to mind.[5]

The constellation of personalities in the new firm served Cleveland well. Laning's prestige and Folsom's magnetism attracted a plentiful flow of clients, and both men were more than happy to take up the courtroom responsibilities that Grover abjured, shouldering the performative, rhetorical burden while he stayed in the office and mastered the substantive details of the cases. The contrast produced a chemistry in their personal lives as well. Cleveland and Folsom became extremely close, with the quarterback-befriends-valedictorian dynamic between them sometimes creating an almost comic juxtaposition. Once, when Folsom—who had the extrovert's gift for conducting all of life as an improvisation—asked Grover for the relevant citation for one of his legal arguments, the future president replied, "Go look it up, and then you'll remember what you learn."[6] The ever-charismatic Folsom won the volley with his reply: "I want you to know that I practice law by ear, not by note."

By the end of the 1860s, Cleveland had settled into a comfortable, if not especially dynamic, professional equilibrium. Laning, Folsom, & Cleveland was successful and, while he certainly wasn't wealthy, his financial situation was more secure. However, his aversion to self-promotion had limited the degree to which he was a figure of public approbation. He was well thought of, if not thought of that often. Had he continued on that trajectory, he likely would have found himself on the bench at some future date, one of those conscientious, workmanlike public officials who wait on an obituary for the appropriate dosage of appreciation. Instead, he was about to take a professional left turn that was, to use the technical term, pretty bananas.

In 1870, the Democratic Party was in need of a warm body. With the midterm elections approaching, retaking Buffalo's seat in the House of Representatives, lost two years prior, seemed within their grasp.[7] They did *not* ask Grover Cleveland. Instead, they turned to William Williams, a banker and railroad president who had done a brief stint in the state assembly. But Williams needed help. The race was going to be close enough that the Democrats recognized that the nominees for down-ballot offices might provide—or deny—the margin of victory for Williams at the top. And this was a problem because the most prominent office after the House seat was sheriff of Erie County, one of those classic public stations only sought by people who should have been allowed nowhere near the job.

The reasons Cleveland was perfect for the sheriff's role were the same that made it a liability for him to pursue it. Even an honest sheriff—something hard to come by in that day and age—was going to improve his financial standing in the job, which was sweetened by a bevy of fees attached to many of its official duties. But for a dishonest one, the opportunities for corruption were legion, encompassing everything from bribes to contracting kickbacks. Most men in the position succumbed to the temptation. For the Democratic Party, the logic was impeccable: nominate a man known as a paragon of virtue for the seediest office in the land.

For Cleveland, the calculus wasn't quite so simple. He had spent fifteen years in Buffalo cultivating a reputation as a man immune to the temptations of partisanship and political expediency, never mind corruption. Was it worth putting all that on the line to pursue an office whose inhabitant, regardless of the facts, would immediately carry the taint of being a political hack?

The answer, surprisingly enough, was yes—though how fervent a yes is a matter of some dispute. Cleveland is recorded as having waived away the possibility at first, noting that the sheriff's office was not usually held by a lawyer. Allan Nevins, author of a magisterial 1932 biography of Cleveland, however, contends that the future president actively courted the role, using Oscar Folsom as an intermediary.[8] The most likely scenario is that both urges were authentic: Grover was likely desperate to place himself back on the political ladder and desirous of a role that could finally give him some real financial security, but also wary of how much his integrity might be impugned in the process. In the end, the temptation to return to politics was too strong to overcome.

Cleveland would win the election (as would Williams), although the Democrats' theory of the case proved to be in error: the incoming sheriff's margin of victory was half that of the new congressman's, a result that owed in part to Grover's aversion to campaigning (an instinct a politician could still indulge in the nineteenth century).[9] While he claimed he valued the office, which came with a surprising amount of free time, for the opportunity it provided to deepen his study of the law, his associates all assumed money was a bigger factor (though Cleveland's legal talents were indeed observed to have improved when he eventually returned to practice). And, in stark contrast to his later stints in government, Grover Cleveland—a man for whom the phrase "work-life balance" could have been invented as a rebuke—brought an uncharacteristic penchant for delegation to the office, assigning most of the day-to-day responsibilities to W. L. G. Smith, the deputy he had inherited and subsequently reappointed. Some of that free time assuredly went to brushing up his legal chops; but a fair bit went to fishing as well.[10]

While the pace was relaxed, any serious audit of Cleveland's time as sheriff reveals that it was not a holiday from his usual scruples: the earnings that provided him a newfound financial security were all above-board.* In fact, many of the local Democrats who had thought him little more than a pawn useful to securing Williams's election would come to rue his selection precisely because of his incorruptibility.

One of the most common sources of graft in the county was vendors supplying only a fraction of the supplies they had been paid to deliver, a practice sustained by elected officials who'd look the other way for a cut of the action. Now, when the county's supplies of cordwood arrived, Cleveland personally measured the delivery, a practice that he would rigorously apply across the board.[11] He also systematized the practice of giving new contracts to the lowest bidder rather than to the politically connected. Many of those snubbed contractors were his fellow Democrats. To his great credit—and at real cost to his political career—Grover Cleveland didn't give a damn.[12]

While Cleveland's reputation for integrity was one legacy of his tenure in the sheriff's office—even his Republican successor admitted how conscientiously he had done the job—the most abiding impression was one that he would have preferred to forget: during his time in office (1871–73), he was twice called on to carry out executions. In both cases, the condemned were murderers. The aforementioned John Gaffney had drunkenly shot a man down after a bad hand of cards; Patrick Morrissey, the first man he led to the gallows, had stabbed his mother to death when she refused him money. In both cases, Cleveland himself pulled the lever that consigned them to the abyss.

There is a long history in American life of bellicose men whose hardness was an essential part of their political appeal. Grover Cleveland, by contrast, was most easily roused to wrath when someone was misquoting Tennyson.[13]† There was thus some irony when, in later

---

*According to the recollection of John C. Level (he of the drunken carriage race with Oscar Folsom), Cleveland claimed to have left the sheriff's office having netted $20,000 (approximately $425,000 in 2019 dollars) over the course of three years.

†Though many biographers seem compelled to emphasize that Cleveland was not an intellectual, he did cultivate concentrated areas of expertise that hinted at his potential had he completed his education. Nowhere was this more evident than in his lifelong love of poetry. One eyewitness account from his presidency describes Cleveland correcting from memory a misquotation of

years, Cleveland's political opponents dubbed him "The Buffalo Hangman," both because the label could have boomeranged in his favor and because it masked the fact that Cleveland was an especially fainthearted executioner.

Grover Cleveland hated the days preceding an execution, when he could think of little else. He'd lose sleep. He'd get ill. On at least one occasion, he asked a local doctor to walk him through all the possibilities of what could go wrong.[14] And yet he didn't *have* to do it. The relevant law allowed the sheriff to pass off the hangman's responsibilities to a deputy for a ten-dollar fee. Indeed, that was the course that Grover's mother—long the person he'd turned to with his anxieties—counseled. But he couldn't accept the reprieve. What kind of man would freely accept all the benefits of his office but fob off its most stomach-turning responsibilities? He had already paid a man to bear his cross once before. He wouldn't do it again.

He was also intent that there would be no morbid voyeurism on his watch. On both occasions, Cleveland barred the general public from attending. (A Buffalo hanging in 1825 had drawn a crowd of 15,000—some estimates range as high as 25,000—at a time when only 5,000 souls lived in the city.[15]) To drive the point home, he employed a team of carpenters to build a frame around the jail yard, then draped the whole edifice in black canvas so that the especially enterprising couldn't get a view from a nearby rooftop. He'd then position himself so as not to be looking at the accused when they made their final descent. Hearing it was enough.

The sheriff's position was not eligible for reelection and so Cleveland returned to private practice after his term expired at the end of 1873. He formed a new partnership with Lyman K. Bass, the man who had defeated him in the district attorney race nearly a decade earlier, and Wilson "Shan" Bissell, a clerk from his previous firm who would wind

---

Tennyson's "Will Waterproof's Lyrical Monologue." Met with the skepticism of his dinner companions, Cleveland insisted on looking it up and was proven correct.

up his closest confidant for the remainder of his life (and virtually the only figure from Buffalo to play a serious role in his political career).

The 1870s would prove to be a decade of loss for Cleveland, with three unexpected deaths weighing heavily upon him. The first two came in 1872, while he was still serving as sheriff. Cecil and Fred, the brothers who had served in the Union army while he tended to the district attorney's office, had, in the years after Appomattox, turned to the hospitality industry. After Fred purchased and successfully operated a hotel in Fairfield, Connecticut, he acquired a lease on a luxury property in the Bahamas, where Cecil was intended to play a management role. In October, the pair boarded a steamship in New York City bound for the Caribbean and their grand opening. They never arrived. The vessel caught fire twenty-five miles off the Bahamian coast and Cleveland's brothers were lost either to the flames or the depths.[16]*

Three years later, in 1875, Cleveland lost the brother with whom he didn't share a surname. Oscar Folsom, his carriage en route to meet Grover, came around a corner and collided with a wagon jutting out into the street. Folsom was thrown from the carriage, severely fracturing his skull. His startled horse then proceeded to run the vehicle over his motionless body. Folsom never regained consciousness and was dead within two hours.[17]

Though the two men were no longer business partners, they had remained extremely close. And Cleveland—approaching forty and still single—had regarded Folsom's wife, Emma, and his daughter, Frances, as his own kin. That sentiment would now be formalized. Folsom, never especially fastidious, had died intestate. Oscar's widow and his daughter—who had turned eleven two days before her father's demise—were made Cleveland's wards, the court deeming the deceased's closest friend (and one of Buffalo's most respected lawyers) as the ideal executor of the estate.

---

*In the aftermath of his brothers' deaths, it fell to Grover to manage their estates and discharge the properties. The process proved protracted because it occurred in the midst of the Panic of 1873, a crisis so deep that it was known in its day as "The Great Depression." The next time the nation faced such an acute economic crisis Cleveland would be president.

Those tragedies aside, the years after Cleveland departed the sheriff's office are notable primarily for how prosaic they were. Indeed, one would be hard-pressed to find a comparable period of inertia in the life of any other man less than a decade away from becoming president. Cleveland continued his law practice, albeit with a revolving cast of characters; Bass did a stint in Congress before removing himself to Colorado to manage a case of tuberculosis, and Cleveland and Bissell later added another young partner, George Sicard.

The esteem in which he was held at the bar only grew, not because he came up with novel arguments or won the day through courtroom oratory, but because he doggedly worked through cases, examining every possible argument and counterargument, until he had so thoroughly mastered the material that he was never caught unprepared. In that era, Buffalo courts had a practice of calling upon outsiders who were regarded as neutral to help adjudicate cases, a sort of proto-arbitrator role. Cleveland, by now widely known for an almost superhuman rigor, his eighteen-hour workdays, and his capacity for impartiality, was always at the top of the list.

Importantly, he had also finally attained a measure of financial independence. Not that it led to a much of a change in his lifestyle: Grover lived in a modest apartment on the floor above his law firm and, especially with the death of his brothers, a substantial part of his budget was still dedicated to his mother's welfare. But shorn of financial imperatives, Cleveland conducted his legal practice to maximize his satisfaction rather than his profits. He generally avoided criminal cases, both because he had a preference for disputes that could be settled out of court and because he had no stomach for defending someone he thought might actually be guilty.*[18] He turned down an opportunity to become general counsel for the New York Central Railroad, a move that would have made him one of the wealthiest and most prominent lawyers in the

---

*This was a lifelong conviction. As a teenager in Fayetteville, Cleveland had organized a debating society in which he argued that it was immoral for an attorney to defend a client he knew had committed the crime of which he stood accused.

state, because he couldn't abide the thought of operating according to the dictates of a corporation rather than his own conscience. And he took on a steady stream of pro bono cases, in addition to many from indigent clients for which he simply never collected.

Nothing about Cleveland's life in this era suggests that he was anticipating being on a ballot again anytime soon. Not only was he turning down work that could've raised his visibility, but he had also largely removed himself from political circles (where, given his disregard for party cronies during his time as sheriff, he wasn't particularly welcome anyway). In fact, he was a virtual nonentity in Buffalo's elite circles. What free time he had apart from the firm was spent largely on hunting or fishing trips—or indulging in the luxuries, such as they were, of being a middle-aged bachelor, which meant lots of drinking, eating, and gaming in Buffalo taverns. And while the details around those pastimes were mostly hazy—a fact that would soon come back to haunt Cleveland—it is evident that they were sometimes taken to excess.

There is a contemporary account of a bar fight that culminated in Cleveland banging a man's head into a gutter.[19] There were instances of indulgence that caused him, by his own later admission, to "lose a day,"[20] as presidential a euphemism as ever there was for a screaming hangover. Ironically, the one aspect of his free time that drew the least comment—perhaps because he had made it known that he enjoyed life as a bachelor—was his love life.

It continued that way for years: long days in the office, often long nights there, too. When that wasn't the case, lost nights in the pubs. Then it all came to a whiplash-inducing halt in the fall of 1881, the night that Grover Cleveland's choice of tavern set him on the path to becoming the next president of the United States.

His Obstinacy, Grover of Buffalo

Grover Cleveland's name would probably have been lost to history if he didn't love beer so damn much. But on October 22, 1881, his appetites inflamed, the sirens steered him to Billy Dranger's restaurant, one of his familiar Buffalo haunts. Cleveland, by now in his eighth year back in private practice, had in large measure drifted away from politics. His failure to play ball during his stint in the sheriff's office had put him on the outs with party regulars, and even when the passage of time weakened that opprobrium, he still didn't seem especially interested, having turned down entreaties to run for an alderman's seat in Buffalo.[1]* He was content with the simple, methodical life his practice afforded him. But that modus vivendi was about to disappear forever, a victim of his preternatural ability to attract jobs that no one else wanted.

Upon entering Dranger's, Cleveland spied a table of familiar Democratic Party men. By the looks on their faces, they had plenty to be drinking about. Pulling up a chair, he soon discovered the cause of their

---

*The term "alderman" in this case and hereafter should be read as the equivalent of the modern term "city councilman." Though "alderman" has, at certain times and in certain locations, carried other meanings, they are not employed in this book. Some jurisdictions—most notably, the city of Chicago—use the term "alderman" for members of their legislative body to this day.

downcast appearances: this quintet had spent the day unsuccessfully canvassing the city's most prominent Democratic businessmen, hoping to convince someone of civic standing to accept the party's nomination for mayor of Buffalo.[2]

Like the sheriff's post before it, the mayor's office had come to stink of corruption. Regardless of which party held the office—and it had seesawed between Republicans and Democrats of late—all recent mayors had either actively participated in or passively tolerated the graft and self-dealing that suffused city government, a trend so pervasive that any attempt to combat it was dismissed as a quixotic use of political capital. Furthermore, the fundamentals of Buffalo politics still favored the GOP—and whoever accepted the nomination would thus also be handed underdog status. With the nominating convention only three days away, the situation was being forced to a head.*

It had a touch of déjà vu to it. At some point in the conversation it dawned on one of his interlocutors that Grover Cleveland just might fit the bill. In hindsight it seems obvious: why not nominate the man with the calling card for integrity, the one who had already shown himself capable of transcending a tarnished office? But beyond the lingering fallout from his tenure as sheriff, there were good reasons Cleveland hadn't been at the top of the list. The mayor's office usually fell to some prominent commercial figure; a lawyer hadn't held the title for a quarter century.[3]

Hagiographic accounts of Cleveland's life tend to give the impression that his career was a series of happy accidents, the political equivalent of the starlet discovered by a director at the soda fountain. More cynical renderings tend to cast his reticence to run for office as little more than calculated image-making (a charge occasionally made against the similarly restrained George Washington). In reality, he appears to

---

*The rhythms of nineteenth-century politics were dramatically different than in our day, with much shorter campaign cycles, especially for local office. Cleveland's first conversation about entering the mayoral race occurred only seventeen days prior to the election.

have been genuinely conflicted, if not actively averse, to elected office in the first half of his career—an understandable impulse given how much he detested Buffalo's corrupt political class.

Still, as his friends continued their entreaties, Cleveland began to entertain the idea more seriously. Despite their local advantages, Buffalo Republicans had made the grievous mistake of choosing as their nominee Milton C. Beebe, president of the city council and a well-known practitioner of Buffalo's darker political arts. Fatigue with that kind of political chicanery had led to disquiet among a contingent of Republicans that the right Democrat could exploit. For Cleveland, that was necessary but not sufficient.

He had a further condition for even considering the race: in an inversion of the usual practice of nominating the mayoral candidate and then selecting down-ticket nominees,[4] he wanted full approval of the Democratic slate. This proviso was targeted squarely at one man: John C. Sheehan, the city's incumbent comptroller and a powerful political boss in Buffalo's Irish community, whose loyalties were known to lie with the (bipartisan) forces of graft rather than with his own party or any guiding principles. Remarkably, it worked. Sheehan stepped aside on the basis of a too-clever-by-half calculation: if Democrats were going to go all in on reform in 1881, he'd let them make their case and suffer the consequent defeat; once it was over, and could be dismissed as a flight of fancy, he and his ilk—the ones who knew how business actually got done—could sweep back in to office and get on with it.[5*]

Cleveland's plan may have worked better than he intended. Among many of his fellow Democrats the suspicion was that demanding veto rights over the ticket—especially given the seeming implausibility of Sheehan voluntarily relinquishing power—was an elegant means by which Grover could pass on the race without being per-

---

*In this era Buffalo held municipal elections every year, so this calculus only entailed Sheehan being out of office for a brief interregnum.

ceived to have slighted the party. If that was the case, his bluff had just been called.

On October 25, 1881—three days after the conversation at Billy Dranger's—Cleveland was in arguments before the New York Supreme Court* when a contingent of party operatives were dispatched from the city's Democratic convention to secure his consent. The presiding judge that day, Justice Albert Haight, described the scene:

> The committee came into court and attracted the attention of Cleveland, who stepped aside and held a brief, whispered confer-ence. Then he came up to my desk, leaning his elbows on it, and talking across in low tones.
>
> "This," he said, indicating the committee with a nod, "is a committee from the Democratic city convention, and they want to nominate me for mayor. They've come over to see if I'll accept. What shall I do about it?"
>
> "I think you had better accept," [was Judge Haight's reply]. "The Republicans have gotten into a tangle. A good many are dissatisfied with the candidate nominated. Your chances may be pretty good." [6]

Cleveland proved persuadable, though his new calling as a politician wasn't going to make him any less conscientious: he departed the court to give some pro forma acceptance remarks at the convention . . . and then came right back to continue his work on the case.

The campaign now joined, Cleveland faced a novel task: putting together an official release that would be widely distributed as the defining statement of his beliefs. Cleveland rarely displayed an ear for rhetoric, but he never lacked for clarity. Four sentences in partic-

---

*In one of the strangest bits of nomenclature in American government, New York's "Supreme Court" refers to the state's trial level, not its highest court.

ular summed up what casting a ballot for Grover Cleveland represented:

> I believe much can be done to relieve our citizens from our
> present load of taxation, and that a more rigid scrutiny of all
> public expenditures will result in a great saving to the com-
> munity. I also believe that some extravagance in our city gov-
> ernment may be corrected without injury to the public service.
> There is, or there should be, no reason why the affairs of our
> city should not be managed with the same care and the same
> economy as private interests. And when we consider that pub-
> lic officials are the trustees of the people, there should be no
> higher inducement to a faithful and honest discharge of a public
> duty.[7]*

Cleveland's acceptance letter laid out with precision his value proposition: the executive as ombudsman. He would make government
cleaner, cheaper, and better at its core duties. That vision, such as it is,
seems cramped today, when holders of executive office tend to behave
like monarchs in style and prime ministers in substance. But for an ad-
herent of the earlier, republican definition of executive authority, the
logic was straightforward: an executive's job was to *administer*—and he
was going to do it more efficiently and honestly than anyone in recent
memory. He would be the proxy for the people of Buffalo against a city
government that too often regarded them as tributaries.

In the two-week window available for campaigning, the broad principles laid out in Cleveland's acceptance would begin to take a more

---

*The slogan associated with Cleveland throughout his career—"A public office is a public
trust"—had its origins in this passage from his acceptance of the mayoral nomination. When presented the crisper version by William Hudson, a staffer on his presidential campaign, Cleveland's
response was "When the deuce did I say that?" Though he'd ultimately sign off on the catchier
formulation, he felt compelled to stipulate, "That's what I've said a little better because more fully."

tangible shape. Cleveland's guiding principle was simple: he was a fiduciary.* He inveighed not only against illicit corruption but also against some practices that had become institutionalized, such as the county treasurer being allowed to keep as personal profit the interest earned on public money. He pledged to shift pay periods for city workers from monthly to weekly, a reform that had been resisted because the former arrangement amounted to an in-kind subsidy to lenders. And he started sharpening his rejection of business as usual, declaring, "We believe in the principle of economy of the people's money, and that when a man in office lays out a dollar in extravagance, he acts immorally by the people." More portentous was a line that put those who chafed at his tenure as sheriff on notice that age and experience had not mellowed Grover Cleveland: "A Democratic thief is as bad as a Republican thief." That was a powerful message for a city full of Republican voters desperate for a rationale to turn against their party without feeling like they were turning against their principles. In the end, Cleveland carried the mayoral election by 3,500 votes—and brought the entire Democratic ticket, save the candidate for city treasurer, along with him. It was the start of what political observers of the day would come to call "the Cleveland luck."[8] But in truth it was more like "the Cleveland method." The Republican Party, in its post–Civil War regnancy, was succumbing to something like political gout. Its dominance seemingly inevitable, it grew indulgent and decadent. Cleveland's great talent was an ability to define himself primarily as an antagonist of the resulting civic decay rather than an avatar of the Democratic Party. As a result, his stratospheric rise through American politics would be fueled every step of the way by a coalition of loyal Democrats and disaffected Republicans. He was in a party, but never *of* it.

If a revolution had come to Buffalo's executive branch, no such

---

*This dynamic was best captured by Cleveland biographer William Osborn Stoddard—himself a former private secretary of Abraham Lincoln's—who wrote of Grover's later tenure as governor, "He was really the attorney and counsellor retained in the great case of *the State and People of New York v. Whomsoever-it-may-concern.*"

transformation was in the offing for the city council. When Cleveland took the oath of office on January 2, 1882, only 10 of the 26 aldermen could be counted on to support his reform agenda.[9] For that reason— and because inertia had broken more than one would-be reformer in the past—many felt that the new mayor might prove more pliant than his rhetoric had implied. That hope was gone by the afternoon of Inauguration Day—when Grover Cleveland made clear that he had come to city hall to break furniture.

If the story of Mayor Cleveland's inaugural message to the city council had to be summarized with one fact it would be this: it so outraged his adversaries that midway through its reading there was a motion to prevent the clerk from finishing it.[10]

> We hold the money of the people in our hands to be used for their purposes and to further their interests as members of the municipality.... There surely is no difference in his duties or obligations, whether a person is entrusted with the money of one man or many. And yet it sometimes appears as though the officeholder assumes that a different rule of fidelity prevails between him and the taxpayers than that which should regulate his conduct when, as an individual, he holds the money of his neighbor.[11]

He'd make a pro forma attempt to place the argument in a velvet glove—"I am fully persuaded that in the performance of your duties these rules will be observed"—but the message was clear enough: go ahead and try it.

That line in the sand having been drawn, Cleveland moved on to particulars. The office of the city auditor, he noted disapprovingly, had been tasked only with double-checking the math on city invoices rather than actually inquiring into whether the claims were legitimate or correctly priced. "This work is certainly not difficult, and might well be done by a lad barely acquainted with figures," he sneered. Were the auditor not empowered to be the watchdog originally envisioned by the city charter, Cleveland pronounced, "his services are worse than use-less." He even railed at the hours put in by city workers, noting "I am sure no man would think an active private business was well attended to if he and all his employees ceased work at four o'clock in the after-noon."

Cleveland had never been the world's most fluorescent personality, but the simplicity and decency of his communiqué gave it broad public purchase. Newspaper sales surged when the inaugural message was published.[12] His bark, if anything, understated the bite to come.

Though Cleveland only commanded the loyalties of a minority of the board of aldermen, his governing style made the math less of a handicap than it may have first appeared. His favorite tool of power—the one, in fact, that would define his mayoralty, as well as his later tenures as governor and president—was the veto. Critically, his allies amid the council numbered just enough to prevent the board from overriding his use of it—in fact, he would never be reversed during his mayoralty.

As a result, he quickly set to cleaning house. He vetoed the council's long-standing practice of paying local newspapers—especially the Ger-man press, with its considerable political power—for publishing the proceedings of the legislative body, coverage that Cleveland argued they would have provided without the subsidy. He rejected every attempt to add new spending that he believed did not serve a public purpose, in-cluding a bill to cover the legal costs of the city attorney, Edward C. Hawks—in a case where Cleveland himself, pre-mayoralty, had served as Hawks's lawyer.* He even took what seemed the politically suicidal step of vetoing an appropriation for the Fourth of July festivities of the Grand Army of the Republic, the influential group of Union veterans of the Civil War,† praising the organization while arguing that, "[T]he

---

*It's unclear whether Hawks was being reimbursed or whether Cleveland, notoriously lax in his billing practices, was never compensated and thus vetoing his own pay for work already performed.
†For a modern analogy, imagine a politician vetoing funds for an organization with the emotional appeal of the VFW and the political power of a major union.

money contributed should be a free gift of the citizens and taxpayers, and should not be extorted from them by taxation. This is so because the purpose for which this money is asked does not involve their protection or interest as members of the community, and it may or may not be approved by them."*

While no bit of city business was too small to attract Cleveland's scrutiny, two issues in particular raised his profile during the year that he spent in the mayor's office, both of them demonstrating that he was beginning to augment sheer grit with considerable political skills.

The first was the seemingly prosaic issue of cleaning Buffalo's streets. In June 1882, the council sent Cleveland a bill awarding a five-year, $422,500 contract† to George Talbot for the upkeep of the city's roadways. Then all hell broke loose. Talbot was not the lowest bidder, nor was he even close: one quote had come in at $315,000, another at $313,500. Compounding matters was the fact that Talbot had resubmitted his bid at a price $50,000 higher than what he had originally quoted the city—a surplus widely understood as spoils to be kicked back to the aldermen who helped to grease the skids. With a growing sense of buyer's remorse among aldermen who realized that, even by the council's debased standards, they were crawling out on a limb— there was a rush to rescind the appropriation before the mayor could get his hands on it. Unfortunately for them, it was hard to get a jump on a chief executive who never slept. The new mayor's veto was returned before the council could act, accompanied by a fusillade on the legislative branch in which he described its action "as the culmination of a most bare-faced, impudent, and shameless scheme to betray the interests of the people, and to worse than squander the public money."[13]

Gone were the formalities with which Cleveland had tempered his

---

*The less-often-told coda of the story: Cleveland made a personal donation equal to 10 percent of the GAR's budget request, then deputized the president of the city council to help raise the rest through private funds. In the end, the organization raised 40 percent more than it had requested from the city treasury.

†Approximately $11.2 million in 2019 dollars.

criticisms in the inaugural message. Indeed, he all but put a bounty on the members' heads:

> We are fast gaining positions in the grades of public stewardship. There is no middle ground. Those who are not for the people, either in or out of your Honorable Body, are against them, and should be treated accordingly.

Given the rapaciousness of the council, Cleveland—by now five months into his tenure—had already had plenty of opportunities to unleash a righteous rage, but by waiting for a piece of legislation so indefensible that even its authors were anxious to disown it, he had scored an unqualified victory. In the aftermath of the veto message, the council, which had passed the appropriation 15–11, hurriedly rescinded it by a vote of 23–2, subsequently awarding the contract to the lowest bidder.[14] The press and the public erupted in support of the mayor, with the *Buffalo Courier* observing, "Rarely have we heard such a universal and unanimous round of public applause as that which everywhere yesterday greeted Mayor Cleveland's message."[15]

Making the whole affair even more remarkable: Talbot, the vendor who had lost the inflated contract, was a close friend and former client of Cleveland's. For Grover, a political monastic, this was irrelevant. "This is neither a personal nor a legal matter," he had informed Talbot. "While I was your attorney, I was loyal to your interests. Now the people are my clients and I must be loyal to them."[16]

The other defining moment of Cleveland's mayoralty—which came to a climax almost simultaneously with the street-cleaning imbroglio—would prove to be his greatest lasting contribution to the city: the construction of a modern sewer system.

Buffalo was not unique in its struggles with public hygiene during this era: cramped quarters, the improper disposal of waste, and the practice of indiscriminately quartering dense groups of animals near human populations caused trouble in many urban areas. With the city located on sloping terrain, gravity would have allowed Buffalo's waste to drain away naturally had it not been for the fact that part of the Erie Canal was built along the drainage path. The result was a fetid stew in that part of the waterway, and a superabundance of infectious disease. In his inaugural message as mayor, Cleveland noted that more than one-third of Buffalo's deaths were due to epidemics, typhoid first among them.[17] A lack of cleanliness pervaded the city: livestock was nourished on unsanitary feed and many of the city's wells provided water too contaminated to be safely consumed.[18]*

The issue of what to do about the sewage problem had lingered for more than a decade—at one point the city had even been sued for maintaining a nuisance—during which time the council had taken two spectacularly unhelpful steps. The year prior to Cleveland's arrival, they had put out bids for a sewer project; but with contractors smelling an opportunity for spoils, the lowest quote came in at over $1.5 million,† and the project fell stillborn.[19] A temporizing effort to install a waterwheel succeeded only in pushing the muck upstream and aggravating the neighborhoods involuntarily drawn into Buffalo's circle of filth.

As it turned out, Cleveland was just as vigorous in catalyzing government to perform its necessary functions as he was in deterring it from indulging in superfluous ones. The opening gambit in this effort shocked the city council. Noting that building the sewer system would be the single largest infrastructure project in the city's history and that it would take at least three years to construct—longer than the terms of office of any city officials—he proposed that state lawmakers allow the city to put the project under the supervision of an independent cit-

---

*One incident precipitated by this fact is worth noting because it puts paid to the facile conception of Cleveland as a thoroughgoing libertarian. When a backlash erupted to the city shutting down an unsafe well, Cleveland vetoed attempts to reopen it, declaring, "My belief is that the citizen should be allowed great freedom in matters pertaining to himself as an individual. And yet this freedom should be no more than is consistent with the ends and purposes of a just and useful government, and there is no place in this enlightened age for the proposition that the authorities of a city may maintain an unwholesome well, known to be such, even though the people are willing to take the risk of life and health in the use of the water."
†Around $40 million in 2019 dollars.

izens' commission that could manage the effort with an eye toward efficiency and economy. What he didn't say—though it was obvious to all who understood the landscape—was that he was proposing to deprive the city council of a shot at a once-in-a-lifetime patronage sump.

Cleveland had stumbled upon a winning political formula: in an environment as corrupt as Buffalo, being a classical liberal also made him a de facto populist. With the press and the public rallying to his side, he proceeded to beat back every effort the council made to parry with the proposal. When they enlisted the city engineer to declare that the commission was unnecessary because the job—which had remained undone for eleven years—would be simple for his office to discharge on his own, Cleveland roared back, ". . . I am utterly amazed to learn at this late day, from the engineer's communication, that the job we have on hand is such an easy one."

When the council attempted to defang the legislation brewing in Albany, suggesting an alternate arrangement in which the members of the citizens' commission would be little more than figureheads, Cleveland publicly excoriated the proposal. The council's rearguard action proved a spectacular failure. The legislation would pass on precisely the terms Cleveland proposed.

Even then the mayor didn't put his guard down. After the commission was approved, the city council passed a resolution calling on Albany to allow Buffalo to float bonds to finance the project. Cleveland vetoed it, arguing that the length of the project—now estimated at ten years—gave the city sufficient time to pay for it without adding debt. In a final, flailing act of petulance, the aldermen then refused to confirm the five nominees Cleveland submitted to sit on the commission. Confident by this point that the electorate was overwhelmingly on his side, the mayor pulled the ultimate power move: he resubmitted the same five names and chalked up the council's previous rejection to "haste and confusion." All five were confirmed. By the time all was said and done, the project cost the city of Buffalo just under $765,000, roughly half the amount of the lowest bid received by the council the year prior.[20]

FIVE

Ugly Honest

In July 1882, Buffalo's ever-vigilant mayor had uncharacteristically abandoned his post. He was two hundred miles away, back at the home in which his mother had abruptly been widowed thirty years prior. Now it was Ann Neal Cleveland who lay dying. Grover had been caught flat-footed by his father's death, and the memory of that Utica newsboy announcing Richard's demise—to Cleveland an eternal reminder of the danger of letting your guard down, even for a moment—haunted him. Death had sneaked up on him too many times before. Virtually every hour that Ann Cleveland had left would be spent in the company of her dutiful son.

There was nothing in that vigil to suggest that the man keeping it had the business of one of America's largest cities on his mind, much less that he had of late developed an urge to upgrade to chief executive of the nation's most populous state. Both, however, were true. By the time Ann Cleveland crossed what Grover once referred to as "the stream of fate" on July 19, 1882, her youngest surviving son had, for the first time in his life, succumbed to something like genuine political ambition. And, in typical fashion, he had spent a few weeks in close quarters with his six living siblings and his dying mother . . . without breathing a word about it to any of them.[1]

We don't know when the thought of higher office first crossed Grover Cleveland's mind, but we have a pretty good handle on when it began to catch fire with the public. In the spring of 1882, the *Buffalo Sunday Times* was the first to editorialize that their mayor, the end of whose one-year term would roughly coincide with the gubernatorial election, was demonstrating the makings of a governor. This was, to put it mildly, something of a stretch. Though Buffalo—at this point the thirteenth-largest city in the country[2]—had more national and statewide relevance in Cleveland's day than it does in our own, it was still the case then, as now, that New York politics was dominated by downstate figures. Up to that time, western New York had produced only one governor and no U.S. senators. It should have been a daunting precedent—but Grover Cleveland was beginning to make a career out of beating exactly those kinds of odds.

There would be no protestations of indifference this time and no pining for the simplicity of life back in the firm. He had conducted his mayoralty on his own terms—terms that it had once seemed might doom his chances at any higher office—and wound up, probably even to his own surprise, loved for it by the people and the press. Why not see exactly how far he could push that advantage?

That was easier said than done. Cleveland had two major problems to overcome. The first was winning over Democrats in other parts of the state. The local press had amplified his reputation in western New York, but he still remained a relatively obscure figure elsewhere,[3*] especially on the all-important turf of New York City. The Cleveland luck in full bloom, unsolicited help on that front came from Edgar Apgar, New York's deputy treasurer and the party's self-appointed talent recruiter. The idealistic Apgar, who had been one of the driving forces behind the election of the reform-minded Democratic governor Samuel Tilden eight years prior, did his reconnaissance work through the insatiable consumption of newspapers from throughout the state. When word of Cleveland's street-cleaning veto arrived on his desk he was transfixed,

---

*When David B. Hill, later to become Cleveland's lieutenant governor and his successor in Albany, told a fellow party activist that Cleveland looked like the most formidable candidate for governor, his interlocutor replied, "Cleveland? Who in hell is Cleveland?"

telling a colleague that the mayor's response "contained sentiments which could only come from an ugly-honest man of good purposes and undaunted courage. . . ."[4] From that moment on, he'd evangelize to all who'd listen—including the mayor himself—on the imperative of making Cleveland the state's next governor. Equal parts campaign strategist and publicity agent, Apgar would soon prove essential to Cleveland's nomination.

Giving his name a familiar ring among New York Democrats, however, would prove a comparatively easy task relative to Cleveland's other great hurdle: navigating the increasingly complicated fissures within the party. Virtually every schism among the Empire State's Democrats in the early 1880s could be traced back a decade earlier, to the fall of William M. "Boss" Tweed, the head of the unfathomably powerful political machine known as Tammany Hall. Though Tweed's electoral summit was a single term in the U.S. House, his role as Grand Sachem of Tammany—there was no truer measure of his power than the ability to inspire fear with so florid a title—gave him such thoroughgoing control of the party machinery that he became the ultimate kingmaker among state Democrats. The power also made him greedy.

Tweed would fall to earth thanks to the poacher's paradox: Successful thieves become emboldened thieves, and emboldened thieves become unsuccessful thieves. In the summer of 1871, an erstwhile ally of Tweed's, spurned by the Grand Sachem, had turned over copies of the city's books to the *New York Times*. The scope of the theft was so monumental—over the course of his career, Tweed defrauded the city of at least $365 million in today's dollars, with some estimates ranging as high as $2.4 billion[5]—that the bond markets, panicked by how leaky Gotham's bucket had become, cut off credit to the city until it got its house in order.[6] Tammany men, having grown appropriately porcine, were led to the slaughter at the next election. While Tweed himself—who dedicated the limited political capital he had left to his own preservation—was able to retain his seat in the state senate, he was living on borrowed time. He'd be jailed in 1873, and again in

1875, even fleeing to Spain at one point via Cuba. Extradited back to the United States, he died of pneumonia in prison in 1878.

In the wake of Tweed's demise, three major factions had formed within the party. Tammany, its head bloody but unbowed, reorganized under the leadership of "Honest John" Kelly, the son of an Irish immigrant (an important advantage given the organization's ethnic constituency) and just enough of a reformer to put an end to the machine's most conspicuous excesses while keeping it firmly in the patronage business.* In the early days of Kelly's reign, the business wing of the party earnestly believed that Tammany could be rehabilitated and assimilated to a more decorous party establishment. When those efforts proved misbegotten, Tilden and many of the Democrats' moneyed elites broke into a faction known as Irving Hall, a pro-business contingent more interested in placing men of stature in public office than doing grubby constituent work in the wards. In 1880, a third wing, the New York County Democracy,† was formed to bind together the conservative and pro-reform members of the party, making it Tammany's de facto antagonist. The County Democracy was the logical home for Grover Cleveland—but no Democrat was going to secure the nomination with the support of only one faction. There was also another complicating factor: the county al-

---

*While Tammany Hall was rife with corruption and influence-peddling, its defenders often note that the organization provided vital social services for many poor New Yorkers, especially immigrants, who were often-treated as second-class citizens (New York's Five Points Mission, for example, once attempted to have poor Irish Catholic children adopted out to midwestern Protestants to hasten their assimilation). There is something to be said for this argument, especially given the lack of any meaningful welfare state during this era. That stipulated, the good the organization may have done does not offset its illicit behavior, much of which was financed by funds taken from the public purse. For a revisionist defense of Tammany, see Terry Golway's *Machine Made: Tammany Hall and the Creation of Modern American Politics*.

†While the phrase may seem inelegant to the modern ear, "The Democracy" was a standard way to refer to the Democratic Party throughout much of the 1800s. The term came into fashion with the presidency of Andrew Jackson, who added a populist flair—including an emphasis on broader suffrage—to the political party that had first come to the White House with Thomas Jefferson in 1801. Indeed, the term was a contrast to the Jeffersonian-era practice of referring to the party as "Republicans," a designation that is often retroactively altered to "Democratic-Republicans" to make clear that the organization eventually morphed into the modern Democratic Party. The organization that we *now* know as the Republican Party was not founded until the 1850s.

ready had a favored candidate for governor in Allan Campbell, the New York City comptroller.

Campbell was far from the only challenger. The landscape for the gubernatorial nomination was unmapped, and it was not immediately clear how Cleveland should navigate it. The two leading candidates for governor were Roswell Flower, a congressman and wealthy financier (who would eventually serve as governor from 1892 to 1894), and Henry Slocum, a retired Union general who had parlayed roles at Gettysburg and in Sherman's March to the Sea into a prominent civic role in Brooklyn and a stint in the House of Representatives. Both, however, were eyed warily by County Democrats for being insufficiently distant from Tammany. Ironically, Tammany itself—demonstrating a discipline that Kelly cultivated in his best moments and tended to destroy in his worst—stood unaligned, waiting to see how the race took shape before deciding which course of action would be most propitious.

Edgar Apgar, anxious to see Cleveland take his rightful place in the party firmament, wrote to the mayor in August 1882, a month ahead of New York's Democratic convention, advising him to set up a meeting with Daniel Manning, the state party chairman, publisher of the *Albany Argus*, and de facto head of the Tilden wing of the party. Cleveland, who by now had grown adept at turning his personal virtues into political ones, rejected the advice. He had no desire to kiss anyone's ring, and whatever advantages he might gain by putting himself in Manning's good graces, he told Apgar, would be outweighed by the accusations that he had chosen sides in the party's internecine struggle.[7] In a protean political atmosphere, he wanted to remain palatable to every faction within the party without seeming like a loyalist to any one of them. It was not a strategy that could succeed in sweeping him to the front of the field, but it could work if the convention failed to produce a quick consensus and had to look beyond the initial favorites.

As in the mayor's race a year prior, Cleveland got an unexpected assist from a GOP cracking under the stress of internal pressures. Beginning with the presidency of Ulysses S. Grant (1869–77), Republicans, their majorities swelled in the aftermath of the Civil War, began to learn that any party with a coalition large enough to achieve electoral dominance is also a party uniquely vulnerable to internal rifts. In the absence of an effective opposition with which to do battle, combative energies had turned inward, concentrated around a strenuous battle over civil service reform. On one side were the Stalwarts, defenders of the spoils system and political machine power, led by New York senator Roscoe Conkling and aligned with Grant. On the other were the Half-Breeds, Republicans who were prepared to forswear the blandishments of patronage and move to a merit-based system.

One of the first flash points in this debate came in 1878, when Grant's Republican successor, President Rutherford B. Hayes, stuck his chin out for reform by firing two prominent civil servants from his own party: Chester A. Arthur, the collector of the Port of New York, and Alonzo B. Cornell, a naval officer who served under Arthur (and moonlighted as the chairman of New York's Republican Party). In the four years between that act and the 1882 gubernatorial election, however, the tables had turned. Arthur, having become vice president on a compromise ticket with the Half-Breed James Garfield, had been elevated to the presidency upon Garfield's assassination. Cornell (son of the Ivy League university's cofounder and namesake) had been elected governor of New York.

Cornell, however, had surprised the Stalwarts by demonstrating an independent streak once in office, defying their wishes for patronage and appointments. Arthur, working in tandem with Conkling[8]* and the railroad magnate Jay Gould (who had been embittered by a Cornell veto),

---

*Conkling was by this point a private citizen, having committed one of the most spectacular own goals in American political history. Incensed that President Garfield hadn't consulted him on the choice of nominee for New York City customs collector—perhaps the choicest patronage perch in the country—Conkling and his fellow New York senator Thomas Platt resigned their seats, confident that the state legislature (which selected U.S. senators up until the adoption of the Seventeenth Amendment in 1913) would reappoint them. In Conkling's calculus, this would humiliate Garfield and send a powerful message about his need to defer to the Senate. In the wake of Garfield's assassination, the New York legislature did not return either man to office.

conspired to deny the popular and well-respected governor renomination. The trio engaged in an elaborate plot that involved replacing many of the delegates to the convention and even engaging in voter fraud.[9]* Every inch of chicanery proved necessary: Cornell was only denied a return to the ballot by a margin of eight votes. His replacement was Charles J. Folger, a New York judge whom Arthur had made his secretary of the Treasury, and who commanded virtually no grassroots support.

The impression was unmistakable: the Republican Party's leadership was willing to cast aside an able public servant in favor of someone who knew that his loyalty to the Stalwarts came before his loyalty to the people of New York. Had anyone at the highest echelons of the New York GOP been paying attention to the still-obscure mayor of Buffalo, they might have realized that they were playing right into his hands. What made this gambit all the more dangerous: two of the last four Democratic presidential nominees had been governors of New York, a state without which the party had almost no hope of recapturing the White House. Chester Arthur had just inadvertently authored the terms on which his party would surrender the presidency.

The news that Folger would replace Cornell on the Republican ticket broke just as Democrats were assembling in Syracuse for their nominating convention—upending their calculations. If Cleveland now saw an opening, the press wasn't as quick to pick up on it. "Only one candidate is mentioned who resides west of Albany, and that is Mayor Cleveland of Buffalo," the *New York Times* reported; "no one here expresses any confidence in his nomination."[10] Prior to the opening of the convention, Cleveland had moved into what looked to be a respectable third place standing among the candidates, ahead of a smattering of minor candidates but still lagging well behind Flower and Slocum. But the combination of Folger's nomination and Cleveland's decision to remain at arm's length from intraparty machinations had piqued the curiosity of the

---

*This was not a novel sin for Arthur, who, at a boozy dinner following the 1880 presidential election, had intimated—in front of an audience that included journalists—that voter fraud from the Stalwart machine had provided Garfield's margin of victory in Indiana.

delegates. With Flower and Slocum looking less viable under the new circumstances, there were signs that Democrats were willing to take one last look at the menu.

Cleveland arrived in Syracuse on the evening of Thursday, September 21, held court with delegates in a hotel lobby, paid the visit to Daniel Manning that Apgar had previously suggested, and was on a train back to Buffalo a few hours after midnight. The visit did not cause the existing coalitions to fracture, at least not immediately. When the first round of balloting took place the next day, there was a virtual tie: 98 votes for Slocum, 97 for Flower. Cleveland had managed 66. Allan Campbell, the County Democracy's candidate, had failed to so much as place. The power brokers were divided. Daniel Manning, despite the visit with Cleveland, was backing Slocum. John Kelly, who cared more about maintaining Tammany's influence than about giving any particular candidate the nod, had hedged, spreading the machine's votes throughout the field. In the second round of balloting, with the minor candidates falling away, the math changed but the dynamics did not. Cleveland inched up a few votes, but not as much as Flower and Slocum, now deadlocked at 123.

What happened next surely owed in part to the impression that Cleveland had made with his visit to the convention; but at least as much, and likely more, of the credit goes to Apgar, the man who had believed in the Cleveland campaign before there ever was such a thing. At the onset of the convention it was Apgar who took to the stage to place Cleveland's name in nomination. The resulting speech—delivered with the kind of eloquence that flows most easily from sincerity— underscored the mayor's reformist bona fides and integrity. But it also made a practical observation: in a state where Republicans held the advantage, he explained, only Cleveland had the potential to draw critical crossover votes, a talent he had demonstrated in the Buffalo mayor's race. The speech so galvanized the room that Roswell Flower's supporters, nervous that their man was especially vulnerable to defections toward Cleveland, attempted to shout Apgar down.[11]

Cleveland, aided by Apgar's star turn, was about to ride his "everybody's second choice" strategy to the nomination. The County Democracy forces, nervous at the prospect that Manning was only a ballot away from swinging the convention to Slocum, went over to Cleveland. Flower's forces, realizing their candidate was no longer viable, did the same, almost to a man. As Cleveland's gravitational pull became too great to resist, even Tammany, which had no priority greater than ingratiating itself with the winner, swung over. Cleveland had shot the gap: not only had he secured the nomination, he had done so without conceding anything to the parts of the party with which he was most ill at ease. It was a fact that would come back to haunt Tammany for years to come.

Navigating the convention proved to be a far more complicated process than the general election to follow.* Cleveland had once again found himself in a "throw the bums out" race where the opposition party went out of its way to identify as the bums. As a result, the 1882 race saw Cleveland elected governor of New York with the largest margin of victory ever recorded in the state up to that time, much of it attributable to Republicans who crossed party lines to vote for him. As had happened in Buffalo, however, there were those who were skeptical that the new chief executive could deliver on the potential the voters saw in him. One wag declared, "He's gone up like a rocket, but he'll come down like the stick."[12]

Those kinds of predictions evinced an unfamiliarity with the subject. The trick to Grover Cleveland was that he could only surprise you if you hadn't been paying attention. The man in office was precisely the man who had been on the ballot, who was precisely the man who toiled long into the night behind his law desk, who was precisely the kid who

---

*Apart from its lopsided outcome, there was one other notable fact about the 1882 New York governor's race: it counted two U.S. Treasury secretaries as combatants. In addition to the Republican nominee Folger, who had briefly held the post under Arthur, Daniel Manning—the Democrats' state chairman and Grover Cleveland's de facto campaign manager in the general election—would run Treasury during the first two years of Cleveland's administration. Manning's brother John would also be elected Cleveland's successor as mayor of Buffalo.

showed up at the Erie Canal at 4 a.m. to get a jump on his competition. To the extent he was profound it was because he was a simple, straightforward man in a Janus-faced profession. To the extent his conduct was shocking it was only because he had a habit of doing exactly what he had said he would do. A letter written to his brother Will on election day underscored that his internal compass remained fixed: "[T]he policy I intend to adopt . . . is to make the matter a business engagement between the people of the state and myself, in which the obligation on my side is to perform the duties assigned me with an eye single to the interest of my employers. I shall have no idea of reelection or any higher political preferment in my head, but be very thankful and happy if I can well serve one term as the people's governor."[13]

Cleveland became governor on January 1, 1883, and, as with his early days in the mayor's office, quickly made his presence felt. But where his stint at city hall had started with a scorched-earth offensive, his tenure as governor would begin on a more magnanimous note: channeling his inner Andrew Jackson,* Cleveland—who, as a rule, chafed at formality and pretense—instructed the staff at the executive mansion to "admit anyone who asks to see the governor."[14] While it's easy to dismiss such gestures as the vestige of a more innocent time, Cleveland was surely aware of the danger: Charles Guiteau, the man who had assassinated Garfield only eighteen months earlier, had been in the White House several times because of precisely this kind of open-door policy (though Garfield's assassination took place at a local train station, not on the White House grounds).[15] There was a method, however, to Cleveland's madness. Most in-person visits to the head of the executive branch were appeals for patronage jobs. Cleveland used the occasions to torment supplicants—and send a message about how business was going to be done in Albany. When visitors asked him for a "favor," he'd narrow his eyes and respond, "I don't know that I understand you."

---

*Jackson famously opened the White House to all comers for his 1829 inauguration, an event that, legend has it, descended into such chaos that he exited via a window.

When they'd attempt to whisper conversation, he'd reply at a volume likely to be heard in the antechamber.[16] So, yes, there was danger in his accessibility, but mostly for his guests.

The governor's residence was a novel experience for Cleveland, who, despite being in his mid-forties and the chief executive of America's largest state, had never before had a home of his own.* Now he was in possession of a mansion far beyond the needs of an unfussy bachelor. He kept a minimal household staff and had no use for any of the home's amenities beyond the work desk. He made only one addition: a billiard table. Not that he'd have much time to use it. Dispensing with the standard gubernatorial carriage, Cleveland would walk to the Capitol every morning, make brief strolls home for lunch and dinner—and return to the office after *both*, often working past midnight (inevitably capping off his labors by telling Daniel Lamont, an aide whom Manning had furnished him, "Well, I guess we'll quit and call it a half-day").

While his work ethic was common knowledge in Buffalo, it was a novelty to the Albany press corps, with one reporter fretting:

> "The eyes of the large man look glassy, his skin hangs on his cheeks in thick, unhealthy-looking folds, the coat buttoned about his large chest and abdomen looks ready to burst with the confined fat. Plainly he is a man who is not taking enough exercise; he remains within doors constantly, eats and works, eats and works, works and eats. . . . There was not a night last week that he departed from the new Capitol before one A.M. Such work is killing work."[17]

For audiences of the day, this was understood as something more than hyperbole. It had only been about thirty-five years since President James K. Polk, possessed of a similar indefatigability, had put in similar

---

*While serving as mayor of Buffalo, Cleveland kept the apartment attached to his law firm—and had, in fact, remained a partner, as it was customary for mayors to keep their day jobs. In practice, however, he had emeritus status.

hours in the White House only to die at the age of fifty-three three months after leaving office.*

Whatever concerns existed that the governor was working himself too hard, however, didn't translate to deference about how he spent what little leisure time he had. On Sundays, Grover would often take time out for a hobby he justified with a creative reading of Richard Cleveland's moral instruction—"My father used to say that it was wicked to go fishing on Sunday, but he never said anything about draw-poker," was the seasoned lawyer's analysis. The local Presbyterian minister, annoyed that the governor had more time for gambling than for God, had made known that he'd like to see Cleveland in church more often. Proving that pastor's kids, like the devil, can cite scripture for their own purposes, the mischievous governor responded, "tell him an ass fell into a pit."[18]†

That kind of confidence was a central element of the new governor's style. Despite his elevated stature—and the proportional increase in scrutiny—he continued to conduct himself with exactly the same kind of self-assurance that had characterized his tenure as mayor of Buffalo. Even though the state legislature was controlled by his fellow Democrats, for example, Cleveland—incorrigible legislative serial killer—still issued forty-four vetoes in his first year in office.[19]

When presented with a bill that would reorganize Buffalo's fire department—and make it easier for local Democrats to stack it with cronies—he issued a swift rejection, paying no mind to pressure from within his own party. In reaction, the *Albany Evening Journal* editorialized that the governor was proving himself "bigger and better than his party."[20]

Sounding every bit like the man who once vetoed funds for a Fourth

---

*Polk was indeed a workaholic—the first gaslights were installed in the White House during his presidency, partially so he could work more efficiently after dark. But while the common narrative that he worked himself to death is a tidy one, at least some of the credit for his demise surely belongs to the cholera outbreak that claimed his life.

†In the gospel of Luke, Jesus, signaling a softening approach to strict observance of the holy day, asks "Which of you shall have an ass or an ox fallen into a pit, and will not straightway pull him out on the sabbath day?"

of July celebration, he killed a bill allowing county commissioners to erect soldiers' monuments, reminding lawmakers that taxpayer money was to be used "for a purpose connected with the safety and substantial welfare of the public."[21] It wasn't a strategy designed to make friends, but then that wasn't the point. As Cleveland explained early in his administration, "Let me rise or fall, I am going to work for the interests of the people of the state, regardless of party or anything else."[22]

Carried to office by a bipartisan coalition, Cleveland was perpetually sensitive to the fact that his mandate was to rise above reflexive party loyalty. As a legislative matter, that meant attempting to stitch together a majority from the reform elements in both parties (the origin of his partnership with a young reformist Republican in the state assembly named Theodore Roosevelt), as well as opposing the equally bipartisan forces of political machine power, known in Albany as the Black Horse Cavalry. To that end, he'd sign a civil service reform bill championed by Roosevelt and outlaw the practice of compelling state employees to pay dues to political parties.

Not that the relationship between the two men was always smooth sailing. Political reporter William Hudson provided an eyewitness account of a confrontation between the future presidents in Cleveland's chambers, when the governor decided to veto a series of bills Roosevelt had introduced making structural changes to the government of New York City. The two men didn't even disagree on the substance. But Cleveland, fastidious as ever, was in the habit of vetoing bills for sloppy draftsmanship, a sin of which this package—which, for instance, specified two different term lengths for the same office—was obviously guilty. Roosevelt, whose rhetoric, when exercised, tended toward a curious mix of God of the Old Testament and petulant child, bellowed, "You must not veto those bills. You cannot! You shall not! I can't have it and I won't have it!"

Cleveland had a trademark tic in moments like this. He would raise his meaty hand in the air. He would clench it into a cannonball. And he would land it swiftly back on the desk in a thunderclap. That sound and

Cleveland's simultaneous declaration—"Mr. Roosevelt, I *am* going to veto those bills!"—are recorded to have landed with such force that the young bull moose fell back in his chair . . . before subsequently excusing himself. Lamont, Cleveland's aide, was recorded by Hudson as going to a window and looking "out on the green in an endeavor to get rid of the broad smile that was plastered on his face."[23]*

That sort of steadfastness extended from Cleveland's relationship with the legislative branch to his management of the executive branch, where it meant handing out appointments to men with technical expertise or demonstrated talent rather than party connections, even when it led to grousing from his fellow Democrats. In an extreme example of the principle, his appointee to be superintendent of insurance, a widely coveted post among the political class, was a man who had worked his way up from being one of the department's couriers.[24]

The hallmarks of his administration—an emphasis on economy, integrity, and good-government reforms—were familiar enough, but his new perch also expanded his intellectual horizons. He proposed that corporations be required to file quarterly financial disclosures, partially to provide transparency for investors, partially to allow better scrutiny of their lobbying expenses.[25] He pushed to reduce the use of force in state prisons, where he suspected the authorities were exceeding the letter of the law.[26] And he signed the first conservation measures to protect Niagara Falls, a proposal his predecessor had rebuffed with the question, "why should we spend the people's money when just as much water will run over the falls without a park as with it?"[27]

That sentiment, though risible by contemporary standards, is noteworthy for another reason: it sounded like it could have been uttered by Grover Cleveland. After all, is it so obvious that the man who vetoed a Fourth of July celebration would recognize some sublime public purpose in preserving a waterfall, no matter how grand?

---

*The incident perhaps confirmed Lamont's observation that "I never see those two together that I'm not reminded of a picture I have of a great mastiff solemnly regarding a small terrier, snapping and barking at him."

If Cleveland's definition of what constituted "the public good" is opaque to us, it is perhaps in part because it was opaque to him, too. He was not prone to introspection and was disinclined toward philosophical abstraction. When, during the first term of his presidency, his quest for tariff reform was bogged down in theoretical arguments about trade, he snapped, "It is a condition which confronts us—not a theory."[28] It was a telling utterance.

Cleveland tended to regard himself as an inductive thinker, reasoning from a series of discrete facts to a logical conclusion. But while that was a reasonably accurate description of the *means* by which he acquired his views, it did not account for the *ends* he had in mind. What did Grover Cleveland think the point of government was?

In reality, Grover Cleveland's view of "the public good" bore a remarkable resemblance to the way economists use that term today. In the dismal science, "public good" is a term of art, referring to goods or services that satisfy two criteria: (1) they are "non-rival," meaning no one person's use of them reduces any other individual's use of them, and (2) they are "non-excludable," meaning no individual can be kept from reaping their benefits. A classic example is national defense. A military protecting America's shores from invasion provides the same benefit equally to all citizens. And no one citizen can be removed from underneath its protective umbrella.

Cleveland, of course, would not have recognized this framework—for one thing, it wasn't articulated in this fashion until well into the twentieth century—and may well have dismissed it as the kind of theorizing that tended to set his eyes rolling. But he nevertheless seems to have intuited it. Scan Grover Cleveland's entire political career and there is but one principle—always articulated, if not always consistently applied—that shaped all the others: government exists to protect the welfare of the people *as a whole*. And any preference government shows to one individual over another is to be regarded as per se suspicious.

That conviction would soon be put to the test in the central drama of his gubernatorial term, which had its roots in a development that should have been obvious to all involved from the day he made his candidacy known: Grover Cleveland was on a crash course with perhaps the most powerful man in his own party, Tammany's "Honest John" Kelly. In another life or another profession, the two may have been friends. Like Cleveland, Kelly had been shaped by the death of his father at a young age. Like Cleveland, he had achieved financial security through a stint as sheriff (though, because Kelly's tenure was in New York City, it was considerably more remunerative). And, like Cleveland, he was notorious for working punishing hours.[29] And while Kelly was not quite the civic moralist Cleveland was, he had evinced genuine political courage over the course of his career. While serving in the House of Representatives (where he was the only Catholic member) during the 1850s—an era when anti-Catholic bigotry had fueled the emergence of the Know-Nothing Party—Kelly had been a lonely voice striking back against the sectarian attacks.

Yet while Cleveland could be self-righteous in moments of indignation, his wrath was rarely the product of impulse; he was too methodical, too controlled for that. Kelly, by contrast, though often a cool and deliberate strategist, had a propensity to turn into a mad dog when he felt slighted. The consequences could be far-reaching. In 1879, frustrated by the party's lack of deference to Tammany, Kelly had staged a walkout from the state Democratic convention, had himself nominated for governor on a schismatic ticket, and thus doomed the reelection of the Democratic incumbent, Lucius Robinson, handing the election to Cornell. The following year, Kelly succeeded in a monomaniacal quest to ensure that Samuel Tilden, a man with whom he had been close before the latter's governorship put them at political odds, was denied another shot at the Democratic presidential nomination.* The conven-

---

*Tilden had been the Democratic presidential nominee in 1876, when he narrowly lost to Republican Rutherford B. Hayes. Perhaps the most indecisive presidential election in American history, disputed vote totals in three southern states prevented the naming of a winner. While Tilden won the popular vote, Hayes was ultimately chosen the victor by a fifteen-member electoral commission created by Congress.

tional wisdom was that to cross John Kelly was to take your political life in your hands.

As with so many instances in Grover Cleveland's career, it's not clear whether he ignored that orthodoxy because he thought he was smart enough to subvert it or because he was simply too stubborn to care. Because of the circumstances under which he had acquired the nomination, Cleveland owed Kelly no debts. Because of the convictions that led him to seek the office in the first place, he also thought he owed him no respect. Cleveland hadn't even offered political perks to his old allies in Buffalo, almost none of whom came with him to Albany, and the last thing he was going to do was to extend that courtesy to the Tammany machine that he reviled. Cleveland refused to hold any meetings with Kelly and ignored all his suggestions for appointments to state office.[30]

Kelly was thus already at a vigorous simmer when Cleveland brought matters to a boil. In March 1883, Cleveland received a bill, passed in the legislature by overwhelming margins, that would have lowered fares on New York City's elevated railway (the city's first form of mass transit, preceding the subway) to five cents per ride (at the time, the five-cent fare only applied during rush hour, with trips costing ten cents during the rest of the day). This was not a purely public question, as the railway was privately owned and operated by the robber baron Jay Gould, though its permissible fares and profits were exhaustively codified in New York law. Given the popular appeal of cutting prices and the contempt in which Gould, who let neither legal nor moral scruples stand in the way of enhancing his wealth, was held, there was wide bipartisan support. This was the rare piece of legislation that could be supported with equal fervor by Thomas Grady, Kelly's cat's paw in the legislature, and Theodore Roosevelt, who rarely saw eye to eye with Tammany but hated Gould with the fire of a thousand suns.[31]*

---

*Roosevelt would say at the time, "If it were possible, I would willingly pass a bill of attainder [an unconstitutional enactment singling out someone for punishment without trial] on Jay Gould and all of Jay Gould's associates."

That, of course, made things awkward when Grover Cleveland vetoed it.

Cleveland carried no particular torch for Gould and conceded the
desirability of lowering fares for commuters. But the governor was nothing if not a constitutionalist and there he had a problem. Article I of the
Constitution prohibits states from passing "any law impairing the obligation of contracts." In Cleveland's reading, the state was attempting to
renege on the contractual guarantees that had created the economic
preconditions for the railway to be built in the first place. In his veto
message he argued that what was at stake was more than just constitutional fidelity:

> The fact is notorious that for many years rapid transit was the
> great need of the inhabitants of the city of New York and was
> of direct importance to the citizens of the state. Projects which
> promised to answer the people's wants in this direction failed
> and were abandoned. The Legislature, appreciating the situa-
> tion, willingly passed statute after statute calculated to aid and
> encourage a solution of the problem. Capital was timid and hes-
> itated to enter a new field full of risks and dangers. By the prom-
> ise of liberal fares, as will be seen in all the acts passed on this
> subject, and through other concessions gladly made, capitalists
> were induced to invest their money in the enterprise, and rapid
> transit but lately became an accomplished fact.... It is manifestly
> important that invested capital should be protected and that its
> necessity and usefulness in the development of enterprises valu-
> able to the people should be recognized by conservative conduct
> on the part of the state government.

Cleveland was characteristically confident that he was right. He was
also confident that he was going to pay a steep political price. Preparing
for bed on the night of the veto, he muttered to himself, "By tomorrow
at this time I shall be the most unpopular man in the state of New

York."[32] In his office the next morning, he studiously avoided the news-papers. His curiosity eventually getting the better of him, he then non-chalantly asked Lamont if he had been mentioned in the day's press. "Why yes, they are all praising you," came the reply. And then, from the governor: "They are? Well here, let me see them!"

As with his street-cleaning veto in Buffalo, Cleveland's exhaustive audit of the relevant law had so decidedly won the day that he had not only earned the media's admiration for taking a stand on principle but had also shamed members of the legislature into public mea culpas. Teddy Roosevelt, not a man known for second-guessing himself, de-clared, "I have to say with shame that when I voted for this bill I did not act as I think I ought to have acted. . . . I have to confess that I weakly yielded, partly to a vindictive spirit toward the infernal thieves who have the Elevated Railroad in charge, and partly in answer to the popular voice in New York." "Nevertheless," he added, ". . . I question whether the bill is constitutional." He wasn't the only one making an about-face. De-spite the fact that the original legislation had passed virtually unop-posed, Cleveland's veto was sustained.

Not among those engaging in self-flagellating apologies was Thomas Grady, Kelly's man in Albany. Tammany had good reason to be put out. By denying them a piece of popular legislation that he could have signed at no political cost, Cleveland was adding insult to the injury of serially denying their patronage requests. Over the coming months, Kelly's oper-ation upped the pressure. When Cleveland had a passel of nominations to make for the state's immigration department and its harbormasters, Tammany, led by Grady, held up the appointees, hoping that it would force the governor to name some of their men to the open positions. Instead, Cleveland let the legislative session expire without action, lead-ing the harbormaster positions to be abolished outright.[33]

Everywhere Cleveland turned, Grady was in his face. Every time, the governor refused to budge. Matters finally came to a head in the fall of 1883, as nominating season was about to get under way for the next leg-islative election. Exercising his power as de facto head of the state party,

Cleveland took the rare step of initiating communication with John Kelly—in the form of a letter informing him that it would be better for all involved if Thomas Grady, Kelly's pit bull, wasn't back in Albany for the next legislative session.

"I do not wish to conceal the fact that my personal comfort and satisfaction are involved in the matter," he wrote. "But I know that good legislation, based upon a pure desire to promote the interests of the people and the improvement of legislative methods, are also deeply involved." Then, in an Olympian display of passive-aggressiveness, this coda: "I forbear to write in detail the other considerations having relation to the welfare of the party and the approval to be secured by a change for the better in the character of its representatives. These things will occur to you without suggestion from me." Even by Cleveland's standards this was a directive that took some chutzpah: kill your man before I do.

Here we must entertain the notion that if Grover Cleveland wasn't a political genius he had an incredible knack for stumbling into situations that made him look like one. The reality is that this gambit should not have worked (indeed, Dan Lamont, Cleveland's aide, advised him against sending the letter). All Kelly needed to do in response was take a page out of Cleveland's playbook and simply ignore the prickly correspondence. But Honest John Kelly had a tendency to lose his mind when someone waved a red cape in front of him, and as he found that intraparty opposition to Grady ran deeper than just the governor—he wound up unable to get Grady renominated despite shopping for a favorable district—his anger only compounded. Reaching a breaking point, he leaked Cleveland's letter to the press, thinking that he would expose the governor as overstepping his bounds and promoting disharmony within Democratic ranks.

The move backfired spectacularly. Cleveland was seen to be preaching exactly the same kind of virtues in private that he was in public. Taking further advantage, he used the wave of support as an excuse to make explicit what had been the subtext of his entire administration all along: he had no interest in party unity if it meant compromising with Kelly and his ilk. In an interview with the *New York Herald*, he predicted, "[T]he time is fast approaching when this odious system [of political bosses] will be swept away and the voice of the people alone be recognized as potent in determining nominees for public offices." But if Cleveland thought his troubles with Grady, now untethered from office, were over, he was mistaken: Grady promptly began spreading the rumor that Cleveland had been bribed to veto the fare-reduction bill. It was perhaps the most incendiary allegation ever made against the governor. Within a year it would look like child's play.

In the two years that had passed since a meal at Billy Dranger's restaurant in Buffalo had altered the course of his life, Grover Cleveland, a man who had spent so much of his life stuck in neutral, had moved from triumph to triumph at breakneck speed. As 1884 dawned, he seemed to be riding higher than ever before. But there was also an ominous undercurrent at work, one that would subtly prefigure his later struggles.

Cleveland's appeal resided in the fact that he was a political purgative in a corrupt era. As demonstrated by his torrent of vetoes and his showdowns with machine politicians, he was constitutionally incapable of making the minor concessions to practicality that lubricate most of political life, a trait that gave him an aura of heroism but that also carried with it tangible consequences. The cleavages within the Democratic Party, for instance, had cost it both houses of the state legislature in the 1883 elections. Having thus diminished the ranks of his legislative allies and stoked a civil war within his own party, the remaining two years of Cleveland's gubernatorial term were almost certain to bring tougher sledding.* This would be something new: he had suffered no such consequences as mayor of Buffalo, a post he only held for a year and had managed to escape before the political bill came due. To the shock of virtually everyone, he was about to do it again.

---

*At the time, New York governors were elected to three-year terms.

SIX

"Rum, Romanism, and Rebellion"

It was the most important night of Grover Cleveland's life—and the phone was dead. Such were conditions at the governor's mansion in Albany on the evening of November 4, 1884, the night of the first presidential election where the candidates could be apprised of returns via the invention Alexander Graham Bell had patented eight years earlier. That was the idea, anyway. But with heavy rain falling all over the eastern United States the connection had gone down. It was a mixed blessing. While the lack of communication was ominous, conventional wisdom also had it that bad weather was a recipe for reduced Republican turnout.[1] With the election looking to be decided by a razor-thin margin, anxiety was running high. It was a fitting end. The process of running for president had made Grover Cleveland miserable. Why should the final hours be any different?

It hadn't started that way. In fact, the genesis of Cleveland's presidential campaign, especially by comparison to his previous races, looked downright conventional. This time around, he wasn't a dark horse or an insurgent. And, yes, he had made the usual noises disclaiming any ambition, reviving the old "I'd rather be back at Mount Vernon" shtick (though his Buffalo apartment—where the most lavish amenity was an icebox filled with watermelons[2]—was not quite a statesman's manor). But by now the protests no longer seemed credible.

It was, of course, possible for a presidential candidate to take his name out of contention, no matter how irresistible the groundswell behind him seemed. Why hadn't Cleveland done so? "I should long ago have made such declarations publicly as I have privately," he somewhat disingenuously wrote his friend Charles Fairchild,* the former New York attorney general, "had I not been restrained by good friends who seemed to think my silence on the subject had better be longer maintained." And then, a few lines later, the final step in this peculiarly Victorian waltz: "I should not feel, perhaps, that I ought to refuse to do what the sentiment of my party shall require of me. . . ."[3]

Duty was surely a part of the equation, even if it wasn't served neat. But Cleveland also had to know what was obvious to all those with even the most rudimentary understanding of the politics of the day: he was uniquely suited to the moment. For Democrats to win a presidential election—something they hadn't done for nearly thirty years, since before the Civil War—they had to field a candidate who could expand the party's coalition to a handful of states outside of the solid South, foremost among them the one that had recently elected him governor by historic margins. With the GOP fracturing over the merits of the spoils system, Cleveland's reformist fides looked likely to attract disenchanted Republicans at the national level, just as they had in Buffalo and New York State. And with Democrats divided as well—there were differences on the issue of whether and how tariffs should be reduced,[4]† the legacy of the Civil War, and the limits of states' rights—Cleveland, who had never held a federal office that compelled an opinion on any of those disputes, was just the blank slate the party needed.

---

*Fairchild would later serve as Cleveland's Treasury secretary during the latter half of his first term as president.

†Modern observers are often confused by the centrality of tariff debates to nineteenth-century American politics. The explanation: prior to the enactment of a permanent federal income tax in 1913 (a temporary one had been imposed during the Civil War), tariffs were the main source of federal revenue. Tariff debates can thus be thought of as a rough analogue to modern arguments over income tax rates. Indeed, more of the federal budget came from tariff revenues in the first year of Cleveland's presidency than comes from individual income taxes today.

The odds tilted even more in his favor in June, when the Republican Party held its convention in Chicago. In the four years since the GOP's last gathering, events within the party had taken astonishing, almost implausible turns. First came President Garfield's assassination, a slow-motion agony in which the president lingered for nearly three months after being shot, losing eighty pounds in the process[5] and essentially leaving the country without a chief executive. Then came his replacement by Vice President Chester Arthur, a man whom reasonable critics suspected because of his long ties to Stalwart cronyism and whom less reasonable ones suspected on the grounds that he may have played a role in Garfield's murder[6] (it did not help matters any that Charles Guiteau, the mentally ill assassin, had proclaimed "I am a Stalwart of Stalwarts! Arthur is President now!" upon gunning Garfield down).[7] Perhaps most surprising of all: Arthur's subsequent about-face as president, when, still smarting from deep Republican losses in the 1882 midterm elections, he signed the Pendleton Civil Service Reform Act, precisely the kind of measure that the Stalwarts existed to defeat. While historians often reward converts, their political contemporaries tend to be more withholding. Rather than being hailed as a statesman, Arthur had triangulated his way out of a constituency. Stalwarts distrusted him because he had betrayed the cause; Half-Breeds, unconvinced that the change owed to anything but political opportunism, remained leery. All of this further diminished Arthur's already weak powers of incumbency. Three previous presidents—John Tyler, Millard Fillmore, and Andrew Johnson—had ascended from the vice presidency on the death of the chief executive. None had subsequently been nominated for a full term by their party.* Arthur looked unlikely to break the streak.

---

*This trend would continue until Theodore Roosevelt, who took office upon the assassination of President William McKinley, was nominated for a full term of his own in 1904. Every subsequent "accidental president" has gone on to receive his party's presidential nomination, and only one, Gerald Ford—who took office under the considerably different circumstances of Richard Nixon's resignation—failed to win subsequent election.

Unbeknownst to virtually everyone except his doctors, Arthur was dying, succumbing to the effects of acute kidney problems known as Bright's disease (the modern diagnosis would be nephritis). Had he somehow managed to pull out a victory, the nation would have endured two presidential deaths within the same decade: Arthur would be dead by the autumn of 1886, just a few months after the fifth anniversary of Garfield's demise.

Why bother campaigning for an office he likely couldn't win and a term he surely couldn't serve out?[8] Arthur's hope was that he could corral enough support to swing the convention to the candidate of his choice once an opportune moment arrived. No one, including Arthur, knew just who that candidate would be. They knew, however, who it *wasn't*: James G. Blaine.

On the basis of his resume alone, Blaine was the most formidable candidate in the Republican field. He had spent thirteen years representing Maine's third district in Congress, the latter half of it as Speaker of the House. After falling just short of the Republican presidential nomination in 1876—Blaine held a commanding lead through the first six ballots at the convention, but persistent allegations about a corrupt relationship with railroad interests led to the eventual nomination of Ohio governor Rutherford B. Hayes—he returned to Capitol Hill as a senator.

In 1880, Blaine again came within hailing distance of the presidential nomination, entering the convention in what looked like a two-man race against former president Ulysses S. Grant, who aimed to make history by being both the first president to serve a third term and the first to serve a nonconsecutive one.* Instead, with both men unable to cobble together a majority, the convention dragged on longer than any in GOP history. In the end—thanks in part to Blaine's machinations—the delegates turned to Garfield, then a relatively

---

*The two-term limit for presidents, while a matter of custom since George Washington, wasn't a matter of law until the ratification of the Twenty-Second Amendment in 1951.

obscure Ohio congressman.* Blaine was rewarded with the position of secretary of state in Garfield's administration, but his tenure was short-lived. Within a few months of the president's death, the Half-Breed secretary of state thought it best to absent himself from the administration of the Stalwart Arthur, a sentiment that the president reciprocated.

Blaine was by no means an implausible opponent for Cleveland. As a Half-Breed, he could go toe-to-toe with Cleveland on civil service reform (in a private letter to Garfield, Blaine had referred to the Stalwarts as "the desperate bad men of the party, bent on loot and booty").[9] Eloquent, erudite, and charismatic, Blaine likely would have run circles around the methodical, workaday Cleveland had the race taken place in the age of broadcast media. And, to the extent that the voters cared, Blaine had the far more distinguished résumé. He had first taken his seat in Congress in 1863, back when a twenty-five-year-old Cleveland was first getting his feet wet as assistant DA in Erie County.

In Blaine's case, however, experience was a double-edged sword. The corruption allegations that had first emerged nearly a decade before continued to dog him. Blaine had purportedly made crooked deals with railroad interests, securing a federal land grant for the Little Rock & Fort Smith Railroad in exchange for an arrangement that allowed him to sell the company's securities at an inflated commission. When those investments went belly-up, Blaine was alleged to have simply played the graft forward, offloading them at a huge premium to the head of the Texas & Pacific Railroad—which also had a land grant bill pending before Congress. Astonishingly, when James Mulligan, a clerk for one of the Little Rock & Fort Smith's contractors, came forward with letters proving Blaine's role in the entire sordid affair, Blaine stole the documents and proceeded to read them on the House floor—taking care to cite only the innocuous passages.

---

*As with Cleveland and Theodore Roosevelt, American history is replete with examples of unexpected interactions between men who would go on to become commander in chief. The first person at the convention to approach Garfield about becoming the nominee was future president Benjamin Harrison.

While the controversy died down after Blaine failed to get the presidential nomination in 1876, there was enough of a residual taint that Cleveland thought it unlikely he would be facing the former Speaker in November. "I have observed that in time of crisis the moral sense of the Republican Party comes uppermost," he declared. "The crisis is here."[10]

Another candidate seemed to share that diagnosis: Blaine himself. In the run-up to the convention, the former secretary of state had admitted to the Republican editor of the *Cincinnati Commercial Gazette* that the GOP's road to the White House ran through New York, "and I cannot carry that state." Nervous about his health (he had become a hypochondriac who would often wear two coats in order to ward off chills) and now more covetous of a second tour as secretary of state than of the presidency, Blaine thought he had found an out: draft the Civil War hero William Tecumseh Sherman to head the ticket. When he wrote the general with that proposition, however, Sherman declined. Ironically, when the convention's anti-Blaine forces were casting about for an alternative the following week, they too turned to Sherman, eliciting a response that would come to be the standard for disclaiming political ambition: "I would not accept the nomination if tendered me. I would not serve if elected."[11]

Just about the only thing that James G. Blaine and his Republican adversaries agreed on was that James G. Blaine should not be the nominee. Neither side got its way. The convention closed with Blaine as the party's standard-bearer and Illinois senator John "Black Jack" Logan—another former Union general—as his running mate.

When Democrats met for their own convention in early July (also in Chicago), it was thus apparent that the Cleveland luck was still in full flower. Reform-minded Republicans, repulsed by the nomination of a man they believed to be venality incarnate, were the Democrats' to acquire—if only the party would provide a nominee who provided a sharp enough contrast. Still, winning the party's nod was not quite effortless for Cleveland. The first hurdle was quashing a restorationist movement for Tilden. Eight years later, the wounds from the 1876 contest had yet to heal. Tilden had won the popular vote by a substantial margin, 3 percentage points. Yet disputes over the outcome in three southern states led a divided Congress—Democrats controlled the House, Republicans the Senate—to stalemate over which results to certify. Gripped by a genuine constitutional crisis, Congress took the unprecedented (and since unrepeated) step of creating a fifteen-member commission to decide the outcome: five representatives, five senators, and five Supreme Court justices.*

The original plan had called for the body to consist of seven Republicans and seven Democrats, with Supreme Court justice David Davis, considered an independent, holding the balance. Then, in a too-cute-by-half gambit, Democrats in the Illinois legislature, hoping to secure Davis's loyalty, appointed him to the U.S. Senate.† It backfired: Davis accepted the Senate seat, but announced he would not serve on the commission, leaving the slot to be filled by Justice Joseph Bradley, a Republican appointee who provided the clinching vote in an 8–7 decision that handed the White House to Hayes. In the years following, it had become a shibboleth in the Democratic Party that this was an act of electoral theft.‡

Given the tensions produced by such a hotly contested outcome barely a decade after the conclusion of the Civil War—President Grant had strengthened the military presence in Washington in anticipation of unrest—Tilden's decision to stand down and accept the result lent him an air of statesmanship, not unlike that which temporarily attached to Richard Nixon after he refused to contest his 1960 loss to John F. Kennedy. By 1884, however, the urge to have Tilden leave his plow (a metaphor unsuited to a man who lived on a 140-acre estate overlooking

---

*The consequences of the 1876 election extended well into the future. In 2021, when Vice President Mike Pence refused to intervene in the official tallying of electoral votes declaring that Joe Biden had defeated Donald Trump for the presidency, he did so in accordance with the Electoral Count Act of 1887, which gives the vice president a purely ministerial role in the proceedings. The bill, intended to avoid a repeat of the chaos of 1876, was signed into law by President Cleveland.
†State legislatures chose U.S. senators up until the ratification of the Seventeenth Amendment in 1913.
‡This claim was hard to take seriously given that it faulted Republican machinations while ignoring the extent to which southern Democrats had gone to suppress the black vote.

the Hudson River) and return to public service was a nostalgia-fueled fantasy. The erstwhile candidate had just turned seventy and lived the life of a recluse. To the extent that he entertained visitors, they found him laid low by a stroke, barely able to speak or walk. When one guest attempted to flatter him with the suggestion that he should be the nominee, Tilden replied, "My boy, don't you see it is impossible?" To another interlocutor he mused that Thomas Hendricks, his running mate in the 1876 campaign, wanted to revive the ticket in 1884, adding, "and I do not wonder, considering my weakness!"[12] Tilden was right: he'd be dead less than eighteen months into the next presidential term.*

In an era when most of the public's knowledge about candidates came via newspaper, however, Tilden's infirmities remained shielded from the voters. In fact, his boosters—likely hoping to keep the old man's prospects alive long enough to allow him (and, by extension, themselves) to play kingmaker in the upcoming contest—regaled the public with wholly invented stories of his renewed physical vitality.[13]

For Daniel Manning, now spearheading the effort to place Cleveland in the White House, the Potemkin candidacy couldn't come to an end soon enough. Tilden still commanded the loyalties of much of the party and, as a fellow New Yorker, posed an especially acute threat to Cleveland, for whom the support of his home state's delegation was an essential step toward the nomination. While there was no realistic scenario in which Tilden could make the race, every day he failed to disclose that fact made it more likely that his supporters would fracture when it came time to pick a second choice.

If Cleveland could acquire most of Tilden's support, he'd be in pole position for the nomination. Cognizant of this, Manning, an old Tilden lieutenant, received Cleveland's blessing to visit the senior statesman at Greystone, his Yonkers estate. The message he bore was simple:

---

*Upon his death, Tilden had actually outlived Hendricks by the better part of a year. Had a Tilden/Hendricks ticket actually won the White House in 1884, the death of both men, under the rules of the day, would have left the presidency to the president pro tempore of the Senate: Ohio senator John Sherman, the brother of William Tecumseh Sherman.

a Tilden administration may no longer be viable—but a Cleveland administration is the closest approximation imaginable. Tilden was even wooed with the prospect of getting a say in the composition of Cleveland's cabinet—provided he'd go public immediately with his intention not to run. Within a few days, Tilden published a lengthy letter in which he declared, "I ought not to assume a task which I have not the physical strength to carry through." The valedictory closed on a note all the more poignant given how narrowly Tilden had missed his shot at political immortality: "Having given to [my fellow countrymen's] welfare whatever of health and strength I possessed, or could borrow from the future, and having reached the term of my capacity for such labors as their welfare now demands, I but submit to the will of God in deeming my public career forever closed."[14]

It was a necessary victory if Cleveland was going to take the nomination—but not a sufficient one. The intermediate step between clearing Tilden from the field and the final battle for the nomination in Chicago was consolidating the support of the New York delegation behind their incumbent governor. The very cussedness that had brought Cleveland to prominence, however, also ensured that process wouldn't be seamless. Yes, there were factions of the New York Democracy that loved him. But there was also Tammany Hall.

At the state party's convention in Saratoga, Tammany made it known that it would not accede to Cleveland's nomination for president as docilely as it had for governor. Realizing that party unity was out of the question, Manning shifted his focus to getting the party to commit to "the unit rule"—the requirement that the New York delegation give the entirety of its votes at the national convention to whichever candidate had a simple majority of support among its members. While the rule passed, it would shortly prove to be less a victory than a deferral of hostilities.

Home state hardships aside, Cleveland was still the front-runner as the convention opened. While a number of "favorite son" candidates were put forward by their home state delegations, the only figures who had any plausibility were Thomas Bayard, an aristocratic senator from Delaware, and Allen Thurman, a former Ohio senator even older than Tilden. Thurman's Jacksonian, anticorporate streak endeared him to Tammany. Bayard struck a classical liberal pose similar to Cleveland's, but was compromised by the fact that he had taken a legalistic view of the Civil War, deeming secession a matter that the federal government's limited powers made it powerless to resist (while many southern Democrats continued to nurse deep resentments over the war, such sympathies were regarded as electoral poison for the national party). Former Speaker of the House Samuel Randall also had a base of support from the pro-tariff wing of the party, but the question of whether duties on international goods were an oppressive form of taxation or a necessary spur to domestic industry was too divisive within Democratic ranks for him to gather much traction.

From the beginning it was clear that the only way a rival could move into serious contention was if Cleveland stumbled. Tammany was more than happy to provide the banana peels. Honest John Kelly worked the conventioneers, citing the veto of the five-cent-fare bill as proof that New York's governor was indifferent to the plight of workingmen, and told the New York Times that Cleveland's nomination was "very much in the light of a party suicide . . ." Questioned as to what he would do if his advice was ignored, Kelly responded, "You can print this as coming from me. I would not oppose any Democratic candidate, but I will not lift a hand to aid in the election of Grover Cleveland if he is nominated."[15]

It was only that sense of party loyalty that imposed some limits on Kelly's vitriol. No such constraints were present on Thomas Grady. Aiming to unnerve the constituency with which they had the most sway, Grady and his associates spread tales of Cleveland the anti-Catholic "Presbyterian bigot," Cleveland the anti-Irish elitist, and Cleveland the degenerate drunkard.

The case rested on a strained and tendentious reading of Cleveland's record. Proof of his religious bigotry was found in a veto Cleveland had issued as governor, rejecting an appropriation for a Catholic protectory for at-risk children. Cleveland's actual rationale for the denial was that the state shouldn't be making direct grants to a sectarian institution— and that New York City already provided funding for the children. If that lawyerly response wasn't enough, the president of the protectory, upon hearing of the chatter in Chicago, issued a letter declaring that despite being rejected for the funding he had never doubted the candidate's motives and "On the contrary, Governor Cleveland is liberal in the extreme. . . ."[16]

Unable to keep his ego out of the affair, Grady located Cleveland's anti-Irish bigotry partially in . . . his hostility to Grady. Perhaps sensing the weakness of that argument, he also expanded the indictment all the way back to Cleveland's mayoral campaign in Buffalo, when he had refused to stand for election unless the corrupt comptroller John C. Sheehan was ejected from the ticket. Cleveland had complicated his own defense in this case, because he had in fact pronounced himself unwilling to run alongside "that damned Irishman." It fell to his campaign associates to explain that Sheehan's extracurricular activities made the adjective rather than the noun the important part of the epithet. The case was easier to make given that three of those associates were themselves Irish Catholics.[17]

Where the record couldn't be stretched, it was fabricated outright. Among the more bizarre rumors Grady trafficked in was an allegation that Cleveland had supported the anti-immigrant Know-Nothing Party in 1856. The nomination would be settled in a matter of days, so even an obvious falsehood was worth a try if it could take enough time to disprove, and indeed, no evidence was furnished to support the charge.*

Despite Kelly and Grady's best efforts, none of the attacks caused

---

*The veteran New York political reporter William C. Hudson—working, at the time, with the Cleveland team—would allege in his memoir that the calumnies against Cleveland were spread in concert with the Blaine forces, looking to knock the Democrats' most formidable candidate out of the running before he could secure the nomination.

Cleveland to lose any momentum. For his part, Manning was empowered by Cleveland to take whatever countermeasures were necessary with but one ironclad rule: "I should not, in any condition of affairs, or under any imaginable pressure, deem it my duty to relinquish the trust which I hold from the people of my state, in order to assume the duties of the Vice Presidency; and the nomination for that office, I could not accept under any consideration whatsoever."[18] (It's a sentiment upon which many men who have held the office would have smiled.)

It didn't take long for the latitude Cleveland had given Manning to come in handy. With the unit rule in place, Cleveland only needed a simple majority of New York's delegation to win the entirety of his home state's votes. The campaign manager—in a gambit at odds with the convictions for which his candidate had become famous—made promises of patronage to win over the wayward members of the delegation and assure the campaign would get the numbers they needed.* It worked. While the Cleveland skeptics hadn't been muted, they had been gelded.

Increasingly backed into a corner, Tammany tried and failed to get the unit rule overturned. In the run-up to the first balloting, pro-Cleveland and anti-Cleveland factions exchanged barbs on the floor. New York congressman Bourke Cockran, an Irish-born wag, seconded a nomination for Allen Thurman by ridiculing the frontrunner's inexperience: "We have been told that the mantle of Tilden has fallen upon Cleveland. The mantle of a giant upon the shoulders of a dwarf!"[19]

The room, however, was on Cleveland's side. By the time the former Wisconsin representative Edward S. Bragg—a onetime brigadier general in the Union army who would later serve as Cleveland's ambassador to Mexico—took to the podium, sparks were all but guaranteed. He opened his remarks with a reference to how Cleveland, whose rapid

---

*In fact, the promises were so at odds with his convictions that Cleveland never delivered on them.

ascent through the political ranks imbued his campaign with a sense of novelty, was energizing the young voters of Wisconsin. "They love him, gentlemen," he informed them, "and they respect him, not only for himself, for his character, for his integrity and judgment and iron will, but they love him most for the enemies that he has made."

The barely subtextual shot at Tammany sent the crowd into a roar—and generated the same effect on Thomas Grady, who marched to the front of the hall and shot back, "Mr. Chairman, on behalf of his enemies I reciprocate that sentiment, and we are proud of the compliment." Grady, whose heart always outpaced his brain, had just stuck his head into a howitzer. Bragg proceed to unleash a rhetorical volley, delivered while staring straight at the Tammany men: "the Governor of the State of New York had more nerve than the machine. They may speak of him—aye, the vilest of the species may defile a splendid statue—but they only disgrace themselves. Wherever the thin disguise can be reached, you will find it covering nothing but personal grievances, disappointed ambition, or the cutting off of access to the flesh-pots to those who desired to fatten upon them."[20] The crowd exploded. Tammany wasn't simply losing—it was being embarrassed.

The first ballots were cast after midnight, as July 10 crept into July 11. Cleveland had a commanding lead, but not a clinching one. He had more than double the votes of the runner-up Bayard, and more than four times as many as Thurman and Randall, both of whom failed to get beyond double digits. The hour was late, however, the convention hall was sweltering, and delegates were retiring to their hotel rooms. Pushing through a second round of balloting under these conditions risked Cleveland's numbers declining simply because of how many attendees had left the building—a development that could give new momentum to a challenger. The proceedings were adjourned until the following morning.

Having mistakenly interpreted the late-night adjournment as a sign of weakness for Cleveland, Tammany cooked up a conspiracy. In the first round of balloting, an Illinois delegate had cast a vote for Thomas Hendricks, the former Indiana governor who had served as Tilden's running mate in 1876. Confident that he would do so again on the second ballot, Tammany hatched a plot to create a "spontaneous" uprising in Hendricks's favor. The machine had sway with the convention's sergeant-at-arms, a fellow Indianan, and instructed him to issue new passes that would pack the gallery with men moved—seemingly by pure inspiration, actually by cash—to support Hendricks. The idea was to show the delegates on the floor that the rank-and-file Democrats in the gallery had made their choice, and that surely the party elders must follow.

The plot was far-fetched to begin with, but it became utterly hopeless when word of the midnight machinations got back to Manning. All through the night, Cleveland staffers worked the delegates, informing them of the plot and instructing them not to react when the moment arrived. It worked.[21] The crowd leased by Tammany went into ecstasy on cue, but the rest of the room remained unmoved. When the Illinois delegation completed its tally, Cleveland's total actually improved.[22] The surge now inevitable, the votes switched over to make it official: Stephen Grover Cleveland, a man who three years earlier was running a law practice in Buffalo, was going to be the Democratic Party's nominee for president of the United States.

All that was left was to choose a running mate. Magnanimity coming easier after a commanding victory—and the Tammany ploy notwithstanding—Thomas Hendricks got the nod, eight years after filling out the ticket with Tilden. Not that it was an act of altruism: Hendricks's native Indiana was one of the northern states that could decide the outcome of the election. In addition, his ties to Kelly and Tammany Hall had the potential to heal, or at least suture, the intraparty wounds. In any event, it wasn't as if there was an abundance of alternatives. The only other finalist for the VP slot was the millionaire former West Virginia senator Henry G. Davis—and his son-in-law was Blaine's campaign manager.[23]

As revelry broke out in Chicago, Grover Cleveland was precisely where fate would have ordained and experience would have suggested:

behind his desk in Albany. When the sound of a cannon shot pierced the air, the staff in the governor's office speculated that it was meant to officially signal his nomination. "Do you think so?" Cleveland said, looking up momentarily. "Well, anyhow, we'll finish up this work."[24]

He wouldn't be able to play the stoic for long. That night, a crowd of five thousand marched through the torchlit streets of Albany to the governor's mansion,[25] where, at their bidding, he delivered brief remarks from the porch, previewing the coming attack on a Republican Party that had grown too comfortable in the White House: "Parties may be so long in power, and may become so arrogant and careless of the interests of the people, as to grow heedless of their responsibility to their masters. But the time comes, as certainly as death, when the people weigh them in the balance."[26]

A few weeks later, in a custom now long forgotten, a party delegation arrived at the executive residence to officially confer the nomination upon him. Among the event's hostesses were two of Cleveland's sisters; the wife of his aide Dan Lamont; and Oscar Folsom's widow and daughter.[27] Surely many of the men in the party delegation believed—and all hoped—that they were in the presence of a future president. Would any of them have suspected that they were also in the presence of *two* future First Ladies?

If they had given the matter any thought, they would've been the exception. Despite being a bachelor in his late forties, Cleveland's love life never attracted much attention, partially because the explanation appeared so simple: the man's entire life was devoted to work. With his weight out of control and no sign that anything was going to be done about the matter—Cleveland hated exercise for its own sake and considered hunting his physical activity of choice*—he wasn't topping any eligible bachelor lists. No one cared about Grover Cleveland's romantic

---

*In his book *Fishing and Shooting Sketches*, Cleveland wrote, "Bodily movement alone, undertaken from a sense of duty or upon medical advice, is among the dreary and unsatisfying things of life. It may cultivate or increase animal strength and endurance, but it is apt at the same time to weaken and distort the disposition and temper."

exploits, or lack thereof, because no one had ever *had any reason* to care. That all changed on July 21, 1884.

The story ran in Buffalo's *Evening Telegraph* with the headline "A Terrible Tale." In an age of journalism by exclamation, there were three consecutive subheadings, but the first—"A Dark Chapter in a Public Man's History"—was sufficient to establish the trajectory. By the time the reader's eyes reached the lede, there was no trace of subtlety remaining: "Grover Cleveland's reputation for morality has been bad in this city for some time."[28] The man known above all for his virtue—the one who carried the nickname "Grover the Good"—was being denounced by a hometown paper as a Jekyll and Hyde figure.

The report began with a general inventory of moral dissipation: Cleveland, in this telling, was a "beastly drunk" and a whoremonger. But this was merely a little mood music before the main event. At the center of the *Telegraph's* reporting was a story that, if true, would tarnish his reputation almost beyond recognition.

The "terrible tale" centered on a young Buffalo woman named Maria Halpin, whom Cleveland was said to have assiduously pursued and ultimately seduced a decade earlier, toward the end of his tenure as sheriff. His conquest complete, Cleveland paid no mind when it turned out that Halpin was pregnant, refusing entreaties to marry her and taking no interest upon the birth of her son, christened Oscar Folsom Cleveland. Apart from providing a measure of financial support, he was entirely absent from both of their lives.

A love child would have been bad enough—that the conception didn't involve the breaking of any marital vows was not especially exculpatory at the time—but it was the events that followed the child's birth that truly marked Cleveland as a moral grotesque. The out-of-wedlock pregnancy had cost Halpin her job. Paired with the father's abandonment, it sent her into a depressive spiral numbed at the neck of a liquor bottle. As Maria's despondency increased, so did Grover's itch to rid himself of the problem. Eventually, the story alleged, he deployed a pair of detectives to abduct Halpin, steal the child away from her, and have her shut up in a mental institution. Only because the asylum found that she did not meet the standards for commitment was she able to emerge to reclaim her child and prepare a lawsuit against those who had conspired to separate them.[29]

On first read the story was remarkable for its lurid revelations. On a second scan, however, a number of the details gave pause. The report suggested that whispers about the scandal underpinned much of the opposition to Cleveland at the Democratic convention. But if that had been the case, why hadn't Tammany—which had been in the market for a kill shot—used the information to finish him off instead of resorting to stunts like the contrived Hendricks boomlet? As the Know-Nothing rumors had demonstrated, Cleveland's opponents wouldn't have held back just because they hadn't confirmed all the facts.

There were also questions about the sources involved. The *Telegraph* identified the *Rochester Union and Advertiser* as the first publication to hint of misconduct—and also noted that its editor, "as a delegate in the national convention, had done his best to defeat Mr. Cleveland. . . ." That wasn't dispositive either way, but it suggested that the investigation had its roots in something less than a dispassionate search for the truth. And though a couple of bit players in the drama—the doctor that had examined Halpin at the asylum and the lawyer she had retained after her release—gave comments to the paper, the full narrative was attributed, with no hint of cognitive dissonance, to a source who "is not anonymous, although we have not published the name of the author."

The report—arguably to the *Telegraph's* credit—also included details that seemed at odds with the overarching narrative that Halpin was a victim at every turn. While the paper repeatedly emphasized that she had been conveyed to the asylum without due process of law, it paused only momentarily to note one of the more salient details behind the intervention: that she had repeatedly threatened to murder both Cleveland and the baby. Readers who endured all the way to the conclusion of the mammoth article also learned that Halpin, described throughout as desirous of nothing more than to be left alone with her son and provided for by his father, had never brought her lawsuit—because she had accepted $500 (about $12,000 in 2019 dollars) to allow the child to be put up for adoption.

Presaging what would become conventional campaign wisdom in a later era, the story aimed not at Cleveland's weakness but at his strength: the idea that he was a pillar of rectitude, especially by contrast to the transactional Blaine. It demanded a response, especially as the story caught on with publications more reputable than the scandal sheet *Telegraph*.[30]* When Cleveland's friend Charles Goodyear inquired as to how the party should handle the matter, the candidate responded not with a strategy but with a principle: "Whatever you do, tell the truth."[31]

That statement is often logged as per se proof of Cleveland's steadfast character, without resorting to the obvious follow-up question: what *was* the truth? At the remove of a century and a half we can still only see it through a glass darkly. As it turned out, Cleveland and Halpin *had* been intimately involved and he had assumed financial responsibility for her child. While Cleveland was unwilling to *deny* paternity—he pushed aside a letter of disavowal prepared by his aides with "No, it isn't true"[32]—his political allies sowed doubts about whether he was actually the father. Halpin had been involved with multiple men, they whispered, and Cleveland was rare among them for being single. That made him the expectant mother's obvious candidate to lure into marriage—and, because the other men included married friends of his who might be disgraced, also gave Cleveland an incentive to accept responsibility. This narrative came into sharper focus when a reporter from the *Detroit Journal* claimed that he had heard from sources close to the candidate that "if the whole truth is ever told it will show Cleveland has taken the part of an honorable man. This intima-

---

*This was not the first time that the *Telegraph* had traded on bizarre stories about a candidate's personal life. A few years earlier the paper alleged that President Garfield had once stolen a cow.

tion involves the memory of a departed friend."[33] The implication was clear enough to those who knew: that Oscar Folsom Cleveland had been named after his biological father.

For Cleveland's part, he displayed far more anger at the sullying of Folsom's name than his own. When word got to him that one of his allies had been offering this alternate version of events to the press, he wrote to his friend and political ally Daniel Lockwood (a former, and future, New York congressman), "Now is this man crazy or does he want to ruin anybody? Is he fool enough to suppose for a moment that if such was the truth (which it is not, so far as the motive for silence is concerned) that I would permit my dead friend's memory to suffer for my sake? And Mrs. Folsom and her daughter at my house at this very time!! I am afraid that I shall have occasion to pray to be delivered from my friends."[34]

Cleveland thought he simply had to endure the controversy, take his lumps, and move on; that feverish attempts to litigate the particulars of the story—many elements of which were false or greatly exaggerated— would only compound its effects. In a letter to Shan Bissell a few months later he wrote that "the policy of not cringing was not only necessary but the only way."[35] Still, his outburst to Lockwood remains curious, not least for someone of Cleveland's methodical, legalistic bearings. Why qualify that the arguments made in his defense were not true "so far as the motive for silence is concerned"? Could there have been any truth to the notion that Cleveland was trying to protect Oscar Folsom's legacy?

As later events would show, Cleveland's penchant for honesty did not necessarily preclude strategic omissions. And nothing about Folsom's sybaritic personality rendered the scenario implausible (though whether that impulse extended to sexual indiscretions is unknown and, at this point, unknowable). Most provocative is the point the candidate himself raised: the effect on the Folsom family. Whatever filial obligations Cleveland may have felt toward Mrs. Folsom were compounded by the fact that he had become enchanted with *Ms.* Folsom—Oscar's now-twenty-year-old daughter Frances. If Grover Cleveland was a man disinclined to sell out his best friend, that instinct would only be compounded by falling in love with the man's daughter.

It's tempting for those inclined to romanticize his character to imagine the entire affair as a heroic exercise in moral restraint: a presidential candidate needlessly suffering through a potentially career-ending scandal to preserve a friend's reputation.* Indeed, Allan Nevins's exhaustively researched biography, which relied on many contemporary sources, claimed that a private letter written during Cleveland's presidency contained an admission that he was never sure of the boy's parentage—but failed to provide any details about the correspondence, which has otherwise remained unseen.[36] The available evidence, however, provides no affirmative reason to embrace the Oscar Folsom theory and at least some to doubt it. Cleveland and Halpin *were* involved. There is no definitive proof that Folsom and Halpin ever were (or indeed that Halpin was involved with anybody else). Some of the details remain baffling no matter which theory is adopted: regardless of who the father was, why name the child after Folsom if there was an organized effort to conceal the parentage?

Apart from the foundational facts that there had been an affair and subsequently a child, however, the offensive launched by the *Telegraph* began to unravel in short order. It would soon be revealed that the source for the stories of Cleveland-as-degenerate was George H. Ball, a Baptist minister from Buffalo. Ball's motivations were not purely to do with moral hygiene; he was a member of the GOP who only days before the scandal broke was recorded in the *Buffalo Weekly Express* pleading with a group of independent-leaning Republicans to stick with Blaine rather than defect to Cleveland, arguing that "the Mr. Blaine of four years ago is not the Mr. Blaine of today. He is certainly a man of unimpeached domestic virtue, which should count for a great deal."[37]

---

*Indeed, a popular novel of the 1890s, *The Honorable Peter Stirling and What People Thought of Him*—widely believed to be a roman à clef of Cleveland's life—featured this scenario as a plot point.

What information Ball possessed was gleaned from an investigation that a group of Buffalo ministers had taken it upon themselves to conduct into Cleveland's moral character. How many of his factual mistakes stemmed from being on the receiving end of a game of a telephone and how many were willful fabrications is a matter of conjecture. It soon became apparent, however, that Ball's "investigations" were less than airtight. In one particularly egregious example he spun a tale in which a drunken Cleveland, after a night of carousing with his Buffalo cronies, had been in the carriage when the equally inebriated Folsom had his fatal crash—a claim easily disproved because it was contradicted by the contemporaneous newspaper accounts of Folsom's death.[38]

In short order, multiple investigations were launched to get to the truth of the matter, most notably by the kinds of independent Republicans who had been tempted by Cleveland's candidacy but, with the premium they placed on character, would have been the first to abandon him if he was revealed to be, as one newspaper editor had put it, "a moral leper." What they found instead was that Ball had constructed a funhouse-mirror version of the story.

Certainly the Buffalonians who knew him best didn't recognize the portrait of Grover Cleveland as a congenital drunk surrounded by prostitutes, neither of which comported with any of the behavior they had witnessed. And while there was no serious dispute of his relationship with Halpin, the details were considerably less dramatic, at least as regards the candidate. Maria Halpin was not, per the original rendering, a naïve young woman exploited by a powerful older man, but rather a widow then in her thirties (only a few years younger than Cleveland) who had come to Buffalo after leaving two children behind with family in New Jersey. Cleveland had not promised to marry her, as some versions of the story asserted. Nor had he conspired to have her abducted, but rather, having grown concerned that her drinking would endanger her son, referred the matter to a retired judge who sat on the board of a local orphanage. The judge, Roswell Burrows, arranged, with Halpin's consent, to have the child placed in the orphanage, with Cleveland paying for the boy's care and also providing Halpin with money to start a new life in Niagara Falls.[39]

Maria Halpin came to regret the decision, however, and, when her legal efforts to regain custody failed, kidnapped the child from the facility. The Telegraph's "terrible tale" was thus the story of the second time her son had been removed from her care, with the authorities intervening at the request of the orphanage, not Grover Cleveland. Nor had there been an effort to commit her to a mental institution. The facility to which Halpin had been removed was a sanitarium of sorts, also used for the treatment of alcoholism. She was free to leave and had, in fact, stayed for more than a week of her own accord. She subsequently acceded to her son's adoption, dropping her legal challenges at the behest of a brother-in-law sent to arrest her downward spiral, and eventually relocated downstate and remarried.

To be sure, contra his more intemperate defenders, there is no version of the story in which Grover Cleveland is a hero. Maria Halpin surely deserved better, though her struggles with alcohol—which even her defenders conceded—may have placed her beyond Cleveland's ability to help. The same was not true of young Oscar. Even if he was genuinely unsure whether he was the boy's father, Cleveland's interest in the child's welfare was distant and contractual in nature (in stark contrast to how he'd later treat the children produced by his marriage). But because Ball's melodramatic tales had landed so wide of the mark, the net effect once the truth came out was relief that Cleveland didn't have cloven hooves rather than outrage at the fact that, at least in this instance, he wasn't quite the paragon of virtue once believed.

In time, Cleveland would, in a bizarre fashion, come to benefit from the Maria Halpin story—or at least the forthrightness that his "tell the truth" quotation signaled. The reversal of fortune occurred a few weeks after the publication of "A Terrible Tale," when the Indianapolis Sentinel introduced a scandal involving Blaine's love life, though one that seems unbelievably quotidian by modern standards. Blaine had impregnated the young woman he would later marry, the story alleged, abandoned her, and only wound up her husband by the intercession of her father's shotgun. The story was patently untrue—a fact as obvious to the authors as to the subject—and Blaine quickly launched a libel suit. But the *Sentinel,* looking to kick up whatever dust it could to obscure the obvious falsehood, managed to unearth a legitimate embarrassment in the Republican candidate's record: Blaine's official campaign biography listed the date of his marriage as March 29, 1851. Yet the couple's first child was born less than three months later.[40]

Given that Grover Cleveland had survived the revelation of the Halpin affair, Blaine—now more than three decades and half-a-dozen children into his marriage to the former Harriet Stanwood—likely could have let matters stand at little cost to his candidacy. Instead, there were furious, increasingly improbable attempts to bat down the allegation. Republicans fed multiple stories to the press exonerating him—all of them contradicting each other. When the candidate finally came forward with his own version of events, he explained that he and Harriet had entered into a secret marriage months prior to the official ceremony— one that had rather conveniently yielded no living witnesses. Upon close scrutiny, several of the details in his account rang false, not least that the date he assigned to the clandestine ceremony fell on a Sunday, something that the Protestant traditions of the day virtually forbade.

Whatever sin Blaine had committed paled in comparison to Cleveland's, yet the latter's candor enhanced his stature when contrasted with Blaine's penchant for what *Harper's Weekly* referred to as "desperate equivocation."[41] In fact, for all the tumult of the campaign, the perception of both candidates had ended up back where it started: Cleveland was a man who'd tell the truth even when it hurt; Blaine was a man who would bob and weave even when the truth was relatively painless.

If Democrats delighted at the tables being turned on Blaine, their nominee was cooler to the development. Cleveland had been personally wounded by the Halpin revelations—it was a scar that he'd carry with him for the rest of his life—but the resultant emotion was disgust rather than vindictiveness. When the governor was approached by a source offering to sell embarrassing information on Blaine's private life, Cleveland bought the papers—then proceeded to tear them up and set the detritus aflame in his office fireplace, telling his aide Dan Lamont, "The other side can have a monopoly of all the dirt in this campaign." When word came later in the race that party officials were considering an offensive based on details of Blaine's marital life, Cleveland informed them that they were free to do so—if they were prepared to have their presidential candidate resign from the ticket.[42]

In truth, Cleveland didn't need to wade into Blaine's personal life; his professional track record provided more than enough ammunition. Though the allegations about Blaine's cozy relationships with moneyed interests were old news by the time 1884 rolled around, a new development brought the issue roaring back to the center of the campaign. A group of Republican Cleveland supporters reopened the case around Blaine's questionable dealings with the railroads, heading straight for one of the players in the original drama: James Mulligan, the clerk from whom Blaine had stolen the incriminating letters nearly a decade prior.

It turned out that Blaine had not retrieved *all* the incriminating evidence. The clerk was in possession of a letter that the candidate had written to Warren Fisher, his intermediary with the railroad, back in 1876, as suspicions about his ties with the industry threatened to derail his shot at the Republican presidential nomination. Any correspondence that so much as hinted at Blaine's involvement with unscrupulous dealings could have been explosive, but Mulligan was sitting on a legitimate bombshell. Blaine had drafted in his own hand the template for a letter he insisted Fisher write, exonerating him of any wrongdoing. Plenty of eyebrows would have raised at Blaine's surreptitious instructions: "Regard this letter as strictly confidential. Do not show it to anyone." But the coup de grace was the then Speaker of the House's unheeded instruction on the back of the message: "Burn this letter!"

The record showed that only a week after the missive was written, Blaine had been on the floor of the House, declaring, "My whole connection with the road has been open as the day. If there had been anything

to conceal about it, I should never have touched it. Wherever conceal-
ment is desirable avoidance is advisable, and I do not know any better
test to apply to the honor and fairness of a business transaction."[43] At
least the Stalwarts took a kind of misbegotten pride in the plunder they
were able to extract from "public service." By contrast, Blaine, the
self-professed reformer, called to mind Emerson's bon mot: "the louder
he talked of his honor, the faster we counted our spoons."

By now, both parties had secured the predicate for declaring the
other's presidential nominee hopelessly morally compromised. Democratic paradegoers marched to the lyric:

> Blaine, Blaine, James G. Blaine,
> The continental liar from the state of Maine
> *Burn this letter!*

Republicans gave as good as they got, filling the air with cries of:

> Ma, Ma, where's my pa?
> Gone to the White House
> *Ha! Ha! Ha!*

While navigating attacks on the nominee's integrity was a problem
for both parties, the political calculations were made all the more difficult by a volatile electorate. By the time the 1884 election came around,
stresses in the existing political coalitions—stresses that would culminate in a national realignment by the end of Cleveland's second term as
president—were already exerting a centrifugal force on American politics. Both Republicans and Democrats had to fight rearguard efforts to
keep some members of their coalition from defecting to the other side,
and others from decamping to third-party efforts.

The most famous, if not the most electorally meaningful, of these
schismatic sects was dubbed the "Mugwumps," a group consisting primarily of elite northeastern Republicans who lined up behind Cleveland

out of a distaste for machine politics.* On first blush, the rough-hewn son of western New York did not seem like an obvious depository for the loyalties of a group of intellectuals with uncallused hands. It's doubtful that men like Henry Adams, the writer directly descended from both presidents of that surname; Harvard president Charles William Eliot; or the *Nation* editor E. L. Godkin would have ever found themselves joining Cleveland for a pint at Billy Dranger's in Buffalo. But as the self-appointed guardians of what they believed to be the old-line American meritocracy—one in which men of their superior learning and social station reigned supreme—they blanched at the transactional quality that Republican politics had taken on, a development that tended to sideline the intellectuals in favor of the political operators.

The loyalty of the Mugwumps was good for some positive press coverage—they were a decidedly literary set, which is surely part of the reason that they are well remembered despite having only a marginal impact upon the election.[44] But their influence was limited by the simple fact that "elite movement" is an oxymoron in a democracy. Indeed, the very name "Mugwump," supposedly derived from the Algonquian word for "big chief,"[45] started out as an epithet to describe the contingent's inherent sense of superiority—but also worked as shorthand for a group that was all chiefs and no Indians. And whatever benefits Cleveland may have reaped from Mugwump support were likely counterbalanced in other parts of the electorate by the stereotype of the group as eye-rollingly effete and supercilious.

The Mugwumps' influence was sufficiently circumscribed that they couldn't even carry the day with all of their fellow Republican reformers. Nowhere was this failure more acutely felt than in their inability to win over Cleveland's erstwhile ally, Theodore Roosevelt. TR had, by this point, decided to leave politics behind, still reeling from the trauma of Valentine's Day 1884, when his wife and his mother died under the

---

*The legendary political cartoonist Thomas Nast, a distinguished member of the group, declared himself unwilling to support Blaine "even if the Democrats should nominate the Devil himself."

same roof on the same day, the former in childbirth. In his last days of political activity, Roosevelt had backed the reform-minded Vermont senator George F. Edmunds for the Republican presidential nomination, writing in his diary during the convention, "All the corrupt element in the Republican Party seems to be concentrated here working in behalf of Blaine."[46] Appalled by Blaine's victory and preparing to decamp to the North Dakota ranch where he'd spend most of the next few years, TR told a reporter in an unguarded moment that he'd offer "hearty support" to any decent Democrat. Yet when Roosevelt returned east later in the year, he declared himself for Blaine. He would tell his mentor Henry Cabot Lodge, "I was sure to lose whatever I did."[47] Though he imagined his political career over for the foreseeable future, he still made the self-preserving choice and resolved the tie in favor of party loyalty.

Tammany had not quite reconciled itself to Cleveland's nomination, either, which was symptomatic of a bigger problem: he was struggling with the traditionally Democratic Irish vote. What made this weakness especially acute was the fact that Blaine, despite his party's history of hostility, had a plausible path to winning at least some of them over. His mother was Irish Catholic (in a practice common at the time, the Blaine family had split, with the boys raised in their father's Presbyterian faith and the girls in their mother's Catholicism*) and cousin Angela Gillespie—sometimes recorded erroneously as his sister, because they were raised for a time as virtual siblings—was a notable figure in the church via her role as mother superior of the Sisters of the Holy Cross, a station in which she was responsible for the creation of dozens of institutions for the education of women. As Secretary of State Blaine had been consistently sympathetic to the Irish cause and—an even surer route to the Celtic heart—hostile to Britain.[48] His protec-

---

*Ironically, to the extent that James G. Blaine's name is remembered today it's mostly for the "Blaine Amendments," provisions in state constitutions (inspired by his failed effort to amend the federal constitution) that prohibit the use of public funds to support education at sectarian schools. This has led to a widely held notion that Blaine was animated by anti-Catholic convictions. In reality, the effort was little more than political opportunism, and Blaine quickly lost interest in the issue once it was no longer politically advantageous.

tionist impulses on trade—free trade being thought of at the time as a distinctly English ideology—also helped.[49] Those fides were augmented by a number of attacks on Cleveland designed to set Irish blood aboil: the veto of the protectory bill; the insinuation that the anti-protectionist Mugwumps were de facto agents of Great Britain; even the allegation— entirely invented—that Cleveland had vetoed a bill abolishing child labor in mills.[50] With a half-million Irish in the crucial state of New York, it was believed that such controversies had the potential to decide the election.[51]*

Niche third parties were also taking gains out of the hides of each party. For Cleveland and the Democrats, the threat came from the anti-monopoly Greenback Party, especially popular *amongst* midwestern constituencies for its populist stance that the inflationary effects of paper currency would be a boon to farmers by reducing the cost of their debt.

The Greenbackers' candidate was Benjamin Butler, a wealthy former governor of Massachusetts with the countenance of an undertaker. Butler had journeyed from Democrat to Radical Republican (during which time he managed the House's impeachment of Andrew Johnson) to Democrat again before defecting in the wake of Cleveland's nomination. Butler would later admit that his candidacy had been funded in part by Jay Gould as a means of denying Cleveland the White House.†

The danger for the GOP lay with the anti-alcohol Prohibition Party. Largely drawn from Republican ranks, they had been humiliated at the

---

*This supposition was likely overstated. As the historian Mark Summers points out in *Rum, Romanism, and Rebellion: The Making of a President, 1884* (the single best volume on the campaign), Irish voters were too weakly organized to move effectively as a block. In addition, Protestant suspicions that Blaine himself was a crypto-Catholic likely offset at least some of the support he gained from Irish voters.

†Jay Gould's money aside, Butler should not be remembered as a cynical figure. Among his virtues was a willingness to stick his chin out on matters of race in a party that still contained many retrograde views on the matter. During the 1884 Democratic convention, when a southern delegate reacted to a controversial Butler proposal by asking "Will this apply to my niggers?" Butler, a former major general in the Union army, replied, "Your niggers? Have you any niggers? I thought I marched down there with my soldiers and settled that. If not, we will march down there again."

party convention—a temperance petition with 20,000 signatures had literally been kicked under the table by the platform committee, where it was later found bathed in tobacco juice[52]—and subsequently broke off to support former Kansas governor John St. John for president. St. John had presided over one of the first prohibition amendments enshrined in a state constitution. He had also birthed a dilemma for Republicans: bow to the prohibitionists to keep them from bolting the party or suffer the wrath of other constituencies (especially German voters) who bridled at the government standing between them and their taps?[53] At one point party leaders entertained a plot to bribe him out of the race. Not only was the effort rebuffed, but St. John was so outraged by it that he shifted his efforts in the homestretch of the campaign almost entirely to New York in an effort to deny Blaine the state's electoral votes. Sauce for the goose being sauce for the gander, Democrats were more than happy to bankroll the effort.[54]

For all the palace intrigue there was still a campaign to be run—though it often looked as if the two major candidates were competing in entirely different races. Blaine, a sparkling orator, adapted a style still novel in that day, barnstorming the country to deliver speeches. Cleveland, characteristically cautious, gave public remarks only twice—once each in the critical states of New Jersey and Connecticut—and then only late in the campaign. That restrained approach was more in keeping with the traditional strictures on a presidential candidate—and certainly more in keeping with his own personal predilections—but Daniel Manning feared his placidity would be his undoing.[55] Cleveland's lack of urgency was so acute that he could be found departing for a vacation in the Adirondacks in August, and writing to Lamont, "[D]on't pledge me to be back at any particular time. I don't want to feel that I cannot stay beyond two weeks if I so desire."[56]

When the campaign was fully joined—and when it was able to transcend arguments about the character of the candidates—it largely revolved around two issues: civil service reform and tariffs. The import of the latter was compounded by the fact that the country was suffering through a brief economic panic in 1884, a consequence of the failure of a handful of New York banks and finance firms (one of which left former president Grant bankrupt).

Because tariffs were the primary source of federal revenue at the time, debates over trade did not hinge on whether they would be applied but at what rate. The central argument was thus whether tariffs were a necessary evil, to be applied at a level no higher than that needed to fund the government's essential operations, or a positive good, which not only filled Washington's coffers but also insulated American industry from ruinous foreign competition. In reality, of course, the distinction between "tariffs for revenue only" and "protective tariffs" was never quite so black and white: no one knew the magical level at which tariffs ceased to be a revenue mechanism and transformed into a protective device (in truth they were both all the time, as well as a de facto tax on consumers). But Blaine, in the best Republican tradition, put himself on the side of protection.* As for Cleveland: he punted. While the party as a whole straddled the issue, pronouncing in its platform that Democrats "pledged to revise the tariff in a spirit of fairness to all interests"— thirteen words in pursuit of a coherent thought—their nominee simply remained quiet on the matter, excusing himself, remarkably, on the basis of his lack of expertise on the issue.

Indeed, most of Cleveland's pronouncements during the campaign echoed those he had made when campaigning for mayor or governor: less specific policy prescriptions than general statements of principle. This was a matter of political convenience, of course, but it also reflected a deeper truth about his conception of the presidency. "It should be remembered that the office of the President is essentially executive in its nature," he wrote in his official acceptance of the party's nomination. "The laws enacted by the legislative branch of the government the chief executive is bound faithfully to enforce," and thus "[N]othing in the

---

*While the word "protectionism" is often interpreted in the modern day to mean a general hostility to trade, Blaine's position was a bit more nuanced. While he was in favor of a high tariff, he also advocated for expanding U.S. trade relations with Latin America.

character of the office . . . requires more from the candidate accepting the nomination than the suggestion of well-known truths, so absolutely vital to the safety and welfare of the nation that they cannot be too often recalled or too seriously enforced."[57] As ever, Cleveland took pains to emphasize that he would be an administrator rather than a prime minister.

As for those "well-known truths," his favorite among them remained that every claim the government pressed upon its citizens in excess of its needs was morally repugnant. In a campaign speech in Newark, New Jersey, he declared "that the people have a right to demand that no more money should be taken from them, directly or indirectly, for public uses than is necessary for [an honest and economical administration of public affairs]. Indeed, the right of the government to exact tribute from the citizens is limited to its actual necessities, and every cent taken from the people beyond that required for their protection by the government is no better than robbery."[58]

Cleveland was singing a libertarian melody, as he had in his letter of acceptance, where he pronounced that "laws unnecessarily interfering with the habits and customs of any of our people which are not offensive to the moral sentiments of the civilized world, and which are consistent with good citizenship and the public welfare, are unwise and vexatious."[59] Yet one had to listen for the harmony as well, which made clear that there was more to his political philosophy than simple laissez-faire. He called for government involvement in "internal improvements" (what we would now call "infrastructure"), though he was careful to note that they must be done within the limits of the Constitution.* He welcomed immigration, but called for restrictions on new arrivals who "do not intend to become Americans, but will injuriously compete with those justly entitled to our field of labor."[60] And he was at pains to note that, whatever adjustments to the tariff might occur, labor had a "right to governmental care."

---

*During his first term, Cleveland would decry the fact that such spending often "contained items more for local and private advantage than for public benefit."

Those dalliances aside, policy was not Cleveland's primary focus. What really concerned him was the moral standing of the people making that policy, a theme he hit with populist élan in Bridgeport, Connecticut, in the campaign's final days:

> There should be no mistake about this contest. It is an attempt to break down the barrier between the people of the United States and those that rule them. The people are bound down by a class of officeholders whose business it is to make money out of their positions. If you are to go on forever choosing your rules from this class, what will be the end? This is a question every one of you can answer for himself.

Republicans chose a different rhetorical tack, focusing on the idea that Cleveland and the Democrats were intent on reversing the gains of the Civil War. In the aftermath of the conflict, it had been standard practice for the GOP to "wave the bloody shirt," evoking the war to remind voters that Democrats were the party of the confederate South and that their return to power threatened to embolden revanchist forces south of the Mason-Dixon Line. That Cleveland had been a Union-supporting northerner whose brothers fought for the cause did nothing to dampen this line of attack. It was alleged that he would end pensions for Union veterans (a rumor spread in part because they were a vital voting block); that former southern slaveholders would be paid reparations for their "lost property"; even that Cleveland would split Texas into five states to ensure permanent Democratic control of the Senate.[61]*

Those charges were more representative of the 1884 campaign than any serious debates about tariffs or civil service reform. Indeed, the cam-

---

*While these accusations were nothing more than campaign season sensationalism, the Texas charge stemmed from a plausible scenario. The congressional resolution admitting Texas to the union contains language allowing as many as four new states to be created from within its borders. In the twentieth century, Texan John Nance Garner—later to serve stints as Speaker of the House and Franklin D. Roosevelt's vice president—was a consistent advocate for Texas to break into multiple states.

paign would close just as it opened: dominated by scandal. The chaos was all unleashed in the space of a few days in late October, less than a week before the election, the product of a Republican effort to end the campaign with Blaine as the last virtuous man in a field full of immoralists.[62]

The offensive began with a shot fired at the prohibitionist candidate, John St. John, who continued to threaten Blaine's chances in New York. St. John had entered into a brief first marriage in his youth—he was only nineteen and it lasted all of two months. The couple split amicably and the former governor would go on to provide, into adulthood, for a son produced by the short-lived union.[63] But the Republican press, knowing that eleventh-hour accusations didn't give the accused adequate time to mount a defense, alleged that St. John had abandoned his first wife, printing a story in which her stepfather supposedly claimed that the young bride had spent seven years fruitlessly waiting for her husband to return and that "his cruel, heartless, and inexcusable desertion wrecked her life, broke her heart, and caused her to fill a premature grave."[64] Left unsaid was that the premature grave didn't become occupied until a decade and a half after the marriage—her passing undoubtedly painful to her second husband. Like the rest of the story, it was a fiction grafted onto a handful of underlying truths salacious by only the most generous definition.

If St. John was a gnat, Cleveland was the big game. Given that the Maria Halpin allegations hadn't felled the target, the tactic of choice might have been to invent a new story. Instead, they opted to renew the Halpin charges with an entirely new set of facts. The *Chicago Tribune* published an affidavit attributed to Halpin herself, heretofore silent, in which she described the circumstances that precipitated her pregnancy. After Cleveland followed her up to her room in a Buffalo boardinghouse, she testified, "he accomplished my ruin by the use of force and violence and without my consent. After he had accomplished his purpose, he told me that he was determined to secure my ruin if it cost him $10,000 or if he was hanged by the neck for it."[65] Calling Grover Cleveland a drunk hadn't worked. Calling him a womanizer hadn't worked. Calling him a deadbeat dad hadn't worked. So this is what it came to: Grover Cleveland was now a rapist.

Here, and only here, we must momentarily depart from Cleveland's life as lived to Cleveland's life as understood in twenty-first-century America, a time and place where the former president's name does not circulate very often—or at least it didn't until the last decade, when the public developed a newfound interest in exhuming historical figures for the purpose of disgracing them. In that time, the Grover Cleveland rape allegation has been taken seriously or even embraced uncritically in publications ranging from *Newsweek*[66] to *Salon*[67] to the *Atlantic*.[68] A story at the *Daily Beast* declared the scandal "The Most Despicable in American Political History."[69] A piece at *Vice* accompanied the headline "Grover Cleveland, a Rapist President" with an image of a $1,000 bill (on which Cleveland's face appears) flecked with blood.

All of these stories take as their source a 2011 book titled *A Secret Life: The Lies and Scandals of President Grover Cleveland*, by Charles Lachman (the author of the aforementioned *Daily Beast* article). It is an exceedingly curious volume. Lachman, a producer of the tabloid television show *Inside Edition*, claimed within the book's pages that the breakthrough in his research came from the discovery of court documents relating to a libel suit that George Ball, the Buffalo minister who had originally spread the Halpin rumors, brought against the *New York Evening Post* for its criticisms of his scandalmongering. These documents were valuable, Lachman claimed, because, "[f]or the first and only time, many of the key people connected to the scandal were compelled to testify under oath about what they knew of Maria Halpin and Grover Cleveland."[70] Despite that tantalizing description, the book's lengthy recounting of the trial sheds no new light on the realities of the relationship and instead describes a legal proceeding that Ball ultimately *lost* thanks to a welter of his own equivocations and uncertainties.

Instead, for his allegations that Cleveland was a rapist—"the worst villain of all" politicians ever caught in sex scandals, in his telling[71]—

Lachman relied entirely on the Halpin affidavit that hit newspapers on Halloween 1884. And why not? It was, after all, the victim's own words. But neither Lachman nor the publications that have since amplified this version of events have explained a rudimentary hole in this thesis: the cover-up it alleges was *unsuccessful.* The story was in print in a major newspaper four days prior to the presidential election. Were a majority of voters in Victorian-era America indifferent to offering a rapist the chair once occupied by George Washington? And if the allegations were true—or, for that matter, even plausible—why did they not factor into Cleveland's subsequent presidential campaigns in 1888 or 1892?

The answer to this question is so simple that the case for Cleveland-as-rapist can only be regarded as the result of either willful misrepresentation or catastrophic oversight: Maria Halpin herself denounced the accusations as a lie within days. In the November 3 edition of the *Detroit Free Press* she revealed that she had signed the affidavit without reading it, having been deceived by someone close to her (the name was not revealed), who told her the document was to be signed at the behest of one of Cleveland's aides, who needed her testimony to defend the candidate. Only because of that personal request did she consent, because otherwise "all the material points had already been published." The woman whose abuse had been understood just days before as the example par excellence of the rage and sin that coursed through Cleveland's veins noted simply, "I have no fault whatever to find in Mr. Cleveland. . . ."[72] A cottage industry of journalists have spent the past decade pleading that Maria Halpin's voice deserves to be heard. In reality, they have been the ones silencing it.

How intimately Blaine was involved in the smears against Cleveland and St. John is purely a matter of conjecture. But whether the accusations bore his fingerprints or those of some rogue aide, it was the candidate himself who would pay the karmic price—and in short order. Blaine had resolved to wrap up the campaign in New York, the state that seemed most likely to determine the next president. Ignoring aides' advice to finish out upstate, where the threat of a Prohibitionist schism was acute,[73] he headed to New York City to attend a gathering of religious leaders intended to underscore his standing as the candidate of moral decency. The assembled clergymen couldn't agree on who from among their ranks should be chosen for the honor of addressing Blaine and the assembled attendees. The compromise choice was the Reverend Samuel Burchard, a relatively obscure Presbyterian minister from Manhattan's Murray Hill neighborhood, who, in his early seventies, was the seniormost minister of the group.[74]

He was also, as it turned out, a man unable to resist a catchy phrase. Proudly contrasting the assembled Republicans with the Mugwumps who had bolted the party, Burchard made the impromptu declaration, "We are Republicans, and don't propose to leave our party and identify ourselves with the party whose antecedents have been rum, Romanism, and rebellion." The triple alliteration was a marvelous rhetorical flourish, instantaneously embedding the phrase in the consciousness of all who heard it—which was the problem: in one fell swoop, Burchard managed to slander all Democrats, all non-prohibitionists, all Catholics, and all southerners, seemingly under the official imprimatur of the Blaine campaign.*

Within days, "rum, Romanism, and rebellion" was a phrase appearing in thousands of pamphlets printed by ecstatic Democrats and chalked, in an act of ironic defiance, onto the doors and windows of offended households. James G. Blaine, son of an Irish Catholic mother and cousin of a mother superior, was sinking under an association with anti-Irish and anti-Catholic bigotry.

Just about the only valuable voting bloc that Burchard had left unscathed in his "rum, Romanism, and rebellion" speech was labor. Further eviscerating his own campaign only hours after Burchard's gaffe, Blaine attended a dinner with wealthy donors—including Jay Gould, whose vast expenditures earned extravagant influence in Republican circles and

---

*The fallout from the remarks would make Burchard a pariah in Republican circles, shunned by members of the political class. The one exception: Grover Cleveland, who greeted him at the White House in 1887.

widespread suspicion everywhere else—at the tony Manhattan restaurant Delmonico's. Everything about the evening—the net worth of the attendees; the candidate's speech pledging that his administration would keep the good times rolling for the assembled grandees; the menu so elaborate that so much as glancing at it would induce gout—could be interpreted as a paean to wealth for its own sake. Predictably, the press caricatured the affair as a celebration of plutocracy occurring in the midst of an economic downturn. Coverage in the *New York World* was accompanied by an elaborate editorial cartoon in which the assembled elites gorged themselves on dishes such as "lobby pudding," "monopoly soup," and "Gould pie," all while a family in rags extended their hands in need. For Blaine, it was yet another public relations fire to extinguish with only a few days left in the campaign.

As the election came to a close, it was clear that it remained a nail-biter, and that projections about New York's centrality to deciding the outcome were going to prove correct. With the Irish and labor voters up in the air, St. John hammering Blaine, and Tammany Hall still lukewarm on Cleveland despite an official armistice, it was anyone's guess. Blaine's attempt to enlist a last-minute endorsement from Roscoe Conkling, the influential former New York senator and Stalwart par excellence, failed. Now it came down to the voters.

As it turned out, the final tally was so close that any number of parties could have claimed to have held the outcome in their hands. As the razor-thin margins became apparent on election night—and the dysfunctional phones in the governor's office kept the candidate from getting timely updates—Cleveland's aide William Gorman Rice headed to the offices of the *Albany Argus* to get the most up-to-date results. With all signs pointing toward the political equivalent of trench warfare—and with seemingly no limit to the lengths enterprising party hacks might go to steer the outcome—the Cleveland staffers in Albany sent telegrams to their colleagues in every New York county dispatching them to their local clerk's office to make sure that the count was untouched by fraud or favoritism. In order to get the operation moving as quickly as possible, they signed the missives, fraudulently, under Daniel Manning's name. As for Governor Cleveland himself, he provided no guidance on strategy. He had gone to bed.

By the time Cleveland arose on Wednesday morning, there was still no decision. Five states—New York, Michigan, Connecticut, Indiana, and New Jersey—would see a margin of victory under 2 percent of the vote. Between them, they represented almost 20 percent of the Electoral College. Blaine took to the press and announced with confidence that he had won New York and that "I do not believe the American people will accept a fraudulent result."[75] Cleveland telegraphed a supporter that "I believe I have been elected president, and nothing but grossest fraud can keep me out of it, and that we will not permit."[76]

It would've been a tense situation under any circumstances, but it was doubly so coming at only eight years' remove from the 1876 election, when Samuel Tilden had been denied the presidency under similar accusations of electoral fraud. The presidential election of 1884 was only the fifth to be held since the conclusion of the Civil War, and it now held the prospect of being the second where one candidate could make a credible case of being cheated out of victory. Especially if Democrats, who were beginning to suspect they would never be *allowed* to win other election, were the aggrieved party, there was no telling where the fallout would end. Indeed, the country appeared dangerously volatile in the days immediately following the 1884 election. Blaine feared that the United States was on the precipice of a second civil war.[77] Cleveland, who was not prone to issue empty threats, declared that if Republicans hadn't been willing to "yield peaceably" he would have "felt it my duty to take my seat anyhow."[78] Republicans in the North sold off stock in anticipation that a Democratic administration would tank the economy. African Americans in the South feared that the return of a Democrat to the White House—the last one, James Buchanan, had happily endorsed the Supreme Court's *Dred Scott* decision, denying constitutional rights to enslaved and free blacks alike—signaled the coming reimposition of slavery.[79] Meanwhile, Democrats, smelling a conspiracy afoot, turned their suspicions toward Jay Gould. Apart from his role as the GOP's chief financial patron, Gould was also in control of the Western Union Telegraph Company, leading to speculation that election results were being delayed or distorted at his direct behest. Democratic crowds in New York City marched to the Western Union offices and to the financier's Fifth Avenue mansion, where they chanted their intentions to "hang Jay Gould from a sour apple tree."[80]

The fever would break by the Saturday following the election, when the numbers became insuperable enough that the Associated Press called the race and Blaine conceded. Gould—anxious, for once, to recede out of sight—had telegraphed his congratulations to the victorious Cleveland the day before, consoling himself with the observation that "the vast business interests of the country will be entirely safe in your hands."[81]

On the final tally, Cleveland had won nearly all of the close states, claiming victories in Indiana, Connecticut, New Jersey, and New York. (Michigan, where St. John's candidacy garnered a far higher percentage of the vote than in any other state, went to Blaine, but the Prohibitionist defection kept the Republican nominee's margin over Cleveland under one percent.) The full accounting revealed a race that was breathtakingly close. Cleveland had won the popular vote with 48.85 percent of the total to Blaine's 48.28 percent. The margins in the Electoral College were wider—Cleveland triumphed 219–182—but even that was misleading. The Democratic nominee had won by 37 votes, 36 of which came from his native New York; and there Cleveland had won by only 1,149 votes. In neighboring Connecticut, he won the state's six electoral votes by fewer than 1,300 votes. Had fewer than 2,500 voters in the Northeast had a change of heart on November 4, 1884, James G. Blaine would have been headed to the White House and Cleveland would have become a historical footnote.

If Grover Cleveland allowed himself a moment of ebullience on becoming president of the United States, it is lost to history. We do know that two emotions gripped him in the immediate aftermath of the election. The first, a near-universal sentiment among those who feel the

weight of the office descend upon their shoulders, was a sense of wonder at, and reverence for, the responsibility he was about to inherit. To
his friend the journalist Harold Frederic, then stationed in London as a
correspondent for the *New York Times*, he wrote:

> Imagine a man standing in my place, with positively no ambition
> for a higher position than I now hold, and in constant apprehen-
> sion that he may be called upon to assume burdens and duties
> the greatest and highest that a human being can take upon him-
> self. I can not look upon the prospect of success in this campaign
> with any joy, but only with a very serious kind of awe. Is this
> right?[82]

To Shan Bissell, he wrote, "I look upon the four years next to come
as a dreadful self-inflicted penance for the good of my country. I can
see no pleasure in it and no satisfaction, only a hope that I may be of
service to my people."[83]

The second sentiment, also expressed only in private—and, even
then, only to his most intimate friends—was a new one for the heretofore imperturbable Cleveland: bitterness. He had, as governor, began to
develop a distaste for the press. When the *New York Times* cited an ex-
cursion to Newport, Rhode Island, as proof that he was overly fond of
junketeering, he replied incredulously that he hadn't even made the trip:
"Alongside of the very columns announcing my presence in Newport
were statements of doings here in this chamber showing that I was here
at work. . . . These papers keep well informed."[84] That attitude had calci-
fied with the Halpin story. But while the press had earned his enmity, an
even darker cloud hung over his feelings for the city of Buffalo, where
the anger was mixed with a palpable sense of betrayal. In the same
above-quoted letter to Bissell, he wrote:

> I am busy all day long receiving congratulations of friends in per-
> son, while through the mail and telegraph they are counted by

the thousand. It's quite amusing to see how profuse the professions of some who stood aloof when most needed. I intend to
cultivate the Christian virtue of charity toward all men except
the dirty class that defiled themselves with filthy scandal and
Ballism. I don't believe God will ever forgive them and I am determined not to do so.

That astringency remained with him for the rest of his life. For the
nearly twenty-five years Cleveland had left on the planet, he would
barely set foot in Buffalo ever again, and then only briefly. Not that the
president-elect would have been in a particularly nostalgic mood under
any circumstances. As he prepared to depart Albany for Washington
there was an anticipation that, given the gravity of the moment, he
might leave New York's capital city with a flourish befitting a future
president. It was an utterly reasonable expectation—if you didn't know
Grover Cleveland. On January 5, 1885, just under two months before
he was to be sworn in as the nation's twenty-second president, Cleveland transmitted his final message to the New York legislature. The
long-awaited valedictory read, in full:

I hereby resign the office of Governor of the State of New York

SEVEN

The Meanest Man
in the World

Introspection was not a practice that came naturally to Grover Cleveland. For a few moments on the morning of March 4, 1885, however, he couldn't help it.* At noon, he would become the nation's twenty-second president, and nearly the youngest in the country's history (he was just two weeks shy of his forty-eighth birthday, about a year older than Grant had been upon taking office). The thought he couldn't shake was about the rapidity of his ascent.[1] That Cleveland was at such short remove from the unremarkable life of a Buffalo lawyer—combined with the fact that his no-frills personality seemed impenetrable by changes in status—went a long way toward explaining the modesty with which he approached the presidential transition. He declined President Arthur's offer to stay at the White House prior to his swearing in, choosing a local hotel instead. He even paid his own train fare for the journey from Albany to Washington, thinking it unbefitting a president to accept any benefits on account of his station.[2] So assiduously was this principle enforced that when a supporter sent him a dog—a hulking Newfoundland—as congratulations for winning the White House, the

---

*Presidential inaugurations were held on March 4 until 1937, when, owing to the passage of the Twentieth Amendment a few years earlier, the ceremony was moved up to January 20.

president-elect responded, "The acceptance of presents of value which could involve an obligation I should deem in my present position entirely inadmissible. And I confess I should feel better if all gifts of any description were discontinued. . . . I shall please myself and I hope not offend you, by sending the dog by express to your address tomorrow at my expense."[3]

Just as his disposition was unchanged by obtaining the highest office in the land, so, too, was his conception of executive responsibility. He continued to believe that he was a civic votary, that his duties were so immense that they required nothing less than working himself to exhaustion, and that the only moral way to exercise his power was to set aside all personal loyalties and govern according to what he deemed a transcendent sense of the public good. During the transition, at a time when most men would be at least a touch beguiled by the trappings they were about to inherit, he complained that he'd prefer to head off alone into the woods for a month to study the issues that would face him as president.[4] On a walk with a Buffalo acquaintance shortly after the election, he declared, "Henceforth I must have no friends."[5] The American presidency is often lamented as the loneliest job in the world. For Grover Cleveland that was a necessity to be embraced rather than a tragedy to be endured.

Both his simplicity and his dogged independence became apparent almost immediately upon his arrival in Washington. Presidential successions are often a matter of stylistic contrasts, and there have been few as vivid as Cleveland, the elephantine, granite-souled political monk accepting the reins of power from Chester Arthur, the epicurean notorious for his extensive collection of designer clothes (it was a matter of public note that the outgoing president reputedly owned eighty pairs of pants), his taste for gourmet meals, and the lavish, monogrammed carriage he had commissioned to ferry him about Washington. One modern-day biographer describes Arthur as "the closest thing to Jacqueline Kennedy that Washington would see until Jacqueline Kennedy."[6] Robert La Follette, a newly elected Republican congressman from Wisconsin (who would later gain fame as a leader of the progressive movement), noted on Inauguration Day, "The contrast with Arthur, who was a fine handsome figure, was very striking. Cleveland's coarse face, his heavy, inert body, his great shapeless hands, confirmed in my mind the attacks made upon him during the campaign."[7]*

The contrasts didn't stop at style. Arthur was rarely in the office before 10 a.m. and inevitably gone by 5 p.m., leading one White House clerk to remark that the president "never did today what he could put off until tomorrow."[8] Cleveland, by comparison, seamlessly transplanted the both-ends-of-the-candle approach he had employed in Buffalo and Albany, with a workday that often ran from 8 a.m. until 2 a.m. Indeed, it was striking how little high office had changed the way he did business. Dan Lamont had come with him from Albany, and, in an era prior to the explosive growth of presidential staff, was virtually the only assistant the president had for day-to-day responsibilities. With the construction of the Oval Office still nearly twenty-five years away, Cleveland worked in quarters within the White House residence, "living above the store" just as he had when he kept an apartment steps away from his law office.

His surroundings were, of course, considerably upgraded from those of his Buffalo flat, thanks largely to the exertions of his predecessor. Arthur may have endured some criticism for his foppish predilections, but his champagne tastes were put to national use when he refused to move into the White House until it underwent a comprehensive renovation. Cluttered, drafty, and full of outdated furnishings, the executive mansion was subsequently given a glittering makeover at the hands of Louis Comfort Tiffany—much of which, as one might expect, was wasted on Grover Cleveland.

Arthur had turned White House gatherings into Washington's most coveted invitation; Cleveland pared the social calendar back considerably, begrudgingly enduring the entertainment duties and always itching to return to his desk. In the absence of a presidential spouse, his

---

*La Follette's autobiography followed this observation by noting, "Later I came to entertain a great respect for Cleveland, to admire the courage and conscientiousness of his character."

sister Rose acted as First Lady—a move that, though born of necessity, proved canny when she won society plaudits likely out of her brother's reach. Capable as she was, however, even Rose often found the responsibilities tedious. Having put the education her older brother financed to good use—their uncle, Lewis F. Allen, declared that "she inherited the brains of the family"[9]—Rose was an accomplished literary scholar, more interested in studying the poetry of George Eliot (a topic on which she wrote a well-received book) than in White House receiving lines. To pass the time during the latter, she would mentally conjugate Greek verbs while greeting the throngs of well-wishers.[10]*

Just as superfluous, for Cleveland's purposes, was the French chef that the gourmand Arthur had installed on the White House's domestic staff. In a carping letter (a genre he excelled at) to Shan Bissell, he signed off with, "I must go to dinner. I wish it was to eat a pickled herring, Swiss cheese, and a chop at Louis' instead of the French stuff I shall find."[11] So intense was his dislike for the haute cuisine that he began searching for workarounds. When one evening's dinner was interrupted by a distinctive aroma coming through an open dining room window, Cleveland asked his steward, William Sinclair (a transplant from the governor's mansion), where the smell was coming from.† Sinclair apolo-

---

*Rose Cleveland went largely unremembered by history after her brother's marriage to Frances Folsom in 1886, at which point she departed the White House and left the duties of the first lady in her sister-in-law's hands. A sudden revival of interest in her occurred with the 2019 publication of the book *Precious and Adored*, a collection of letters revealing that she had carried on a decades-long lesbian relationship with Evangeline Simpson Whipple, a wealthy widow. While the relationship was interrupted by Whipple's marriage to the Episcopal bishop of Minnesota, the two rekindled their relationship after his death in 1901, eventually living together in Italy until Rose died of Spanish influenza in 1918.

†Cleveland and Sinclair were close, a fact made more salient in that day by the fact that the latter was mixed-race. The president likely spent more time with Sinclair than anyone else during his two terms, and the pair even conducted weekly sessions to review the White House bills, a task that Cleveland refused to delegate. The majordomo earned perhaps the highest praise the president could hand out: "He is the most economical man I have ever known." Though Sinclair was brought on to the White House staff because of his previous relationship with the president, he would remain—apart from private-sector service to Cleveland during the four-year interregnum between terms—in the employ of the executive mansion until 1902, when he was dismissed by Theodore Roosevelt.

getically explained that the source was the corned beef and cabbage the servants were having for dinner. Cleveland immediately had the French delicacies arrayed before him hustled off to the waitstaff in exchange for a serving of their meal. He later boasted to a friend that it was "[t]he best dinner I had had for months."[12] In short order, Cleveland—the man who prided himself on putting official duty before his personal needs—was taking time out of the presidential schedule to write a pleading letter to David B. Hill, his successor as governor of New York, as to whether his old cook from Albany might be available to join the White House staff.[13]

If Cleveland was slow to adjust to the trappings that accompanied his new role, he had no such learning curve when it came to his official duties. The poise that he was to bring to the executive branch was first vivified when he rose to deliver his inaugural address and—completely in character but to the utter shock of the crowd, most of whom were laying eyes on this political neophyte for the first time—delivered the entire speech without notes. Watching the new president fold his hands behind his back and begin delivering the remarks from memory, the Kansas senator John J. Ingalls exclaimed, "God, what a magnificent gambler!"[14]

Like most of his speeches, Cleveland's inaugural was more notable for the degree of difficulty inherent in memorization than for any great rhetorical flourishes. As for substance, it hit on many of the themes that had elevated him to the office: the importance of economy in government, the need to lower tariffs, the urgency of civil service reform, and the necessity of maintaining a sound money supply (delivered as a warning shot to the advocates—most of whom were in his own party—of expanding the use of silver as a means to inflate the currency).

There were also signs that his field of vision was expanding: on foreign policy, he pledged his loyalty to the Founding Fathers' vision of neutrality, rejecting both foreign interference in U.S. affairs and American intervention abroad. He called for Native Americans to be treated "fairly and honestly," and put on a path toward American citizenship.

And he called for breaking up the "purloining schemes and unlawful occupation" by which lands in the American West, intended for wide-scale homesteading, were being gobbled up by corporate interests.

While each of these issues would come to play a significant role in his administration—Cleveland never pledged himself to a policy he didn't subsequently pursue—the speech's most important theme lay elsewhere. In the dying days of the campaign, Republicans had portrayed a Cleveland victory as portending a Confederate restoration. With a Democrat back in the White House for the first time in nearly twenty-five years, the South, it was cautioned, would regain the whip hand in Washington. African-Americans were warned that they were living on borrowed time. In the shadow of those allegations, Cleveland struck a note of national unity reminiscent of Thomas Jefferson, who had famously declared in his 1801 inaugural (marking the first time that the White House had changed party hands), "We are all Republicans, we are all Federalists."

Cleveland, of course, had no capacity for such epigrams, but he implored the country to "cheerfully and honestly abandon all sectional prejudice and distrust, and determine, with manly confidence in one another, to work out harmoniously the achievements of our national destiny . . ." An entire paragraph was dedicated to easing the fears of the nation's black population:

> In the administration of a government pledged to do equal and exact justice to all men, there should be no pretext for anxiety touching the protection of the freedmen in their rights, or the security in their enjoyment of their privileges under the Constitution and its amendments. All discussion as to their fitness for the place accorded to them as American citizens is idle and unprofitable, except as it suggests the necessity for their improvement. The fact that they are citizens entitles them to all the rights due to that relation, and charges them with all its duties, obligations, and responsibilities.

The last Democrat to be elected president, James Buchanan, had used his inaugural address to explicitly pre-endorse the Supreme Court's *Dred Scott* decision,* foreclosing the possibility of black citizenship. Twenty-eight years to the day, the next Democratic president announced that black citizenship was an immutable fact of American life. No less a figure than Frederick Douglass declared it "all any friend of liberty and justice could reasonably ask."[15]†

With the twentieth anniversary of Lee's surrender at Appomattox coming barely a month after his swearing-in, Cleveland was convinced that the time had come for the country to put the legacy of the Civil War to one side—for the South to look with optimism toward its future rather than bitterness toward its past; for the North to relinquish the suspicion that the Confederacy lay dormant in every southern heart, only awaiting the trumpet that would signal its resurrection; for the mass of former slaves to be assimilated into American society rather than kept at its margins. As a northerner who headed the party of the South, he was in a unique position to make that case, even if his failure to don a Union uniform—he was the first nonveteran elected president in the postwar era—was occasionally employed to diminish the effort.

Any fair assessment of Cleveland's efforts on this front has to begin with the stipulation that his efforts at reconciliation were aimed largely at the *white* population. Though his views on race were tolerant by the standards of the era—remarkably so for a Democrat—they did not cause him to rethink his convictions about the rightful limits of federal power. The last federal troops tasked with enforcing Reconstruction had been removed from the South during Rutherford B. Hayes's admin-

---

*The ruling had not yet been made public, but Buchanan had been tipped off to the outcome by Supreme Court justice Robert Cooper Grier.
†Though Douglass—serving as Washington D.C.'s recorder of deeds at the time—was a Republican, Cleveland refused pressure to remove him from office. The president also frequently hosted Douglass and his wife at the White House despite widespread controversy over the couple's interracial marriage, an act that Douglass noted in his autobiography, "drew upon [Cleveland] fierce and bitter reproaches from members of his own party in the South." In a nearby passage, Douglass wrote that "[t]his manly defiance, by a Democratic President, of a malignant and time-honored prejudice, won my respect for the courage of Mr. Cleveland."

istration, contingent on a (subsequently broken) vow that local authorities would ensure the protection of civil rights. And during the Arthur administration, the Supreme Court had found the Civil Rights Act of 1875 unconstitutional, holding that the federal government could not restrict racial discrimination by private parties. The worst was yet to come—the depravations of Jim Crow were still inchoate in Cleveland's first term—but the contours of the problem were already becoming clear. Yet the president, whose reverence for the Constitution was nearly boundless, never seemed to entertain the idea that black progress was contingent on a more aggressive role for the federal government. Whether this owed to a lack of imagination or a rare lack of courage—it almost certainly would have spelled political suicide within the Democratic Party—is a question his silence leaves unanswered.

Well-intended as Cleveland's efforts to balm the remaining wounds of the Civil War were, it became apparent in short order that the effort posed a practical problem. There were two fronts on which a president could launch this offensive: through rhetorical leadership and through specific policy actions. Cleveland went light on the former—his conception of the presidency was too brass tacks, too cramped to imagine what Theodore Roosevelt would later refer to as the "bully pulpit" as a central element of presidential leadership. And on the latter, he soon found that there was a direct conflict between his belief in a fiscally continent federal government and his aim of retiring the Civil War as one of the animating forces of American political life.

The president's initial steps toward sectional reconciliation were easy enough. Cleveland's first official act as president was to sign the commission restoring Ulysses S. Grant—by then destitute and dying of throat cancer—to the rank of General of the Army, thus reinstating his military pension.* On the other side of the ledger, he also appointed to

---

*Grant had forfeited his military benefits upon assuming the presidency. He was not otherwise entitled to retirement income, as ex-presidents did not begin receiving pensions until the passage of the Former Presidents Act in 1958, a piece of legislation inspired by the financial hardships experienced by Harry Truman in his post-presidency. At the time of the law's passage, the only

his cabinet two ex-Confederates who had publicly reconciled themselves to union: Mississippi senator Lucius Quintus Cincinnatus Lamar (whom Cleveland would get confirmed to the Supreme Court in 1888*) as secretary of the interior and Arkansas senator Augustus Garland as attorney general. These would be the last easy victories he'd score for the cause of healing old wounds.

One factor loomed larger than any other in preventing Cleveland from making further progress: Union veterans. Going back to his mayoral veto of funds for the Grand Army of the Republic's Fourth of July celebration in Buffalo, he had made clear that his admiration for the men who had fought to preserve the union was both heartfelt and insufficient to make him any less vigilant a guardian of public funds when they were the claimants. In Washington, the implications of that principle were far more dramatic.

When Cleveland came to office, pensions for Union veterans represented the second-largest category of federal expenditures, trailing only interest payments on the national debt.[16] Legislation passed early in the war had promised federal support for any member of the Union military injured in the course of the conflict, as well as for widows, orphans, and, in some cases, mothers or underage siblings of those killed.[17]† Cleveland may have been a skinflint, but he was also deeply patriotic; he had no objection to the basic arrangement.

The situation became more complicated, however, in 1879, when President Hayes signed the Arrears Act, allowing pensions to be awarded retroactive to the date of injury rather than the date of application, meaning that a successful claim could bring a financial windfall.

---

other living ex-president was the multimillionaire Herbert Hoover, who nevertheless accepted the pension in order to spare Truman embarrassment.

*Over the course of his career, Lamar did more to inflame racial tensions than heal them. On the Supreme Court, he, like all four justices appointed by Cleveland, voted in favor of *Plessy v. Ferguson*, the decision codifying the legality of segregation. While some sources erroneously claim that Cleveland praised the decision, he is not known to have made any statement on the matter.

†The pension program proved to have a remarkable life span. The final beneficiary of a Civil War pension, Irene Triplett, died in May 2020. Triplett had been born in 1930 to an eighty-three-year-old Union veteran.

With the eligibility process notoriously porous (in part because award-ing pensions doubled as constituency-building for the Republicans doing the dispensing), the result was a tidal wave of claims on the Trea-sury. As Cleveland himself would later note, applications jumped from fewer than 37,000 in the year prior to the new law to over 110,000 once it took force—despite the fact that the country was presumably not churning out any new injured veterans.[18]

By the time Cleveland took office, the profligacy had taken on a new form: private pension bills. In many cases where veterans had claims de-nied by the Pension Bureau, the recourse was to turn to their members of Congress, who would file a bill to award them the payout via direct legislative appropriation. Members were anxious to provide a direct benefit to their constituents, while their colleagues were often only too happy to help, knowing that their assent would be reciprocated when their own voters came pleading. Whether the applicant was actually qualified for the benefit was often superfluous. The process was thus conducted with casual disregard, with most of the bills passed by voice vote in nearly empty chambers.[19] In many ways the exercise mirrored the modern practice of congressional earmarks, with concentrated dis-tributions of federal money earning the political loyalty of recipients but going largely unnoticed by taxpayers because the cost was opaque and broadly distributed.* It also helped, of course, that providing assistance to veterans was a popular cause in the abstract, even if many of the cases proved cynical upon closer inspection.

A president possessed of a broader vision—one who was willing to absorb any number of inefficiencies, minor injustices, or political accom-modations as long as they didn't impede his pursuit of two or three major goals—would likely have let the issue lie or, at most, criticized it without undertaking any major exertions to unwind it. Grover Cleve-land, however, who regarded being a night watchman for taxpayers as a

---

*This is a long-standing problem in political economy, famously identified by the economist Mancur Olson in his book *The Logic of Collective Action*.

core responsibility of his office, was not in the business of cutting cor-
ners. What followed was something of a revolution in the use of the
veto as a tool of presidential power—a series of executive assertions that
would, to some degree, distort subsequent generations' understanding
of the Cleveland presidency.

Among connoisseurs of presidential trivia, it is widely known that no
president ever vetoed as many bills in a single term as Cleveland, with
414, did in his first. What made that number all the more remarkable
was that it was more than double the number of vetoes issued *by all previous presidents combined.*[20] Considered in a vacuum, that statistic invites
visions of a president resisting an adversarial legislative branch intent on
enacting sweeping policy change. In reality, however, Cleveland spent his
entire first term with a divided Congress (Republicans controlled the
Senate, Democrats the House) and more than half of the vetoes (228)
were of private pension bills.[21] Of the remainder, many involved the distribution of land to railroads (a topic discussed in the next chapter). The
fervor with which Cleveland rejected legislation was less the act of a
counterrevolutionary than of an especially irritable auditor.

Whatever political cost Cleveland may have paid for devoting so
much energy to the pension issue, there was a practical one as well: the
burden it placed upon his time. Though his energies would almost
surely have been better spent elsewhere, the president insisted on personally interrogating each of the claims. The effort, though nobly intended, was ultimately exhausting. By little more than a year into his
term, he was complaining in one veto message that he was "thoroughly
tired of disapproving gifts of public money to individuals who in my
view have no right or claim. . . ." And though he was doing his best to
weed out the undeserving, he fretted that it was still not enough: "I have
now more than 130 of these bills before me awaiting executive action. It
will be impossible to bestow upon them the examination they deserve,
and many will probably become operative which should be rejected."[22]

The fatigue would show through in the character of his veto messages, many of which called to mind the disdainful tone he had show-

ered down on Buffalo aldermen only a few years earlier. This was especially the case when the claims proved outlandish. There has likely never been an executive missive quite like Cleveland's veto of a bill to increase pension benefits for a veteran by the name of John W. Farriers, in which the president of the United States found himself compelled to write, "The ingenuity developed in the constant and persistent attacks upon the public Treasury by those claiming pensions . . . is exhibited in bold relief by this attempt to include sore eyes among the results of diarrhea."[23] Another veto issued a few days before concluded with the similarly surreal presidential pronouncement that "there seems to be no allegation of present disability either from Army service or the injury sustained while gathering dandelions."[24] In fact, the applicant in this case, one John Hunter, claimed that he broke a leg stepping in a ditch while collecting flowers, and that the injury healed a few weeks slower than it otherwise would have due to a gunshot wound he had suffered in the same limb roughly fifteen years earlier. Hunter, of course, could have been eligible for the pension on the grounds of the original injury alone. Cleveland's research, however, revealed that there was no record of such a wound and that Hunter had been on sick leave for a fever during the time he claimed to have been shot. "We are dealing with pensions," the frustrated chief executive huffed, "and not with gratuities."[25]

Whether one's inclination is to dismiss the armada of vetoes as a measure of Cleveland's deep-seated humbuggery (that was the view of former president Hayes, himself a Union veteran, who accused Cleveland of penny-pinching[26]) or a triumphant defense of the taxpayer, it is worth noting that the president himself regarded a deeper moral issue as being at stake. In the same message in which he carped about his inability to inspect all the claims with adequate thoroughness, Cleveland struck a solemn note:

Heedlessness and a disregard of the principle which underlies the granting of pensions are unfair to the wounded, crippled soldier who is honored in the just recognition of his Government. Such a man should never find himself side by side on the pension-roll with those who have been tempted to attribute the natural ills to which humanity is heir to service in the Army. Every relaxation of principle in the granting of pensions invites applications without merit and encourages those who, for gain, urge honest men to become dishonest. Thus is the demoralizing lesson taught the people, that as against the public treasury the most questionable expedients are allowable.[27]

The earnestness of this conviction is revealed by a fact too often overlooked in tales of Cleveland-as-scold: despite the daunting volume of vetoes, the president approved nearly 90 percent of the private pension bills that came to his desk.[28] In a spasm of almost touching naïveté, he even told his friend Richard Watson Gilder that he thought his patrolling of the pension rolls would earn him the support of the Grand Army of the Republic, suggesting that a pamphlet placed at GAR posts listing his vetoes would be the most effective campaign literature he could imagine.[29] No such appreciation was forthcoming from the GAR, which had long since transitioned from a purely fraternal organization to a powerful lobbying force.

In fact, Cleveland and the veterans' organization were headed for a showdown. In 1887, Congress, no longer content to handle the issue piecemeal, passed by wide margins the Dependent Pensions Act, a bill that would extend benefits to any veteran having served more than ninety days and suffering from a disability that impeded their ability to work, regardless of whether the affliction was incurred as a result of military service. It represented the most expansive approach to veterans' benefits ever seriously considered by the federal government—and seemingly guaranteed that the kinds of claimants the president had worked so hard to exorcise from the system would find themselves on the federal rolls in perpetuity.

Cleveland believed the law would strain the Treasury (in 1887, pension payments already cost more than $2 billion a year in 2019 dollars); that the language of the bill was so imprecise—and the bias in favor of applicants so strong—that it would induce a spate of fraudulent claims; and that projections of the number of new beneficiaries it would spawn were risibly low (he noted that the actual costs of an 1853 pension expansion ended up 750 percent higher than initial projections; another widening of benefits in 1818 had outpaced projected costs by more than 4,500 percent).[30] He issued a veto. Far from praising his concern for the sanctity of the pension rolls, the GAR considered his rejection of the legislation an in-kind contribution to its plans to deny him a second term.

Shortly thereafter, the president, in a further attempt at postwar reconciliation, made matters worse for himself. His secretary of war, William C. Endicott—a former judge on the Massachusetts Supreme Judicial Court and failed candidate for governor—forwarded the president a memo from Adjutant General Richard C. Drum, a northern veteran serving in the higher ranks of the War Department. Drum suggested that a variety of Civil War battle flags (both Union and Confederate) stored at the department ought to be returned to surviving members of the corresponding regiments (a practice that was already employed for Union veterans on a by-request basis). Cleveland, imagining it a healing gesture, approved the plan. Upon its publicization, the reaction in northern quarters was sheer indignation. The idea that the flags of the Confederacy would once again find their way to southern soil was, in the words of the Republican governor of Kansas, "an insult to the heroic dead and an outrage on their surviving comrades.[31]" The GAR, sensing how seamlessly the controversy played into their offensive against Cleveland, went into high dudgeon. Lucius Fairchild, the former Wisconsin governor who served as the head of the organization, was sufficiently aroused to request divine retribution, thundering, "May God palsy the hand that wrote that order. May

God palsy the brain that conceived it. And may God palsy the tongue that dictated it."[32]

The backlash was enormous. Cleveland beat a rare retreat, rescinding the order on the technical justification that he had discovered it was not within his power to release the flags and that any disposition of the banners required congressional approval. Nevertheless, the indignities continued. The president had been invited to review a GAR encampment and parade in St. Louis in September, a moment that, as originally conceived, would give visual testimony to the new era of American unity. As the event approached, however, ominous signs emerged that a gathering of Union veterans might not provide the most receptive audience.

During a veterans' event in Wheeling, West Virginia, in August, a contingent of the assembled Union alumni ostentatiously refused to march under a banner bearing the phrase "God bless our president," choosing to proceed around it and fold their flags. When a nervous Cleveland inquired with the mayor of St. Louis whether he would still be welcome for the city's festivities, the former reported—perhaps with more tact than honesty—that while he found local GAR members receptive to a presidential visit, there was concern that Cleveland's presence might deter members of other posts from attending. The president, by now clearly losing ground, withdrew from the event, noting that he could endure whatever hostility might be directed at him in an individual capacity but that he was unwilling to damage the prestige of his office.[33] It was not an especially persuasive distinction. And it was not the last time the GAR would draw blood.

If Union veterans had a bone to pick with the commander in chief, however, they needed to take a number. For while the outrage occasioned by the pension vetoes was at least limited to a discrete constituency, the president's other great reformist crusade, cleaning up the civil service, had given just about everyone—Republican and Democrat, friend and foe—a reason to resent him.

There was, as Cleveland prepared to assume office, some skepticism that his pledges to flush the federal government of party patronage were anything but campaign season cant. This, of course, betrayed a fundamental misunderstanding of the incoming president, who had the baffling quality of always telling people exactly who he was. For any other candidate, however, it would have been a perfectly reasonable supposition. Republicans had just enjoyed a nearly twenty-five-year window of executive branch dominance, during which time they stacked federal offices with their compatriots. Was the first Democrat to interrupt that streak really going to forswear the chance to fill the ranks with his own men? And if he was fool enough to do such a thing, whose applause did he expect for the effort? Rank-and-file Democrats didn't swoon at the idea of being denied office in service of an abstract principle. The only voters whose pulse quickened at the idea of civil service reform were the Mugwumps, a contingent vital to Cleveland's success only if the next election was going to be decided by a few of the toniest blocks in Boston.*

During the presidential transition, Cleveland had written to George W. Curtis, president of the National Civil Service League and erstwhile chairman of President Grant's commission on civil service reform—a body whose efforts amounted to naught because Congress, jealous of the power that came along with appointments, refused to fund any serious reform measures[34]—to assure him that his campaign promises were sincere. "I regard myself as pledged to [civil service reform]," he wrote; ". . . I have in effect promised the people this should be done."[35] Elided in the letter—perhaps because Cleveland himself had yet to fully grasp it—was that the way he intended to go about it would chafe Curtis and his fellow Mugwumps just as often as it rankled the spoilsmen at Tammany Hall.

The passage of the Pendleton Civil Service Reform Act in 1883

---

*The Mugwumps' relatively thin ranks were part of the inspiration for the historian Geoffrey Blodget's bon mot that Mugwumpery "was not an organization, but a mood."

had given Cleveland all the tools he required. That law had shifted the way certain federal jobs were filled, doing away with political appointments and creating a process in which the posts could be pursued by application, with hires made on the basis of competitive examinations. It had also left it within the president's power to expand the number of jobs that fell into this protected category. Most consequentially, it had prohibited the practice of "assessments," a change that would forever alter American politics. Prior to the law's passage, the man who received a government job because of his partisan ties was expected to kick back part of his salary to the party, a financial stream so deep that it was estimated to provide up to 75 percent of party revenue.[36] After the Pendleton Act became law, politicians were forced to look for other sources of financial support, a dynamic that ultimately led to a reliance on wealthy individuals and interest groups to fund the machinery of electoral politics.[37]

The law had been a blow to defenders of the spoils system but, apart from the prohibition on assessments, its impact was slighter than it initially appeared. The number of federal jobs shifted over to the civil service exam process was vanishingly small—only about 12 percent at the time Cleveland took office.[38] As far as many party regulars were concerned, that meant it was open season on the other 88 percent. The Mugwumps and like-minded reformers had precisely the opposite idea in mind. They longed for the president to expand the number of federal employees covered by civil service protections as broadly as possible, envisioning a Washington staffed by a cadre of competent, disinterested men who could do the work of government free of low-minded partisan concerns (one did not have to listen to a Mugwump's description of the ideal government servant for long before realizing they were describing . . . Mugwumps). It was a vision that in many ways presaged the progressive moment's conception of government administration as a quasi-scientific endeavor meant to be carried out by experts insulated from the political process.

Like the Mugwumps, Cleveland believed that there were an abundance of government jobs in which ideological loyalty to the president was immaterial and, if made the paramount hiring criterion, unlikely to yield the most qualified appointments.* There was, after all, no Republican or Democratic way to deliver the mail (postal appointments represented a huge chunk of federal personnel). At the same time, the president recognized that trying to completely divorce the administration of government from the ideological predilections of the men administering it was a fool's errand. When it came to positions that had more direct influence on policy, indifference as to whether his subordinates agreed with the orders they were asked to carry out was tantamount to indifference about whether those orders were ever executed.[39]

With those principles in mind, Cleveland developed a rough set of guidelines: he would gradually expand civil service protections to cover more of the truly nonpartisan roles. The number of workers under this umbrella nearly doubled during his first term, going from 14,000 to 27,000. By the end of his second term nearly 40 percent of federal employees were subject to civil service rules.[40] He would also remove Republican appointees who were clearly using their offices for political ends, retain until their terms of office expired those who were doing their jobs in a competent fashion, and even reappoint exceptional Republicans who he believed were yielding a valuable service for taxpayers. As for the long line of Democrats queuing up for jobs, he'd assiduously inspect the candidates to make sure the appointments were being made on the merits rather than as political favors. And he would count his own personal ties to any candidates for nothing—or, in some cases, as a demerit.

---

*So seriously did Cleveland take this principle that during his second term he even hired a politically active Republican as his personal clerk, a position with immense behind-the-scenes access to the president. The young man tried to decline, worrying that Cleveland could never be fully candid with him because of the possibility that he would leak privileged information for partisan purposes. The president responded, "I don't care anything about your politics: all I want is somebody that is honest and competent to do my work." On the strength of Cleveland's recommendation, the clerk, George Cortelyou, was kept on in William McKinley's White House; eventually held multiple cabinet posts in Theodore Roosevelt's administration; and served a stint as chairman of the Republican National Committee.

In one particularly painful application of this principle, the president found himself alienating perhaps his closest friend, his former law partner Shan Bissell, denying him, in turn, both a desired cabinet role and a consulship . . . and then complaining that Bissell was the uncharitable one for not understanding that "I have something on hand here that cannot be interfered with; and if my Buffalo friends or any other friends cannot appreciate that, I can't help it."[41] For the rest of his life Cleveland would defend this austerity, though at one point he confessed to a reporter, "I go to bed after a long day with the feeling that I must be the meanest man in the world, for I seem to say only 'no' where I would be only too glad to say 'yes.'"[42]

And there was plenty of mean to go around. When Mugwumps complained that the reforms weren't sweeping enough, Cleveland groused that they "with supercilious self-righteousness discredit every effort not in exact accord with their attenuated ideas, decry with carping criticism the labor of those actually in the field of reform, and, ignoring the conditions which bound and qualify every struggle for a radical improvement in the affairs of government, demand complete and immediate perfection."[43] When Democratic regulars would lobby for positions currently held by an incumbent Cleveland had decided not to remove, he would glower at them and respond, "I was not aware that there was a vacancy in that position" (a witness to one of these scenes reported "If you see him once and look at that face and jaw, you will believe he means what he says").[44] He would have Honest John Kelly to the White House to make his case for installing a favored Democrat as New York City's postmaster—and then turn around and reappoint the Republican incumbent.[45] Party insiders smarted, not least because Republicans loved to taunt them with slogans like, "You got your president, but you can't get your postmaster."[46]

Principled or not, none of this amounted to good politics on Cleveland's end. Members of his inner circle got a steady stream of complaints from loyal Democrats wondering why their commander in chief seemed to take so much pleasure in denying them a seat at the table.

Manning, now his secretary of the Treasury, and Secretary of the Navy William Whitney both sided with the partisans, worrying that the president was straining party loyalties. Those anxieties were made flesh in the person of David B. Hill, Cleveland's former lieutenant governor in New York, who had ascended to the governor's mansion upon his resignation. Hill shared virtually none of Cleveland's reformist sympathies, proudly stacking offices with party cronies. When he was elected to a full term in the fall of 1885 with margins significantly larger than those by which Cleveland had carried the state in the presidential election, murmurs instantly arose among the Democratic rank-and-file that another New York governor was available for the White House should the current occupant continue to dismiss the needs of his party.[47] Vice President Hendricks, who shared none of Cleveland's convictions on the matter of appointments, was among those whose public praise of Hill was so effusive as to call his loyalties into question.

Feeling the pressure, Cleveland began to soften his stance, though he did not reverse it. The standards by which Republicans could be dismissed grew a bit more elastic and the allowances for loyal Democratic men to replace them grew proportionately. It was worth getting his fellow Democrats off his back, not just for the sake of party unity, but also because the fight was expanding to a second front: Republicans were now intent on using the issue against him as well.

Had Cleveland chosen to liquidate Republican officeholders en masse, it would have looked like nothing more than the partisan turnabout that came standard in the wake of the White House changing hands. But because removals were being made à la carte, the reputations of the men being ejected from office were suffering in the process. Every firing suggested some breach of public duty. In the Republican-controlled Senate, this inspired a strategy to pull the president down from his Olympian heights—and inadvertently gave Grover Cleveland an opportunity to strengthen the institutional power of the presidency.

The offensive was launched through the Senate Judiciary Committee, chaired by Vermont senator George Edmunds (the reformist

Republican whom Theodore Roosevelt had supported over Blaine). The weapon of choice was the Tenure of Office Act, a law passed in 1867 as Republicans in Congress sought to restrain the powers of President Andrew Johnson. Johnson had been chosen as Abraham Lincoln's running mate for a second term largely as a gesture of national reconciliation (indeed, Lincoln ran for reelection not on a Republican ticket but on a one-off National Union ticket). He was a southerner and a lifelong Democrat, but he was also the sole southern senator to reject the Confederacy and keep his seat in the upper chamber throughout the war. His elevation to the presidency upon Lincoln's assassination, however, exposed that the accord he had with Republicans on the importance of union did not extend in the slightest to the issue of Reconstruction, where he judged Republican methods toward his native South heavy-handed. Congress, looking to rein in Johnson's ability to install sympathists in the administration (especially in the War Department, overseeing the military occupation of the former Confederacy), attempted a legislative gelding. The Tenure of Office Act essentially gave the Senate a veto over the president's ability to remove appointees from office. Just as confirmation required the advice and consent of the Senate, so too would removals.*

However, by the time Cleveland came to office, the law—the constitutionality of which was always in question†—had become nearly a dead letter thanks to amendments made at the beginning of the Grant administration. What remained on the books amounted to little more than uncontroversial assertions of the power to confirm appointees that the upper chamber had always possessed. That didn't stop Senate Republicans, however, from attempting to resurrect it as a vehicle by which to chase Cleveland off the moral high ground.

---

*The law passed over Johnson's veto. When he challenged it by removing Secretary of War Edwin Stanton, his violation of the act was used as grounds for impeachment. Johnson was acquitted by one vote, the closest any president has ever come to being removed from office by Congress.
†Though the Tenure of Office Act was never litigated before the Supreme Court, the Court's 1926 opinion in the case of *Myers v. United States* included analysis declaring that the law—by then long repealed—had been unconstitutional.

The strategy upon which they alighted was to insist that the law compelled the administration, when removing appointees from office, to submit all relevant documents leading to the employee's dismissal (a category that included private correspondence) to the Senate. Cleveland took no exception to turning over materials relating to the men he nominated to the resulting vacancies, a request he saw as perfectly in line with the Senate's responsibility to provide advice and consent; but he was utterly unwilling to comply with the request when it came to officials who were being dismissed, regarding a decision to remove appointees as entirely outside of the Senate's purview. For their part, the senators had no expectation that their efforts would materially change who got booted from office—if Cleveland wouldn't even appease his own party, he damn sure wasn't going to offer any flexibility to the opposition. Rather, they hoped it would embarrass the administration if the public was convinced that there was no high-minded civic principle at work; that Republicans were being removed purely to clear the way for Democratic Party hacks starved for a shot at public office.

It was a baffling strategy. Why prosecute an exceedingly weak legal case against an exceedingly stubborn president for exceedingly small symbolic stakes? It was also, as it turned out, not particularly well executed even on its own terms. Republicans chose as their battleground Cleveland's decision to remove a U.S. attorney in Alabama, George M. Duskin. In early 1886, Senator Edmunds pushed through a resolution instructing Attorney General Garland to turn over all papers related to his termination. Garland, at Cleveland's instruction, refused, at which point the Judiciary Committee issued the dual threat of a censure for the attorney general and the obstruction of all of Cleveland's subsequent nominees until the administration began cooperating.

In response Cleveland issued a blistering letter to the Senate. After a long audit of the relevant legal principles—and a sly suggestion that at least some of the Republicans removed from office had been excused from duty at the suggestion of certain Republican senators—he closed on an unambiguous note: "I am not responsible to the Senate, and I am unwilling to submit my actions and official conduct to them for judgment."[48] The constitutional design of the Founding Fathers, Cleveland believed, meant the power to remove inhered entirely in the presidency, subject to no outside scrutiny.

For all the intensity surrounding the conflict, it would wind up defused on the most prosaic of terms: by the time the fight came to a head it was revealed that the term of Duskin, the official in question, had expired. The U.S. attorney's office was now a vacancy like any other, and the question of the Senate's jurisdiction was mooted. A replacement was confirmed, passions cooled, and—almost a year to the day of Cleveland's defiant message to the Senate—he was signing the repeal of the Tenure of Office Act, which even some Republicans were now willing to concede was useless and likely unconstitutional. The presidency, largely regarded as enervated in the postwar period, was permanently strengthened, a harbinger of the aggressive growth in power the office would realize in the near future.

As with his scrutiny of the private pension bills, Cleveland refused to delegate decisions on appointments. Indeed, he was more prone to obsess over minor, insignificant offices than major ones. While that may have been a frivolous use of presidential time—one is hard-pressed to ignore the parallels with Jimmy Carter's famous insistence that he personally manage requests to use the White House tennis court[49]—there was, as ever, a principle at work. The president believed he didn't have to fret as much over major positions, where hundreds of people—well-wishers and pests alike—would make their opinions known about the right man for the job. But for the minor post on some distant frontier? The wrong man, deputized by his president, might do damage for years before it ever came to the attention of anyone who could do anything about it. Grover Cleveland could not abide that thought.[50] The results of his passion for competent men would reverberate throughout the government. Many of Cleveland's appointees demonstrated the same obsessive attention to detail as their president. At the Treasury Department, Daniel Manning discovered that customs houses had been colluding with importers to undervalue goods and thus lower tariff costs. Even though Manning was an advocate for cutting tariff rates, he was not willing to see them reduced by corruption. He broke up the practice and, upon finding that most of the men charged with fraud prevention were political cronies, cut their department's budget by nearly 85 percent.[51] At the Navy Department, Secretary William C. Whitney entered office intent on building a modern fleet, noting in his first annual report that, after spending $75 million, "It is questionable whether we have a single naval vessel finished and afloat at the present time that could be trusted to encounter the ships of any important power."[52] So dogged was Whitney in his pursuit to transform the Navy into a powerhouse that when he became convinced that one of the department's bureau chiefs—who couldn't be fired thanks to civil service protections—would impede progress, Whitney taught himself the ins and outs of naval construction so thoroughly that his subordinate couldn't answer any of his probing questions about the work. Humiliated, the man resigned.[53]

EIGHT

Points West

W hile economics and national defense are standard areas of emphasis for a presidential administration, many of Cleveland's other important efforts came through an unlikely channel: the Department of the Interior, charged with managing the nation's public lands. In the West, once a beacon of new beginnings, the frontier was closing. Moneyed interests of the kind that Grover Cleveland had so often been accused of serving were gobbling up land at a staggering scale. If they were counting on a pliant president, they were in for an exceedingly rude awakening.

Cleveland had singled out Native Americans for special attention in his inaugural, calling for their "care and education . . . with an ultimate view towards their citizenship."[1] His view was simple in its precepts, if complex in its implications: the moral and practical dimensions of the "Indian problem" were in alignment. The United States owed members of the various tribes—some 260,000 Indians spread over 134 million acres of reservation land[2]—basic respect for their rights; respect that had been denied every time a supposedly sacrosanct treaty had been invalidated due to white encroachment.

While Cleveland could be strident when referring to Native Americans, using terms that make modern readers grimace—in his

1886 message to Congress* he referred to Geronimo and his confederates as "murderous savages"[3]—those outbursts were always in reference
to specific actions taken by specific individuals.† In general, however, his
instincts toward Native Americans were protective. Cleveland had a
long-standing aversion to seeing powerful interests run roughshod over
groups without the resources to defend themselves. That sentiment was
especially pronounced when it came to the Indians, with their long history of exploitation at the hands of the federal government.

Indeed, Cleveland's rhetoric around Native American issues was notable for the palpable indignation that it conveyed. In one message to
Congress, he referred to "the sin of their oppression."[4] A veto message
late in his first term put the matter in stark moral terms: "The idea is
too prevalent that, as against those who by emigration and settlement
upon our frontier extend our civilization and prosperity, the rights of
the Indians are of but little consequence. But it must be absolutely true
that no development is genuine or valuable based upon the violence and
cruelty of individuals or the faithlessness of a government."[5]

There was also the fact that, as a practical matter, the frontier was
closing. As the western states and territories grew, natives and whites
would wind up living cheek-by-jowl despite the fact that by every significant measure—language, culture, economy—they belonged to different
civilizations. For Cleveland, the only answer was assimilation. Before
preparing the Indians for the future, however, he had to arrest the injustices of the present.

Upon coming to office he had discovered that President Arthur, in
the final days of his tenure, had opened up nearly half a million acres of
land in the Dakota Territory—lands pledged by treaty to the Win-

---

*The annual message to Congress was the written equivalent of the modern State of the Union
speech, though the messages tended to be far less florid than their modern analogues (most of
them read like corporate annual reports). From 1801 until 1913, all presidents opted for a written
message rather than an oral one.

†The phrase was more descriptive than hyperbolic. As one biographer notes, "In both Mexico
and the United States, [Geronimo] lived up to his reputation as a ruthless butcher. Especially in
Mexico, he shot, slashed, tortured, and murdered almost anyone he came across."

nebago and Crow Creek Indians—to white settlement. Despite the fact that the law had yet to go into effect, thousands of homesteaders had already poured in, while thousands more camped on the borders awaiting the lawful opening. Cleveland, believing there to be no legal justification for Arthur's unilateral abrogation of the treaty, declared the order unlawful and ordered the whites already present to evacuate.

In the Indian Territory (largely coextensive with modern Oklahoma), he took a similarly firm stance. White ranchers had encroached on the lands of the Cheyenne and Arapahoe Indians, claiming that their use of the acreage for grazing was lawful because they had contracted with the Indians for its use. This was less of a defense than it sounded because such leases were inoperative unless blessed by the federal government in its superintendency, a legal nicety with which none of the ranchers had bothered.

Commanding General of the U.S. Army Philip Sheridan, dispatched by Cleveland to investigate, reported back that the result was a systematic exploitation of native credulousness. The leases had been negotiated at appallingly low rates—rents were a cent or two per acre—and the Indians were made liable for any losses to the herd.[6] It was an arrangement under which it was perfectly possible that the Indians would wind up net payers. The president gave sixty days' notice for the ranchers to vacate the territory, under threat of military intervention. However firm his convictions, the order would eventually haunt him: driven from their normal grazing areas out to less forgiving country, approximately 80 percent of the ranchers' livestock subsequently died in the midst of a brutal winter.[7]

There were smaller mercies, too. Native Americans came in for special consideration when it came to presidential pardons and commutations. Cleveland, despite his reputation for obduracy, was always liberal in his use of the pardon power. And on multiple occasions he vetoed congressional appropriations of Indian land intended for the use of railroads, insisting that it was not the federal government's place to award the acreage without the consent of the relevant tribes.

He even deflected criticism of the fearsome violence some Native Americans had demonstrated—an especial anxiety given the trail of carnage the recently escaped Geronimo had left in the West, where he was prone to murder whites without pretext[8]—if only to counter those who would use it as a pretext for ethnic cleansing. "It is useless to dilate upon the wrongs of the Indians," he told Congress, "and as useless to indulge in the heartless belief that because their wrongs are revenged in their own atrocious manner, therefore they should be exterminated."[9]

By all accounts, his conviction that Native Americans deserved treatment as equals was in earnest, and it earned him the admiration of some of their defenders. Helen Hunt Jackson, whose 1881 book, *A Century of Dishonor*, chronicled the long legacy of Indian mistreatment, was not known for mincing words with politicians. When the volume was released, she sent copies to members of Congress emblazoned with the inscription "Look upon your hands! They are stained with the blood of your relations." Yet from her deathbed, she wrote to Cleveland, then barely six months on the job, "I am dying happier for the belief I have that it is your hand that is destined to strike the first steady blow toward lifting this burden of infamy from our country and righting the wrongs of the Indian race."[10]

As his presidency progressed, Cleveland became convinced that the reservation system was a millstone around the Indians' neck; that its net effect would be to retard their development and exacerbate the inevitable tensions with white settlers. The only solution, in his judgment, was assimilation. That meant education, English language acquisition, and, most important, doing away with the practice of collective landownership on the reservations and transitioning to a system of private property that would allow for economic initiative and capital formation.*

---

*Contra what has become conventional wisdom, it was not the case that private property rights were unheard-of among Native Americans. In reality, attitudes toward property prior to the reservation system had varied widely between tribes, running the gamut from collective ownership to arrangements not unlike conventional fee simple property.

While Cleveland grew increasingly persuaded that this was the only means by which the Indians could be fully reconciled to American life, he remained cautious about taking any affirmative steps. Mindful of how divergent the circumstances were between tribes, he dispatched federal commissioners early in his term to make reports on their varying levels of "civilization." He was dedicated to their betterment, but convinced that a one-size-fits-all policy that failed to account for tribal variation might be only marginally less harmful than outright neglect. Some tribes, he argued, longed for private property, while others resisted it. Some were on land that would be appropriate for grazing, but had no flocks; some on land ideal for farming but with no agricultural implements. There were cultural divisions, too, which he expressed in ugly terms consistent with the paternalistic view most policymakers took at the time: "While some are lazy, vicious, and stupid, others are industrious, peaceful, and intelligent."[11]

In 1887, Massachusetts senator Henry Dawes authored a piece of legislation—officially titled the General Allotment Act but known ever after as the Dawes Act—that would open the door to private property for Native Americans. Under the terms of the law, reservation lots between 40 and 160 acres (depending on whether the land was being given to an individual or a family) would be converted into privately owned parcels, though it was stipulated that the land could not be sold for twenty-five years, on fears that the newly propertied Indians would accept unreasonably low offers to sell. Upon taking one of these allotments, the property owner gave up his tribal status and became a U.S. citizen, obligated to pay taxes and able to vote (although, in practice, many jurisdictions went to great pains to keep Native American voters from casting a ballot).

Grover Cleveland signed the Dawes Act and demonstrated genuine enthusiasm for its goals. Still, he kept his ambitions modest, stating when he first began considering proposals for individual property ownership, "I should desire to do much and place it among the achievements of my administration, yet probably I can only make a

beginning."[12] And even well after the legislation was in force he continued to sound cautious notes, writing at one point to his second-term
secretary of the interior, Hoke Smith, that "the good and welfare of
the Indian should constantly be kept in view, so that when the end is
reached citizenship may be to them a real advantage, instead of an
empty name."[13]

Those cautious notes would prove well founded. The policy of
"assimilation" proved a disaster, though many of the ills frequently attributed to the law Cleveland signed are actually the consequences of
policy changes that occurred later on. In 1891 (between Cleveland's two
terms), the Dawes Act was amended to allow the properties to be leased
to non-Indians, a response to the rapacious white appetite for western
lands.[14] Though Dawes had provided that any land remaining unallot-
ted after the division into private parcels could be sold to the federal
government, it stipulated that the provision required tribal consent
and had to be negotiated "on such terms and conditions as shall be
considered just and equitable between the United States and said tribe
of Indians."[15] The Supreme Court's infamous ruling in the 1903 *Lone
Wolf* case, however, left the tribes virtually powerless to resist federal
coercion. In 1906, the Burke Act augmented Dawes by stipulating
that natives would only receive title to their land at the end of the
twenty-five-year period if the Department of the Interior deemed them
"competent," a judgment left to the discretion of federal employees.
Moreover, it delayed their acquisition of citizenship until title was
granted, whereas Dawes had provided it at the time the property was
allotted.

The result was a debacle. By 1934—when the Indian Reorganization Act halted outsiders' access—nearly 50 percent of the lands were
no longer in Indian hands.[16] That may have been a tolerable price to pay
if the natives were flourishing. Many tribes, however, had resisted the
push toward private property as anathema to their traditions. And even
many others who did opt into the system found themselves stuck with
lands unsuited for farming or ranching (160 acres was often insufficient

for a viable farm in dry western climates[17]), despite the fact that federal officials were charged with helping them find productive parcels. In fact, Indian farming would actually decline under the arrangement.[18] Perhaps the situation would have wound up otherwise if the men on the ground had the same fiduciary convictions as the president they served. But how commendable was a policy that could not be successfully carried out unless placed in the hands of extraordinary men? Whatever the Dawes Act occasioned, it was not the renaissance for which the president had hoped.

Cleveland's concerns about western lands were not limited to the areas inhabited by Native Americans. From his inaugural address forward, he had expressed an anxiety that the vision underpinning the Homestead Act—in which Americans were given free property on the frontier if they worked the land—was being undermined. That legislation had been designed to turn the West into a reservoir of opportunity, open to all with the pluck and tenacity to mix sweat with soil. By the time he came to office, however, the president warned, "Laws which were intended for the 'common benefit' have been perverted so that large quantities of land are vesting in single ownerships."[19]

Corporate interests had learned how to game the system. The railroads—which Congress had given the right to claim new territory if the lands granted them by the federal government proved unusable—would wait until settlers had improved tracts and then claim them for their own. Government surveyors, working in collusion with business, would draw lines favorable to their under-the-table benefactors. And ranching, mining, or timber interests would have their employees claim homesteading acreage on prime land only to turn around and sell it to the employer. So extensive was this practice that in one area of Minnesota more than 4,300 homestead claims were made on a territory in which fewer than 100 people were actually homesteading.[20]

The Cleveland administration, getting little in the way of assistance from Congress, struck back through executive action, at one point freezing nearly all new land grants pending a massive investigation into the malfeasance afoot. Railroads were forced to cede back lands they had claimed under specious justifications. Fraudulent homestead claims were systematically invalidated and returned to possession of the federal government. By the end of Cleveland's first term, he had thus clawed back 80 million acres—a territory about the size of Malaysia—to be used for "actual husbandry and genuine homes." Ever the perfectionist, however, he felt compelled to note that this was "less than the greater areas . . . unjustly lost."[21]

While these efforts were aimed primarily at maintaining home-steading as a viable option, there was also a minor theme for which American politics didn't yet have a name: conservationism. Years before Theodore Roosevelt would become famous as the pioneer of presiden-tial environmentalism, it was Cleveland who set aside for preservation forests in Wyoming's Grand Tetons, Washington's Olympic Peninsula and Mount Rainier, and South Dakota's Black Hills, part of an effort that would see the National Forest Reserve double by the end of his time in office.[22] It was even Cleveland, in 1894, who signed the first leg-islation ever to protect wildlife on federal lands: a law preventing the killing of animals in Yellowstone. Though the president was himself an avid hunter (albeit mostly of birds and small game), he saw no contra-diction in that fact, later writing in his book *Fishing and Shooting Sketches* that:

> [T]hose who . . . by instinct and birthright belong to the sport-ing fraternity and are actuated by a genuine sporting spirit, are neither cruel nor greedy nor wasteful of the game and fish they pursue; and I am convinced that there can be no better conser-vators of the sensible and provident protection of game and fish than those who are enthusiastic in their pursuit, but who, at the same time, are regulated and restrained by the sort of chivalric fairness and generosity felt and recognized by every true sports-man.[23]

If the fate of the West's vast landscapes and the plight of its Native American population seemed exotic topics to entrust to a lawyer who had never so much as seen the region, they were downright pedestrian compared to two other topics that traveled from the frontier to his desk: Mormon polygamy and Chinese immigration.

The question of how to handle the Latter-day Saints had vexed the country virtually since the first publication of the Book of Mormon in Palmyra, New York (only about seventy-five miles west of the president's childhood home in Fayetteville), in 1830. Consistently ostracized and harassed in whichever jurisdiction they settled, Mormons traversed the Midwest for a decade and a half, often meeting with violence, as in the 1838 Mormon War in Missouri (which led to around twenty deaths and the sect's expulsion from the state) or the 1844 murder of the faith's founder, Joseph Smith, alongside his brother in Illinois. While the subsequent Mormon exodus to what would become Utah successfully isolated them from hostile neighbors, it didn't eliminate government scrutiny: in 1857, President James Buchanan dispatched the military to the Utah Territory on fears that Mormon hostility to Washington's oversight augured open rebellion. Warfare never resulted, but the territory had existed in an uncomfortable equilibrium ever since, with the issue of polygamy barring any serious prospect for statehood.

During the 1884 election Republicans had used the shadow cast by the Halpin scandal to suggest that Cleveland had yet to meet a vice he couldn't embrace. Among the ensuing allegations was that the Democratic nominee would not only tolerate polygamy (opposition to which had been a longtime point of emphasis in the GOP) but that he was so firmly committed to the cause that the LDS church was running a slush fund on his behalf.[24] He had quickly dispelled the notion once in office, writing in his first annual message, "The strength, the perpetuity, and the destiny of the nation rest upon our homes, established by the law of God, guarded by parental care, regulated by parental authority, and sanctified by parental love. These are not the homes of polygamy."[25]

In the same missive he also proposed that Mormon immigration—the work of LDS missionaries abroad had led to a steady, though by this time declining, stream of migrants from Europe—be prohibited.[26]*

By the end of Cleveland's first term, the crusade against polygamy—indistinguishable, for many of its advocates, from a crusade against Mormonism itself—had reached a confrontational climax. In 1887, Congress passed the Edmunds-Tucker Act, a piece of legislation that amounted to a federal program of de-Mormonizing the Utah Territory. Not only did the law include a raft of anti-polygamy provisions—among them prohibiting the children of such unions from inheriting property—but it also gutted Mormon power structures. The LDS church was disincorporated, its property to be confiscated by the federal government (though, in practice, much of the church's real estate was left untouched).[27] The Perpetual Emigration Fund, an entity set up to help finance Mormon relocations to Utah, was similarly disestablished. The federal government asserted control over the territory's schools, courts, and legislative districts. Women's suffrage, allowed in Utah since 1870, was abolished.[28]

Cleveland made no public utterance about the legislation, but it became law without his signature.† Because it had passed both houses of Congress by overwhelming margins, a presidential veto would have been superfluous. In all likelihood he sympathized with the law's broader aims of extinguishing polygamy but had qualms about the constitutionality of the aggressive assertions of federal power (which would be upheld by the Supreme Court in the 1890 case of *Late Corporation v. United States*). While it certainly wouldn't have been out of character for him to issue a veto message despite knowing he'd be overruled—if only

---

*Mormon immigration itself was never outlawed, though immigration officials would often look for pretexts to turn LDS arrivals away. In 1891, however, polygamists were added to the classes of those denied entry to the United States.

†Per the Constitution, presidents have ten days (excluding Sundays) to sign legislation passed by Congress. If, by the end of that period, they have neither signed nor vetoed the bill it becomes law—unless Congress has adjourned, in which case the bill is rejected, a practice known as the "pocket veto."

to make his objections a matter of public record—it's plausible that he imagined a heavy-handed resolution of the matter preferable to no resolution at all.

Regardless, the law's secularizing effect on Utah laid the predicate for statehood—and some measure of reconciliation—in Cleveland's second term. In 1890 the Mormon church publicly renounced the practice of plural marriage, and four years later Cleveland issued an amnesty for polygamists. Two years after that the president was issuing a proclamation admitting the state of Utah to the union, a gesture enabled by a provision in the state constitution that "polygamous or plural marriages are forever prohibited."[29]*

The Mormons were not the only group that called Cleveland's attention to matters of immigration. In 1882, President Arthur had signed the Chinese Exclusion Act, prohibiting for ten years the importation of Chinese laborers to American shores. The law, though now remembered mostly for the racist motivations of some of its proponents, in truth owed just as much to protectionist instincts. The presence of Chinese workers in western states and territories had engendered local hostility, both because they were willing to work for wages lower than domestic labor and because, tending to cluster together, they were accused of refusing to assimilate. Despite its wide reach, the Exclusion Act had not entirely dissipated the tensions. While the law barred *new* entrants, it did not expel those already present in the country (though it did require them to receive certification to reenter the country if they departed at any point, in addition to prohibiting them from receiving citizenship).[30]

Cleveland came to office sensitive to the complaints that had precipitated the legislation, declaring in his inaugural that he would rigidly enforce "the laws . . . which prohibit the immigration of a servile class to compete with American labor, with no intent of acquiring citizenship, and bringing with them and retaining habits and customs repugnant to

---

*Though it is still illegal, Utah effectively decriminalized polygamy in 2020.

our civilization."[31] The sentiment, with its odor of ethnic essentialism, falls hard on modern ears. It also represents a complexity that tends to get lost—either whitewashed away or magnified beyond reason—in most accounts of Cleveland's life. While Cleveland was not a bigot under any reasonable understanding of the word—in fact, he would've been much more popular within the Democratic Party of the day if he was—he was also not a thoroughgoing racial egalitarian. It's a duality for which modern observers have few reference points. Grover Cleveland could, on the one hand, help Booker T. Washington raise funds for the Tuskegee Institute[32] and, on the other, squirm about appearing at an event with the famed black educator.[33] He could tell an audience in his post-presidency that he came before them "as a sincere friend of the negro," and conclude the very same paragraph with "I believe that neither the decree that made the slaves free, nor the enactment that suddenly invested them with the rights of citizenship any more purged them of their racial and slavery-bred imperfections and deficiencies than it changed the color of their skins."[34] With the Chinese, as with African-Americans and Native Americans, he tended to define their collective shortcomings by the degree to which they were removed from the mainstream culture of white America. He perceived that trait as a deficiency but did not regard that deficiency as innate. In the case of Indians or the black population, this led to what he considered a compassionate emphasis on education as the key to assimilation. For the Chinese—who, unlike those groups, were not permanent residents—his response was less paternal even if it still displayed a measure of empathy.

The situation erupted six months into Cleveland's tenure, in the Wyoming Territory town of Rock Springs. Ten years earlier, a strike by white miners at the town's Union Pacific coal mines had led the company to shift the composition of its labor force, with the new roster including 150 Chinese miners and only 50 whites. By 1885, there were 331 Chinese to 150 whites.[35] Though the proportions had shifted in their direction, the latter still resented the former's presence, especially because the Chinese had refused to join the whites in collective bargaining with the mine operators.[36]

On September 2, 1885, a contingent of white miners (themselves largely immigrants) who had been agitating for the Chinese to be expelled from Rock Springs took their campaign to barbaric new lengths.[37] That morning, they attempted to intimidate Chinese laborers in an especially productive mine into leaving (because the miners were paid according to how much material they extracted, a good location corresponded to a bigger payday). When they didn't evacuate, the white posse brutally beat three of them, one of whom eventually died from a blow to the skull with a pickaxe. This, however, was only a prelude.

A few hours later a white mob of somewhere between 100 and 150 descended on the community's "Chinatown," cutting a path of carnage. They robbed the Chinese of their valuables, beat their faces in with rifle butts, and shot many where they stood. As the Asian workers fled in panic, the aggressors set their homes on fire, in some cases with people still trapped inside. When a few brave residents of Chinatown returned after dark to bury their dead, they found that there was nothing left. Seventy-nine homes had been burned. Twenty-eight of the Chinese workers had been murdered. Many of the bodies were nearly unidentifiable, burned beyond recognition or eaten at by dogs or pigs. Fearing for their lives, the surviving Chinese followed railroad tracks by moonlight to make the fifteen-mile trek to the nearest town.[38]

When word of the massacre reached him, Cleveland was horrified. He deployed federal troops to Wyoming to restore order (he would subsequently do the same in Seattle to stave off the potential of a similar attack there).* After the crimes went unpunished—sixteen miners were arrested, but, with no eyewitnesses willing to come forward, charges were never pressed—Cleveland fulminated that it was "a ghastly mockery

---

*In a statement to the Chinese consul in New York, the survivors of the Rock Springs Massacre singled out Cleveland ("The great President of the United States") for thanks for deploying federal forces. Troops would remain in the Rock Springs area to prevent any further incidents for thirteen years.

of justice" and "a palpable and discreditable failure of the authorities."[39] When the Chinese government requested compensation for the carnage, the president, mindful of avoiding a potentially damaging precedent, went to great pains to stipulate that the federal government bore no responsibility for the crimes and had no treaty obligations to provide relief—but still recommended that Congress approve the money "in aid of innocent and peaceful strangers whose maltreatment has brought discredit upon the country."[40]

The president did not mince words in his diagnosis of what had happened at Rock Springs. "Race prejudice is the chief factor in originating these disturbances," he wrote, "and it exists in a large part of our domain, jeopardizing our domestic peace and the good relationship we strive to maintain with China."[41] But while Cleveland didn't approve of those racist attitudes, he reasoned that he had more control over the men receiving the hatred than those generating it. In his 1886 message to Congress, he argued that "[i]n opening our vast domain to alien elements, the purpose of our lawgivers was to invite assimilation, and not to provide an arena for endless antagonisms. The paramount duty of maintaining public order and defending the interests of our own people may require the adoption of measures of restriction, but they should not tolerate the oppression of individuals of a special race."[42]

Ultimately, Cleveland would come to the conclusion that relations between Chinese laborers and their white counterparts were so fraught as to be unmendable, declaring at the end of his first term, "The experiment of blending the social habits and mutual race idiosyncrasies of the Chinese laboring classes with those of the great body of the people of the United States has been proved by the experience of twenty years . . . to be in every sense unwise, impolitic, and injurious to both nations."[43] His administration would negotiate with the Chinese government a treaty to extend the period of exclusion for Chinese laborers to twenty years, compensate Chinese victims who had suffered at the hands of Americans, and eliminate the Chinese Exclusion Act's provision allowing Chinese workers to reenter the United States after departing. When the Chinese government attempted to reopen negotiations after the two sides had already agreed on terms, the president—who, with only six weeks to go before election day, was animated in part by a desire to have his name attached to a popular policy[44]—instead bypassed the treaty process entirely and signed the Scott Act, a piece of legislation unilaterally barring the reentry of Chinese laborers. The decision prevented an estimated 20,000 workers who were abroad at the time from returning to the United States. While the circumstances were not quite as tidy as some modern-day critics imagine—contemporary observers are often too quick to elide the genuine difficulties presented by the clash of cultures—the Scott Act's human toll would nevertheless mark it as one of the most lamentable actions of the first Cleveland administration.

It was, however, an aberration. For the most part, Grover Cleveland's views on immigration stressed acceptance and accommodation. Only two days before leaving the White House for good, one of his final acts as president would be the veto of a bill prohibiting immigration by the illiterate (who made up more than a quarter of immigrants at the time).[45] To this proposal he responded:

> In my opinion, it is infinitely more safe to admit a hundred thousand immigrants who, though unable to read and write, seek among us only a home and opportunity to work than to admit one of those unruly agitators and enemies of governmental control who can not only read and write, but delights in arousing by inflammatory speech the illiterate and peacefully inclined to discontent and tumult. Violence and disorder do not originate with illiterate laborers. They are, rather, the victims of the educated agitator.[46]

The president believed not only that America could successfully absorb immigrants, but that it was a vital factor in the nation's success.

"A century's stupendous growth," Cleveland declared in the same veto, "largely due to the assimilation and thrift of millions of sturdy and patriotic adopted citizens, attests the success of this generous and free-handed policy which, while guarding the people's interests, exacts from our immigrants only physical and moral soundness and a willingness and ability to work."[47]

Sentiments like those made it all the more appropriate that Grover Cleveland was in New York City on October 28, 1886, for a rare instance of pageantry in his administration. The president served as master of ceremonies for a parade witnessed by at least several hundred thousand observers, and perhaps as many as a million (it would, in fact, turn out to be the progenitor of the city's tradition of ticker-tape parades)[48] before traveling across a New York Harbor choked with flag-waving vessels to Bedloe's Island for the day's main event: the dedication of a statue gifted by the French government to the United States, christened *Liberty Enlightening the World*. In later years Bedloe's Island would only be remembered as Liberty Island, *Liberty Enlightening the World* only as the Statue of Liberty, and Grover Cleveland's remarks not at all. That last fact ranks as an injustice because the president who read poetry as a pastime demonstrated a rhetorical ability far in excess of his reputation:

> We are not here today to bow before the representation of a fierce and warlike god, filled with wrath and vengeance, but we joyously contemplate instead our own deity keeping watch and ward before the open gates of America, and greater than all that have been celebrated in ancient song. Instead of grasping in her hand thunderbolts of terror and of death, she holds aloft the light which illumines the way to man's enfranchisement.
>
> We will not forget that Liberty has here made her home; nor shall her chosen altar be neglected. Willing votaries will constantly keep alive its fires, and these shall gleam upon the shores

of our sister republic in the east. Reflected thence and joined with answering rays, a stream of light shall pierce the darkness of ignorance and man's oppression, until Liberty enlightens the world.[49]

Not bad for a beer-guzzling ex-hangman.

NINE

Grover, at Ease

Every presidency is, at some level, music. George Washington's was a stately, majestic march. Lincoln's was a sweeping, melancholy pastoral. FDR's—at least pre–World War II—was pure jazz, largely improvised but irresistibly energetic. Up through the summer of 1886, Grover Cleveland's felt a bit like a harpsichord recital: exacting, precise, and joyless. No one doubted that the president was taking his responsibility seriously. In fact, his sense of duty bordered on an obsession. Less clear was whether he was actually enjoying any of it.

Grover Cleveland was not a mirthless man. But then, when acting in his official capacity, it wasn't clear that he was a man at all. Friends described a figure who, in moments of repose, was accessible, warm, and quick to laugh. The second matters of state intruded, however, he reverted to a somber, immovable piece of granite. There was no humor, no flexibility, and no respite. Given the extensive hours he devoted to duty, that dour face became the one by which the world knew him.

It was for precisely this reason—the man simply did not allow room for a personal life—that no greater commotion was occasioned by the fact that the president of the United States, nearing fifty years of age, was still a bachelor. In Cleveland's era, an unmarried president was not quite the novelty it would later appear. In the late 1850s, the never-wed James Buchanan had turned over the duties of First Lady to his young niece, Harriet Lane (who quickly became a sensation in Washington society).* Jefferson, Jackson, Martin Van Buren, and Chester Arthur had all come to office as widowers. John Tyler's first wife had suffered a fatal stroke in the White House. Thus, the fact that Cleveland was unaccompanied in the executive mansion was more curiosity than anomaly. Add to that the widely held notion that the president was a coarse, inelegant figure—Henry Adams wrote to his wife that "we must admit that . . . the Lord made a mighty common-looking man in him"[1]—and the idea of the most powerful man in the nation sitting down to dinner alone seemed an altogether explicable state of affairs.

If the public didn't expect much from the president's love life, they didn't get much, either. While there was occasional speculation about romantic interests—the most common rumor involved Emma Folsom, the widow of his best friend Oscar and a frequent guest at the White House—it was entirely idle. Cleveland had always chafed at the intrusions of journalists but had been radicalized into an all-out hatred of the press after enduring the living autopsy of the Halpin scandal. That aversion to the media combined with his naturally laconic temperament to ensure that the president's private life, to the extent it existed, occurred far from the public stage; so far, in fact, that reporters on the Cleveland beat were unaware that a presidential marriage unlike any other was taking shape right under their noses.

Emma Folsom was indeed a regular visitor to the White House, but the object of the president's affection wasn't the widow of his deceased best friend; it was her daughter.

Much has been made in subsequent years of the fact that Frances Folsom Cleveland became her future husband's ward at the age of eleven. When combined with a few other details—that Cleveland bought her first baby carriage, or that the future president once answered his sister's inquiry about when he'd finally settle down by saying

---

*In recent decades it has been suggested that Buchanan was gay and in a long-term relationship with Alabama senator (and later vice president) William Rufus King. The evidence for these claims, however, is entirely circumstantial. No definitive proof has yet emerged.

"I am only waiting for my wife to grow up"[2]—and then placed alongside the more wild-eyed versions of the Maria Halpin story, the implication of Cleveland as sexual predator is too obvious to ignore.

Like the Halpin story, however, the vision of Cleveland as a figure out of Nabokov ignores or misunderstands many of the relevant details: chief among them that Frances was never actually his ward, at least not in the sense in which that term is commonly understood. True, Cleveland had been made the executor of Oscar Folsom's estate, but, in something of a departure from the legal norms of the day—minor children were usually assigned a male guardian upon the death of their father, even if the mother was still alive—the future president's role was purely administrative.[3] The Folsoms never lived with him—in fact, they didn't live in Buffalo for much of Frances's childhood, even relocating to Minnesota for a time. And when they returned to the city, her romantic interests lay elsewhere: while still a teenager she became engaged to a young seminarian who eventually called the wedding off, having fallen for another woman.[4] As for the much-cited "waiting for my wife to grow up" line, Cleveland's sister, Susan, connected it to Frances only as a matter of ironic coincidence. According to the account in which she presented the story, the conversation in question happened prior to the outbreak of the Civil War—at a time when Frances Folsom had yet to be born and Grover Cleveland had likely not even met her father.[5]

Even shorn of its scandalous aspects, the relationship between Grover Cleveland and Frances Folsom was nevertheless unusual. Cleveland was twenty-seven years older than his bride. Only President Tyler, whose second marriage was to a woman thirty years his junior, had a bigger age gap with his First Lady.* And the courtship, such as it was, took place under abnormal circumstances.

The relationship seems to have begun while Frances was studying at Wells College in New York's Finger Lakes region—a matriculation fa-

---

*The second Mrs. Tyler's other contribution to presidential history was her insistence that "Hail to the Chief" be played when her husband entered the room, a tradition that stuck.

cilitated in part by her future husband, who, as the newly elected mayor of Buffalo, had interceded to gain her admission despite the fact that she had not finished high school. In keeping with the social protocols of the day, Cleveland had received Emma Folsom's permission to begin corresponding with her daughter, his letters soon augmented by regular flower bouquets.[6] Even by the liberal standards of a later era, a powerful, forty-something politician pursuing an undergraduate with whom he had been acquainted since birth is difficult to sanitize. Yet what was perhaps most remarkable about the relationship was how unexceptionable it seemed to those in close proximity. Emma Folsom would later remark, seemingly without any unease, that her daughter had "made a hero out of [Grover Cleveland] before she was out of short dresses and [looked] at him through the glamour of love's young dream."[7]*

Despite the fact that Grover and Frances were physically separated for most of the courtship—she was likely the only First Lady in American history kept from her husband's inauguration because her college dean didn't want her to miss final exams[8]—the relationship's ultimate course seemed set from an early date. Frances had accepted Grover's proposal, delivered via letter, in August 1885, shortly after her graduation from Wells. The president's sister Rose later indicated that both families had considered the matter a fait accompli since before Cleveland had even won the presidency.[9] And yet the White House managed to keep the news out of the papers until April 1886, only about six weeks prior to the wedding—and only issued official confirmation on May 28, less than a week before the ceremony.

There was good reason that the engagement managed to evade detection by the press: the future Mrs. Cleveland had spent the run-up to the wedding on a different continent, embarking on a postgraduation tour of Europe with her mother. Their return to New York at the end of May coincided with the height of journalistic speculation about the

---

*In the same interview Emma Folsom gave perhaps the most concise description of Grover Cleveland extant: "He is a peculiar man, but one of the noblest in the world."

First-Lady-to-be, forcing Cleveland to dispatch Dan Lamont to retrieve them from their ship and keep them at arm's length from a ravenous press corps. When the president arrived in New York City a few days later—officially to participate in Memorial Day observances—the public got its first-ever view of Grover Cleveland's softer side. As the president observed a parade proceeding down the Manhattan streets, Frances fluttered her handkerchief at him from the window of her nearby hotel room. Grover Cleveland winsomely tipped his hat in acknowledgment, a military band broke into the wedding march, and the crowd erupted in cheers. In his short time in public life this great gruff man had always commanded respect. Now, for the first time, he seemed to be commanding genuine affection.

The outpouring of public approbation continued through the wedding day, when crowds massed on the White House lawn (completely open to the public in that era) in a vain attempt to catch a glimpse of the bride (the groom would have been easier to locate; the president, playing to type, spent the first half of his wedding day at his desk). That the ceremony took place inside the executive mansion was itself notable—no president before or since has been wed on the White House grounds[*]—and something of an improvisation. The original plans had called for the ceremony to take place near Buffalo, at the farm owned by Frances's paternal grandfather. Colonel John Folsom had died, however, during Frances's return voyage across the Atlantic. Because the president didn't belong to a church in Washington and balked at the idea of marrying in a hotel, the couple settled on the world's most glamorous backup plan.

Given Cleveland's aversion to pomp and the pall cast by the death of the incoming First Lady's grandfather, the ceremony was far more modest than the setting might imply. The *New York Times*' account of the proceedings even went out of its way to note that the decorations were no better than had "been seen on many occasions when the different cir-

---

[*]Cleveland was one of three presidents to marry while in office. John Tyler remarried in 1844 in New York City. Woodrow Wilson remarried in 1915 at his new wife's Washington home.

cles of society have been invited to meet each other and pay their respects to the president."[10] Fewer than thirty guests—a smattering of friends, family, and cabinet members*—gathered in the Blue Room to witness the service. The wedding music was provided by the Marine Band, conducted by no less than John Philip Sousa himself (so fervid was the public's desire to witness the proceedings that Sousa had turned away a fifty-dollar bribe from an onlooker who wanted to pose as the band's triangle player).[11]

In one noteworthy detail, the bride's vows had been altered, rendering the promise to "love, cherish, and obey" as "love, cherish, and keep"—a somewhat surprising departure from tradition given that Cleveland, an opponent of female suffrage, did not hold especially progressive views on the role of women.[12] The thoroughly Presbyterian ceremony—Frances not only shared her husband's faith, but was decidedly more devout in her observance—was presided over by Dr. Byron Sunderland, the pastor of the First Presbyterian Church in Washington, but it was another man of the cloth who pronounced the blessing at the ceremony's conclusion: the president's brother, the Reverend William Cleveland.

While Grover Cleveland did not view his new wife as a political asset—he was, if anything, overzealous in attempts to keep her from the public eye—it would be the case from their wedding day forward that Frances—young, big-hearted, and beautiful—was the member of the Cleveland family who truly captivated the public. Not quite twenty-two years old, she had become the youngest First Lady in American history.† The effect she had on Washington would be unrivaled until Jacqueline Kennedy's tenure nearly a century later.‡ The *New York Times'* coverage

---

*In one of the more peculiar developments of an already surreal day, Attorney General Garland was said to have skipped the ceremony because of a well-known aversion to wearing tails.

†More precisely, Frances Cleveland was the youngest *wife* of a president. Andrew Jackson's niece, Emily Donelson, and Martin Van Buren's daughter-in-law, Sarah Angelica Van Buren, both assumed the duties of first lady at an even younger age.

‡Mrs. Kennedy, the modern benchmark for a young, vivacious First Lady, was a decade older than Frances Cleveland when she assumed the role.

of the wedding established the fawning tone that would dominate throughout her public life, declaring in its description of Frances's wedding dress, "Nature did more to make the picture pretty than had the art of the costumer, for the delicate profile of the bride, her shapely head and self-reliant carriage, all subservient to the timid look of her eyes, the compression of her well-formed lips, and the statuesque firmness of her face, made the fabrics she wore a simple and harmonious drapery. It was the woman at whom the women looked rather than the dress."[13] The language was purple, but then so was public sentiment.

Praise for Frances came from all quarters. There were the regular encomia from the *Times*, which would pronounce in 1887 that no First Lady (a term that had yet to harden into standard usage, and one that the president disliked) had "more widely and generally endeared herself to the people of the United States than the wife of President Cleveland."[14] The sentiment was seconded by those who saw her behind closed doors. After an unbroken stint as a staffer for every president from Abraham Lincoln to Theodore Roosevelt, William H. Crook wrote in his memoirs, "I am an old man now and I have seen many women of various types through all the long years of my service in the White House, but . . . Mrs. Grover Cleveland was the most charming woman and the most lovely character that I have ever known in the course of my life. When one remembers that in addition to this she was physically beautiful, one can easily understand her extraordinary influence upon all who saw her."[15]

The public at large was equally enraptured, sometimes to a hysterical extent. When news hit the papers, for example, that Mrs. Cleveland had decided to forswear the bustle as a part of her wardrobe, the popularity of the garment collapsed almost instantaneously. What made the trend all the more remarkable was that the precipitating story was false, the creation of a newspaper columnist who knew that any story involving the First Lady made for good copy. Frances Cleveland *did* end up abandoning the bustle . . . but only to comply with what, by that time, her adoring public expected of her.[16] It was far from the only time she would be conscripted for commercial purposes. So ubiquitous was the use of the First Lady's image on consumer products—everything from arsenic pills to tobacco—that Congress even considered legislation prohibiting the unauthorized use of a woman's likeness.[17]

While the average American's closest brush with the First Lady might be the image that appeared on a commemorative ashtray, the handful that saw her up close testified that the appeal was more than skin-deep. Crook's memoir notes that, shortly after taking up residency in the executive mansion, Frances had been encouraged to stop hosting White House receptions (open to anyone in Washington who wanted to attend) on Saturday afternoons, as they tended to attract the type of young women who spent their weekdays as department store clerks, a demographic that was deemed unsuitable company for the first family. Frances took the advice to heart: it inspired her insistence that the events would *continue* until there were no more of Washington's shopgirls left for her to meet.[18] By the end of her time in public life she may have come to regret being quite that accessible: she had greeted so many visitors that her right hand had swollen half a size larger than her left.[19]

The First Lady had many fans, but no one was more beguiled by Frances Cleveland than her husband. Put aside the fact that mere rumors about her taste could disrupt the American fashion industry; her most stunning accomplishment was surely getting Grover Cleveland to loosen up, if only a little. Reports from the connubial White House were uniform: the president had begun to show signs of a previously elusive ease. The ceaseless days behind his desk were now subject to afternoon interruptions—time enough for a carriage ride with his new bride. Reports from the couple's honeymoon in the mountains of western Maryland even described a scene where "[t]he bride picked some wildflowers and whipped the President's chin with them. He stood it as a mastiff regards the playfulness of a cocker spaniel, plainly thinking it very nice for her and harmless to him."[20] Thus did the man who had once cowed Theodore Roosevelt into submission yield to the teasing of a twenty-two-year-old girl.

Wedded bliss had not entirely stripped Grover Cleveland of his edge, however. The reports that endeared Frances Cleveland to the public, for example, sent her husband into a rage. It was in keeping with the president's vision of his role—he was a custodian, not a national totem—that he believed the press had no rightful claim on his private life. Already disdainful of the media's prying eyes, he found the situation intolerable once his wife was thrown into the mix. Part of this defensiveness surely owed to Frances's age—armchair Freudians have had a field day attempting to demarcate the line between conjugal and paternal affection in their relationship—but just as much owed to the extreme measures the media took to uncover the smallest details about the woman who had suddenly become a national sensation.[21]* Some of the yellower papers even speculated about the toll the president's weight might take on the First Lady when the time came to consummate the marriage.

In a moment of self-indulgence, Cleveland allowed himself to vent his spleen on paper. The missive delivered to the *New York Evening Post* complained of the offending reporters that they "have used the enormous power of the modern newspaper to perpetuate and disseminate a colossal impertinence, and have done it, not as professional gossips and tattlers, but as the guides and instructors of the public in conduct and morals. And they have done it, not to a private citizen, but the President of the United States, thereby lifting their offence into the gaze of the whole world and doing their utmost to make American journalism contemptible in the estimation of people of good breeding everywhere."[22]

His inability to contain his emotions when it came to his wife's privacy would be a recurring theme. In the fall of 1886, Cleveland was

---

*The crush of media would later inspire Cleveland to suggest that a single journalist, charged with distributing news to all other media outlets, follow the first couple on trips. The idea was an embryonic form of what would be later known as a "pool reporter."

invited to speak at Harvard on the occasion of the school's 250th anniversary.* What garnered the most attention at the time, however, was the fact that the president's usual self-discipline melted away . . . in public. While delivering a dinner speech to Harvard alumni, Cleveland caught sight of Frances in the gallery and was overcome with emotion. Departing from his prepared remarks, he launched into a harangue of the reporters who had ceaselessly harassed her (some of whom were seated right in front of him), a tongue-lashing that included a reference to "those ghouls of the press." Even more surprising: by the time he was done with the convulsion his cheeks were stained with tears.[23]

The urge to be out of the public eye would culminate in an unusual development: Cleveland decided to become a commuter president, at least part-time. A few months before the marriage, the president had purchased a home on twenty-seven acres in an area of Washington then known as Georgetown Heights (it is now known, thanks to his residency, as Cleveland Park). Located about a half mile north of the present-day site of Washington National Cathedral, the stone farmhouse (which the Clevelands Victorianized with the addition of red porches and turrets, leading the public to christen it "Red Top") would function as the president's home during the summer and other quiet interludes in the White House social calendar, with a carriage dispatched for daily trips to and from the White House. The property was brimming with crops and animals—in addition to the couple's four dogs, there was everything from quail to foxes[24]—and Cleveland referred to it, with only slight exaggeration, as his farm. In a story that appeared in the *Washington Post*, Frances (predictably described therein as "A Greek goddess, pure in every curve and outline") told an interviewer that "when we go to the farm, he walks all about there, and it rests a man's

*The visit is usually remembered for the fact that the president, acutely aware of his limited educational pedigree, turned down an offer to receive an honorary degree (a decision "based upon a feeling which I cannot stifle and which I hope may be humored without any suspicion of lack of appreciation or churlishness").

mind to talk of potatoes and hay and corn, and where he is going to put the roads and all that. Oh, the farm is indeed a godsend for us!"[25] The president may have fancied himself master of the property, but it was clearly Frances who was engaged in the more heroic act of domestication.

Red Top was to be only the first step in Cleveland's efforts to extricate himself from the four walls of the White House. In 1887, arrangements were made for the decidedly provincial president—prior to Cleveland's inauguration he had only been to Washington once[26]—to venture out and see the country for the first time. A dry run of sorts was conducted in the summer, when he engaged in a mini-homecoming tour of upstate New York, returning to visit Clinton, Fayetteville, and Holland Patent. That the man had been reborn was clear from the tenor of the speeches. For once, the lawyerly remarks were put aside for impromptu reminiscences of his early years. There was even a rare display of impulsiveness in Holland Patent, where he decided to tag along on a house call with an old friend who worked as a local doctor. In the *New York World*'s telling, "The president entered the house of the patient and conversed with the lady of the house, and it was not [until] he was leaving that the doctor introduced him as the President of the United States. The good woman with whom he had been talking so freely was so surprised that she nearly fainted." Frances was equally at ease, despite reports that one of the well-wishers who turned up at a reception for the couple in Holland Patent was an ex-girlfriend of the president's (Cleveland, the paper nonchalantly noted, "once presented her with a pony").[27]

The president's subsequent tour of the South and the "West" (he got as far as Omaha) was a more stately affair: a three-week journey on a specially appointed presidential train with stops in Indiana, Missouri, Illinois, Wisconsin, Minnesota, Nebraska, Tennessee, Georgia, and Alabama. The journey was constructed with great care, as the track record for presidential tours was decidedly mixed. The gold standard remained the visits George Washington insisted on paying to every state in the union (the trips, intended to unify the young nation, also birthed the iconic—and often erroneous—"George Washington slept here" sign). The example to be avoided at all costs was Andrew Johnson's "swing around the circle," a catastrophic 1866 speaking tour in which Johnson—irascible, consumed by a persecution complex, and often drunk—would get into shouting matches with hecklers and occasionally compare himself to Jesus.[28]* Safety was also an issue: when President Arthur had made a trip west a few years earlier, it was rumored that a group of outlaws had plotted to kidnap him and hold him for ransom near Yellowstone.[29]

The journey, widely hailed as a success, proved to be a kaleidoscopic sampling of late-nineteenth-century America. The tour began in Indianapolis, where the Clevelands called on the widow of Thomas Hendricks. Cleveland's vice president had died less than a year into his term, his health having been in decline since a stroke a few years earlier. With the vice presidency vacant (the modern procedure, in which a replacement vice president can be nominated by the president and confirmed by Congress, was not established until the ratification of the Twenty-Fifth Amendment in 1967), Cleveland had subsequently signed the Presidential Succession Act, putting cabinet secretaries in the line of succession so as to avoid a constitutional crisis if he, too, perished.† The tour came perilously close to testing out that arrangement. While in transit to Memphis, word reached the party in just enough time that a trestle the presidential train was scheduled to traverse had burned down, allowing them to reroute.[30] It was neither the trip's only brush with death nor its strangest one. When Cleveland arrived in Memphis, his speech was introduced by Henry T. Ellett, a former judge on the

---

*The "swing around the circle" was considered so disgraceful that it actually formed the basis for one of the articles of impeachment brought against President Johnson.

†Prior to the Presidential Succession Act's passage, the only offices in the line of succession behind the vice president were president pro tempore of the Senate and Speaker of the House (in that order). The law signed by Cleveland removed both of those offices at the same time that it elevated the cabinet secretaries. In 1947, a law signed by Harry Truman restored them to the line of the succession but reversed the order, making the Speaker first in line should both the presidency and vice presidency fall vacant.

Mississippi Supreme Court. Moments after the president began his speech, Ellett dropped dead onstage.[31]

It was the southern leg of the trip that provided many of the journey's most memorable moments. In Nashville, the president and First Lady met with the eighty-four-year-old Sarah Childress Polk, widow of the eleventh president, who by then had already outlived her husband by nearly forty years. In Atlanta, while visiting the home of Georgia senator Alfred Colquitt, Cleveland arrived through a driving rain and immediately requested a drink. It was unclear whether he didn't know or didn't care that Colquitt was a leading prohibitionist (genteel as could be, Colquitt managed to procure bourbon from a neighbor). Atlanta was also the site of rumors that Jefferson Davis would turn up at one of the president's events. Cleveland, thinking the whole point of the southern leg was to look toward a future in which sectional differences were muted, threatened to boycott any gathering where the former Confederate president was in attendance. Davis never turned up.[32]

Despite his noble aims, however, the tour also provided early evidence that Cleveland had inadequately grasped the scope of the challenge facing blacks in the South. In a speech in Montgomery, Alabama, the president told his audience that "you still have problems to solve, involving considerations concerning you alone, questions beyond the reach of federal law or interference, and with which none but you should deal. I have no fear that you will fail to do your manful duty in these matters...."[33] He should have feared, of course. But the president's devotion to the Constitution meant that the paramount consideration in his mind was procedural—that Washington not impinge on matters the Constitution reserved to the states—rather than humanitarian. Cleveland believed, as he would say moments later, that education was the key to elevating the black population in the South. He simply did not acknowledge—whether because of a lack of imagination or because of a willful blindness—that much of that audience had no regard for the elevation of the formerly enslaved, and that many of them actively opposed it.

That the tour was met with such a warm reception was at least partially attributable to the fact that many audiences regarded the president as the support act—the people came to see Frances. The First Lady grew mildly obsessed by the fear that the size and passion of the crowds would end with an innocent bystander being trampled to death (an anxiety likely attributable to the circumstances around her own father's demise).[34] One Ohio newspaper remarked that at least ten thousand men were as suited to be president as Grover Cleveland . . . but that no one seemed quite as perfect for First Lady as his wife.[35] At least there was a compliment buried in the abuse. The days ahead would provide no such silver linings.

TEN

Turned Out

The reason that Grover Cleveland lost the presidential election of 1888—indeed, the reason for nearly every loss he suffered throughout his political career—boiled down to eleven words that appeared in the *New York Sun*'s post-election obituary: "The President of the United States has to be a politician."[1]

All the traits that had propelled him to higher office—the refusal to deviate from principle; the unwillingness to genuflect to purely partisan interests; the confidence in his convictions that could, at times, bleed into self-righteousness—tended to shrink rather than expand his political coalition. The practical consequence of his oft-repeated vow to serve "the public interest" rather than those of any particular faction was to harden the opposition of his enemies without creating proportionate loyalty among his friends, most of whom were never more than half-satisfied.

The pattern began even before he had moved into the White House. In February 1885, approximately a month before he was to take the oath of office, Cleveland had received a letter from Abraham Hewitt, the New York representative who chaired the House Ways and Means Committee, conveying the news that any incoming president fears most: a crisis was about to be dumped in his lap.

This crisis, it bears noting, tends to seem inscrutable to modern Americans. In Cleveland's day, the country was on the gold standard, meaning that the paper currency that had been introduced during the

Civil War could be redeemed at any time for its equivalent worth in gold. The theory of this system was that the gold represented the real value, with the greenback dollars simply serving as a proxy that made for easier financial exchanges than actually being forced to transfer metals. Because the supply of gold was not limitless, however, this necessitated limits on the country's money supply—and, correspondingly, the availability of credit. As a result, a growing pressure emerged, especially from those who felt that such a tight money supply was limiting their economic opportunities, to switch to a system of "bimetallism," in which silver also made up part of the country's monetary base. The impetus for this movement was twofold: wage laborers and farmers, many of whom had sank deep into debt trying to finance their operations, hoped that it would lead to inflation, reducing the cost of paying back their obligations. Meanwhile, the western states where silver was mined coveted an arrangement whereby they could make Washington a client in perpetuity.

The movement had already met with some success in the years before Cleveland came to office. Ever since the passage of the Bland-Allison Act in 1878 (over the veto of President Hayes), the federal government had been obligated to purchase and coin between $2 million and $4 million of silver per month. The problem with this arrangement— the critics of which included Hayes, Arthur, and virtually the entire eastern financial establishment—was that silver was worth less than gold. By the time Cleveland was preparing to assume office, the actual value of a silver dollar was approximately 85 percent that of a gold dollar.[2] This led to a predictable pattern: every financially literate American had an incentive to pay their bills with silver while hoarding gold.* This was an especially acute problem for the federal treasury, which was obligated to *issue* payment in gold but also to *accept* payment made in silver. Compounding the difficulty: The Treasury was also required to

---

*This behavior represented the economic principle known as Gresham's law, usually formulated as "Bad money drives out good."

maintain gold reserves of at least $100 million (a measure taken to en-
sure the redeemability of the greenbacks).[3]

Hewitt's letter had warned that the gold draining out of federal
coffers was about to cross the threshold at which the reserves would
be endangered and Washington would have to suspend payments in the
metal. Banks and financial interests were already engaging in stockpiling. It was a currency crisis in the making, and the outgoing Arthur
administration was intent on forestalling it just long enough to give
Grover Cleveland sole responsibility.

Representative Hewitt, along with Samuel Randall, a Pennsylvania
congressman who'd previously served as Speaker of the House, had implored Cleveland to assume the mantle of leadership despite the fact
that he had not yet been sworn in. It was an appeal that cut against the
grain of Cleveland's formal, legalistic interpretation of his duty. Yet, convinced that a crisis was in the offing, he conceded to the request, though
stipulating to Randall that "I have some delicacy in saying a word that
may be construed by anybody as interfering with the legislation of the
present Congress."[4] The resulting statement from the president-elect
found him endorsing the Pennsylvanian's proposal to suspend the coinage of silver, arguing that otherwise:

> . . . Such a financial crisis as these events would certainly precip-
> itate, were it now to follow upon so long a period of commercial
> depression, would involve the people of every city and every state
> in the union in a prolonged and disastrous trouble. The revival
> of business enterprise and prosperity so ardently desired, and
> apparently so near, would be hopelessly postponed. Gold would
> be withdrawn to its hoarding places, and an unprecedented con-
> traction in the actual volume of our currency would speedily
> take place.[5]*

---

*New to the issue of monetary policy, Cleveland's silver letter was the sole instance in his career
where he relied on a ghostwriter. The document was authored by Manton Marble, an ally of
Samuel Tilden's and a former editor of the *New York World*. Tilden was no fan of Cleveland's in-

It was a bold assertion of presidential leadership, especially coming from someone with such a restrained view of the office's powers. It was also an utter political disaster—and a portent of the factors that would keep Grover Cleveland from reelection four years later.

The impropriety of adding silver to the nation's monetary mix was by no means an article of Democratic Party orthodoxy. In fact, the question split the party in two—and Cleveland was in the minority camp. A Democratic congressman from Missouri wrote to the president-elect, "This House will not aid in stopping [silver's] coinage, the next House will not do it, and there must be a wonderful change in the South and West before such action can be expected from the Fiftieth Congress. The question, then, is what necessity there can be for a Democratic administration to press a measure with no hope of its success, with at least three-fourths of the Democratic Party opposed to it. . . ."[6] He was right. Less than twenty-four hours after the publication of Cleveland's letter, the House defeated the move to suspend silver coinage 152–118. Grover Cleveland had racked up his first legislative defeat before he had even acquired the keys to the White House.

To protect the gold reserves, Treasury secretary Manning had the department's payments made in greenbacks where possible and halted the previous administration's policy of expediting bond redemptions (a policy undertaken because the federal government was running a massive surplus at the time). In fact, Cleveland had managed to increase gold reserves by more than 20 percent during his first year in office (a move that had the perverse effect of convincing his critics that the previous fears of a crisis had been overblown).[7]

But while the president had arrested the short-term threat, he hadn't changed the fundamental dynamics at work. In his 1885 message to Congress, he had attempted to puncture what he regarded as the illogic of the inflationists, arguing that, "if the laboring man should

---

sistence on self-sufficiency, declaring him "the kind of man who would rather do something badly for himself than to have somebody else do it well."

receive four depreciated dollars where he now receives but two, he will pay in the depreciated coin more than double the price he now pays for all the necessaries and comforts of life."[8] The argument, along with the president's repeated calls to suspend silver coinage, proved unpersuasive to most of his party. By the time of his 1886 message to Congress, Cleveland was reporting that the value of a silver dollar—which had been a little over 94 cents at the time of the Bland-Allison Act's passage—had declined to less than 72 cents.[9]

It didn't help matters any that Cleveland had engaged in a baffling act of autocastration on the matter. As the issue began to bubble up again in early 1886, the *New York Herald* published a report predicting a resurgence of the chin-first presidential leadership he had displayed in writing his silver letter. Instead, for reasons that remain a mystery, he now responded with a rediscovery of his modest conception of presidential power. Cleveland would not intervene with Congress, he declared, pronouncing, "I believe that this is an executive office, and I deem it important that the country should be reminded of it. I have certain duties to perform; when that is done my responsibility ends."[10]

Democrats who had counted on the president to take the lead couldn't hide their mortification. One member of Congress told the *Herald*, "The opposition to his policy was melting away like snow in a thaw. He need not have done anything. If only he had said nothing, we should presently have had a united party, confident and happy, with the President as our natural and proper leader. It makes me sad—for what he so needlessly said is an invitation to confusion and discord."[11]

Cleveland's weakness would prove provocative on the other end of Pennsylvania Avenue. With the president pre-committing to supineness, the pro-silver forces in Congress went on the offensive. First came a maximalist bill that would abolish all limits on how much silver could be added to the money supply (the "free silver" policy that would later come to be associated with William Jennings Bryan). It failed, but with enough Democratic support to show that the members of Cleveland's party on Capitol Hill were unafraid of crossing the White House on the issue.

Next came a far more formidable challenge. Given the extraordinary size of the national surplus (in the previous fiscal year, the federal government had collected over $322 million and left more than $63 million unspent*),[12] significant pressure existed to get the excess funds back into circulation. Representative William Rawls Morrison, the Democrat who had taken over the chairmanship of the House Ways and Means Committee, found in that fact an opportunity to advance the silver cause, authoring legislation that would compel the Treasury to spend down its gold to pay off the country's outstanding bonds. Cleveland was appalled at the proposal, surmising that it could break the gold standard for good. Yet he once again kept a studied distance from the legislative branch.

Having spared the rod, the president soon found his fellow Democrats correspondingly spoiled. The Morrison Resolution—a direct rebuke to the president's stated views on monetary policy—passed the House with the support of 143 of his fellow Democrats. Only 14 took the president's side.[13] The only factor that staved off full-blown internecine warfare was the Republican Senate, which diluted the bill to the point that its provisions became entirely subject to the discretion of the Treasury secretary, making the contents of the legislation little more than advisory. Cleveland nevertheless disposed of it with a pocket veto.† The silver campaign was stalemated, with neither the conservative push to stop coinage nor the populist one to radically expand it able to gain any ground. The veto of the Morrison Resolution would, for all intents and purposes, mark the end of the issue in

---

*Why wasn't money from the budget surplus used to bolster the tottering gold reserves? It would have required an act of Congress. With silver Democrats holding the reins in the House, the money was thus unavailable to be applied toward staving off a currency crisis.

†A pocket veto occurs when the president fails to sign a piece of legislation and the bill can't be reconsidered on Capitol Hill because Congress is out of session.

Cleveland's first term, though it would come back to haunt him in his second.

In March 1886, Daniel Manning, returning to the Treasury Department from a cabinet meeting, suffered a brain aneurysm while climbing the building's front steps. The president, both keenly dependent on and deeply fond of his Treasury secretary, went to elaborate lengths to retain him, turning down Manning's resignation on multiple occasions despite the fact that the secretary's enfeeblement clearly prevented him from discharging the duties of his office. While Manning would retain his title for more than a year before Cleveland finally acquiesced to his departure, he was no longer a member of the cabinet in any meaningful sense, spending most of that time convalescing away from Washington, at times overseas.[*] The lack of his guidance would be acutely felt in Cleveland's ensuing tariff crusade, which managed the impressive feat of being both passionate and desultory.

The federal tax system that Cleveland inherited was one in which, as of 1884, customs duties made up just under 60 percent of federal revenues, with another 37 percent coming from excise taxes on products like tobacco and liquor (the remainder came from the sale of federal lands).[14][†] Cleveland had come to office inclined to reduce the tariff, but cautious about making any bold gestures. The problem was that Democrats were divided between those who regarded it as an instrument of oppressive taxation and those who considered it a safeguard against ruinous foreign competition. Making matters all the more complicated was that Democratic support for tariff reduction tended to be strongest in the parts of the country where opposition to the president's stance on silver was most intense.

At least some of the president's initial tentativeness on the issue likely owed to a belief that he was over his intellectual skis. Carl Schurz, one of the leading Mugwump reformers of the era, claimed that when

---

[*]Daniel Manning officially left office in April 1887 and died before the year's end.
[†]Though a federal income tax had been implemented during the Civil War, it was subsequently repealed in 1872.

he implored Cleveland to take up the tariff issue (unlike the fractious Democrats, Mugwumps were overwhelmingly and intensely in favor of reductions) the new president buried his face in his hands and ruefully declared, "I know nothing about the tariff."[15] The vignette has been treated with skepticism by Cleveland biographers, and not without reason: the president's humility rarely crossed the line into self-abasement. But Schurz's tale likely falls into the untidy category of "untrue but accurate." There had simply been no need for Cleveland to acquaint himself with the issue prior to arriving in Washington. The president's track record, however, was unambiguous: the less he knew about an issue, the more intensely he set to studying it.

As he delved deeper into the tariff question, Cleveland became characteristically immovable in his convictions. He had long argued that every cent in taxes that the federal government collected in excess of its "legitimate needs" was not only unjustified but also morally indefensible. Given that the federal government in the 1880s was taking in $1.40 for every dollar it spent,[16] the president now found himself party to what he could only regard as a betrayal of the fiduciary duty he owed to taxpayers. For all of the protectionist homilies about how trade barriers were essential to protecting American jobs and increasing wages, the rates tended to be set at the behest of corporations looking to minimize competition. With a steady surplus, a reduction in tariff rates posed no serious threat to the health of the federal budget. Moreover, Cleveland noted, whatever increase the tariffs generated in wages tended to be offset by the higher prices workers would have to pay for goods subject to the duties.

Thus, in contrast to how the issue would often be framed in future generations, Cleveland came to the conclusion that *lowering* tariffs was the true populist position. He was not alone in that conviction. When pro-tariff advocate David Wells had been made Special Commissioner of Revenue by Congress in the late 1860s, his exposure to the process by which rates were actually set led him to privately confess that "I have changed my ideas respecting tariffs and protection very much

since coming to Washington. . . . I am utterly disgusted with the ra-
pacity and selfishness which I have seen displayed. . . ."[17] And even
Republicans, traditionally the foremost defenders of tariffs, had conceded in the prior election that high taxes were adversely affecting the
economy.

The first sign that the tariff issue might inspire Cleveland to abandon the reticence that had characterized his approach to silver came in
early 1886. Representative Morrison—the very same member who had
been the thorn in his paw on the currency question—was attempting to
advance a modest tariff reform bill through the House. In a further sign
of how topsy-turvy the coalitions were, Samuel Randall—who had
spurred Cleveland to write his silver letter—was the foremost opponent
of Morrison's initiative. This time the president tried to assert executive
leadership, calling members of Congress to the White House to make
his case for the bill's passage. The effort was unsuccessful. Not only did
Cleveland have to overcome his self-imposed irrelevance to the legislative process, but he was also not especially gifted as an arm-twister; "this
kind of missionary effort does not seem to be in his line," the *New York
Herald* reported with the resignation of a disappointed parent.[18] The
bill never came up for consideration, blocked from debate by a margin
of 157–140.

Serious action on the tariff now had to await the next Congress, the
product of an 1886 midterm election that resulted in further muddle.
Democrats took losses in the House (including Morrison), barely hanging on to their majority. In the Senate, by contrast, Republican ranks declined, with the GOP retaining control of the chamber by a margin of
just two seats. The results suggested a public not especially aroused in
either direction. Cleveland would soon get to work making sure that
such ambivalence was no longer an option.

The congressional calendar of Cleveland's era—indeed, of all of
American history up until the 1930s—was, by modern standards, baffling. Though the members of the Fiftieth Congress were elected to
office in November 1886, they did not actually assemble in Washington

until more than a year later, in December 1887.* When they arrived, they discovered a president resolved that he would no longer be relegated to the passenger seat.

The December gathering of Congress was the traditional occasion for the delivery, by letter, of the president's annual message. In Cleveland's day, such a document tended to be a turgid, discursive exercise, touching on every element of federal business but rarely yielding a clear upshot. In an uncharacteristic bit of innovation, however, he now jettisoned that approach entirely: the entire document was to be a cri de coeur about the need for tariff reform. Never before had an American president taken such a step.

Cleveland had been laying the groundwork for this offensive for months. In September, he had summoned the Democratic leadership—including Speaker of the House John Carlisle and incoming Ways and Means chairman Roger Mills—to Red Top to set the mechanics for a serious reform effort in motion. In what would prove to be a grievous mistake, no invitation was forthcoming for former Speaker Randall, the Pennsylvanian whose protectionist convictions made him the leading foe of rate reduction within the president's party. Rather than being courted, Randall was to be marginalized. "From my standpoint," the president wrote, "there is but one policy to be pursued: we have got to take Mr. Randall by a flank movement, and, if possible, draw his supports from him one by one."[19] No longer content to be battered by his own party, the president also let it be known that anyone who allied with Randall on the matter would find patronage opportunities closed off to him.

Not everyone in Cleveland's inner circle was convinced of the wisdom of his newfound assertiveness. George Hoadly, the former governor of Ohio, warned him of "the danger of alienating large bodies of

---

* The new Congress technically began on March 4 of the year following an election (it was altered to January 5 with the ratification of the Twentieth Amendment in 1933), but sessions weren't held until December, an arrangement originally devised because of the rhythms of the agricultural calendar and sustained because of the brutal summertime heat in Washington.

workingmen, who are thoroughly organized, whose ignorance is crass, and whose employers are extremely jealous of any danger of loss of profits."[20] Upon seeing a draft of the annual message, William Whitney, Cleveland's secretary of the Navy, suggested not only that he not send it to Capitol Hill but that he also destroy the document.[21] The anxieties were almost universally rooted in one concern: pressing this hard on the tariff so late in his term virtually guaranteed that it would become the defining issue of the 1888 reelection campaign—and, given that it divided Democrats and united Republicans in opposition, it was weak territory on which to make a stand.

Appeals to strategy, however, fell on deaf ears with a president who seemed unable to take up any issue without casting it as a moral crusade. To one staffer, he uttered an aphorism that was, in every sense of the word, a fitting epitaph: "What is the use of being elected or reelected unless you stand for something?"[22]

There was a great deal of courage in this gambit—and a great deal of foolishness. One elementary fact should have halted the initiative in its infancy: with Republicans still controlling the Senate, there was no serious prospect that tariff reductions were actually going to make it into law. Simply choosing the issue as a point of emphasis for the campaign would have been dangerous enough: it was a banner Cleveland knew that some men in his party would refuse to march under. But launching a full-scale legislative assault that, even under the best-case scenario, would yield nothing more than a symbolic victory in the House before being starved of oxygen in the Senate was utterly reckless.

The president did not have a specific program in mind—he was still mindful enough of the separation of powers to refrain from substituting his judgments for those of Congress—but he did have a few key principles: tariffs on raw materials should be eliminated, as the increased costs to the manufacturers that required those supplies would simply seep into the American economy. The welfare of workers employed in tariff-protected industries should not be forsaken, though it was inevitable that "relief from [tariffs] may involve a slight reduction of the advantages which we award our home productions. . . ."[23] Cleveland also sniffed at the most common Republican rejoinder: that tax reductions should come from abolishing domestic levies on tobacco or liquor rather than reducing tariffs.

Despite the protests of his aides, the tariffs-only annual message was deployed to Congress. Measured by the reaction from the intellectual classes, Grover Cleveland had scored a triumph for the ages. The Mugwumps at the *Nation* declared it "the most courageous document that has been sent from the Executive Mansion since the close of the Civil War."[24] James Russell Lowell, the eminent man of letters who had served Republican administrations as ambassador to both Spain and the United Kingdom, told an audience at Harvard, "I confess that I feel myself strongly attracted to Mr. Cleveland as the best representative of the higher type of Americanism that we have seen since Lincoln was snatched from us."[25] George F. Parker, an editor who had played a minor role in the 1888 campaign and eventually became Cleveland's biographer, would later write of the annual message that "it is probable that no document of its length ever had so wide a reading."[26]

Perhaps, but the intelligentsia was unlikely to move the vote count in Congress. For that Cleveland had to rely on Roger Mills, the Texas congressman who had just assumed the chairmanship of the House Ways and Means Committee. Mills's personality was radiant. (He was best known for his supposed remark, "If lightning were to strike all the drunkards, there would not be a live prohibitionist party in Texas.") For the president's purposes, however, Mills could've done with a little less verve and a lot more discretion.

Mills's bill was worked up in secret, without committee hearings or input from persuadable critics—but with plenty of consultation from the relevant commercial interests. The result was a dog's breakfast. Contra Cleveland's recommendation, the legislation included cuts to internal taxes on tobacco and liquor. More damagingly, it evidenced a clear regional bias. The southern Democrats who had steered the legislation saw to it that duties were cut the deepest on products that came out of the North or Midwest. Products that competed with southern commerce—such as sugar, rice, and tobacco—were only grazed. Items associated with other regions—such as paper, glassware, and lumber—came in for much more sweeping changes.

Had the bill had any real shot at enactment, its shoddy design may have occasioned more defections from within the president's party. Amid the centripetal pressures of an election year, however—and with Cleveland's lieutenants having successfully executed their charge to neutralize Randall's protectionist faction—the bill narrowly passed the House with only four Democrats dissenting. Party loyalty had won the day.

The same was true on the other side of the aisle. Republicans who had, in 1884, stipulated the need for at least *some* reform of the tariff system now proposed that the surplus be reduced entirely through the reduction of internal taxes and accused Democrats of betraying the laboring classes. Leading the pack was the man widely believed to be headed back to the top of the Republican presidential ticket: James G. Blaine.

In an interview with the *New York Tribune*, Blaine announced that his preference would be to reduce the surplus by repealing the tobacco tax, because "tobacco to millions of men is a necessity. The President calls it a luxury, but it is a luxury in no other sense than tea and coffee are luxuries." As for the tax on whisky? Blaine was against repeal, because "there is a moral side to it."[27] True enough, though there was also the issue of keeping prohibitionist voters from abandoning the Republicans for a third party. A politician par excellence, Blaine left no angle unplayed.

If the former candidate's skills were undiminished, however, it was not clear whether the same could be said for his ambition. Though considered the front-runner for the Republican nomination by nearly all involved, Blaine was genuinely ambivalent at the prospect of running again, fearing (as he always did) that his health was in decline. In February 1888, only a few months after taking the lead in the battle against tariff reform, he shocked the party faithful with a pair of public statements announcing that he would not be a presidential candidate again. Why two? Because his reputation for both ambition and coyness was so widespread that no one believed the first was anything more than a feint. So implausible was the idea that James G. Blaine would voluntarily sit out the race that his allies continued to labor on his behalf right up through the Republican convention, on the eve of which bookmakers were still offering two-to-one odds that he would walk away with the nomination.[28]

By the time the Republican delegates assembled in Chicago in June, Senator John Sherman of Ohio was the perceived front-runner, a view vindicated when he came in first in the initial balloting (albeit with only about half the votes needed to secure the nomination). Among his closest competitors were Walter Q. Gresham, a federal judge who, with his support of civil service reform, aversion to machine politics, and moderate views on the tariff, presented an insufficient contrast to Cleveland; and Chauncey DePew, a New York railroad executive whose business ties made him toxic to Republicans in the West.

It was the man who came in a modest fourth in the initial balloting, however, who would ultimately become the party's standard-bearer. Benjamin Harrison began his pursuit of the White House with at least one advantage: his name. The grandson of the nation's ninth president, William Henry Harrison (whose death thirty-two days into his term gave him the shortest tenure of any chief executive in American history), and the great-grandson of a signer of the Declaration of Independence, Harrison could have run a plausible campaign solely on the basis of genetics. Having risen to the rank of brigadier general in the Union army during the Civil War and subsequently served as a U.S. senator from Indiana, however, he would have been formidable even without the gilded surname.

Those accomplishments were all the more notable given that Harrison had enjoyed none of the benefits that might be assumed to come with a presidential bloodline. Though the candidate's father, John Scott Harrison, represented an Ohio district in the House of Representatives

for a two-term stint in the 1850s, that was the extent of the family's prestige. The Harrisons subsisted on the relatively modest income of the
family farm, were chronically in debt, and plowed most of their disposable income into the education of their children.* Benjamin Harrison
had made his own way in life, relocating to Indianapolis and ultimately
rising through society on the basis of a successful law practice.

Harrison was well situated to be his party's standard-bearer in
1888. He came from Indiana, one of the states almost certain to determine the outcome of the election. His status as a Union veteran gave
him a powerful pull on the Grand Army of the Republic, which Cleveland had alienated through his pension vetoes (Harrison had taken special offense at Cleveland's caustic veto language, declaring the rejections
"tipped with poison arrows").[29] And Harrison, as devout a protectionist
as could be found, would be the perfect foil for Cleveland in a campaign
that the latter seemed hell-bent on making a single-issue referendum on
tariffs.

The incumbent began the campaign in an awkward position: during
his first run for the White House, Cleveland had argued that presidents
should be limited to one term lest they succumb to the temptation of
putting their electoral interests ahead of the national welfare. Now given
the opportunity to become the first Democratic president in nearly fifty
years to be nominated for a second term, he was also on the record having said that the Constitution should be amended to prevent just such
an outcome. In his 1884 acceptance of the Democratic nomination, he
had written:

When we consider the patronage of this great office—the
allurements of power; the temptation to retain public place once

---

*John Scott Harrison had neither a charmed life nor a charmed death. On the day of his funeral,
his children noted that the nearby grave of a family friend had been robbed (at the time, corpses
were often stolen for use in medical schools). Benjamin Harrison's brother, Carter, pursued investigation of the matter to a Cincinnati medical school—where he was shocked to discover his
own father's corpse with the jugular vein severed, the body having been similarly pilfered shortly
after burial.

gained; and, more than all, the availability a party finds in an incumbent whom a horde of officeholders (with a zeal born of benefits received and fostered by the hope of favors yet to come) stand ready to aid with money and trained political service—we recognize in the eligibility of the President for reelection a most serious danger to that calm, deliberate, and intelligent political action which must characterize a government by the people.

Not content to let those remarks go forgotten, Cleveland's enemies forged a letter under his name declining a second term and fed it to the *Albany Times* in early 1888. The point was less to mislead the public— Cleveland could declare the correspondence a forgery in short order— than to suggest to the voters that the man known for his moral steadfastness applied considerably more elastic standards to himself. He had to admit that he was running again. "The temptation to retain public place" proved too great to overcome, even if the "zeal born of benefits received . . . and favors yet to come" wasn't quite up to snuff.

Unsurprisingly, Tammany was cool to the idea of four more years of Cleveland, flirting with a potential candidacy by his successor as governor of New York, David B. Hill, who had restored the machine's standing in Empire State politics. Protectionist Democrats entertained similar thoughts about Samuel Randall, the one man who seemed to stand between them and the transformation of the party into a vehicle singularly focused on tariff reduction. Many of the Mugwumps had cooled on Cleveland as well, though his move in their direction on trade had brought some of the waverers back into the fold. All in all, it was an inauspicious way to begin the pursuit of a second term.

While Cleveland was able to scuttle any serious challengers from emerging at the Democratic convention in St. Louis,* it would be virtually the last good news he received that year. What followed for Demo-

---

*When aides went to inform Cleveland of his renomination, they found the president—always a bit more interested in policy than in politics—reviewing a textbook used to educate Native American children.

crats was a campaign conceived in strategic miscalculation and executed with an incompetence that verged on comic. That trend first emerged when it came time to pick a running mate for Cleveland, who had been operating without a vice president since the death of Thomas Hendricks in 1885. The nod went to Allen Thurman, the former Ohio senator who had been one of Cleveland's rivals for the nomination four years earlier.

Harrison's choice of ticket mate, Levi Morton, emerged from a sound, if uninspiring, rationale: Morton, a former congressman and ambassador, was from New York, and his personal wealth (he had made a fortune as an investment banker) promised to keep the campaign afloat down the stretch. Thurman, by contrast, offered no valuable real estate (Democrats had no real hope of victory in Ohio), no resources, and, at the age of seventy-four, would have been the oldest vice president in history. One member of Ohio's congressional delegation japed, "The Democratic Party will be obliged to transport the old gentleman about the country to show the people that he is alive."[30] Remarkably, that was a serviceable description of the Cleveland campaign's actual strategy.

The president, abjuring campaign speeches once again, put the lion's share of the work on Thurman, leading to a series of public embarrassments. None was worse than when the vice presidential nominee began a speech to a crowd at Madison Square Garden by pronouncing, with seeming defiance, "I have heard it said since I was nominated for the Vice Presidency of the United States that Allen G. Thurman is an old, weak, broken-down man." He proceeded, however, to confirm the thesis rather than refute it: "I don't know what to reply to this. It seems to me, though, that I am not quite as well as I ought to be, and I am in no condition to speak to an immense audience like this tonight. I want to speak. But I am too unwell."[31] The candidate was then helped off the stage and the crowd of twenty thousand was sent home with the explanation that Allen Thurman had the flu.

By contrast, Harrison launched a decidedly modern campaign that zigged everywhere Cleveland's zagged. While the president limited his campaign rhetoric to a single letter issued more than three months after he had secured the nomination, Harrison would give around ninety speeches, reaching almost 300,000 listeners.[32] The remarks usually began on the front porch of his Indianapolis home, but that was not where they ended. Campaign aides would distribute the speeches through wire services, landing Harrison's message in the newspapers virtually every day. It was a media distribution network that would have been recognizable to political professionals a century later. In contrast to the Cleveland campaign's use of Thurman (whom they seemed determined to kill in the saddle), Harrison's most visible proxy was Blaine, still considered foremost among Republican orators. Unlike Thurman's failed speaking engagement in Manhattan, Blaine's appearance at Madison Square Garden inspired one journalist's summary that "[n]o pen can describe the madness with which the uncrowned king was greeted."[33]

The contrast between the two campaigns was just as apparent behind the scenes. Harrison had entrusted his operation to Matthew Quay, a Pennsylvania senator and master tactician who organized the campaign calendar and communications strategy, and, perhaps most important, drove fund-raising from the business interests threatened by Cleveland's tariff policy, raising an at-the-time unfathomable $4 million (in the aftermath of civil service reform, the parties, no longer able to rely on dues from civil servants, increasingly leaned on the private sector for campaign funds).[34] As for Cleveland, he had . . . nothing. As Charles W. Calhoun, historian of the 1888 election, has written, "Ten days after his renomination, Cleveland wrote to a friend that if anyone had 'any very clear ideas' on who should run the national and New York state campaigns, 'I am not aware of it.'"[35] When a decision was finally made, it did little to inspire confidence. Cleveland turned the campaign over to William Barnum and Calvin Brice, both successful businessmen and both chilly at best to the president's tariff initiative. So lukewarm were the men in charge that after Cleveland's defeat one of his friends wrote of Brice, "I do not think that he was heartbroken at the result of the election."[36]

Personnel was a problem, but it paled in comparison to Cleveland's decision to build the campaign around the tariff at a time when he was clearly running ahead of the electorate on the issue. He was far from the only president ever to imagine that he could turn the tide of public opinion based on an educational campaign. He *was*, however, perhaps the only one to do so and then proceed to remain behind his desk while leaving the spadework to others.* The strategy was not merely ineffective; it was actively counterproductive. Up until Cleveland took the initiative, Republicans had been on defense over tariffs, knowing that the voters were growing restless with high rates, especially at a time of consistent surpluses. Now, however, they had no need to defend the status quo—just to prove that Cleveland's alternative was inferior. They rallied to the cause with alacrity. The populist fusillade delivered by Ohio representative William McKinley, one of the GOP's leading spokesmen on the issue, indicated just how readily Republicans, often dismissed as beholden to moneyed interests, seized on the opportunity to redefine themselves as the party of the common man:

> This measure is not called for by the people. It is not an American measure. It is inspired by importers and foreign producers, most of them aliens, who want to diminish our trade and increase theirs; who want to decrease our prosperity and augment theirs; and who have no interest in this country except what they can make out of it.
>
> To this is added the influence of the professors in some of our institutions of learning, who teach the science contained in books and not practical business. I would rather have my political economy founded upon the everyday experience of the pud-

---

*Cleveland simply believed his official duties were a more pressing concern than politicking. In fact, the president's work ethic was so unflagging that he never even found time to register to vote for his own reelection.

dler or the potter than the learning of the professor, the farmer and factory hand than the college faculty.

Then there is another class who want protective tariffs overthrown. They are the men of independent wealth, with settled and steady incomes, who want everything cheap but currency; the value of everything clipped but coin—cheap labor, but dear money. These are the elements arrayed against us.[37]

Another member warned that if Congress "let some free trade Samson pull down one of these pillars . . . the whole temple of American industry must fall."[38] The drama was not limited to Capitol Hill. The owner of an ironworks in upstate New York issued employees envelopes in which to make contributions to the Harrison campaign, a measure undertaken to ensure their jobs weren't lost in the inevitable shutdown of the industry it was implied would result from Cleveland's reelection.[39] The criticism of the tariff plan—that it was the product of intellectual abstractions detached from the concerns of American labor (and suspiciously British in their provenance)—was far more intelligible than the administration's argument that the legislation was a necessary overhaul of a deeply flawed system . . . *but* likely to be so mild in its effects that it would barely merit notice from the average laborer. Grover Cleveland had chosen to fight the campaign on only one issue—and it was getting away from him.

At least it could be said that, unlike the contest against Blaine four years prior, the 1888 election turned largely on policy issues rather than personal attacks. There were, however, a few attempts to renew questions about Cleveland's character. While the Maria Halpin story was not revived (further proof that Republicans had never really believed its more salacious aspects), its spirit lived on in new allegations that the president regularly beat the First Lady. In one particularly overwrought version, the abuse was even said to extend to Cleveland's mother-in-law, whom he had supposedly exiled to Europe so as not to provoke his further wrath.[40] When Frances would travel without the president by her side, the more tawdry journals reliably reported that, finally pushed to her breaking point, she was leaving for good. Perhaps because the previous campaign's allegations had reached such high dudgeon—how was the press ever going to top Cleveland the baby-stealing rapist?—the rumors never gained much traction. It also helped that Frances—whose stock with the electorate was so high that she probably would have swept the Electoral College had she been on the ballot—publicly denounced the allegations.

The one legitimate controversy to emerge from the campaign put the president in an uncomfortable light, although its details were so bizarre as to be barely intelligible to later generations. As in the previous campaign, Republicans used Cleveland's tariff position to insinuate an affinity for England, which had begun liberalizing its trade policy mid-century. In a general sense, the charges were meant to portray the president as insufficiently nationalistic. In a specific one, they were intended to arouse the suspicions of Irish voters, for whom "English" was an adjective that condemned whatever noun followed in its wake.

Believing that a paper trail would help make the case, a California Republican named George Osgoodby wrote to the British ambassador to the United States, Sir Lionel Sackville-West, posing as a British-born immigrant to America by the name of Charles F. Murcheson. "Murcheson" sought the ambassador's candid advice: which presidential candidate should he support if he hoped for a better relationship between the United States and the United Kingdom? (At the time, Cleveland's State Department was involved in a highly publicized dispute with British Canada over fishing rights, an issue that allowed the president to put himself at arm's length from charges of Anglophilia.)

Sackville-West inexplicably replied, declaring that "there is every reason to believe that . . . [Cleveland] will manifest a spirit of conciliation." The sentiment would have been less damning had it not been for Sackville-West's spectacularly unhelpful preface: "You are probably aware that any political party which openly favored the mother country at the present moment would lose popularity, and that the party in power is fully aware of this fact."

Osgoodby had somehow managed to snare a fox with a mousetrap. Politically savvy, he resisted the temptation to release the letter upon receipt, holding it back from the press until only two weeks before the election.[41] When the story hit the newspapers, Cleveland flew into a rage. It was bad enough that the representative of a foreign government had weighed in on an American election; but it was entirely indefensible that he had done so with an implication that the president was deceiving his constituents in order to curry their political favor (though Sackville-West's diagnosis was closer to the truth than not). With London refusing to recall Sackville-West, Cleveland took matters into his own hands and had the ambassador dismissed.

For all the tumult it caused, the Osgoodby letter did not have its intended effect—Cleveland's margins with Irish voters actually increased in many precincts.[42] In fact, he defeated Harrison in the popular vote, and by wider margins than he had beat Blaine four years earlier.* The problem was that the votes were inefficiently distributed. Harrison managed to flip Cleveland's home state of New York, winning with only about 1 percent more of the vote than the Empire State's former governor. Harrison's home state of Indiana also moved into the Republican category, even though the native son won it by only about half a percentage point.[43] The result was a 233–168 victory for Harrison in the Electoral College. For only the third time in American history—the elections of John Quincy Adams in 1824 and Rutherford B. Hayes in 1876 were the first two—the winner of the popular vote was to be kept from the presidency.

The razor-thin margins birthed a welter of conspiracy theories that the election had been stolen from the incumbent. In New York, it was

---

*As with all vote totals in the decades after the end of Reconstruction, the final tally has to be viewed in light of the widespread suppression of the black vote in the South, without which Cleveland (and all other Democrats of the era) would have found their presidential ambitions nearly hopeless.

alleged that the reelected Governor Hill, whose frosty relationship with Cleveland was by now an open secret, had made a swap with Republicans: Democratic votes for Harrison in exchange for GOP votes for himself.[44] In Indiana, Republicans were said to have purchased the margin of victory. In truth, while neither state was free from election year skullduggery, it's unlikely that it provided the margin of victory. Hill's win in New York seems to have been the product of crossover appeal to German Republicans.[45] As for the Indiana vote-buying scandal, the scheme was exposed prior to the election, leading to enhanced scrutiny come election day—and whatever chicanery existed on the Republican side was almost certainly matched by that among Democrats.[46] The allegations persisted nonetheless and played a key role in the adoption of the secret ballot, which would be in use in thirty-eight states by the time of the next presidential election.[47]

One man who did not entertain the notion of a stolen election was the loser. Asked by journalists why he believed he had lost, Grover Cleveland replied, "It was mainly because the other party had the most votes."[48] Cleveland knew that making the campaign about the tariff had been one of his magnificent gambles—and that he had lost (the Mills bill had died a predictable death in the Senate shortly before the election). Yet he did not regard the matter with regret. In the early days of the debate, he had told Speaker of the House Carlisle that "[i]f every other man in the country abandons this issue, I shall stick to it."[49] In a postelection letter to the Massachusetts Tariff Reform Association, he wrote:

In the track of reform are often found the dead hopes of pioneers and the despair of those who fall in the march. But there will be neither despair nor dead hopes in the path of tariff reform, nor shall its pioneers fail to reach the heights. Holding fast to their faith and rejecting every alluring overture and every deceptive compromise which would betray their sacred trust, they them-

selves shall regain and restore the patrimony of their countrymen, freed from the trespass of grasping encroachment.[50]

It was a hopeful note, if also a self-righteous one, laying the blame
on the false consciousness of the electorate rather than any of his own
shortcomings in pressing the case.

That he was not chastened by the outcome of the election became
undeniably apparent in December, when he issued his final annual message to Congress. Given the circumstances, it would have been entirely
predictable, not to say appropriate, to issue a gentle valedictory. Instead,
the president, seemingly relishing his new status as a man unencum-
bered by the constraints of propriety, delivered a red-hot populist jere-
miad. Americans were losing touch with their limited-government
roots, he argued, and, in the process, allowing for an expansion of the
federal government that weakened individual initiative and created endless opportunities for private interests to bend public power to their
will. In one especially pungent passage, he wrote:

[W]e find the wealth and luxury of our cities mingled with poverty and wretchedness and unremunerative toil. A crowded and
constantly increasing urban population suggests the impoverish-
ment of rural sections, and discontent with agricultural pursuits.
The farmer's son, not satisfied with his father's simple and labo-
rious life, joins the eager chase for easily-acquired wealth. We
discover that the fortunes realized by our manufacturers are no
longer solely the reward of sturdy industry and enlightened fore-
sight, but that they result from the discriminating favor of the
government, and are largely built upon undue exactions from
the masses of our people. The gulf between employers and the
employed is constantly widening, and classes are rapidly form-
ing, one comprising the very rich and powerful, while in another
are found the toiling poor.[51]

In another searing passage, he warned:

Communism is a hateful thing and a menace to peace and organized government; but the communism of combined wealth and capital, the outgrowth of overweening cupidity and selfishness, which insidiously undermines the justice and integrity of free institutions, is not less dangerous than the communism of oppressed poverty and toil, which, exasperated by injustice and discontent, attacks with wild disorder the citadel of rule.

Grover Cleveland may have been leaving office with fire in his belly, but there was also peace in his heart. In June, long before the electoral die had been cast, he had written to Shan Bissell that he was not overly enthusiastic about the idea of a second term, adding, "I tell you, Bissell, I am sure of one thing: I have in [Mrs. Cleveland] something better than the presidency for life.... I absolutely long to live with her as other people do with their wives. Well! Perhaps I can after the 4th of next March."[52]

Frances, while certainly reciprocating the affection, was less persuaded that the proper course for her husband was a quiet retirement. When March 4 finally came and the Clevelands gathered up their belongings to depart the White House, the First Lady turned to Jerry Smith, a veteran of the executive mansion's household staff since the days of Ulysses S. Grant, and instructed, "Now, Jerry, I want you to take good care of all the furniture and ornaments in the house, and not let any of them get lost or broken, for I want to find everything just as it is now, when we come back again." Smith, slightly taken aback, asked when the couple would be visiting the building, so that he could make proper arrangements.

With a confident smile, Frances Cleveland announced "We are coming back just four years from today."[53]

ELEVEN

Interregnum

F rances Cleveland may have been confident that her husband's absence from power was merely a sabbatical, but word had yet to reach the other side of the marital bed. Little more than a month after being evicted from the White House, Cleveland wrote to Shan Bissell, "You cannot imagine the relief which has come to me with the termination of my official term. There is a good deal yet which seems to result from the presidency and the kindness of people ... which keeps me in remembrance of Washington life, but I feel that I am fast seeking the place I desire to reach—the place of a respectable private citizen."[1]

"Washington life" was indeed nothing more than a memory. The Clevelands had left town immediately upon Harrison's inauguration, selling off Red Top and the menagerie of animals that populated it. Disposing of the property meant the former president surrendering his rustic pretensions ... but they were, after all, pretensions. At one point, having received a flock of quail as a gift, Cleveland had taken it upon himself to construct a pen to house them. Only upon completion of the structure—and the sight, moments later, of the birds scurrying away—did the president of the United States realize he had chosen wire so wide that the creatures could simply hop out of the enclosure.[2] The decades spent in a Buffalo bachelor pad had not produced a horny-handed son of the soil.

In recognition of that fact, the Clevelands set their sights on more

urban trappings. Buffalo was out of the question, since the former president still nursed an indiscriminate grudge against the entire city as a result of the Halpin scandal (in a letter to William Vilas, a member of his
first-term cabinet, Cleveland referred to Buffalo as "the place I hate
above all others").³* Only fifty-two, Cleveland—existing in an era when
ex-presidents had no surefire way to monetize their experience and,
indeed, often found themselves on the brink of poverty—settled on a
return to legal practice. He joined up with the prestigious New York
City law firm of Bangs, Stetson, Tracy, & MacVeagh, an outfit whose
prominence owed in part to the fact that J. P. Morgan was a client. He
and Frances moved into a mansion on Manhattan's Upper East Side, his
fantasy of a normal domestic life seemingly fulfilled.

In truth, life at the firm was more valuable for giving the former
president something to do than adding to his financial well-being.
Cleveland wasn't a partner, didn't bring in an especially lavish salary,
and—apart from the sale of Red Top for a handsome profit—had no
real assets of which to speak. He had studiously avoided investing,
thinking it improper for a man with his inside knowledge of the economy to play the markets. He had also declined any claims on Frances's
share of her father's estate, leaving the money entirely to the former
First Lady's disposal. None of this, however, seemed to cause him much
anxiety. In a continuation of the trend that ran all the way back to his
days at the Buffalo bar, he abjured lucrative cases and barely saw the inside of a courtroom, functioning primarily as an arbitrator. In fact, one
of the few times he found himself before the bench was in Washington,
where he argued a case involving municipal debt, *Peake v. New Orleans*,
in front of the Supreme Court . . . and lost.† Of the three justices who

---

*Cleveland would return to Buffalo for a speech in 1891, at which point his hostility seemed to
cool. Nevertheless, he never again took up residency in the city.

†Cleveland is one of eight presidents to have argued before the Supreme Court. The others were
John Quincy Adams, James K. Polk, Abraham Lincoln, James Garfield, Benjamin Harrison,
William Howard Taft, and Richard Nixon. Taft would serve as chief justice of the Court in his
post-presidency. In the years before he ascended to the White House, Adams had been nominated
to the Court by James Madison and confirmed by the Senate—yet declined the position.

took his side, two—Chief Justice Melville Fuller and Justice Lucius Quintus Cincinnatus Lamar—were men he had appointed.

The goal of Cleveland's retirement, so far as he saw it, wasn't wealth, fame, or a return to political relevance; it was the thing that had eluded him during all those years of backbreaking work: freedom. He no longer wanted to mix in political circles. Indeed, he was virtually a ghost on the New York political scene, only keeping up with a few old friends acquired earlier in his career, and specifically steering visitors to his office rather than his home so as not to intrude on his private existence. He did not want to function as a sort of monarch in exile. It's insufficient to say Grover Cleveland was indifferent to the prospect of a political comeback. Indifference would have implied that he bothered to give it any thought.

This was probably for the best, as political matters would likely have lost the battle for his attention in any case. In a midlife reversal, he no longer wanted to be chained to his desk. His summer calendar at the firm would be kept clear for prolonged hunting and fishing trips. Indeed, though long one of his favorite pastimes, fishing grew into an obsession during his first post-presidency. During the president's first term, the Clevelands had become friendly with Richard Watson Gilder, the editor of the *Century Magazine* (formerly *Scribner's Monthly*). It was Gilder who, in Cleveland's first summer out of the White House, convinced him to vacation in a remote part of Barnstable County, Massachusetts, on the upper cape (the section closest to the mainland) of Cape Cod. So seduced was the former president—and so healthy was the haul a fisherman could extract from adjacent Buzzards Bay—that he and Frances would spend nearly every summer there for the next decade and a half, purchasing a home, dubbed "Gray Gables," in the town of Bourne in 1891.

The intensity that Cleveland had once applied to official duty was now transferred seamlessly to rod and reel. Gilder would recall how, when daydreaming while his line was in the water, he'd often hear the former president's voice boom out, "If you want to catch fish, attend strictly to business!"[4] Cleveland's focus could not be broken even by the elements. Gilder marveled that his partner fished through searing heat, thunderstorms, and while being pelted with hailstones. "This, I have discovered, is the secret of 'Cleveland luck,'" Gilder observed; "it is hard work and no let up."[5] When it was time to bring the boat in for the evening, the former president would, with metronomic regularity, plead for just a few minutes more.

Landbound, however, it was a different story. Cleveland, tempered by marriage, loosed of the stresses of office, and surrounded by a new and eclectic set of friends drawn from outside the world of politics, began to reveal a more carefree side of himself—and a previously hidden sense of fun. Though shy in the company of strangers or those he imagined his intellectual superiors, Gilder noted that Cleveland, when comfortable, "was one of the very raciest of talkers and raconteurs."[6] Among the friends most frequently present at Gray Gables was Joseph Jefferson, one of the most distinguished actors of the era. Jefferson, in Gilder's telling, "used to say that Mr. Cleveland missed his vocation when he went into politics instead of going up on the stage."[7] Given the right circumstances, the president was even known to do impressions.

Even more notable, though largely forgotten by history: around this time Cleveland's sense of humor began to seep into his public persona as well. In the early years out of office he consciously avoided any public remarks that veered into politics, both because he imagined it indecorous given his stature and because he believed it could only hurt his business prospects. He would, however, occasionally accept invitations to address industry groups or participate in ceremonial occasions. While there was always a sober message at the heart of his remarks— usually an exhortation for the audience to become more engaged citizens and do more to hold their elected officials accountable—there was also a surprisingly agile wit.

In an address before a group of medical professionals, he launched into an extended riff on how doctors and lawyers both had to deal with ungrateful customers, noting, "The defeated client is left in a vigorous and active condition, not only in the complete enjoyment of his ancient privilege of swearing at the court, but also with full capacity to swear at his lawyer. The defeated patient, on the contrary, is very quiet indeed and can only swear at his doctor if he has left his profanity in a phonograph to be ground out by his executor."[8] In remarks to the local townspeople in Cape Cod he underscored the awkwardness of life as an ex-president, noting, "Of course the subject would be relieved of all uncertainty and embarrassment if every president would die at the end of his term."[9]

If Cleveland seemed dangerously close to contentment, it was only magnified in October 1891 with the birth of his first child, a daughter named Ruth. Writing to Shan Bissell, himself soon to be a first-time father, the former president's heart overflowed: "I, who have just entered the real world, and see in a small child more of value than I have ever called my own before; who puts aside, as hardly worth a thought, all that has gone before—fame, honor, place, everything—reach out my hand to you and fervently express the wish—the best my great friendship for you yields—that in safety and in joy you may soon reach my estate."[10] His aide George Parker records him saying less than a year after his defeat:

> Why should I have any desire or purpose of returning to the presidency? It involves a responsibility almost beyond human strength for a man who brings conscience to the discharge of his duties. Besides, I feel somehow that I made a creditable showing during my first term, all things considered, and I might lose whatever of character and reputation are already gained in it.[11]

One reason Grover Cleveland had accepted his defeat in the 1888 election with poise was that he admired the man who beat him. Cleveland judged Benjamin Harrison intelligent and capable, and even approved of some of his substantive decisions, later telling an aide, "I thought I realized the importance of the federal courts, resisting party pressure and giving to my appointments the most jealous care, but I must confess that Harrison has beaten me."[12] Judicial appointments, however, would be the exception. As it became increasingly clear that the legacy of the Harrison administration would be undoing the legacy of the Cleveland administration, the former president began to chafe.

Where Cleveland had emphasized strict frugality, the first two years of Harrison's term (in which the GOP controlled the House, Senate, and White House for the first time in fifteen years) saw the biggest spending spree up to that point in American history, earning the legislators of 1889–90 the nickname of "The Billion Dollar Congress." Making matters worse, at least in Cleveland's eyes, was that one of the major expenditures was the Dependent Pension Act, a version of the same legislation he had vetoed in 1887. The law's enactment had at least one salutary effect: it proved correct Cleveland's theory that the measure would explode the budget. In the three years after the Dependent Pension Act's passage, the number of pensioners more than doubled, from just under 456,000 to more than 935,000—despite the fact that the country wasn't producing any new veterans. Spending on the program increased from $89 million to $157 million, representing a remarkable 40 percent of the federal budget.[13]

There were other indignities as well. The election results having convinced members of the GOP that they had won on the trade issue, the Republican Congress passed the McKinley Tariff, entrenching protectionism by increasing the average tariff rate from 38 percent to 49.5 percent.[14] The law also *eliminated* the tariff on sugar (which would lower its price) but did so by replacing the duties with an equivalent subsidy direct from the federal government (which would protect the profits of the sugar companies). Between the loss of federal revenue from sugar duties and the cost of payments to the industry, the sugar provisions alone would cost the Treasury more than $60 million[15]—at a time when the entire annual surplus was $105 million.[16]

Six western states—North and South Dakota, Montana, Washington, Idaho, and Wyoming—were admitted to the union within

Harrison's first sixteen months in office. That only increased the political power of the region, particularly in the Senate, which brought the
silver issue back to the fore. In fact, many westerners made their support for the McKinley Tariff contingent on the expanded use of silver
in the money supply, resulting in the passage of the Sherman Silver
Purchase Act in 1890, which required the government to purchase 4.5
million ounces of silver per month, roughly double the standard under
the Bland-Allison Act—and nearly equal to all the silver the nation
produced. Perhaps even more noxious to Grover Cleveland: his own
party was drifting further and further into the pro-silver camp.

As early as the fall of 1889 there were signs that the swing in
national policy was getting to the former president, who wrote to former secretary Vilas, "I feel badly and sad to see the result of so much
hard labor undone. . . . And yet I sometimes think that God has ordered
it all for the enlightenment and awakening of our people."[17] If he was
hoping for signs of divine intervention, he needed look no further than
the midterm elections a little more than a year later.

Grover Cleveland's conception of the tariff as a populist issue may
have been unpersuasive in the abstract—but it proved entirely correct
upon implementation. With prices increasing for basic necessities like
food, canned goods, and woolens, shopkeepers placed signs in their
windows encouraging customers to buy before the new rates went into
effect.[18] The public backlash was swift. While the GOP maintained
control of the Senate (albeit while losing four seats), the results in the
House were a bloodbath. The Billion Dollar Congress had 179 Republican members in the House; in the next session, there would be only
86. It remains to this day the third-largest loss any party has suffered in
the lower chamber.

The 1890 midterms imbued Grover Cleveland with a sense of vindication. In a letter to a friend, he referred to the outcome as "a moral
awakening" that "reinstates one's faith in human nature."[19] It would be
tempting to conclude that it emboldened him—if boldness was a trait
he ever lacked. As if to underscore that point, his first public act after

the Democrats' triumph was one almost universally reckoned as political suicide.

In February 1891, Grover Cleveland received an invitation from E. Ellery Anderson, president of New York's Reform Club, to address a meeting of the organization to discuss the silver issue. The Republican press had invented rumors that the former president had softened his position on the matter, an allegation intended to put him in an impossible position: if he publicly acknowledged changing his view (or simply remained silent) it would destroy his reputation for candor, making it seem as if he stood ready to compromise his principles in the pursuit of a second term. If he remained immovable, he'd be signing his own death warrant in a party that had evolved beyond him on the silver question.[20] Grover Cleveland chose death.

The former president was unable to attend the event but determined to make himself known to the public on the silver question. Cleveland drafted a response to Ellery, then refined it through multiple editions—each one shorter in length and sharper in tone—until the final product ran to only three paragraphs.[21] The scene among Cleveland's inner circle as he prepared the letter for publication recalled the equally intrepid drafting of his tariff message: a blend of horror and disbelief. Dan Lamont advised him to dismiss silver as an issue on which neither party was united and respond instead with a homily on the tariff. William Whitney, his former Navy secretary—who was quickly growing into Daniel Manning's old role as Cleveland's political aide-de-camp—warned that the statement was premature and would likely foreclose any possibility of a future presidential run. Indeed, that was precisely the reaction from much of the Democratic rank and file when it was published. But to Cleveland, that was part of its virtue. Richard Watson Gilder noted "his satisfaction at having been able to show that he was not 'waiting around' for a third nomination." Invoking the parallel with the tariff message, Gilder wrote, "Every once in a while, Cleveland 'threw away the presidency,' and I never saw him so happy as when he had done it."[22]

Had the silver letter actually doomed his candidacy, it would perhaps have been a more fitting capstone for Cleveland's career than the one that would eventually take shape. There would have been a certain symmetry to his political future being foreclosed by one last stand on principle. Instead, the same dynamic that had allowed him to defy the laws of political gravity so many times before reasserted itself: whatever controversy attached to the substance of his remarks ended up being overtaken by the respect his candor inspired. Furthermore, his stance on silver was particularly heartening to the eastern financial establishment, desperately casting about for any candidate who didn't seem hell-bent on blowing up the financial system.

While Cleveland continued to proclaim himself uninterested in another run at the White House, his personal correspondence began to demonstrate less certainty. Though he claimed to regard the prospect of pursuing office again distasteful, he wrote to Lamont, "I am far from believing that I have a right to set up my own judgment and wishes against those of personal and political friends. . . ."[23] While it is too cynical—and too inconsistent with his personality—to imagine that Cleveland's appeals to duty were entirely insincere, it's equally clear that he was developing more enthusiasm for a comeback than he was publicly letting on. While he would continue for some time to argue that Democrats would be better advised to find him a worthy successor than to attempt his rehabilitation, the factor that finally pulled him into the race was the prospect of the party's presidential nomination going to someone with the potential to erase his legacy: his former lieutenant governor in New York, David B. Hill.

Hill's presidential ambitions had been manifest ever since ascending to the governor's office—and Cleveland regarded them with dread. In a letter to Bissell, he fretted that a Hill presidency would be one that saw the Democratic Party "fall back to shiftiness and cheap expediency."[24] Where Cleveland had labored to clean up the Augean stables of the civil service, Hill was a machine man without the slightest compunction about using patronage to his benefit. Where Cleveland wanted to undertake a wholesale revision of the tariff system, Hill, disinclined to tangle with protectionists, was content to return to something like the pre–McKinley Tariff status quo. Where Cleveland regarded the infusion of silver into the money supply as a potentially catastrophic risk, Hill straddled the issue in an attempt to win over the West.

Witnessing Hill's machinations, the former president simmered, and eventually boiled. By December 1891, by which time Hill's associates were proclaiming his nomination a fait accompli, Cleveland wrote a fiery letter to Bissell in which he declared that "the only way for a decent Democrat to live in New York and to maintain his self-respect and at the same time stand by his party is to break this thing up."[25] He could, perhaps, have tolerated a future in which Grover Cleveland was not at the center of the Democratic Party. He would not abide a future in which Clevelandism itself was discarded.

The success of Grover Cleveland's 1892 presidential campaign was in many ways dependent on his failures in the 1888 election. That he had first taken up the tariff issue at a time when it cut against his political self-interest left no doubt of the sincerity of his convictions. Equally important, however, were the organizational lessons he had taken from the ramshackle operation that helped to doom his first attempt at reelection. This time around, the campaign would operate with a level of efficiency and systemization unlike anything previously seen in his career.

The former president had inadvertently begun building this infrastructure through his practice of responding to every message he received after leaving the White House with a handwritten letter, developing a constellation of loyal admirers throughout the country.[26] When, shortly after leaving office, Cleveland enlisted George F. Parker to help distribute copies of one of his speeches to the press, the aide saw an untapped opportunity. Parker began pushing for the publication of Cleveland's correspondence in local newspapers. Overcoming the former president's aversion to the media (though not without some resistance), he began developing a nationwide network of correspondents who would push Cleveland's speeches and interviews to local media outlets, ensure their distribution to nearby Democrats, and mobilize the party faithful in his support. The operation was aggressively decentralized, delegating significant amounts of authority to men sometimes thousands of miles away. So assiduous was Parker in its development that by the time the election was in full flower, Cleveland had a nationwide organization built entirely from scratch, free from the influence of the national or state parties.[27]

By the time the race began in earnest in the spring of 1892, this network stood ready to be harnessed by the campaign's high command. The reins were handed to William Whitney, who had already proved his genius for management as Cleveland's secretary of the Navy (and who, unlike Cleveland's 1888 campaign managers, was a trusted confidant of the president's). In the months leading up to the Democratic convention in Chicago, Whitney was thus able to absorb intelligence about Cleveland's prospects in virtually every state as quickly as the technology of the late nineteenth century would allow—and, where necessary, to deploy the resources necessary to bolster his candidate. Though every inch of his personality would have seemed to militate against it, Grover Cleveland was now sitting atop a thoroughly modern campaign machine.

As valuable as that infrastructure proved against David B. Hill, there was one other factor that proved essential to earning Cleveland the Democratic Party's nomination: Hill's capacity for self-sabotage. Two maneuvers, in particular, demonstrated that New York's governor was more cunning than canny.

The first was Hill's successful effort to get himself appointed to the U.S. Senate by New York's legislature in January 1891.* On its own, the gambit was unremarkable: Hill clearly hoped that a federal perch might burnish his presidential credentials. What was utterly baffling, however,

---

*Cleveland had hoped the seat would go to Shan Bissell. It was a measure of how little prestige the former president had with the state party that his friend was never seriously considered for the role.

was his refusal to give up the governor's mansion upon receiving the appointment. Because Hill would not be officially seated in Congress until December, he declared himself perfectly able to hold both roles simultaneously, a practice that had been outlawed in several states and one that led the New York Tribune to declare that "no other man in public life today would be guilty of such misconduct and continue to hold up his head."[28]

A more sensible politician would have taken the backlash to dual officeholding as sufficient caution that he was pushing up against the ceiling of public patience. Hill, however, succumbed to the sort of hallucinations that often lead those gripped with presidential fever astray. The governor/senator had a strong hand to play: he commanded the machinery of New York's Democratic Party in a way his predecessor never had. A decisive show of support from the Empire State—especially because it would be a key swing state in the general election—could well have left Cleveland hobbled. In his intemperance, however, Hill pressed the advantage too hard.

Thanks to the intervention of Hill's agents, the state party—which would normally hold the convention at which it backed a presidential candidate in late spring—announced, on short notice, that it would convene in Albany on February 22. Calling a convention in the middle of the winter snows would have the practical effect of preventing many rural delegates from attending, granting disproportionate power to the urban areas where Hill's support was concentrated. Moreover, moving New York's convention so far up would strike an early blow for the Hill campaign and touch off a chain reaction in which he began to appear the inevitable nominee. That was the theory anyway.[29]

In reality, the strategy produced a brutal backlash among Democrats throughout the country. Hill likely would have appeared ruthless and unprincipled in any set of circumstances, but that effect was compounded by the fact that the intended victim of the plot was a man known for his sense of propriety and fair play. In New York, an alternate delegation of Cleveland supporters was assembled to attend the national convention in defiance of Hill's chicanery. Throughout the rest of the country, the senator suddenly fell into bad odor, even in states where he had previously looked ascendant. As for Cleveland himself, he embraced the wisdom that one should never kill a man who's in the process of committing suicide. Asked by a reporter to give a quote on the summoning of what soon came to be derided as the "snap convention," he simply replied: "The State committee has selected a historic day. I hope the weather will be fine."[30]

If Hill was beginning his campaign in a fashion that looked utterly, crassly political, Grover Cleveland was doing precisely the opposite. In February, he delivered a speech at the University of Michigan to commemorate George Washington's birthday. It is often considered the moment when he officially remerged into political life. It was, to put it mildly, perhaps the most unusual kickoff to a presidential campaign in American history. It was also perhaps the finest speech of his career.

In his remarks to the students in Ann Arbor, Cleveland did not discuss American politics, public policy, economics, or foreign affairs. Instead, he delivered an extended philosophical monologue on the importance of *sentiment* in American life; on the idea that those in public service must not simply meet the material needs of their citizens but also uphold a spirit of public morality. In one remarkable passage, he observed:

> [S]entiment is the very lifeblood of our nation. Our government was conceived amid the thunders that echoed "All men are created equal," and it was brought forth while free men shouted "We, the people of the United States." The sentiment of our fathers— made up of their patriotic intentions, their sincere beliefs, their homely impulses, and their noble aspirations—entered into the government they established. And unless it is constantly supported and guarded by a sentiment as pure as theirs, our scheme of popular rule will fail.
>
> Another and a different plan may take its place; but this

which we hold in sacred trust, as it originated in patriotism, is only fitted for patriotic and honest uses and purposes—and can only be administered in its integrity and intended beneficence by honest and patriotic men. It can no more be saved nor faithfully conducted by a selfish, dishonest, and corrupt people than a stream can rise above its source or be better and purer than its fountainhead.[31]

In his peroration, Cleveland seemed to compress his entire theory of political morality into one passage, delivered as an exhortation to his undergraduate audience:[*]

I beg you, therefore, to take with you, when you go forth to assume the obligations of American citizenship, as one of the best gifts of your alma mater, a strong and abiding faith in the value and potency of a good conscience and a pure heart. Never yield one iota to those who teach that these are weak and childish things, not needed in the struggle of manhood with the stern realities of life.

Interest yourselves in public affairs as a duty of citizenship; but do not surrender your faith to those who discredit and debase politics by scoffing at sentiment and principle, and whose political activity consists in attempts to gain popular support by cunning devices and shrewd manipulation. You will find plenty of these who will smile at your profession of faith and tell you that truth and virtue and honesty and goodness were well enough in the old days when Washington lived, but are not suited to the present size and development of our country and the progress we have made in the art of political management.

---

[*]Cleveland, never overly solicitous of his audiences, also told the group of undergraduates, "The college graduate may be, and frequently is, more unpatriotic and less useful in public affairs than the man who, with limited education, has spent the years when opinions are formed in improving contact with the world instead of being within college walls and confined to the study of books."

ABOVE: President Cleveland's parents, Richard Falley Cleveland and Ann Neal Cleveland.
NEW JERSEY DEPARTMENT OF STATE

LEFT: Cleveland at approximately twenty-seven years old, around the time he was assuming the position of assistant district attorney of Erie County.
BUFFALO HISTORICAL SOCIETY

RIGHT: Cleveland's uncle, Lewis F. Allen. A leading citizen of Buffalo, he persuaded a young Grover to make the city his home and helped him land his first legal job.
BUFFALO HISTORICAL SOCIETY

A young Grover Cleveland, at far left, pictured with seven of his eight siblings.
GROVER CLEVELAND BIRTHPLACE

LEFT: The Maria Halpin scandal threatened to derail Cleveland's 1884 presidential campaign and gave rise to partisan taunts like this one, bitingly titled "Another Voice for Cleveland."
LIBRARY OF CONGRESS

RIGHT: James G. Blaine, the veteran Maine politician who faced off with Cleveland in the mud-slinging presidential election of 1884.
LIBRARY OF CONGRESS

LEFT: A Thomas Nast cartoon shows a dejected Tammany Hall reacting to Grover Cleveland's 1884 presidential victory, with a bandaged "Honest John" Kelly leading the procession.
LIBRARY OF CONGRESS

RIGHT: The young Frances Cleveland, whose beauty and charm would make her a First Lady whose popularity was unrivaled until the days of Jacqueline Kennedy.
LIBRARY OF CONGRESS

LEFT: A *Harper's Weekly* sketch of Grover and Frances Cleveland's 1886 White House wedding. Given the absence of photographs from the ceremony, it came to be the defining image of the presidential nuptials.
LIBRARY OF CONGRESS

LEFT: Cleveland in an official photograph from 1888, as he was embarking on an ultimately failed reelection campaign. LIBRARY OF CONGRESS

RIGHT: Benjamin Harrison, the Indiana Republican who eked out a narrow win over Cleveland in the 1888 presidential election, only to lose the rematch in 1892.
LIBRARY OF CONGRESS

Gray Gables, the Clevelands' summer home on Buzzard's Bay, served as a salubrious haven for the President's recovery.

An artist's rendering of "Gray Gables," the Cape Cod home that served as Cleveland's summer retreat and the site of his recovery from a secret cancer surgery.
ELSIE GUTCHESS GREAT WOMEN OF THE USA COLLECTION, HOWLAND STONE STORE MUSEUM

Cleveland seated aboard the deck of the *Oneida*, the yacht on which his secret cancer surgery was performed. The figure at right is E. C. Benedict, the New York banker who owned the vessel and become one of the president's closest friends. NEW JERSEY STATE PARK SERVICE

N THE PRESIDENT'S MIND.

An editorial cartoon from Cleveland's second term, underscoring the torrent of controversies that accompanied his return to the White House. NEW YORK PUBLIC LIBRARY

Cleveland, late in his second term, in his natural environment: at his desk, often until the wee hours of the morning. NEW YORK PUBLIC LIBRARY

LEFT: William Jennings Bryan, the populist Nebraska Democrat who supplanted Cleveland as the head of the Democratic Party and lost presidential elections in 1896, 1900, and 1908. LIBRARY OF CONGRESS

ABOVE: Cleveland in the midst of one of his many hunting trips. An avid outdoorsman, his exploits would inspire the only book he ever wrote, *Fishing and Shooting Sketches*. GROVER CLEVELAND BIRTHPLACE

Cleveland, in his retirement, alongside then President Roosevelt. Acquainted since their days in New York politics, the two occasionally butted heads, but each man exhibited a lifelong respect for the other. LIBRARY OF CONGRESS

Cleveland, on the porch of his Princeton home in 1907, with Frances and the couple's four living children. NEW YORK PUBLIC LIBRARY

Cleveland, circa 1908, in what was likely the final photograph taken before his death. LIBRARY OF CONGRESS

Be steadfast. The strong and sturdy oak still needs the support of its native earth, and, as it grows in size and spreading branches, its roots must strike deeper into the soil which warmed and fed its first tender sprout. You will be told that the people no longer have any desire for the things you profess. Be not deceived. The people are not dead but sleeping. They will awaken in good time and scourge the moneychangers from their sacred temple.[32]

When the speech hit the national press, the voters were reminded of why they had loved Grover Cleveland. They were also given an instructive contrast: the University of Michigan speech took place the same day that the snap convention was meeting in Albany.

By the time the Democratic convention rolled around in late June, David B. Hill's campaign had become hemophilic—and William Whitney's masterful coordination of the delegates had left no room for surprise. At one point it had been imagined that the disputed New York delegation might end up holding the keys to the nomination. Yet by the time the delegates gathered in Chicago they were superfluous. Cleveland had so dominated in the other states that he was nominated on the first ballot.

For most other men, it would have been an unsurpassed moment of vindication: only Andrew Jackson had previously held the honor of being the Democratic Party's presidential nominee three times. For Grover Cleveland? As the president, his wife, and a group of intimates monitored the results from a specially installed telegraph at Gray Gables, the man of the hour interrupted the affair by exclaiming, "I forgot to dry my lines today!" The once and future president of the United States headed outside and missed the final tally . . . in order to tend to his fishing gear.[33]

The rest of the convention proceeded with mixed results. Cleveland was pleased with the selection of Adlai E. Stevenson, a former Illinois representative who had served as an assistant postmaster general in his first term, as the vice presidential nominee.* Stevenson had been chosen in part as a sop to the party's silver supporters, but Cleveland perceived his real value to the ticket as an increased chance of flipping Illinois to the Democratic side, a valuable insurance policy if, as was widely feared, an embittered Hill and Tammany conspired to deny him New York. Less helpful, in the nominee's view, was the platform that the party adopted (a matter then taken much more seriously than it is today), which went beyond Cleveland's advocacy for a lower tariff to declare that any duties set in excess of revenue needs were per se unconstitutional, a position that Cleveland thought was incorrect as a matter of legal analysis and unhelpful as a matter of politics.

The field was now set. Benjamin Harrison had secured renomination from the Republican Party a few weeks earlier at the GOP convention in Minneapolis, albeit not without a touch of drama. In recognition of his service to the 1888 campaign—and his powerful influence within the party—Harrison had given the most prestigious role in his cabinet to James G. Blaine, restoring him to the secretary of state role he had previously filled in the Garfield administration. As the years went by, however, the two men developed an increasingly frosty relationship (which, compounding matters, invited the bitterness of both their spouses). Blaine's name had been bandied about as a possible replacement for Harrison on the 1892 ticket and, in a now predictable fashion, the secretary of state publicly dismissed any interest in the matter while privately making it known that he was keeping his options open. On June 4, three days before the convention was to open, Blaine tendered his resignation in what was widely believed to be a bid for the nomination. The tactic worked about as well as David Hill's. The Republicans proceeded to renominate Harrison—along with a new running mate, Whitelaw Reid, who had served as his ambassador to France—on the first ballot.

---

*Stevenson was the grandfather of Adlai Stevenson II, who would be the Democratic Party's presidential nominee in 1952 and 1956.

The resulting presidential race proved to be one of the most unusual the country has ever seen. It marked the only time in the history of the republic that two men with experience serving as president have faced each other in a contest for the White House. Despite that novelty, however, the campaign failed to arouse much public ardor. Henry Adams recorded, "A presidential election was to take place in November, and no one showed much interest in the result. The two candidates were singular persons, of whom it was the common saying that one of them had no friends; the other, only enemies."[34]* Both were also, as the previous campaign had demonstrated, wed to a sense of propriety that prevented them from indulging in personal attacks against the other.

That likely would have made for a quiet campaign under any circumstances, but it was exacerbated by periods of incapacitation for both candidates. Cleveland once again resisted efforts to get him out on the stump, giving only a single speech at Madison Square Garden, but his health provided some measure of excuse. The candidate spent significant chunks of the year laid up with gout (in several letters of the period he refers to problems with his hands, in one missive confessing that the ailment had forced him to dictate the message to Frances for transcription). Harrison, meanwhile, was coping with his wife Caroline's fight with tuberculosis, which culminated in her death in the White House only two weeks prior to the election.†

One of the few events to puncture the general listlessness of the campaign took place outside of Pittsburgh only a few weeks after the conclusion of the Democratic convention. On July 6, chaos broke out at the Carnegie Steel plant in Homestead, Pennsylvania. Henry Clay Frick, Andrew Carnegie's business partner, had, with Carnegie's blessing, resolved to break the Amalgamated Association of Iron and Steel Workers union at the plant. With their contract expiring, the union had

---

*Cleveland, of course, bore the enemies. Harrison was regarded as a singularly aloof personality, giving rise to his nickname "the human iceberg."
†Harrison would remarry in 1896. The bride, Mary Dimmick, was his late wife's niece. Harrison's children were scandalized by the union.

proposed a new agreement that would include wage increases. Frick countered with an offer for pay *cuts*, setting the stage for a walkout and laying the predicate for the firm to bring in nonunion labor. At Frick's direction, the workers were locked out and the plant was fortified with barbed-wire fencing. Within a few days Frick would fire the laborers en masse and ship in a force of three hundred Pinkerton security guards to secure the facility for the arrival of the "scabs" who would supplant the union workers. When the Pinkertons attempted to make a boat landing at the facility, however, an angry crowd of thousands of workers and their families engaged them in what proved to be a twelve-hour battle. Gunshots were fired from both sides (accounts differed as to who fired first) and at least ten individuals were dead before the fighting ceased. The workers captured and occupied the plant, only to be dispossessed of it a few days later, when Frick prevailed on Pennsylvania's governor to deploy 8,500 National Guardsman to take back the facility.

Though public sentiment stopped short of endorsing the workers' use of force, there was still widespread sympathy for the strikers, not least because Carnegie Steel was precisely the sort of company whose profits, swelled by the tariff regime, were supposed to translate into higher wages for workers. Cleveland used that fact to his advantage, noting in his acceptance of the Democratic nomination, "Our workingmen are still told the tale, oft repeated in spite of its demonstrated falsity, that the existing protective tariff is a boon to them, and that under its beneficent operation their wages must increase, while, as they listen, scenes are enacted in the very abiding place of high protection that mock the hopes of toil and attest the tender mercy the workingman receives from those made selfish and sordid by unjust governmental favoritism."[35]

Cleveland's formulation—that labor could be most effectively aided by *less* government intervention—would, within the very near future, seem decidedly out of place within the Democratic Party. Regardless of whether or not it was true, it demonstrated a consistent pattern in his thought: the former president rarely perceived any tension between his abstract principles and their tangible consequences. In virtually every situation, it seemed clear to him that his overarching convictions—public-sector frugality, a respect for the limits imposed by the Constitution, a light hand from the government—would, of necessity, generate a morally optimal outcome. This point bears noting in relation to the 1892 election because it was there that this tendency most badly disserved him.

Though it would prove of only negligible consequence in the election, one of Cleveland's minor themes in the race was opposition to the Lodge Bill, a piece of legislation endorsed by the Harrison administration that would have given the federal government the power to superintend federal elections (otherwise controlled by the states). The measure, which had narrowly passed the House and then succumbed to a filibuster in the Senate, was intended primarily to prevent discrimination against black voters in the South—yet Cleveland seemed incapable of viewing it in anything beyond the narrowest partisan terms. In a speech to a gathering of Democrats at Cooper Union in 1891, he referred to the Lodge Bill as a plan "to retain partisan ascendancy by throttling and destroying the freedom and integrity of the suffrage through the most radical and reckless legislation."[36] It should be stipulated that Cleveland's characterization is not quite as far-fetched as it appears to modern eyes. Given the amount of skullduggery in the politics of the era, it was not unfathomable that a greater federal role in election regulation *could* be manipulated for partisan gain. But that, of course, was of secondary importance when compared with the certainty of widespread disenfranchisement on the basis of race. It was one issue on which Harrison, who backed the Lodge Bill at considerable political cost, inarguably held the moral high ground.

What makes the issue all the more vexing was that Cleveland, loath to pander to any audience on any topic, never displayed an inclination to do so on race. At an address in Boston delivered only three weeks after he inveighed against the "force bill" (Democrats' term of opprobrium for Lodge's legislation) at Cooper Union, he paid fulsome tribute to the memory of Charles Sumner, the Massachusetts senator whose career had been defined by his opposition to slavery (and who was nearly killed on the Senate floor in an attack by the proslavery representative Preston Brooks of South Carolina). Sumner, in Cleveland's telling, was "the great senator who unhesitatingly braved executive displeasure and party ostracism in loyalty to his sense of right . . . and who, throughout a long public career, illustrated his belief that politics is but the application of moral principle to public affairs."[37] Cleveland believed neither in more expansive federal power nor in the subjugation of black Americans. His tragedy was that he perceived no tension in those positions.

If the issue of race and federal power wasn't to be decisive in the 1892 contest, one issue that had the potential to be was the hostility of the Democratic machine in New York—the members of which had believed themselves finally rid of Cleveland for good four years earlier. Though Cleveland had consistently dismissed the reports that David B. Hill and his allies had undermined the 1888 campaign, a pervasive anxiety remained that a tepid showing from New York Democrats could once again deny him the White House. By all rights, Cleveland should have been the man most disturbed by the prospect—but that distinction belonged to Whitney, who believed too much in his candidate to see him fail because of a stubborn insistence that he would not make peace with Tammany and Hill's allies.

Had Grover Cleveland taken as little interest in tweaking Tammany during his temporary retirement as he had in other political matters, the tensions would perhaps have dissipated. Instead, he took every opportunity to deliver gratuitous reminders of their moral inferiority. When Tammany sent him a pro forma invitation to attend their Fourth of July gathering in 1890, the former president—rather than simply sending his regrets or ignoring the request entirely—fired off what was ostensibly an essay on the American character but was clearly intended as a thinly veiled broadside against the entire institution. In it, he observed that the American people "will, as long as their love and veneration for their government shall last, revolt against the domination of any politi-

cal party, which, entrusted with power, sordidly seeks only its own con-
tinuance, and which, faithlessly violating its plain and simple duty to the
people, insults them with professions of disinterested solicitude while it
eats out their substance."[38] A simple "I send my regrets" likely would
have sufficed.

Whitney, believing New York hanging in the balance, was determined to salve the wounds. The difficulty was in getting the boss to go
along. Not only was Cleveland uncooperative—he wasn't even in town.
Despite being in the midst of a presidential campaign, he still insisted
on spending virtually the entire summer at Gray Gables. When Whitney wrote to Cape Cod pleading for Cleveland to pen a letter that
would smooth over the differences, the nominee groused to Shan Bissell, "I'll see the whole outfit to the devil before I'll do it."[39] Whitney
refused to take no for an answer, with Cleveland noting that "he wrote
me a very petulant and unpleasant letter" after the refusal. The candidate further informed Bissell that "[Whitney] was here yesterday and
we had a little talk—nothing unpleasant, but I can see that he is not
satisfied, and he seemed to be on the point of exploding."[40]

Cleveland self-servingly reasoned that by picking up a few marginal
states in the Midwest he could make the question of whether or not he
won New York irrelevant—but the Democratic nominee eventually
succumbed, if only to avoid being the first presidential candidate ever
murdered by his campaign manager. Rather than a letter, arrangements
were made for Cleveland to return to New York City and dine with
members of the Tammany leadership. The former president laid down
one precondition: he would make no binding promises.

In early September, Cleveland and a trio of aides were to sit down
for dinner with three of Tammany's leading men: Richard Croker, who
had succeeded Honest John Kelly as Grand Sachem;[*] New York's
lieutenant governor, William Sheehan (the younger brother of John
C. Sheehan, the Irishman whom Cleveland had controversially ejected

---

[*]Kelly's health declined precipitously after the 1884 election, and he was dead by 1886.

from the Buffalo ticket so many years before); and Charles Francis Murphy, who would become the next Grand Sachem in 1902. In the hours
before the meeting at New York City's Victoria Hotel, the candidate's
anxiety was beginning to morph into petulance. One moment, Cleveland was threatening to give up the nomination rather than make concessions to Tammany; the next he was threatening to barnstorm the
state and whip up the party faithful over the machine's disloyalty.

In the end, the theatrics proved unnecessary. The political discussion was tabled until after-dinner coffee, at which point Sheehan and
Murphy complained of the abuse heaped on them in the press by Cleveland's reformist allies. They also insisted on a promise that a second
Cleveland term would provide Tammany the kind of patronage benefits
denied them by his first. The candidate was characteristically immovable. Cleveland refused to make any pledges and, when the matter was
pushed harder, repeated his threat to surrender the nomination rather
than truckle.* It could have been a powder keg, if not for the fact that
Croker—having taken a lesson from the self-destructive rage of his
predecessor—broke the tension, suggesting to his companions that
Cleveland's insistence on refusing pledges was an utterly reasonable
position.[41] Whitney was equally energetic in playing peacemaker. The
campaign manager had one advantage that the candidate did not: personal relationships. Years earlier, Whitney had successfully defended
Croker in a murder trial.[42] It would be an overstatement to say that the
dinner at the Victoria Hotel resulted in a resolution, but it did yield a
modus vivendi. Tammany would not stand in Grover Cleveland's way.

As it turned out, the entire engagement would prove superfluous.
Cleveland's seemingly far-fetched notion of earning enough votes in
the Midwest to make the outcome in New York immaterial proved
prophetic. Not only did the Democratic nominee win back the two
states most decisive in his 1888 loss—New York and Harrison's native

---

*Some versions of the story have Cleveland pounding the table and bellowing his refusal at the
Tammany men. The most reliable accounts, however, suggest that Cleveland was firm in his refusal but intentionally restrained.

Indiana—but he also tallied victories in Illinois, Wisconsin, and California, three states that had eluded him in both of his previous campaigns. Ironically, Cleveland managed his best ever performance in the Electoral College—277 votes to Harrison's 145—while simultaneously earning the lowest percentage of the popular vote (46 percent) in any of his three races.

The explanation for both outcomes was James B. Weaver, the former Iowa congressman who ran as the presidential nominee of the newly formed People's Party. The Populists, as they were commonly known, feared that great concentrations of wealth threatened the very fabric of American democracy. Regarding understatement as a foreign tongue, they pronounced in the preamble to their platform, "A vast conspiracy against mankind has been organized on two continents, and it is rapidly taking possession of the world. If not met and overthrown at once it forebodes terrible social convulsions, the destruction of civilization, or the establishment of an absolute despotism."[43]

Running on an agenda of strengthened labor unions; free and unlimited silver; government ownership of railroads, telegraph, and telephone lines; and a federal income tax, the Populists' appeal was aimed squarely at the "plain people" of the West and the South. In the former, they were aided by Democrats looking to undermine Republican dominance; in the latter they were aided by Republicans looking to undermine Democratic dominance. Indeed, it was even feared at one point that Weaver could play enough of a spoiler to deny either Harrison or Cleveland a majority in the Electoral College, throwing the race into the House of Representatives.[44] The tide would not rise quite that high, but Weaver wound up carrying Colorado, Idaho, Kansas, Nevada, and North Dakota, collecting 22 electoral votes in the process. It was a showing less significant for what it meant in the moment than for what it presaged.

Benjamin Harrison, having returned to Indianapolis to bury his wife, met his defeat with a note of fatigue similar to Cleveland's four years earlier: "It does not seem to me that I could have had the physical strength to go through what would have been before me if I had been re-elected, with the added burden of a great personal grief. I have often said that I did not want to die in a public building or to have an official funeral." As for the causes of his loss, the outgoing president placed the blame squarely on public distemper over the tariff: "The workingman declined to walk under the protective umbrella because it sheltered his employer also. He has smashed it for the fun of seeing the silk stockings take rain."[45]

Even by the rarified standards of American presidents, Grover Cleveland had found himself in elite company. Only Andrew Jackson had matched his record of winning the popular vote in three consecutive elections. Only Franklin Roosevelt would surpass it. And yet, as the festivities broke out in New York City on election night (and into the early hours of the following morning), Cleveland was stoic rather than effusive. "While we find in our triumph a result of popular intelligence which we have aroused, and a consequence of popular vigilance which we have stimulated," he cautioned, "let us not for a moment forget that our accession to power will find neither this intelligence nor this vigilance dead or slumbering. We are thus brought face to face with the reflection that if we are not to be tormented by the spirits which we ourselves have called up, we must hear, above victorious shouts, the call of our fellow countrymen to public duty, and must put on a garb befitting public servants."[46] If it seemed an oddly downbeat note from a victorious presidential candidate, it was nevertheless a prophetic one. Cleveland couldn't begin to imagine just how much torment the spirits would visit upon him in the next four years.

TWELVE

The Crash

The largest building in the world was reduced to ashes overnight. Chicago's Manufactures and Liberal Arts Building, the architectural centerpiece of the "White City" constructed for the 1893 World's Columbian Exposition, was 1,687 feet long and 787 feet wide, covering more than thirty acres. So cavernous was the facility that the Sears Tower, that great icon of a later Chicago—and, until 1996, the tallest building in the world—could have fit inside if laid horizontally. That was the case on the evening of July 5, 1894, anyway. By the morning of July 6, the colossus was nothing more than a smoldering pile of rubble.[1]*

With the country in the grips of a devastating depression, the abandoned facilities of the Columbian Exposition were now teeming with Chicago's unemployed. The blaze that destroyed this symbol of almost unfathomable prosperity had exploded out of control from a cooking fire set by a band of homeless men.[2] That the destruction of this landmark isn't better remembered owes to the fact that it wasn't even the biggest story in Chicago *that week*. The city was also occupied by federal troops, inserted over the objections of Illinois's governor. The cause: a labor strike that had paralyzed commerce throughout much of the country and threatened to expand into a nationwide walkout of laborers

---

*This was not the first time the building had been under siege. Only six months earlier, another fire had spread to its roof. In fact, the July 1894 fire was the last of a series of blazes that combined to destroy nearly all the facilities constructed for the Columbian Exposition.

in practically every vocation. Even normally sober observers began to fret that America stood on the precipice of a second civil war, this one to be fought on class lines rather than regional ones. This was America in Grover Cleveland's second term.

On paper, the conditions surrounding Cleveland's second inaugural seemed propitious. Not only had he achieved a restoration unprecedented in American history, but he had done so with coattails. Grover Cleveland's second term would begin with Democrats controlling the White House and both houses of Congress for the first time in thirty-five years. A more accurate guide to the trajectory of the second term, however, could be found in the omens that seemed to be everywhere in the administration's earliest days.

The definition of the "Cleveland luck" had grown capacious enough to include a belief that the president's public remarks would always be accompanied by fair weather, but his inaugural (where, perfectly to type, Frances received louder applause than he did) was held on an unseasonably cold March day in which Washington was blanketed with snow (the president still insisted on holding the ceremonies outdoors, so as not to disappoint those who had traveled for the occasion). During the celebrations later that evening, a wire in the Blue Room of the newly electrified White House ignited a fire.[3] This wasn't even the only problem *in the executive mansion.* The Clevelands, their caution magnified now that they had a young daughter in tow, had to find accommodations elsewhere in Washington because of a White House outbreak of scarlet fever during the final days of the Harrison administration.[4]

The president's luck wasn't much better when it came time to get down to business. Setting to the work of assembling a cabinet, he was rebuffed by nearly all his top choices, leading him to grouse to his friend L. Clarke Davis that "I am dreadfully perplexed and bothered. I cannot get the men I want to help me. . . ."[5] He could take some solace in having persuaded John Carlisle, the Kentucky senator who had served as Speaker of the House during his first term, to become Treasury secretary. Cleveland gave the role top priority not only because he anticipated economic issues would be central to the administration but also because he hoped to position Carlisle as his successor.[6] The indignities, however, were otherwise legion. They even extended to a declination from his former secretary of state, Thomas Bayard, whom he had hoped to restore to his old station (Bayard preferred, and received, an appointment as ambassador to the United Kingdom instead). To the surprise of many observers, the role would go instead to Walter Q. Gresham, the Republican judge who had been one of Harrison's rivals for the 1888 presidential nomination. Given Cleveland's career-long insistence on a strict separation between his personal affections and his political duties, it was even more noteworthy that he gave cabinet roles to two of his closest friends. Longtime aide Dan Lamont, no longer content to play Boswell, was elevated to secretary of war. Shan Bissell was made postmaster general on the theory that the patronage-rich department could be most effectively supervised by someone in total communion with Cleveland's reformist sensibilities.*

Bissell's appointment was a sign of maturity insofar as it evinced a president who no longer thought himself capable of personally scrutinizing every federal appointment. Indeed, the task now felt like an imposition rather than a sacred duty. So fatiguing did the crush of office seekers become—partially because Cleveland had taken the inadvisable step of barring any official from the first term from joining the second administration—that he eventually removed himself from the entire affair, declaring in an open letter to the public, "A due regard for public duty (which must be neglected if present conditions continue) and an observance of the limitations placed upon human endurance oblige me to decline, from and after this date, all personal interviews with those seeking appointments to office, except as I, on my own motion, may invite them." He warned members of Congress that the rule applied equally to their own efforts to introduce potential appointees,

---

*The postmaster general was a member of the cabinet—and thus in the presidential line of succession—up until the Post Office Department was abolished and replaced by the United States Postal Service in 1971.

noting, "Applicants for office will only prejudice their prospects by repeated importunities and by remaining at Washington to await results."[7]*

Even if his involvement in the issue wasn't as thoroughgoing this time around—and even if many men he surely would have rejected had he been paying closer attention managed to slip into federal jobs as a result—Cleveland continued the transformation of the civil service into a more professionalized, less partisan force. By the time he left office, civil service protections that prevented government employees from being removed for political reasons would be extended to more than 40 percent of the federal workforce.[8] In an early signal that his desire to keep civil service reform a bipartisan affair remained intact, he even retained Harrison's hard-charging civil service commissioner. The decision was less surprising than it would have otherwise been given that Cleveland already trusted the man, having worked with him on the same issue in New York. So, Theodore Roosevelt kept his job.

A new ease with delegating power was the first of many signs to come that Grover Cleveland was adopting a markedly different approach to the presidency in his second term than he had in his first. Indeed, the two terms seem to belong to different eras, with the assertive style of the second strikingly more modern than the often-ministerial sensibilities of the first. The change was overdetermined. First, Cleveland was sensitive to the political price he had paid for his occasional bouts of passivity in the first term. Second, changes in his personal life (as we will see in the next chapter) rendered him increasingly impatient. The most important factor, however, was also the most straightforward: in his second term, Grover Cleveland was presiding over a country in peril.

---

*One supplicant who took Cleveland's desire to be undisturbed to heart was Mark Twain. Twain, hoping to ensure his friend Frank Mason was retained as consul general in Frankfurt, addressed a letter to that effect . . . to Cleveland's then two-year-old daughter, Ruth. Cleveland wrote back that his daughter "took the liberty of reading it to the president" and that Mason would be left undisturbed.

The term "wartime president" connotes heroism, regardless of the underlying facts; no one, by contrast, has ever referred to himself as a "depression president." Economics has the capacity to overmatch the office in a way that even warfare does not. One word from the president of the United States can send troops to the front. If there's a formula by which an increase in GDP or a decline in the unemployment rate can be spoken into existence, alas, no president has yet divined it. Franklin D. Roosevelt, perhaps the only president to emerge from a severe economic downturn with his reputation enhanced, is likely the exception that proves the rule: his economic challenges ended up overshadowed by— and arguably ameliorated by—the military conflict that would come to define his time in office.

There would be no such mitigating factors for Grover Cleveland. Nor would there be any time to acclimate to a term of office far more volatile than the one he had previously served. Cleveland returned to office with America's economy already on a knife's edge. Ten days prior to his inauguration, the Philadelphia & Reading Railroad—one of the nation's oldest and, only a few decades earlier, the largest corporation in the world—filed for bankruptcy. With the Sherman Silver Purchase Act driving fears that America would abandon the gold standard, gold flew out of the country ($50 million worth went overseas in 1892).[9] The Treasury's gold reserves stood imperiled in precisely the manner that Cleveland had warned about in his first term. The outgoing administration had administered triage in its final days, floating a bond issue to keep it from sinking beneath the talismanic $100 million figure.* The measure bought the Cleveland administration time—but not much of it.

Only an act of God had kept the chaos of what later generations would dub the Panic of 1893 (those who lived through it referred to it,

---

*In his post-presidency Cleveland would admit that the $100 million figure was important more as a symbol that the country would remain on the gold standard than as a precise inflection point for monetary health. That judgment would later be echoed by Milton Friedman in his landmark *A Monetary History of the United States, 1867–1960.*

as they had with the severe downturn of the 1870s, as "The Great Depression") from Benjamin Harrison's doorstep. Compounding the anxiety induced by the more accommodationist silver policy Harrison had signed into law, the passage of the McKinley Tariff had led to Americans stockpiling imported goods in anticipation of the higher duties, creating a sudden trade deficit and a corresponding drawdown of gold reserves. At the same time, the spending bonanza of the Billion Dollar Congress was sending the country's previous budget surplus nosediving toward a deficit. All indications were that the United States had given itself over to economic hedonism. That British banks were increasing interest rates at the same time drove even more capital overseas. By the summer of 1890, the economy had dipped into a shallow recession and the Treasury had begun paying out some debts in paper money, further stoking concerns about the stability of the currency. The godsend that allowed Harrison to escape largely unscathed: inclement weather in Europe led to a catastrophic crop failure at the same time American farmers were experiencing record yields. The resulting exports of America's agricultural output temporarily spurred the economy and reversed the flow of gold across the Atlantic.[10] By the time the economy began weakening again, Harrison was already turning the corner into the end of the administration.

For Cleveland, the necessary remedy was obvious: the Sherman Silver Purchase Act had to be repealed. This remained for him a moral necessity just as much as a practical one. When William J. Northen, the free silver Democrat serving as governor of Georgia, wrote to him pleading the silver case, an irritated Cleveland responded by declaring, "I will not knowingly be implicated in a condition that will make me in the least degree answerable to any laborer or farmer in the United States for a shrinkage in the purchasing power of the dollar he has received for a full dollar's worth of work or for a good dollar's worth of the product of his toil."[11] The sentiment, though by this point unshakably held, was not quite correct. For a classical liberal like Cleveland the primary goal of the monetary system was stability; a currency that retained a consistent value would be a neutral vehicle. It would produce neither inflation that benefited debtors at the expense of their lenders nor deflation that did the opposite. This surely also appealed to the fastidious lawyer in him, since a change in the value of the currency was tantamount to a change in the terms of contracts denominated in it.

In reality, however, a limited dosage of silver—though not the free and unlimited coinage for which the populists agitated—was a necessary precondition of that stability. The gold standard had been exerting *deflationary* pressures on the economy, part of the reason that the populists found so much support in the West. The vast acreage thrown open to settlement by the Homestead Act and other initiatives aiming to create a new generation of yeoman farmers yielded a frontier populated by men whose livelihoods were financed by debt. Those settlers watched helplessly as the real value of their liabilities increased—and their crop prices fell—according to the supply of gold. As the Nobel laureate economist Milton Friedman would later write, "Loans that would have been good and banks that would have been solvent if prices had been stable or rising became bad loans and insolvent banks under the pressure of price deflation. And doubtless, also, the collapse of some banks caused runs on others and their suspension, in turn, even though many would have remained fully solvent in the absence of the runs.[12]"

Cleveland and most of his contemporaries, however, did not apprehend the issue in quite that light. Most of them did not understand the debate as a narrow dispute over how to fine-tune the currency to ensure maximum stability; they understood it as debate over whether silver mania would be allowed to entirely overthrow the gold standard, a move that could leave the country isolated in international trade (at the time only India was on a silver standard, and it was to abandon it that very year). That this question had reached a boiling point at a moment when the Democratic Party—deeply divided on the matter—controlled nearly all the mechanisms of federal power only added to market uncertainty over which route the country would choose. Congress was the only body that could resolve that question, but Cleveland was faced with a familiar problem: how to move with expediency when the legislature wouldn't be in session until the end of the year.

There were, from the start, calls for Cleveland to call Congress back into a special session, and he gave the matter serious consideration. Here, however, the president had not quite shaken the diffidence that at times bedeviled him in his first term. Calling a special session could be seen as an unbecoming interference in legislative affairs; it could be interpreted as genuflecting to the interests of Wall Street, a considerable liability when much of the country—including a huge swath of Cleveland voters—regarded themselves as unjustly indentured to the financial class; and it also risked trading speed for effectiveness. If anything, the Democratic Party had moved away from its president on the silver question. He would need more time to win over the opponents in his own caucus. That last calculation proved true, though less because of any gift for persuasion on Cleveland's part than because of the economy's deterioration in the interim.

Matters only got worse in the months before Congress reconvened, sometimes because of political mismanagement and sometimes because of economic fundamentals. Cleveland and Carlisle, his new Treasury secretary, worked assiduously to build the gold reserve back up, swapping paper currency or silver out to banks in exchange for bullion. In a trend that would continue for years, however, every increase in reserves was inevitably followed by another drawdown. This led to an unforced error in April, when Carlisle announced that the government would continue to pay out demands in gold "as long as it has gold lawfully available for the purpose." The conditionality of the statement was interpreted in many quarters as a signal that the administration was about to abandon the gold standard (the effect was amplified by the fact that

Carlisle had voted for the Bland-Allison Act, reintroducing the coinage of silver, during his time in the House).[13] Cleveland was forced to reassure the public that the ambiguity on his Treasury secretary's behalf owed to a slip of the tongue rather than a change in policy.

Some problems the president couldn't talk his way out of. May 4 was the day that the dam burst, with the National Cordage Company, a ropemaking trust that had issued a splashy 100 percent dividend only months earlier, succumbing to insolvency. The already jittery markets tanked. Banks began to call in loans that proved unpayable. Depositors, in turn, tried to remove funds for which the banks had insufficient liquidity. The already overbuilt rail industry suffered a cascading series of failures with the Erie, Northern Pacific, Union Pacific, and Atchison, Topeka, & Santa Fe railroads joining the Philadelphia & Reading in receivership.[14] As the crisis rolled on, New York banks, now operating under a "kill or be killed" mind-set, slowed their release of deposits held for banks in the nation's interior. As a result, the roughly six hundred banks that would eventually close were disproportionately in the South and the West, only fanning the populist flames. National unemployment would eventually crest somewhere between 17 and 19 percent.[15]

On June 30, Cleveland made the announcement that he was calling Congress into a special session. The body convened on August 7, greeted by a message from the president delineating the parade of economic horribles the nation was facing. Though he continued to maintain that there could be some limited role for silver in the national currency mix, he nevertheless argued that the Sherman Act had gone too far and had to be repealed.

The chaos permeating the economy had brought some previously recalcitrant Democrats to his side. For the rest, the president was willing to engage in some realpolitik that would have sent the first-term Grover Cleveland to his fainting couch. Daniel Voorhees, for instance, would have seemed an unlikely ally. The Indiana senator chaired the body's

Finance Committee, was a committed free silver advocate, and had steadfastly opposed Cleveland's renomination. Yet he wound up on the side of repeal ... after Cleveland gave him something approaching carte blanche on the choice of presidential appointments in the Hoosier State. The first-term Grover Cleveland would have unleashed a self-righteous tirade at so much as the idea. This new incarnation of the president was said to have ruefully noted that "a man had never yet been hung for breaking the spirit of the law."[16]

Certain Democrats, however, could not be won over at any price. Among them was a young Nebraska representative who had just a few years earlier written Cleveland admiringly over his forceful stance on the tariff issue. On the silver question, however, the two were irreconcilable. The congressman would hold forth in a three-hour floor speech in opposition to the repeal of the Sherman Act, demonstrating both a substantive mastery of the issue and remarkable rhetorical gifts. Warning his Democratic colleagues that they could not simply substitute the president's judgment for their own, he cautioned:

> [I]t is before the tribunal established by our constituencies, and before that tribunal only that we must appear for judgment upon our actions here. When we each accepted a commission from 180,000 people, we pledged ourselves to protect their rights from invasion and to reflect their wishes to the best of our ability, and we must stand defenseless before the bar if our only excuse is "he recommended it." And remember, sir, that these constituencies include not bankers, brokers, and boards of trade only, but embrace people in every station and condition of life; and in that great court from whose decision there is no appeal every voter has an equal voice.[17]

For most men, it would have been a career-defining speech. For the thirty-three-year-old William Jennings Bryan, it was but a prelude. Even the colleagues he had most impressed that day would likely have been surprised to learn that they had just heard from the Democratic Party's nominee in three of the next four presidential elections.*

Bryan and his less silver-tongued confederates notwithstanding, Cleveland would ultimately get his way, though not without some hardship. By the end of August, the repeal bill passed the House on a bipartisan basis, though a higher percentage of Republicans voted with the president than Democrats (138 of whom were in favor, 78 of whom were opposed).[18] It would languish in the Senate until the end of October, partially due to continued Democratic infighting. When a contingent of Democrats floated a watered-down version that would have slowed silver purchases instead of ceasing them outright, Cleveland proved immovable, ceasing all patronage appointments until the bill was passed on the terms he demanded. It would eventually pass out of the Senate 48–37. Cleveland earned plaudits from much of the press for the forceful show of presidential leadership, but it would prove something of a pyrrhic victory. Resentment over his strong-arming and the growing ideological fissures in the Democratic caucus meant he would never again ride herd over his party in such a fashion. There was another problem, too: the policy didn't work. As we will see, the gold reserves would continue the cycle of being replenished (often through bond issuances) and then drawn back down again for years. In some instances, the results would have been comical if the stakes hadn't been so high. A few of the bond issues, for instance, failed to increase the reserve by the intended amount because the buyers had themselves cashed out gold to make the purchase.[19]

With the repeal of the Sherman Silver Purchase Act behind him,

---

*They would likely have been even more surprised to learn that they had heard from a man whose influence would echo in American popular culture well into the twenty-first century, albeit in a roundabout way. In 1990, the economist Hugh Rockoff penned an influential paper arguing that *The Wizard of Oz* was an extended allegory for the monetary fights of the late nineteenth century. The cowardly lion, in his analysis, represented Bryan. Grover Cleveland factored into the story, too: he was the Wicked Witch of the East, crushed by Dorothy's house at the beginning of the story. For the full analysis see Rockoff's "The Wizard of Oz as Monetary Allegory" in the *Journal of Political Economy* 98 (1990).

Cleveland immediately moved on to the issue that had consumed him for the past five years: tariff reform. In principle, the Cleveland administration should have been on surer footing here. Unlike the money question, party divisions on trade had actually abated in the years since Cleveland's first term. This owed in part to the obvious excesses of the McKinley Tariff, which had left consumers smarting over higher prices, compounded the effects of the economic downturn, and—at a time when the federal budget was already groaning under the weight of the Harrison administration's spending—actually *reduced* federal revenues (primarily because it had moved sugar, previously a major source of funds, to the duty-free list).[20]

By December 1893, Representative William L. Wilson of West Virginia, chairman of the House Ways and Means Committee, was moving a bill that embodied the tariff principles that Cleveland had now been espousing for years: raw materials like coal, lumber, and wool were to be placed on the duty-free list. For most other protected industries, the reductions were modest. So determined was Cleveland to avoid giving Republicans any fodder for their well-worn argument that he was steering the country toward free trade that many of his ideological allies (including Wilson) thought the legislation insufficiently ambitious. But Cleveland had been defeated on the tariff issue once before and if bowing to political reality was the price he had to pay for a passable bill, it seemed a tolerable one.

There were other concessions as well. Westerners disliked tariffs for their regressive qualities: the rich man and the poor man had to pay the exact same duty. To win their support, an amendment was attached imposing a modest federal income tax (2 percent on incomes over $4,000, roughly equivalent to $120,000 in 2019 dollars). While Cleveland had concerns about the constitutionality of the levy (concerns that would be validated when the Supreme Court struck the provision down in 1895), he let it ride. It was another sign of how much he had changed since the first term, as was his continued use of patronage as both carrot and stick in wooing wavering members of Congress. But as events were about to demonstrate, he hadn't entirely lost his trademark bullheadedness.

The tariff bill escaped the House more or less intact, by a vote of 204–140, with fewer than 10 percent of Democrats dissenting. In the Senate, however, it was an altogether different matter. Given the chamber's close margins (Democrats held 44 seats, Republicans 38, and Populists 3), the president needed every last man—which meant that every last man had extraordinary leverage. This was especially empowering for Democrats from states that housed key industries affected by the legislation. If the distinctive feature of the Mills tariff bill in Cleveland's first term had been its regional biases, the most salient aspect of the House version of the Wilson-Gorman Tariff (as it came to be known) was its lack of them—and these members set out to change that. West Virginia couldn't stomach duty-free coal. Alabama wanted a tariff on iron ore. Louisiana desired protection for sugar. Once again, albeit more reluctantly, Cleveland was in the concession-making business.

What followed in the five months that the bill sloshed around the Senate was a total transformation. Cleveland understood that the proposal would be reshaped, perhaps dramatically, in the upper chamber, but consoled himself with the idea that a conference committee to reconcile the differences between the House and Senate versions would strip out most of the excesses. It was a total miscalculation. By the time the bill passed out of the Senate Finance Committee, it had been amended more than 400 times. Another 200 or so would be added before final passage by the full body.[21] The most enduring quote about the debacle came from a disenchanted member who pronounced, "this is a free-lunch counter—walk up and help yourself."[22]

The final product bore only the faintest resemblance to Cleveland's original vision. The provisions for duty-free raw materials were almost entirely gone, with wool and copper the only exceptions. Many duties had been revised *upward*, and sugar in particular came in for lavish protection, with a 40 percent tariff placed on the raw variety.[23] By the time all was said and done, concern for the bill's passage hinged not on the senators who had originally been wavering but on the devout tariff reformers, who had come to regard the legislation as a betrayal of the cause. They would eventually assent, with the bill passing the Senate 39–34, though some of those "yeas" were surely cast by men who shared Cleveland's hope that the bill could be improved in bicameral negotiations. That hope would soon be dashed, not least because Cleveland himself inadvertently sabotaged the process.

By the time members from both chambers met in the conference committee, the president had already accepted that he could expect nothing better than a partial victory. In a self-pitying letter to his friend Everett Wheeler during the prolonged Senate process he had complained, "There never was a man in this high office so surrounded with difficulties and so perplexed, and so treacherously treated, and so abandoned by those whose aid he *deserves*, as the present incumbent."[24] Determined to come out of the process with at least something that instantiated his principles, Cleveland insisted that Chairman Wilson and the House delegation push for iron and coal to be restored to the duty-free list, as well as for the lowering of sugar tariffs. The Senate side, possessing all the leverage, refused to budge.* This catalyzed Cleveland to take matters into his own hands.

One of the secrets to Grover Cleveland's unlikely success as a politician was his ability to channel one of his political idols, Andrew Jackson, by appealing directly to public sentiment rather than trying to play the inside game of wooing recalcitrant legislators. His strategy in this case was reminiscent of his days as the veto mayor of Buffalo: he attempted to shame the legislature into submission. But while that could be a viable strategy when the goal was to shift public sentiment over the long term, it was less appropriate in the eleventh hour of a fight that would

---

*Cleveland's old nemesis, New York senator David B. Hill, was not a member of the conference committee, but his keen political mind made him one of the first to intuit that it would deadlock. Inspecting the food trays being removed from the room where negotiations were taking place, he noted that "[m]en who are in agreement and making progress never send for sweet milk and corn bread; when you see the trays carrying a decanter and a box of cigars, you can bet then an agreement has been reached."

be determined by a handful of congressmen meeting in private. Nevertheless, Cleveland, seeking to electrify the tariff debate, allowed William Wilson to release to the public a private letter he had written upon the opening of the conference committee excoriating Senate Democrats for their betrayal of party principle. In the missive, Cleveland noted that he had been willing to make accommodations on issues like the income tax and sugar duties, but that what he had received in return fell far short of what Democrats had been promising the country since he made tariff reform the center of his annual message more than six years earlier:

> Every true Democrat and every sincere tariff reformer knows that this bill in its present form and as it will be submitted to the conference falls far short of the consummation for which we have long labored, for which we have suffered defeat without discouragement, which, in its anticipation, gave us a rallying cry in our day of triumph, and which, in its promise of accomplishment, is so interwoven with Democratic pledges and Democratic success that our abandonment of the cause of the principles upon which it rests means perfidy and party dishonor.[25]

What exactly did Cleveland hope to achieve by making this sentiment public? Exactly what job did he think he had signed up for? All of the metaphysical pretense of trying to define what constituted a "true Democrat" was pure surplusage. There were no true Democrats or false Democrats; there were just congressional Democrats. They held the fate of his signature legislation in their hands. And he had just grabbed them by the tail.

The reaction on Capitol Hill was swift and nowhere more vicious than from Maryland senator Arthur Pue Gorman, one of the architects of Cleveland's 1884 victory. Gorman had been skeptical from the start of tariff reductions in the middle of an economic crisis and had been a central figure in watering down the bill—but he had done so believing that he was rendering service to a politically clumsy president. Now under attack for the assistance he had provided, he delivered a blistering speech from the Senate floor, accusing Cleveland, that great defender of the separation of powers, of having flaunted them: "Never since the Declaration of Independence was such action taken by a President of the United States," Gorman declared.[26]

Cleveland had learned of the speech in advance and called Gorman to the White House in an attempt to dissuade him from delivering it, but he was in no position to win even that modest concession. Yet delusions of that sort were ubiquitous in the White House as the process headed to its underwhelming denouement. In the coming days, Cleveland would entertain the bizarre idea of keeping the Senate in session longer to wring out at least a few concessions. He would also float to the press that he might even veto the legislation altogether—a self-defeating move if ever there was one given that, for all its messiness, the bill did indeed lower tariff rates from the 49 percent average under the McKinley Tariff to 42 percent.[27] In the end, he split the baby: the Wilson-Gorman Tariff would pass into law on the Senate's terms—and without Grover Cleveland's signature. A more enterprising politician, particularly given the strain he had placed on his own party, might have signed the bill and attempted to dress up this modest accomplishment as a monumental success. Grover Cleveland, however, couldn't shake his bitterness at having his signature policy issue made into a mockery by members of his own party. In a letter to Mississippi representative Thomas Catchings, he unburdened himself of the sentiment in Manichean terms:

> I take my place with the rank and file of the Democratic Party who believe in tariff reform and who know what it is, who refuse to accept the results embodied in this bill as the close of the war, who are not blind to the fact that the livery of Democratic tariff reform has been stolen and worn in the service of Republican protection, and who have marked the places where the deadly blight of treason has blasted the counsels of the brave in their hour of might. The trusts and combinations—the communism

of pelf*—whose machinations have prevented us from reaching the success we deserved, should not be forgotten nor forgiven.[28]

There was a bit of blindness in Cleveland believing that he was in a position to hand out forgiveness at that moment. In reality, he was on the demand side of that market. Every step of his second term thus far had strained the bonds that held the party together. Silver repeal had alienated the populists of the West and the Midwest. His petulance on the tariff had put a chill on his relationship with Congress. Most damagingly, his reaction to the depression and his green-eyeshade view of the economy was increasingly feeding the impression that Grover Cleveland—the head of a party that claimed to represent the plain American workingman—was a tool, intentionally or not, of Wall Street and financial interests.

Despite the depression, the idea of direct federal support for the unemployed was foreign to the world of 1894. It was doubly so to Grover Cleveland. In one of his few quotations to have earned much notoriety with future generations, an 1887 veto of a bill to provide seeds for a drought-stricken part of Texas included his pronouncement that

> I can find no warrant for such an appropriation in the Constitution, and I do not believe that the power and duty of the general government ought to be extended to the relief of individual suffering which is in no manner properly related to the public service or benefit. A prevalent tendency to disregard the limited mission of this power and duty should, I think, be steadfastly resisted, to the end that the lesson should be constantly enforced that though the people support the government the government should not support the people.
>
> The friendliness and charity of our countrymen can always be relied upon to relieve their fellow-citizens in misfortune. This

---

*An archaic word referring to money, usually ill-gotten.

has been repeatedly and quite lately demonstrated. Federal aid in such cases encourages the expectation of paternal care on the part of the government and weakens the sturdiness of our national character, while it prevents the indulgence among our people of that kindly sentiment and conduct which strengthens the bonds of a common brotherhood.[29]

It was sentiments like these that separated Cleveland from the rising generation of populists within the Democratic Party. The distinction was not that Cleveland was indifferent to the plight of the common man; it was that he believed, as in the case of the tariff, that the common man would be safe as long as the government didn't grant special privileges to those looking to exploit him. That answer, however, was becoming increasingly unpalatable for broad segments of the population, not least those in the laboring classes who believed they were being held hostage to the power of concentrated capital.

That burgeoning resentment spilled out into the open in the summer of 1894 in Chicago. Workers at the Pullman Palace Car Factory, a maker of luxury railroad sleeping cars, were restive over the conditions imposed on them by the firm's owner, George Pullman. In the face of the depression, Pullman had cut wages by 20 to 35 percent, in addition to reducing workers' hours.[30] When a group of steamfitters and blacksmiths had called a strike over the conditions the year before, Pullman had ended it with a simple offer: accept the reduced wages or join the masses of the unemployed.

Pullman's logic may have been cruel, but so was the depression's. With the firm's business declining, wage reductions were by no means unthinkable. Conditions in the company town of Pullman, the Chicago suburb where most of the workers lived, were harder to countenance. While rents in Chicago had plummeted with the downturn, some by nearly half, Pullman had refused to cut rates on worker housing. The cost of services was similarly extractive. As the historian Jack Kelly notes in his history of the Pullman Strike, *The Edge of Anarchy*:

"George Pullman sold them water at a 500 percent markup. He forced them to pay $2.25 for gas that neighbors bought for 75 cents. Painters received 35 cents an hour on the open market, Pullman painters only 23 cents."[31] Nor was moving a viable option, as the company gave preference to residents when labor markets were slack.[32]

The situation reached a breaking point in May, when a delegation of Pullman workers appealed to the company's president to either raise wages or lower rents. Pullman denied the appeal—and the next day three of the men bold enough to make the request were relieved of their jobs (though the Pullman Company maintained the decision was unrelated). In solidarity with their brethren, 80 percent of Pullman workers walked off the job. There would be no work even for those who didn't, as Pullman, intent on crushing the uprising, shuttered the factory until further notice.

Had the conflict been limited to George Pullman and his workers it likely would have slipped forgotten into history. What turned it into a matter of federal import was that each side of the dispute was quickly reinforced by organizations with a national reach. The Pullman workers had the backing of the new American Railway Union (ARU), whose leader, Eugene Debs, had recently created the organization to represent the interests of all railroad workers regardless of occupation (previous attempts to organize by trade having proved ineffective).* As for Pullman, he could rely on the muscle of the General Managers' Association (GMA), a confederacy of railroads that did business in Chicago. Though originally organized for the prosaic purpose of coordinating logistics, it quickly morphed into a cartel intent on combatting union influence.[33]

For approximately a month, the Pullman Strike, while at an impasse, caused no larger disturbance. While the Pullman workers be-

---

*In his post-presidency Cleveland called the ARU's involvement "an exceedingly unfortunate proceeding, since it created a situation which implicated in a comparatively insignificant quarrel between the managers of an industrial establishment and their workmen the large army of the Railway Union."

seeched the ARU to intervene, Debs made the utterly sensible suggestion that they first attempt to resolve the dispute by arbitration. This sentiment was seconded by the Civic Federation of Chicago, and, according to a later government report, the mayors of more than fifty of America's largest cities.[34] It was also consistent with the past pronouncements of no less a figure than Grover Cleveland. During his first term, Cleveland had become the first president to suggest a federal role in labor disturbances, proposing a standing three-member commission that could arbitrate disputes between workers and management (in that message, the president, now caricatured as a handmaiden of capital, had pronounced that "[t]he discontent of the employed is due in a large degree to the grasping and heedless exactions of employers...").[35] George Pullman, long since departed for his beach home in New Jersey, refused to deal, regarding any recognition of the workers as a collective body as an unacceptable concession. At that point, the ARU joined in solidarity: beginning June 26, railroad workers throughout the country boycotted work on any train that included a Pullman car.*

At this point, the implications of the strike were no longer confined to Chicago. The demobilization of the railroads' workforce was tantamount to the suspension of commerce, at least in places where the plan caught hold (in keeping with the broader political divisions of the era, the sympathy strikes were much more widespread in the Midwest and the West than in the great cities of the Northeast). Companies already battered by the depression had to lay off employees as they found themselves unable to get goods to market or restock inventory. (At the peak of the unrest, ARU work stoppages would disrupt rail traffic in twenty-seven states and territories.) Food prices skyrocketed, with reports that the cost of ice in steamy summertime Chicago had quadrupled from $2.50 to $10.00 a ton.[36] Within a week, rail traffic in Chicago was run-

---

*Many versions of this story emphasize that Congress made Labor Day a national holiday the day after the strike began, often painting it is an empty, symbolic gesture that took the place of meaningful action. In truth, Labor Day had already been celebrated in the majority of states by 1894 and the bill had been moving through Congress before the Pullman Strike even began.

ning at 10 percent of its normal volume and mail was going undelivered.[37] The *New York Times* declared it "the greatest battle between labor and capital that has ever been inaugurated in the United States."[38]*

With more than 200,000 workers throughout the country participating in the boycott, the Pullman Strike had become the largest coordinated work stoppage in the country's history.[39] For Debs and the ARU it was a delicate dance. Public sympathy tended to be on their side, in part out of a sense that Pullman workers' treatment was genuinely exploitative, in part because Pullman himself had proved so truculent. Whether that sentiment could survive the resulting paralysis of the American economy, however, was a closer question. Seeking to keep the workers from inflaming the situation by harassing the men brought into replace them, Debs cautioned the strikers that "if the railroad companies can secure men to handle their trains, they have that right. Our men have the right to quit, but their right ends there. Other men have the right to take their places, whatever the opinion of the propriety of so doing may be. Keep away from the railroad yards or rights-of-way, or other places where large crowds congregate. A safe plan is to remain entirely away from places where there is any likelihood of being an outbreak [of violence]."[40]

Debs's problem was that he was a hostage to forces beyond his control. One troublemaking striker could disturb the entire equilibrium— and there was no shortage of those looking to inflame the situation. Who was responsible for actually throwing the match remains a matter of historical dispute. There were varying reports at the time—which continue to be contested to this day—about how much of the chaos that subsequently gripped Chicago owed to restive workers; to saboteurs hired by the railroads to turn public opinion against the strikes by inciting violence; to the hordes of itinerant men in Chicago (a subsequent government investigation referred to this contingent as "shiftless

---

*From his perch in Cincinnati, the federal judge (and future president) William Howard Taft delivered the reprimand, "The starvation of a nation cannot be a lawful purpose of combination."

adventurers and criminals attracted to [the city] by the Exposition and impecuniously stranded in its midst");[41] and how much was exaggerated by sensationalistic press reports. This much is clear: by the final days of June, there were sporadic incidents of mobs holding up trains or forcing them to detach their Pullman cars. The Diamond Special, a luxury train headed for St. Louis, narrowly avoided a catastrophic crash only because of a quick-thinking engineer's reflex on the brake upon hitting a stretch of track where the spikes had been removed.[42] In some instances, railroad employees who continued working were beaten by strikers.

In its early days, when the conflict seemed to be a localized labor dispute, there was no real reason for it to command Grover Cleveland's attention. Chicago, after all, had gone through similar tumult in his first term, with 1886's Haymarket Riot, a conflict between law enforcement and labor protesters that left seven police officers and a comparable number of civilians dead. In keeping with the sensibility of the times— and the sensibility of the president—there had been no role for the federal government to quell the violence. Another important factor was keeping the events at Pullman from the top of his agenda: the entire controversy was playing out at the same time that Cleveland was trying to see tariff reform through to a satisfactory conclusion. That meant that the administration's point man on the Pullman Strike was Attorney General Richard Olney, a fact that has come to be regarded as a blemish on Cleveland's record.

Olney was one of many second choices to be found in Cleveland's second-term cabinet. The president had originally hoped to recruit Senator George Gray, who had previously served as attorney general in his home state of Delaware.[43] Upon Gray's declination, he turned to Olney, a highly regarded corporate lawyer from Massachusetts, but a virtual unknown whose high-water mark in electoral politics was a single term in the Bay State's legislature. That background raised eyebrows when the Pullman case came to his desk, because the source of Olney's legal prestige was the extensive work he had done with railroads. Astonishingly, he had even remained on retainer from the Chicago, Burlington, & Quincy Railroad after being installed as attorney general.[44]

Many accounts of Olney's decisive role in the Pullman Strike rely heavily on the implication that his financial connections to the railroads prejudiced his actions in the case. While that can't be ruled out, it's a diagnosis that likely gets the causation backward: Olney wasn't a zealot for the railroads because they paid him so well; they paid him so well because he was a zealot for the railroads. In defending them against what he regarded as the depredations of organized labor, Olney believed that he was defending the very principle of private property itself. Indeed, Olney resembled the president insofar as he was a man who became immovable once he had settled his views on any given issue. Unlike, Cleveland, however, who was prone to periodic eruptions of temper that tended to subside, Olney was positively irascible—and seemingly incapable of deescalation.

It was with that mind-set that the attorney general set out to quash the disorder, appointing a special counsel to work with the U.S. attorney in Chicago, Thomas Milchrist, on a request for an injunction to halt the obstruction of rail traffic. The Justice Department's strategy seamlessly blended justifiable uses of federal power with pure excess, often crossing ethical lines in the process. The first such trespass was Olney's selection of Edwin Walker, an attorney for the railroads who came recommended by the General Managers' Association, as special counsel. The second was the U.S. attorney enlisting the very judges who were to hear the request to help revise the application (unsurprisingly, they granted the injunction). The third was the staggering scope of the ensuing order.

Most of the writ issued by the U.S. Circuit Court for the Northern District of Illinois on July 2, 1894, could be justified as a matter of keeping vital infrastructure online. Strikers were ordered not to interfere with the operations of train traffic, not to destroy railroad property, and not to enter onto railroad grounds with an eye to either purpose. It also, however, prohibited strikers from "compelling or inducing (or attempting to compel or induce) by threats, intimidation, persuasion, force, or violence, any of the employees of any of said railroads to refuse or fail to perform any of their duties. . . ."[45] By the inclusion of the word "persuasion," the writ had the effect of prohibiting virtually all support of the strike.

In short order, it became apparent that no piece of paper issued by a court would quiet the disturbances. On July 2, a dispatch to the attorney general from John W. Arnold, the U.S. marshal for northern Illinois, reported that in Blue Island, outside of Chicago, a group of 2,000–3,000 strikers had refused to disperse from the area's railroad tracks, tipped over a series of railcars to obstruct traffic, and, in the ensuing melee, stabbed a deputy marshal. Noting, "We have had a desperate time here all day and our force is inadequate," Arnold suggested that only federal troops would be sufficient to restore order. This was precisely what Olney longed to hear. The attorney general cabled Milchrist, the U.S. attorney, and not so subtly requested another, more forceful version of the statement, which he immediately deployed to convince Cleveland that the time for federal intervention (which the president and most of his cabinet had heretofore resisted) was at hand.[46]

It is easy, and surely correct, to blame the attorney general for his willingness to cut every corner to enlist first the courts and then the military to break the strike, as well as for his serial exaggeration of the threats on the ground. Yet the urge to turn Olney into a villain has often led later generations to underestimate the legitimate problems that the administration faced. After all, it's not as if Olney had fabricated the entire situation. National commerce really was grinding to a halt, forcible disruptions of train service really were happening, and outbreaks of violence really had taken place. The perception of danger was inflamed by a sense that such unrest could presage the breakdown of society. Only a week earlier, the popular president of France, Sadi Carnot, had been stabbed to death by an Italian anarchist.

Once Olney conveyed the warnings coming from Chicago, Cleveland and his previously reticent cabinet members flipped: troops would be sent into the field. It was a bold step: a president who professed a belief in limited government and states' rights deploying federal troops into the nation's interior, despite the fact that there had been no request from Illinois itself. Cleveland believed he had legal justification, even without petition from the governor, by dint of his responsibility to ensure the preservation of interstate commerce. As for his moral justification, he'd later explain that "I woke up one morning and as I got out of bed, I asked myself: Did the people elect Eugene Debs or Grover Cleveland president? And that settled it."[47]*

Whether the presence of federal troops—nearly 2,000 were deployed between July 3 and 10[48]—inflamed the situation or anticipated an inflammation that would have occurred anyway is unknowable, but there were flames nonetheless. Even the previously temperate Debs lost his head, seemingly laying the groundwork for the class war his critics had feared: "The first shots fired by the regular soldiers at the mobs here will be the signal for a civil war. I believe this as firmly as I believe in the ultimate success of our course. Bloodshed will follow, and 90 percent of the people of the United States will be arrayed against the other 10 percent. And I would not care to be arrayed against the laboring people in the contest or find myself out of the ranks of labor when the struggle ended."[49] Cleveland had expressed a different theory of the case: "If it takes the entire army and navy of the United States to deliver a postal card in Chicago, that card will be delivered."[50]

Federal troops arrived on July 4. In the days immediately after the holiday, a general sense of chaos ensued, as mobs roamed the city, tipping over railroad cars, harassing the troops, and setting fires. Though the fire that engulfed the facilities built for the Columbian Exposition was unrelated, its sheer enormity, when added to the blazes set by the rioters, lit the city in a nighttime orange glow, giving Chicago the feeling of a war zone.

Saturday, July 7, 1894, marked the culmination of the conflict. A

---

*While Cleveland meant the question rhetorically, Debs may have taken it literally. He became the Socialist Party's candidate for president in 1900, 1904, 1908, 1912, and 1920, his final campaign taking place while he was in prison.

company of troops from the Illinois National Guard, at work clearing a section of track, were surrounded by an aggressive crowd that began throwing rocks and, in short order, whatever implements they could find. When they failed to heed orders to disperse—and the projectiles became more frequent and more dangerous—the guardsmen fired into the crowd. An all-out riot ensued and at least four people were killed. A similar incident occurred with federal troops in Indiana the same day. The war that Eugene Debs had promised seemed to be upon them.

Over the weekend, the strikers had begun seriously discussing a city-wide mass walkout of workers in all the trades. They even bandied about the prospect of attempting it on a national scale.[51] In the face of chaos, Cleveland issued a remarkable proclamation. On July 8, he put Chicago under something approaching martial law, ordering all parties obstructing federal forces to disperse by noon the following day and warning:

> Those who disregard this warning and persist in taking part with a riotous mob . . . can not be regarded otherwise than as public enemies.
>
> Troops employed against such a riotous mob will act with all the moderation and forbearance consistent with the accomplishment of the desired end, but the stern necessities that confront them will not with certainty permit discrimination between guilty participants and those who are mingled with them from curiosity and without criminal intent. The only safe course, therefore, for those not actually unlawfully participating is to abide at their homes, or at least not to be found in the neighborhood of riotous assemblages.
>
> While there will be no hesitation or vacillation in the decisive treatment of the guilty, this warning is especially intended to protect and save the innocent.[52]

Within thirty-six hours of the proclamation, the dominoes began to fall. Even though it seemed like the ARU had gained extraordinary leverage, George Pullman, characteristically unbowed, once again re-fused to negotiate. Hours later, Debs, along with other union leaders, was arrested for having violated the injunction and engaging in a con-spiracy to interfere with interstate commerce. (The conspiracy case was later dropped, but Debs appealed the application of the injunction all the way to the Supreme Court, which ruled unanimously in favor of the federal government. He would serve six months in jail.)* With labor's leadership decapitated, the strike began to fall apart. By midweek, Debs, free on bail, was proposing that the strike end only on the modest terms that the Pullman workers "be restored to their former positions without prejudice."[53] In the end, the terms were that Pullman workers would be welcomed back . . . as long as they withdrew from the ARU.[54]

A return to the status quo ante came at a high price. A report issued by a commission Cleveland set up in the wake of the strike was riddled with grim arithmetic. Twelve people had been fatally shot, 575 arrested. Between federal troops, state militia, a makeshift contingent of deputy marshals (many of whom were essentially double agents of the rail-roads), deputy sheriffs, and the Chicago police, a force of more than 14,000 had been required to restore order to the city. Total revenue losses to the railroads came out to more than $138 million in 2019 dol-lars. The total wage loss to Chicago railroad employees was estimated at over $41 million in 2019 dollars.[55]

There was also a political cost to pay for the president who had so forcefully inserted himself in the proceedings. Cleveland had touched off a bitter spat with Illinois governor John Peter Altgeld, a fellow Dem-ocrat who objected to the president's unilateral insertion of federal troops in a biting letter that proclaimed "that the state of Illinois is not only able to take care of itself, but it stands ready to furnish the federal

---

*This was not to be Eugene Debs's final stint behind bars. He was arrested again in 1918 for violating the Espionage and Sedition Acts with his outspoken opposition to World War I. As with the Pullman case, Debs appealed all the way to the Supreme Court. As with the Pullman case, he lost. Given a ten-year sentence, he would be freed in 1921 thanks to a commutation from President Warren G. Harding, who sought to roll back the restrictions on civil liberties imposed by the wartime administration of Woodrow Wilson.

government any assistance it may need elsewhere."[56] When Cleveland issued a matter-of-fact response articulating his legal justifications, Altgeld fired back an even more bracing letter in which he compared Cleveland to a European monarch and accused him of embracing a theory of the state that could entirely destroy local government. The clearly irritated president responded with a one-sentence telegram: "While I am still persuaded that I have neither transcended my authority nor duty in the emergency that confronts us, it seems to me that in this hour of danger and public distress, discussion may well give way to active efforts on the part of all in authority to restore obedience to law and to protect life and property."[57]

The president surely could have handled an uncomfortable relationship with a single governor, but Altgeld was representative of a bigger trend. While there was an initial wave of support for Cleveland's decisive stance in Chicago—a gambit that some credited with staving off revolution—the affair only put him at a further remove from the Democratic Party. Proponents of federalism blanched at the casual disregard of states' rights, while union men believed he had betrayed them. In a time of economic depression, the one man who had unambiguously benefited from Cleveland's leadership was the already fantastically wealthy George Pullman. It was not a selling point in a party growing more populist by the day.

Facing a party that regarded him with increasing fatigue, a listless economy, and a country that at times seemed to be coming apart, it was difficult to imagine things getting any worse for Cleveland. There was, however, another hardship in his life, unknown to the public.

THIRTEEN

How Weak the Strongest Man

Four men have killed a president of the United States. W. W. Keen could well have been the fifth. While that distinction alone would have landed him in the history books, it would have come with a special distinction: he would've been the first one to do it by accident.

To all external appearances, Grover Cleveland's personal life seemed charmed in his second term. He had contentedly settled into the role of husband and father. And unbeknownst to official Washington, young Ruth Cleveland also had a sibling on the way. In September, Frances would become the first (and, to date, only) First Lady to give birth in the White House. Continuing the family's predilection for Old Testament nomenclature, the president's new daughter was christened Esther. The public, however, was less interested in the name than the sex—which proved a great letdown to those who hoped a mini-Grover might soon be roaming the White House grounds. So ubiquitous was the popular regret that Frances hadn't had a boy that she punctuated a letter to Daniel Manning's widow with the update that "[a]ll here are pleased that she is a girl, however disappointed the nation may be."[1]

As during Cleveland's first term, the public's fascination with the members of the first family oftentimes seemed to outstrip its interest in the president himself. It was not long into the second term, for instance, that Frances had to request that the gates to the South Lawn of the White House be closed in order to ward off the crowds that tried to get a glimpse of (or, more disquietingly, a hug from) little Ruth.[2] Given the president's jealous defense of his family's privacy, it thus came as little surprise when he once again opted to separate their personal lives from his public duties. The Clevelands rented a private home in Washington dubbed Woodley, not far from their first-term retreat at Red Top.

It should've been a recipe for domestic bliss, a respite from the chaos swirling around the administration. Instead, Cleveland's life became imperiled at almost precisely the same moment his presidency did. On May 5, 1893—the day after the failure of the National Cordage Company had sent the economy into a tailspin—the president noticed a rough spot on the roof of his mouth. When he asked the First Lady to take a look, Frances reported the presence of a "peculiar lesion."[3] The implication was terrifying. Not only was Cleveland an enthusiastic cigar smoker but his use of chewing tobacco was so extensive that the White House staff claimed to measure the length of his work nights by how full the presidential spittoon was the next morning.[4] It was difficult to imagine the prospect of so imposing a man brought low by an uncompliant cluster of cells. Yet the country, and Grover Cleveland, already knew that no amount of virility was sufficient to protect from a disease so dreaded that it was usually spoken of only in euphemism.

The knowledge that the president of the United States might have cancer would be destabilizing in any setting—but it was doubly so in the late nineteenth century, a time when the diagnosis was regarded as an almost certain death sentence. It had been only eight years since the nation had watched Ulysses S. Grant, ravaged by throat cancer, shrink to less than 100 pounds and eventually fall mute before dying at his cabin near the Adirondacks. The decision to select a running mate for his ability to smooth over intraparty differences now took on ominous implications. If anything happened to Cleveland, Vice President Stevenson—an outspoken proponent of free silver—would take the helm.*

---

*According to his second-term aide, Robert O'Brien, Cleveland regretted having picked Stevenson for vice president.

Had the country known it was facing the prospect of changing horses (and policies) midstream, the ensuing panic almost surely would have accelerated the depression. So, the president resolved, the public would not know. The first in a long series of subterfuges came when the First Lady, alarmed by her husband's condition, made an unannounced stop in Jersey City, New Jersey, on a June 19 trip from Washington to Gray Gables. The purpose: a clandestine meeting with Dr. Joseph Bryant, the president's friend and personal physician in New York.* On the day prior, Cleveland had submitted to an inspection by the White House physician, Dr. Robert O'Reilly, who "found an ulcer as large as a quarter of a dollar, extending from the molar teeth to within one-third of an inch of the middle line and encroaching slightly on the soft palate, and some diseased bone."[5] A biopsy sent out under cover of anonymity yielded a report that, whoever the patient was, his condition was almost certainly malignant. O'Reilly, regarding the need for surgery as a near inevitability, encouraged Cleveland to consult with Bryant, an appointment facilitated by Frances's surreptitious stop in New Jersey (she couldn't risk making the request via telegram). Upon arriving at the White House and examining the patient, the president's friend didn't mince words: "Were it in my mouth I would have it removed at once."[6]

"At once" was not an option for a president attempting to fend off an economic meltdown, so the time frame would have to be carefully calibrated. Cleveland had one advantage of which a modern president could not avail himself: no one had any expectation of seeing him during the summer, when Congress was out of town and prolonged presidential absences were unremarkable. In addition, his habit of repairing to Gray Gables for the season was well established. Under normal circumstances, that would've been cover enough. But there was still the matter of the special session to be called on the silver issue. Cleveland drew disparagement in some quarters for picking the late date of August 7 for

---

*Bryant was also the brother-in-law of Cleveland's former assistant, and now secretary of war, Dan Lamont.

Congress to reconvene. Surely, they carped, the body would be able to reassemble sooner. Little did the critics know that the president, having settled on a July 1 surgery, was advised by his physicians that it was the earliest he could return to Washington without displaying physical evidence that something was amiss.[7]

It may seem strange to attach the word "lucky" to a cancer-stricken president engaged in a massive cover-up while managing an economic crisis, but, given the circumstances, Cleveland had drawn a high card. The placement of the tumor allowed for all surgical work to be done from inside his mouth. That meant there'd be no visible scarring, nor would he have to part with his trademark mustache. His body could keep the secret. Whether the same could be said of the retinue that would be party to the deception was a closer question.

As Cleveland attempted to keep the economy from taking on water, Bryant went to work assembling a medical team that would be up to the formidable task of a clandestine, invasive surgery on the president of the United States (no previous president had so much as been put under anesthesia while in office). The most important recruit was W. W. Keen, the Philadelphia physician regarded as the nation's foremost surgeon. Barely five years before, Keen had conducted what was likely the first surgical removal of a brain tumor in American history.[8] Despite that illustrious track record, the doctor's nerves were still on edge. Keen would later write, "The operation [on Cleveland] was as nothing compared with scores that [I] had performed; but on it hung the life not only of a human being and an illustrious ruler but the destiny of a nation. It was by far the most responsible operation in which I ever took part."*[9]

Joining Bryant and Keen would be O'Reilly; his assistant, John Erdmann; another New York surgeon, E. G. Janeway; and Ferdinand

---

*Keen would later be called on to treat another (in this case, future) president. In 1921—by which time he was in his eighties—the doctor was summoned to the island of Campobello to determine what exactly had brought on the partial paralysis of Franklin Delano Roosevelt. He incorrectly told FDR it was likely a blood clot or a spinal cord lesion.

Hasbrouck, a dentist (who would handle the anesthesia in addition to the requisite work on Cleveland's teeth). With Frances already at Buzzards Bay, the only person present from outside the president's medical team would be Dan Lamont, who, though now serving as secretary of war, couldn't quite shake the role of Cleveland's man Friday. Right up through the moment that Cleveland went under the knife, not even Vice President Stevenson had the faintest clue that he might be one nick of the scalpel away from the presidency.

Another difficulty: the surgery would have to take place at sea. There was simply no place on land that could provide both an adequate space for the medical team to operate and the privacy necessary to keep the president's condition under wraps. Thus a plot was hatched to enlist the use of the *Oneida*, the luxury yacht of Cleveland's friend and prominent New York banker E. C. Benedict, under the pretense that the vessel was ferrying Cleveland from Manhattan to Gray Gables for his summer vacation. The plan added an extra degree of difficulty to the surgery but compensated for it by shrinking the universe of potential witnesses. The story told to the ship's crew was that the president would be having a dental procedure while on board. Because the sheer volume of medical personnel present might suggest that description was incomplete, the *Oneida*'s hands were told the doctors were a necessary precaution in case Cleveland suffered blood poisoning.[10]

Late in the day on June 30, Cleveland issued a proclamation calling Congress into special session on August 7; or rather, the office of the president issued a proclamation. In point of fact, the White House, already attempting to muddy the timeline, had held the announcement until a few hours after Cleveland and Lamont had departed for the train that would carry them to New York. Throughout the day, the surgical team had been making their way to the *Oneida*'s position in the East River, each departing from a separate pier to avoid arousing suspicion.[11] By the time that Cleveland and Lamont arrived, it was nearing midnight. If the president was racked with anxiety, he wasn't showing it: Cleveland took a seat on the deck . . . and lit a cigar.[12]

Subsequent generations with the luxury of knowing the procedure's outcome can scarcely imagine the fears that dogged Cleveland's medical team. It was bad enough that they were being asked to operate on the president of the United States, that the entire affair had to be kept secret, and that they were forced to convert the saloon of a yacht into an operating room; there was also a host of potential liabilities. Keen fretted that putting a man of the president's substantial girth under anesthesia could induce a stroke, a complication he had experienced with a previous patient.[13] What would the nation do with a half-dead commander in chief, especially in an age before the Twenty-Fifth Amendment created a legal framework for dealing with presidential incapacitation?

The team had brought both nitrous oxide and ether, hoping only to use the former but keeping the latter on hand in case nitrous was insufficient to keep the president under. A pre-op urinalysis, however, found that Cleveland was in the early stages of a kidney disease that ether could severely aggravate.[14] What about the blood loss that could result? At sea, there was no hope of a transfusion. Moreover, the course of the cancer itself might conspire to ruin the entire cover-up. If it had spread far enough it could necessitate the removal of the lower part of his left eye socket, leaving that side of his face permanently sagging and potentially altering his vision.[15] And this was all before factoring in the nautical complications that inspired Bryant to command, mordantly but understandably, "If you hit a rock, hit it good and hard, so that we'll all go to the bottom."[16]

If Bryant and even Cleveland had taken on a sort of gallows fatalism, there was one participant in the affair with no such impulse. Imagine the dread that must have plagued Frances. The First Lady was not yet thirty. Her daughter Ruth was still shy of two years old. She was entering the third trimester of pregnancy with Esther. Her entire adult life had revolved around her husband—and her entire childhood had featured him as a kind of surrogate father. Frances Cleveland sat pensively at Gray Gables, unable to receive word from the *Oneida*. All she could

do was look to the horizon, knowing that Grover was out there somewhere, bobbing on a distant tide. She could not know whether he was
doing it alive or dead.

On the morning of July 1, the *Oneida* set sail up the East River (the
doctors were dispensed belowdecks until the ship cleared the city, a precaution against any of them being recognized as the vessel passed Bel-
levue Hospital).[17] As the craft turned northeast toward Long Island
Sound, a makeshift operating room was set up in the vessel's saloon,
which had been cleared of furniture save for an organ bolted to the floor.
There was nothing to use as an operating table, so Cleveland was placed
in a large chair tied to the mast at the room's center and stripped almost
entirely naked, a detail that weighs heavy in the counterfactual.[18] Abraham Lincoln and James Garfield had death set upon them in moments of
leisure. William McKinley and John F. Kennedy were assassinated in the
course of official business. How merciful were the fates that kept Grover
Cleveland from the eternal notation "killed in his underwear on a yacht."

The ensuing procedure was surprisingly efficient—it was over in approximately ninety minutes. The details of what happened during that
time, however, are grisly, at least in the telling. The operation took place
under the light of a single bulb. With the president under nitrous (he
had required two doses), the dentist Hasbrouck took the lead, extracting
a pair of teeth (an electrical burn was applied to cauterize the wound) to
clear the way for Bryant's incisions in the roof of the president's mouth.
As the doctor began the process of cutting through Cleveland's soft palate and gums to excise the tumor, however, there was a complication: the
president appeared to be regaining consciousness. Janeway frantically administered another dose of nitrous and Cleveland was successfully kept
at bay.[19] Once the tumor was removed, the real gore began, necessitating
a dose of the dreaded ether. In Keen's telling:

> The entire left upper jaw was removed from the first bicuspid
> tooth to just beyond the last molar, and nearly up to the middle
> line. The floor of the orbit—the cavity in the skull containing

the eyeball—was not removed, as it had not yet been attacked. A small portion of the soft palate was removed. This extensive operation was decided upon because we found that the antrum— the large hollow cavity in the upper jaw—was partly filled by a gelatinous mass, evidently a sarcoma.[20]*

With the procedure complete, Cleveland's mouth was packed with gauze, a dose of morphine was administered, and the president was relocated to his cabin. A sense of propriety disappointing to subsequent historians proscribed any eyewitness accounts of what it took to move a man of Cleveland's size back to his private chambers. Post-operation, the president's vitals were strong. And if there were any doubts as to whether he'd emerge with his temperament intact, it was put to rest when he awoke to find Erdmann by his bedside and immediately began questioning the physician on the qualifications of an office seeker from Erdmann's hometown. When Cleveland asked, "is he so poor that he needs a job from me?" and Erdmann replied in the negative, the president bellowed "Well, then he won't get one!"[21] It seemed like the boss was going to be fine.

There was, however, a serious difficulty ahead. Cleveland now had a noticeable disability. As Keen would later report, "With the packing in the cavity his speech was labored but intelligible; without the packing it was wholly unintelligible, resembling the worst imaginable case of cleft palate."[22] Even under the era's more austere expectations for executive oratory, it was a problem for the president of the United States to be functionally without the use of his voice. That this development didn't give away the entire game owed solely to the ingenuity of a New York dentist named Kasson Gibson. Recruited by Bryant, Gibson was installed at Gray Gables, where, using a plaster cast of the hole inside Cleveland's mouth, he was able to fashion a prosthetic out of vulcanized

---

*Twentieth-century analysis would reveal that the "gelatinous mass" was not cancerous, but rather the result of infection.

rubber that restored the proper shape to Cleveland's face and allowed him to regain his articulation.[23] Though Robert O'Brien, the president's assistant, would later claim that there was a noticeable difference in Cleveland's voice thereafter,[24] there are no accounts to suggest that anyone who wasn't aware of the surgery ever picked up on it.

With the president recovering admirably, the medical staff (with the exception of Bryant, the only one who had a plausible reason to be traveling with Cleveland) were deposited along the banks of Long Island Sound. By July 5, Cleveland—who by now had been ambulatory again for two days—arrived at Gray Gables and walked into his summer home on his own power.[25] For all the drama, the surgery itself had been amazingly free of complications. There was, however, still fallout yet to come, both in terms of the cover-up and the president's health.

One early complication was the length of the voyage. It had taken the *Oneida* four days to make what was typically a thirteen-hour journey from Manhattan to the Upper Cape. Thankfully, an onset of thick fog along the coast had provided a plausible cover story.[26] Plausible, but not necessarily persuasive. The press gathered on the Cape began to ask questions. What had happened onboard the boat? The administration's line was that the president, wary of dentists, had put off some much-needed dental work for far too long and finally submitted to a procedure on board. But if that was the case, why hadn't he been seen performing his usual hunting and fishing exploits since arriving at Gray Gables? "Laid up with a particularly unpleasant bout of rheumatism," came the answer.

Ironically, it was Bryant, choreographer of the entire affair upon the *Oneida*, who nearly blew the president's cover. Unexpectedly cornered by a reporter, he regurgitated the official story but then nervously cut the conversation off when specifically questioned as to whether there had been a surgery. On July 8, a story ran in the *Boston Herald* arguing that "there is a disposition manifest to treat [the official denials] with incredulity, and to assume with absolutely no warrant in information or authority, that [Cleveland] must be suffering from some disease more serious in character than the one which was mentioned in the official statement given out by Colonel Lamont yesterday."[27] It had been only a week and already the narrative was at the risk of unraveling.

Cleveland's alibi was saved only by his reputation for candor and the unrefined instincts of the press corps. Lamont, in an attempt to smother the suspicions in their cradle, decided to call a sort of impromptu press conference, inviting the mass of reporters stationed at Buzzards Bay to Gray Gables for a session in which he would set the record straight. Strategically choosing a barn far enough removed from the main home to keep the president (who was in a bathrobe and confined largely to bed) out of sight, Lamont retold the tale of harrowing dentistry with enough élan—and the intimation that the reporters were entertaining stories surely planted by Cleveland's political opponents—that he managed to break the fever. Remarkably, the tactic worked only because the assembled journalists did business as a cartel. Roughly half of the press corps didn't believe the story—but they had made it standard practice to agree upon which version of events they'd publish.[28] Cleveland stood alongside Washington and Lincoln in the pantheon of presidents known for honesty. His reputation broke the tie, and word went out throughout the country that the fears about the president's health were overblown.

The deception went far beyond Lamont's attempt at hypnotizing journalists. Indeed, John Erdmann would later recall that he never lied so much in his life as he did that summer.[29] Friends and colleagues were misled with the same verve as the press. The campaign of deception could have gone off without a hitch—if not for the dentist.

Ferdinand Hasbrouck had not been allowed to leave the *Oneida* on his preferred schedule (a request Bryant had denied because he believed he'd need the dentist if Cleveland required a second surgery) and had, as a result, missed a scheduled procedure in Greenwich, Connecticut. When he showed up a day late and was met by a doctor angry at his unexplained absence, Hasbrouck excused himself by recounting the entire story. The doctor, Carlos MacDonald, then proceeded to share it throughout the Greenwich medical community, by which means it eventually ended up in the hands of E. J. Edwards, the New York correspondent for the *Philadelphia Press*, who wrote under the nom de plume "Holland."[30]

Edwards was extraordinarily responsible in his handling of the story. He managed to track down Hasbrouck, who was dumbfounded not only that the reporter had correctly ascertained the broad outline of the story but that he seemed to have mastered most of its details as well. Hasbrouck confessed and on August 29, the day after the repeal of the Sherman Act had passed the House, the story ran under the headline "The President a Very Sick Man." That was about as sensationalistic as it got. Edwards's report was measured, precise, and sympathetic to the president—and it was nevertheless savaged. All the usual defenders reasserted the party line: it was dental work and nothing more. Had it simply been Edwards's word against theirs, the façade may have cracked. But there were several mitigating factors working in the administration's favor. For one, Cleveland had by then returned to Washington in seemingly good health (in private, Bryant would pronounce him all healed on September 1). For another, one of the stewards on board the *Oneida*, Charles Stewart, had taken the extraordinary step of telling the press that he had seen nothing strange on board the ship and that Cleveland had walked the deck every day.[31] There was also a coordinated attack directed at Edwards from the *Philadelphia Press*'s crosstown rival, the *Philadelphia Times*, whose publisher was a devoted Cleveland loyalist. Branding Edwards "a calamity howler," the paper ran story after story dedicated to tarnishing his reputation and, by extension, his reporting on the surgery at sea.

In the end, Edwards's story faded from the headlines, crowded out by news of extraordinarily violent hurricanes in New York City and the Sea Islands of Georgia and South Carolina and, a few weeks later, by news of the birth of Esther Cleveland.[32*]

---

*Edwards's reputation would not be rehabilitated until 1917, when W. W. Keen, one of the last surviving participants in the surgery on the *Oneida*, published an account of the proceedings, a step he took with Frances Cleveland's blessing. In the recounting, Keen took special care to note that Edwards's "dispatch was substantially correct, even in most of the details."

There had been more to the story than even Edwards had known. On July 17, two and a half weeks after the original procedure, Cleveland had once again been taken to sea for surgery, this time a much more modest procedure to remove some suspicious tissue remaining at the site (the follow-up never leaked to the press because Bryant, suspicious that Hasbrouck couldn't be trusted, did not invite the dentist back).[33] The president's recovery had also proceeded more unevenly than it may have appeared. In the days immediately after the surgery, Attorney General Olney had visited Gray Gables to consult with the president on the silver issue. In a later description of the visit, he recalled that "[the president] had changed a great deal in appearance, lost a great deal of flesh, and his mouth was so stuffed with antiseptic wads that he could hardly articulate. The first utterance that I understood was something like this: 'My God, Olney, they nearly killed me.' He did not talk much, was very depressed, and at that time acted, and I believe he felt, as if he did not expect to recover."[34] There were lingering side effects, too. Cleveland would later note in a letter to Kasson Gibson, the creator of his prosthesis, that he had developed problems with earaches, perhaps because the surgery had displaced his uvula.[35]

The changes were not purely physical. Cleveland was also said to have developed a more brittle personality. His personal assistant, Robert O'Brien, would later recount that "he worried more easily, and was more sensitive. The economic period was disturbing, and Cleveland was very anxious." He had developed, O'Brien reported, a "disposition to dismiss things that would trouble him rather peremptorily."[36]

The irony of it all was that Cleveland endured this hardship for a medical issue less severe than had been imagined at the time. The tumor, which was saved and eventually donated to the Museum of the College of Physicians in Philadelphia, was placed under examination for the first time in 1975. It could've undergone inspection earlier, but the Cleveland family was reluctant to permit it because of an oddity noticed at the time of the operation: the tumor had perforated the president's palate, a potential indicator of syphilis.[37] Once his relations finally consented, the subsequent analysis not only revealed that Cleveland had not had the venereal disease, but also that the tumor was an extremely rare form of oral cancer known as a verrucous carcinoma. While technically malignant, it does not metastasize; it was more likely to kill Cleveland by becoming too large for him to eat or breathe properly (and its growth is so slow that even that would have been an extremely prolonged process).[38]

Of course, Cleveland did not have the luxury of knowing the comparatively modest lethality of his cancer, and the creeping sense of mortality would inform his presidency thereafter. In September, a few days after Esther's birth, he confessed the cover-up to his former secretary of state Thomas Bayard by letter, marking the only time he revealed the details to anyone not proximate to the surgery. In a poignant reflection, he wrote:

The truth is, officeseeking and officeseekers came very near putting a period to my public career. Whatever else developed found its opportunity in the weakened walls of a constitution that had long withstood fierce attacks. I turned the corner to the stage of enforced caretaking almost in a day. And this must be hereafter the condition on which will depend my health and life. Another phase of the situation cannot be spoken of with certainty, but I believe the chances in my favor are at least even.

I have learned how weak the strongest man is under God's decrees and I see in a new light the necessity of doing my allotted work in the full apprehension of the coming night.[39]

FOURTEEN

The Moralist Abroad

Foreign policy had not been a major focus of Cleveland's first term, nor was it a matter to which he ever dedicated prolonged thought. The president believed that the wisdom of the Founding Fathers rarely required updating, and this was especially true when it came to America's role in world affairs. The sum of his thinking on the matter had been expressed in a single paragraph in his first inaugural:

> The genius of our institutions, the needs of our people in their home life, and the attention which is demanded for the settlement and development of the resources of our vast territory, dictate the scrupulous avoidance of any departure from that foreign policy commended by the history, the traditions, and the prosperity of our republic. It is the policy of independence, favored by our position and defended by our known love of justice and by our power. It is the policy of peace suitable to our interests. It is the policy of neutrality, rejecting any share in foreign broils and ambitions upon other continents and repelling their intrusion here. It is the policy of Monroe and of Washington and Jefferson—"Peace, commerce, and honest friendship with all nations; entangling alliance with none."[1]

The few international issues Cleveland handled during the first term fell neatly into that schema. One of his first acts in office was withdrawing from Senate consideration a treaty negotiated by the Arthur administration that allowed for the construction of a transoceanic canal across Nicaragua, to be jointly owned by the two nations. While the president was enthusiastic about the prospect of creating a direct passage between the Atlantic and Pacific, he couldn't countenance the agreement's requirement that Nicaragua become an American protectorate, thus permanently intertwining the affairs of the two countries.

As for "repelling intrusions," Cleveland applied that principle most notably to Samoa, then an independent kingdom, but one that had signed treaties with the United States, the United Kingdom, and Germany allowing for trade and the construction of naval bases. When the German government under Otto von Bismarck attempted to replace the Samoan king with a rival more sympathetic to Berlin's interests— widely interpreted as a prelude to rendering the kingdom a German protectorate—the United States objected, calling an ultimately inconclusive conference between the three outside powers. After a faction of Samoans resisting German influence inflicted significant casualties on the chancellor's forces, the tensions threatened to spill into open war.

Cleveland had no desire to bring Samoa under the American umbrella (he recalled a consul who accepted, without authorization, an offer to make the kingdom an American protectorate), but he was equally unwilling to see the country absorbed by Germany. In what would ultimately prove perhaps the sharpest foreign policy leadership of either term, he met the German naval presence around the islands by deploying three American warships, an escalatory move tempered by an immediate State Department remonstrance that the United States desired nothing so fervently as a diplomatic solution. Bismarck was already in the process of backing down when a devastating cyclone struck Samoa in March 1889, wrecking most of both countries' fleets. The dispute would eventually be resolved by diplomatic means, with the United States, the United Kingdom, and Germany agreeing to a tripartite protectorate. Cleveland, by then out of office, disapproved of the resolution, having hoped to preserve Samoan autonomy and keep the United States from getting further enmeshed in the situation.*

A similar sense of justice—and a similar aversion to expansionism—would animate his response to the Hawaiian controversy in the early days of his second term. There had been an American presence in the islands since the 1820s, when the first New England missionaries sought to bring Christianity to the Pacific. In the ensuing decades, however, the focus of Hawaii's American population had grown decidedly less spiritual. With the rise of a lucrative sugar industry in the islands, the expats came to play a dominant role in the kingdom's economy. Two-thirds of Hawaii's plantations were owned by its white population,[2] with Americans holding 80 percent of the island nation's wealth despite making up less than 20 percent of the population.[3] As their capital grew so, too, did their impatience with the Hawaiian monarchy, which many American and European elites regarded as feckless and unaccountable. The result was the imposition of the "Bayonet Constitution" in 1887, an upending of the Hawaiian government forced on King Kalakaua by the implied threat of force.

The gambit had been engineered by the Hawaiian League, an alliance of American planters and foreign business interests, many of whom took American annexation of the islands as their ultimate goal. The new constitution neutered the monarchy at the expense of the Hawaiian legislature, placed property requirements on the franchise, and expanded the right to vote to American and European resident aliens (but not to those from Asia).[4] Though the upheaval took place during Cleveland's first term, it attracted little attention from the White House, where it was regarded (as was typical for the time) as a purely

---

*The tripartite protectorate would prove short-lived. Another civil war broke out within a decade, culminating in a convention of the three powers in which Germany was given possession of the present-day nation of Samoa, while the United States acquired the eastern islands that now constitute the territory of American Samoa. Control of the western islands would transfer from Germany to New Zealand during World War I, with Samoa ultimately obtaining its independence in 1962.

internal affair. The only consequence for Washington was that an ener-vated Kalakaua acceded to giving the United States exclusive access to Pearl Harbor as a coaling and refueling station.

In the years between the adoption of the Bayonet Constitution and Cleveland's return to office, Kalakaua had died of kidney failure, leaving the throne to his sister Liliuokalani, the only queen in the kingdom's history. The new monarch regarded herself as the avenging angel of native Hawaiians, aiming to restore their influence along with the power of the throne. In January 1893, Liliuokalani sent Hawaii's legisla-ture out of session and announced that she would propound a new con-stitution: one that limited the franchise to male Hawaiian citizens—either native-born or naturalized—and left her virtually unchecked by her cabinet (the body to which the Bayonet Constitution had shifted most meaningful executive power). The proposal was unilateral and made no pretense of following a sanctioned legal process, though criticism on those grounds was difficult to sustain given the equally lawless origins of the existing constitution. If adopted, her constitution would have made the monarchy even more powerful than it had been before Kalakaua was forced to the negotiating table.[5]

It was a risky effort, not least because it united Hawaii's white elites and the foreign diplomatic corps—all of whom attempted to dissuade the queen—in opposition. The stakes were enormous: many of Liliuo-kalani's detractors already believed that the fall of the monarchy was a question of *when* rather than *if.* That was especially true of John L. Stevens, the Harrison administration's minister to the islands, a disciple of James G. Blaine, and a dedicated proponent of annexation. Indeed, as events unfolded in Honolulu, Stevens wrote to John Foster, Blaine's suc-cessor as secretary of state, that "the Hawaiian pear is now fully ripe and this is the golden hour for the United States to pluck it." That the senti-ment may not have been universally shared by the locals did not trouble the ambassador, who noted that "the main part of the opponents of an-nexation are the lower class of natives, led by unscrupulous foreigners of little property...."[6]

It is an underappreciated feature of American history that much of the nation's territorial expansion owes to diplomatic or military officials operating with near autonomy because of their distance from Washington. James Monroe and Robert Livingston came into the negotiations that ultimately produced the Louisiana Purchase authorized only to spend $10 million to acquire New Orleans and/or France's share of Florida. When they discovered that Napoleon was willing to part with all of his territorial holdings on the continent for $15 million, they took the deal without being able to secure President Jefferson's approval. Sixteen years later—by which time Monroe himself was president— America acquired the rest of Florida from Spain as the result of a dispute that began when General Andrew Jackson crossed into Spanish territory without authorization from Washington. John Stevens, America's man in Honolulu, was intent on adding his name to that list.

Liliuokalani's plans for a new constitution precipitated an immediate backlash. With both her cabinet ministers and the foreign diplomatic corps opposed, she agreed to a delay, but not to a retreat. This was enough to lead her opponents—now organizing under the banner of the Committee of Safety—to move on a permanent resolution: removing the queen from power. When the committee presented this possibility to Stevens, he replied that, though he had always supported the monarchy in the past, "in this case he considered the position taken by the Cabinet and people a just and legal one, and the attempt made by the Queen a revolutionary one; and that if asked by her for his support he would not give it; and on the contrary he should recognize the Cabinet as the supporters of law and as possessing the authority of Government so long as they were supported by any respectable number of responsible citizens...."[7]

It was this prospect that led Stevens to give orders for the Marines aboard the USS *Boston* to come ashore, ostensibly for the protection of American lives and property (this was not an unprecedented move—Marines had been called into Hawaii during a minor rebellion in 1889, a fact Stevens would later use in his defense). On January 16,

1893, 162 U.S. Marines arrived on Oahu, and while the landing party would not actively be involved in efforts to topple the government, their presence alone tamped down any possibility that the monarchy would resist. On January 17, the day after the Marines came ashore, members of the Committee of Safety occupied the Aliolani Hale, the seat of government—a surprisingly easy task, given that most of the royal officials were away trying to negotiate a diplomatic modus vivendi. A new government was declared, the queen's ministers (most of whom had already accepted the situation as terminal) capitulated, and Liliuokalani agreed to step aside on the condition that her abdication be regarded as temporary pending an appeal of her claim to the U.S. government. Stevens conferred America's recognition of the aborning government before the sun went down.

Within two weeks, Hawaii's new leaders would request that the United States accept the island nation as a protectorate, claiming that American military forces were necessary to keep other powers like Britain from staking their own claims. Stevens granted the request, and Old Glory replaced the Hawaiian flag in the skies over the capitol. At the same time, delegations representing both the provisional government and the monarchy sped to Washington to make their case.

The Harrison administration had not authorized Stevens's excesses, nor did it accept them without reservations. Secretary of State Foster, though an expansionist, was careful to stipulate that American protection could not extend to an intrusion upon Hawaiian sovereignty. The White House, however, regarded the events in the islands as something of an inevitability. Harrison thus had no compunctions about fast-tracking an annexation treaty to the Senate, a document he accompanied with the observation:

> It is quite evident that the monarchy had become effete and the Queen's Government so weak and inadequate as to be the prey of designing and unscrupulous persons. The restoration of Queen Liliuokalani to her throne is undesirable, if not impossible, and

unless actively supported by the United States would be accompanied by serious disaster and the disorganization of all business
interests. The influence and interest of the United States in the
islands must be increased and not diminished.[8]

There was a reason for the rush: Harrison had less than a month
left in office. In private, he lamented that "the Hawaiian question did not
come six months sooner or sixty days later, as it is embarrassing to begin
without the time to finish. Still, we may be able to mark out some policy
that will be safe and that my successor will follow."[9] On that latter front,
he would be sorely disappointed.

A few weeks before his inauguration, Cleveland called together John
Carlisle, his soon-to-be secretary of the Treasury, and Walter Gresham,
his soon-to-be secretary of state, to discuss the annexation treaty at the
Lakewood, New Jersey, cottage where he was vacationing. Whether
because of his inherent aversion to expansionism or because of the
specifics of the Hawaiian case (circumstantial evidence suggests that the
president-elect may have received a dispatch relaying Liliuokalani's
version of events), he dispatched the two men to Washington to inform
the Senate that he wanted to consider the events in more detail before
settling on a course of action. On March 9, a few days after his inauguration, Cleveland withdrew the annexation treaty entirely.[10]

Though subsequent events might imply that Cleveland had a plan
in mind from the start, contemporary evidence suggests that the president's ambivalence was in earnest. As with many of the most momen-
tous issues he faced during his time in office, he genuinely desired more
time to study the matter before settling on a course of action, telling his
advisors that he hadn't made up his mind on annexation, and that "we
ought to stop, look, and think."[11] While the stopping and thinking
would happen in the White House, the looking was delegated to James
Blount, a newly retired Georgia congressman who had chaired the
House Foreign Relations Committee and was deployed to Honolulu to
investigate and report back.

Blount was an odd choice insofar as he could hardly be imagined neutral on the question. The former representative was notoriously opposed to expansionism, and, as an outspoken believer in white superiority, no fan of territorial acquisition that would necessitate bringing "alien populations" into the American family. If he could be convinced of the case for annexation it would surely have passed the Senate by overwhelming margins. But Blount could not be convinced.

Upon arrival in Honolulu, Blount was intent that the United States cease to bare its teeth. He ordered the Marines sent back to the *Boston* and the American flag lowered from in front of the capitol. He also went to great pains to demonstrate his neutrality, refusing an offer to use the queen's carriage while also rejecting the posh accommodations offered him by the wealthy annexationists.[12] He was, from the perspective of both sides, maddeningly opaque. No one knew exactly what Blount was going to tell Grover Cleveland—in fact, no one knew the exact nature of his orders from the president—but as time passed the annexationists began to whisper that Blount was falling under the sway of the royalists. Whether that disposition was driven by a sober analysis of the facts, Blount's ideological priors, or a combination of the two, it was certainly the case that the report that arrived at the White House in the summer of 1893 came down firmly on the side of Liliuokalani. It was the Committee of Safety, Blount averred, rather than the queen that had committed the real act of revolution. The usurpation had occurred in opposition to the will of the Hawaiian people, he concluded—and it would not have succeeded without the criminal complicity of agents of the United States government.[13]

Whether there was ever a serious chance that Cleveland could have come to any other conclusion—there was initial speculation that he withdrew the treaty simply to slow the process and get more credit for the eventual annexation—it was now certain that he would oppose American acquisition of the islands. Moreover, he was not even interested in an American protectorate, the fallback option upon which the provisional government had settled. Grover Cleveland was a man who often thought of foreign policy questions as equity suits. The United States—or, rather, John Stevens cloaked in the power of the federal government—had done wrong by the Kingdom of Hawaii. The remedy was straightforward: restore the status quo ante.

This prescription was easier said than done—and wasn't even a matter of consensus within the cabinet. Secretary of State Gresham, who shared Cleveland's legalistic disposition and his moralistic streak, presented the matter as a simple ethical equation: "Should not the wrong done to a feeble but independent state by the abuse of the authority of the United States be undone by restoring the legitimate government? Anything short of that will not, I respectfully submit, satisfy the demands of justice."[14] Olney, however, worried that Gresham's position was long on idealism and short on feasibility. It was already October by the time that Cleveland and his cabinet were deciding how to proceed. Was it practical, with the provisional government having been in control of Hawaii for nine months, for the official position of the United States government to become "give it back"? And what if Hawaii's new rulers refused? Would the United States then be willing to use force to restore Liliuokalani to her throne? Wouldn't that require a declaration of war from Congress? And what would happen were the queen to be reinstated? The Cleveland administration may have believed the annexationists were in the wrong, but they had nevertheless been operating under what they believed to be the blessing of the federal government. Was the fate of those men, certain to be branded insurrectionists, to be left to a revanchist queen to decide?

They were eminently reasonable questions, though Cleveland and his cabinet did not answer them in an eminently reasonable fashion. Their solution: Cleveland's newly appointed minister to Hawaii, former Kentucky representative Albert S. Willis, would handle the matter diplomatically, securing a restoration for the queen on the condition that she would grant amnesty to her usurpers. Liliuokalani's consent was to be secured first.

It did not go well. Willis paraphrased the results of their initial November 13 meeting in a telegram to Gresham that simply read "Views of first party so extreme as to require further instructions."[15] What that meant, according to Willis's subsequent description, was that the queen's counteroffer to the amnesty proposal was "that such persons should be beheaded and their property confiscated to the government."[16] (Liliuokalani would later dispute that she ever referred to beheading, though she did not quibble with the allegation that she had suggested execution.)

Willis chipped away at the queen for more than a month before she finally agreed to Cleveland's terms. Unfortunately, two factors made the outcome moot. First, there had been a basic flaw in the American diplomat's methods: if Willis had hoped to make any meaningful progress, he should've been shuttling back and forth between Liliuokalani and the provisional government in order to determine if a mutually satisfactory set of terms existed.* Instead, he had conducted negotiations solely with the queen, hoping to have everything in place before presenting an offer to Sanford B. Dole, the head of the new Hawaiian government. When the terms were offered a few days before Christmas, Dole not only rejected them out of hand but also refused to recognize the American government's right to adjudicate such matters in the first place. Even that act of defiance, however, was somewhat academic in light of the second development of December 1893: Cleveland had already washed his hands of the matter.

As Willis's dispatches from Honolulu began to make clear that there would be no diplomatic resolution to the Hawaiian controversy,

---

*Given the high stakes involved, why didn't Secretary of State Gresham travel to Hawaii to conduct the negotiations himself? There *was* precedent for sending a secretary of state abroad: William Seward had visited the Caribbean during Andrew Johnson's administration. Moreover, the nearly five-thousand-mile journey to Hawaii could be made with surprising speed given the transportation constraints of the day: Cleveland noted that it took the diplomatic delegations from the islands about two weeks to reach Washington. In a sign of the changing times, diplomatic travel for the secretary of state would become normalized beginning with the administration of Cleveland's successor, William McKinley.

Cleveland came to the conclusion that no further progress could be made through the powers of the presidency. It was unlikely that force would be used—public opinion in the United States ran heavily on the side of the Republican expansionists and even some congressional Democrats regarded the acquisition of Hawaii as unexceptionable— but on the off chance that the military *was* called in, authorization would have to come from Congress. Thus, on December 18, 1893, the president sent to Capitol Hill a special message turning over the Blount Report, laying out his diagnosis of the situation in the Pacific, and shifting responsibility to the legislative branch, the only move he imagined consistent with the constraints of the Constitution.

The Hawaii message is one of the most poignant documents to issue from either of Cleveland's terms, both because of its deeply felt sense of injustice and because of the utter impotence that underpinned it. It is easy to canonize Cleveland on the basis of the sentiments therein. It is just as easy to criticize him for the fact that they were, from the moment of their delivery, a dead letter.

The document's opening was remarkable, providing a perhaps un-precedented example of a commander in chief so ashamed of the nation's conduct that he questioned whether he even understood the country he ostensibly led: "I suppose that right and justice should determine the path to be followed in treating this subject. If national honesty is to be dis-regarded and a desire for territorial extension or dissatisfaction with a form of government not our own ought to regulate our conduct, I have entirely misapprehended the mission and character of our govern-ment and the behavior which the conscience of our people demands of their public servants."[17]

Cleveland did not tar Harrison or the Senate that took the annex-ation treaty under consideration as complicit in injustice; he laid the blame squarely on the shoulders of Stevens for deceiving them. The moral indignation that spilled forth was extraordinary, not just a con-demnation of a plot hatched in Honolulu, but an indictment of a school of thought that traced all the way back to the adage in Thucydides's

Melian Dialogue that "the strong do what they can and the weak suffer what they must."[18] The passage deserves to be quoted in full:

[I]n the present instance our duty does not, in my opinion, end with refusing to consummate this questionable transaction. It has been the boast of our government that it seeks to do justice in all things without regard to the strength or weakness of those with whom it deals. I mistake the American people if they favor the odious doctrine that there is no such thing as international morality; that there is one law for a strong nation and another for a weak one, and that even by indirection a strong power may with impunity despoil a weak one of its territory.

By an act of war, committed with the participation of a diplomatic representative of the United States and without authority of Congress, the government of a feeble but friendly and confiding people has been overthrown. A substantial wrong has thus been done which a due regard for our national character as well as the rights of the injured people requires we should endeavor to repair. The provisional government has not assumed a republican or other constitutional form, but has remained a mere executive council or oligarchy, set up without the assent of the people. It has not sought to find a permanent basis of popular support and has given no evidence of an intention to do so. Indeed, the representatives of that government assert that the people of Hawaii are unfit for popular government and frankly avow that they can be best ruled by arbitrary or despotic power.

The law of nations is founded upon reason and justice, and the rules of conduct governing individual relations between citizens or subjects of a civilized state are equally applicable as between enlightened nations. The considerations that international law is without a court for its enforcement, and that obedience to its commands practically depends upon good faith instead of upon the mandate of a superior tribunal, only give additional sanction to the law itself and brand any deliberate infraction of it not merely as a wrong, but as a disgrace. A man of true honor protects the unwritten word which binds his conscience more scrupulously, if possible, than he does the bond a breach of which subjects him to legal liabilities. And the United States, in aiming to maintain itself as one of the most enlightened nations, would do its citizens gross injustice if it applied to its international relations any other than a high standard of honor and morality.

On that ground the United States cannot properly be put in the position of countenancing a wrong after its commission any more than in that of consenting to it in advance. On that ground it cannot allow itself to refuse to redress an injury inflicted through an abuse of power by officers clothed with its authority and wearing its uniform; and on the same ground, if a feeble but friendly state is in danger of being robbed of its independence and its sovereignty by a misuse of the name and power of the United States, the United States cannot fail to vindicate its honor and its sense of justice by an earnest effort to make all possible reparation.[19]

It was perhaps the rhetorical high-water mark of his entire eight years in office. And it was utterly inert. Cleveland imagined a world governed according to his own sense of forbearance, yet ultimately lacked any of the resources necessary to make that world a reality. There had been a time when the mayor of Buffalo bellowed and his city aldermen stood at attention. Now President Grover Cleveland roared . . . and Congress yawned. The legislative branch would do nothing to bring about the reparation he proposed. It was John Stevens's vision that would win out, albeit by inches.

Congress would commission another report on the events surrounding the Hawaiian Revolution, this one produced by John Tyler Morgan, an expansionist Democratic senator from Alabama. The final document contradicted Blount's account at nearly every turn, including in its judgment that Stevens had not exceeded his rightful authority.* In 1894, the Senate passed the Turpie Resolution, locking in the status quo: no further attempt to annex the islands, but also no attempts to restore Liliuokalani or unseat the provisional government. It also signaled America's commitment to keeping other foreign powers out of Hawaii, making the country a de facto protectorate if not a de jure one. The same year, a new constitution was adopted creating the Republic of Hawaii. The members of the provisional government allotted themselves a majority in the constitutional convention, drawing up a document that disenfranchised a greater proportion of the native population and completely denied the vote to the islands' immigrant Asians. The following year, an unsuccessful attempt by natives to put the queen back in power led to Liliuokalani being put on trial in her own throne room and sentenced to five years in prison at hard labor (it was later reduced to an eight-month sentence served in her palace).

The affair came to its inevitable conclusion in the summer of 1898, when President McKinley, citing the Spanish-American War as proof of the need for an American outpost in the Pacific, pushed the annexation of Hawaii through Congress. When asked for comment by the Associated Press, the retired Cleveland responded bitterly: "I regarded, and still regard, the proposed annexation of those islands as not only opposed to our national policy, but as a perversion of our national mission."[20]†

Having already provided a dramatic example of his opposition to American imperialism, the second term would also provide Cleveland

---

*To this day, the Blount Report and the Morgan Report—the two most comprehensive accounts that rely on contemporaneous testimony—jostle for primacy when it comes to interpreting the events of the Hawaiian Revolution. Both documents provide tendentious renderings of what happened in 1893, which led the late Ralph Kuykendall, perhaps the most distinguished historian of Hawaii, to compare them to opposing lawyer's briefs.

†That point of view would eventually get another hearing in the White House, but it would take a century: in 1993, on the hundredth anniversary of Liliuokalani's ouster, President Bill Clinton signed a congressional resolution issuing an official apology for America's role in the Hawaiian Revolution—a document that cited the Blount Report and Cleveland's message to Congress.

with an equally grand stage for his opposition to foreign intrusions into America's sphere of interest. The precipitating circumstance was a long-simmering border dispute between Venezuela and the neighboring colony of British Guiana. The two nations had been arguing the matter intermittently since 1841, when the British-employed, German-born surveyor Robert Schomburgk drew boundary lines giving the United Kingdom control over the mouth of the Orinoco River, the vital 1,500-mile-long waterway running from deep in the Venezuelan interior out into the Atlantic. During Cleveland's first term, the United States had offered its good offices to help facilitate a resolution of the controversy, but the British government was perpetually cool to proposals to submit the dispute to arbitration. In 1887, a frustrated Venezuela broke off diplomatic relations with the United Kingdom.

When Cleveland returned to office, Caracas became intent on pressing the matter, mounting a full-court press through their diplomatic corps, a campaign catalyzed by the Venezuelan government's retention of William L. Scruggs, a former American minister to the country, as a lobbyist. Scruggs mounted an aggressive advocacy campaign, penning a widely distributed pamphlet titled *British Aggressions in Venezuela, or the Monroe Doctrine on Trial*. He also succeeded in getting a unanimous resolution through Congress in early 1895 endorsing Cleveland's call for the border dispute to be put to arbitration. In fact, Cleveland had perennially raised the point in his annual messages to Congress, but the coordinated lobbying campaign—along with the news that gold had been discovered in some of the disputed territory—quickly elevated it to a top-tier issue.

The Venezuelan crisis would showcase many of the same shortcomings that had plagued Cleveland's conduct regarding Hawaii: an overly legalistic view of what were, at their core, pure power struggles; a disposition toward moral grandstanding even if it proved counterproductive to achieving the desired ends; and a certain recklessness about overplaying the diplomatic hand the United States had been dealt. In March 1895, Cleveland deputized his secretary of state and kindred spirit

Walter Gresham to prepare a comprehensive report on the border dispute for the cabinet's consideration. The report got finished, but so did the secretary. By the end of May, Gresham was dead of pneumonia. (Cleveland, aboard the train that returned his secretary of state's body to Chicago, was said to have gone missing only to be found weeping over Gresham's coffin. He had been there for over an hour.[21])

The president's subsequent decision to make Richard Olney Gresham's successor meant that the Venezuela controversy was going to be handled with just as much self-righteousness, but also with a healthy dose of the Massachusetts lawyer's signature truculence. Why exactly Cleveland allowed Olney to take the lead on drafting another report—this one to be transmitted to London as the definitive statement of America's position on the controversy—is a mystery. The new secretary of state was a man of many gifts; a capacity for pacification wasn't one of them. Why the president encouraged Olney's report even upon reading the combative draft is even more baffling. Remarkably, Cleveland pronounced that "I do not think that, in all my experience, I have ever had to deal with any official document, prepared by another, which so entirely satisfied my critical requirements."[22] That was a different reaction than it would engender on the other side of the Atlantic.

Had Olney or Cleveland been thinking like statesmen they would have realized their task was relatively straightforward: convince the British government that a diplomatic resolution of the border dispute would involve less pain and less potential risk than letting the situation fester. Instead, Olney penned a windy, supercilious homily full of pronouncements that seemed to serve no purpose apart from antagonizing Westminster. In one especially gaseous passage, he wrote:

> The people of the United States have a vital interest in the cause of popular self-government. They have secured the right for themselves and their posterity at the cost of infinite blood and treasure. They have realized and exemplified its beneficent operation by a career unexampled in point of national greatness

or individual felicity. They believe it to be for the healing of all nations, and that civilization must either advance or retrograde accordingly as its supremacy is extended or curtailed.

Imbued with these sentiments, the people of the United States might not impossibly be wrought up to an active propaganda in favor of a cause so highly valued both for themselves and for mankind. But the age of the Crusades has passed, and they are content with such assertion and defense of the right of popular self-government as their own security and welfare demand. It is in that view more than in any other that they believe it not to be tolerated that the political control of an American state shall be forcibly assumed by an [sic] European power.[23]

There were likely better ways to win the cooperation of Her Majesty's government than by suggesting it was playing a role in civilizational regression. In one spectacularly ill-advised passage, Olney even crowed, "Today, the United States is practically sovereign on this continent, and its fiat is law upon the subjects to which it confines its interposition." This surely came as a revelation to a British government exercising dominion over next-door Canada, as did Olney's confident declaration, "That distance and three thousand miles of intervening ocean make any permanent political union between an [sic] European and an American state unnatural and inexpedient. . . ."[24] It was all in service of the new secretary of state's larger argument: the Monroe Doctrine, propounded to prevent further European colonization of the Americas, was to be applied just as strenuously to resist European expansion of existing holdings.

Even in later years, neither Cleveland nor Olney seemed to appreciate how spectacularly counterproductive the letter had been. In his retirement, the former president would refer to the document approvingly as Olney's "twenty-inch-gun"[25] and compare the dispute between Venezuela and Britain to a pair of neighbors fighting over a fence line "until all account of cost and all regard for the merits of the contention give place to a ruthless and all-dominating determination, by fair means or foul, to win. . . ."[26] This view fundamentally misapprehended the situation by failing to consider the dispute from the perspective of either party. Britain fretted that submitting to arbitration in this case would open the door to such tactics elsewhere around the globe, and that an infelicitous placement of the borderline could leave British citizens living on Venezuelan soil. Venezuela, meanwhile, faced the prospect that one of its most vital trade routes would fall under undisputed British sovereignty. It is unlikely that either party regarded the stakes as comparable to those concerning the placement of a fence.

The British prime minister, Lord Salisbury, responded to the American statement in two separate missives—one devoted exclusively to deconstructing Olney's theory of the Monroe Doctrine, one to litigating his account of the border dispute. Both documents displayed a mix of annoyance with American impudence and condescension at how poorly executed the effort had been. While acknowledging that the Americas were rightly closed for new settlement, Salisbury denied that the Monroe Doctrine had any bearing on the subject at hand, writing that the border dispute was "a controversy with which the United States have no apparent practical concern. It is difficult, indeed, to see how it can materially affect any State or community outside those primarily interested, except perhaps other parts of Her Majesty's dominions, such as Trinidad. The disputed frontier of Venezuela has nothing to do with any of the questions dealt with by President Monroe."[27] As for Olney's account of the border dispute, Salisbury derided its one-sided narrative as the clear product of Venezuelan influence. He reasserted what had become London's standard position on the issue: the British government was open to arbitration, but only within narrow parameters that would exclude consideration of much of the territory to which Venezuela felt it had a rightful claim. Wrote Salisbury, "Her Majesty's Government are convinced that in similar circumstances the Government of the United States would be equally firm in declining to entertain proposals of such a nature."[28]

Already in for a penny, Cleveland reacted to Salisbury's dispatch by going in for a pound. If the British government was going to obstruct arbitration, the president resolved to simply go around them. He thus submitted a special message to Congress in December 1895 in which he turned over Salisbury's correspondence and proposed an American-made solution to the impasse: a congressionally created commission that would determine the boundaries impartially. Once the lines were settled, the president pronounced, "it will, in my opinion, be the duty of the United States to resist by every means in its power, as a willful aggression upon its rights and interests, the appropriation by Great Britain of any lands or the exercise of governmental jurisdiction over any territory which after investigation we have determined of right belongs to Venezuela." Underscoring the implicit threat of conflict, he added, "In making these recommendations I am fully alive to the responsibility incurred and keenly realize all the consequences that may follow." Cleveland concluded with a peroration reminiscent of his language during the Hawaii controversy:

> I am . . . firm in my conviction that while it is a grievous thing to contemplate the two great English-speaking peoples of the world as being otherwise than friendly competitors in the onward march of civilization and strenuous and worthy rivals in all the arts of peace, there is no calamity which a great nation can invite which equals that which follows a supine submission to wrong and injustice and the consequent loss of national self-respect and honor, beneath which are shielded and defended a people's safety and greatness.[29]

Why would Cleveland so dramatically up the ante? To be sure, there were legitimate national security interests in play. Gresham had noted before his death that Britain's territorial claims had "silently increased by some 33,000 square miles" during a relatively brief period in the 1880s and only expanded thereafter.[30] The American position that claims at that scale were de facto new colonization, and thus in violation of the Monroe Doctrine, was not as far-fetched as Lord Salisbury made it seem. Cleveland also worried that the border dispute would lead to open warfare between Venezuela and Britain, and hoped that forcing the issue toward a resolution would forestall that possibility. Secretary of the Interior Hoke Smith recalled of the note to Congress that "I heard him refer to this message . . . as his 'peace message,' and as 'the only way, in his judgment, to prevent a probable collision between the two nations.'"[31]

It was also the case, however, that Cleveland and Olney were seduced by a strain of idealism that prefigured early-twentieth-century initiatives like the League of Nations and the Kellogg-Briand Pact (the 1928 international agreement renouncing the use of war) in its conviction that civilization had advanced to a point where legal mechanisms could obviate the use of force. In his letter to Salisbury, Olney had dismissed the prospect of settling the border dispute through "an appeal to arms—a mode of settling national pretensions unhappily not yet wholly obsolete." Warfare, he editorialized, was "condemnable as a relic of barbarism and a crime in itself."[32] Cleveland would later sound a similarly utopian note, referring to arbitration as "the refuge which civilization has [built] among the nations of the earth for the protection of the weak against the strong, and the citadel from which the ministries of peace issue their decrees against the havoc and barbarism of war."[33]

If Cleveland was intent on playing peacemaker, someone forgot to tell Congress—and the public. Popular sentiment was overwhelmingly on the president's side and the legislative branch made the requested appropriation for a border commission within just a few days. The reaction, however, stemmed not from a belief that Cleveland was a farsighted statesman but from the supposition that he had succumbed to the war fever of the expansionist jingo movement. That was certainly the case in England, where Cleveland aide George Parker, then serving as consul in Birmingham, reported that "talk was heard of the necessity for the mobilization of the army and other war preparations."[34] The message to Congress had been met with a similar reception stateside, where the *Washington Post* reacted with a delighted, "It is the call to the arms; the jingoes were right after all, and it is not to be the fashion henceforth to sneer at patriots and soldiers."[35] Massachusetts senator Henry Cabot Lodge, one of the leading lights among the jingos, was said to be "bubbling over with delight."[36] Everyone seemed convinced that the president meant war—except the president. Cleveland could draw a straight line in his mind between his opposition to Hawaiian annexation and his attempt to resolve the Venezuelan controversy—yet all the same people who hated him for the former seemed to love him for the latter.

It was indeed militarism that brought the Venezuela crisis to its conclusion—just not the militarism of any of the parties to the dispute. Only two weeks after Cleveland's message, Germany's Kaiser Wilhelm II issued a congratulatory telegram to the president of Africa's Transvaal Republic for repelling a British raid. News of the communication, widely interpreted as an escalation of German hostility to Britain—and a potential foreshadowing of German intervention in British national interests—prompted outrage in the United Kingdom and pushed the Venezuela controversy to the back burner. Recognizing the comparatively modest stakes, London agreed to negotiations, eventually accepting arbitration with the stipulation that any area occupied for more than fifty years would not be subject to review (this led to rioting in Caracas, as Venezuela had rejected similar terms on multiple occasions in the past).[37]

The ultimate result of arbitration—which didn't reach its conclusion until 1899, long after Cleveland had left office—would be that Britain retained most of its territorial claims, though Venezuela did manage to win back the mouth of the Orinoco River. Much like the Hawaii controversy, the ratio of effort to outcome was decidedly lopsided. Cleveland's grander vision of arbitration as a tool to stave off conflict was also disappointed. Simultaneous with the Venezuela negotiations, an American and British treaty pledging both countries to arbitration as a future means of dispute resolution was hammered out, winning widespread support from the public, the press, and, eventually, Cleveland's successor, William McKinley. The Senate, however, was not nearly as enthusiastic. The treaty was gutted through the amendment process and ultimately went down to defeat in the early days of McKinley's administration. Cleveland would later tell friends that the defeat of the treaty was the greatest disappointment of his second term.[38] Given the storm clouds that gathered in his final two years in office—a point at which he was virtually abandoned by his own party—it's amazing that he could choose just one.

FIFTEEN

In Due Time

On July 7, 1895, while the first family was vacationing at Gray Gables, Frances gave birth to her third daughter, Marion. It was virtually the only good news that accompanied her husband's final two years in office.

The tone for those years was set early and unmistakably with the outcome of the 1894 midterm elections, one of the most decisive party repudiations in American political history. Between the anemic economy and the administration's refusal to indulge the public's growing appetite for overseas adventurism, the table was set for a Republican resurgence. Moreover, the deepening schisms within the Democratic Party had left the president utterly isolated. Republicans and dissenting Democrats could point to the same set of facts: while the ordinary farmer watched his crop prices nosedive and the ordinary worker saw federal troops called in to put down labor strikes, Grover Cleveland's main obsession seemed to be preserving a monetary system that satisfied Wall Street. Whether it was a fair caricature or not was beside the point; it was a politically profitable one. Thomas Reed, the Republican congressman from Maine who had served as Speaker of the House for two years during Harrison's administration (and who would soon be restored to the position), predicted of the midterms, "The Democratic mortality will be so great . . . that their dead will be buried in trenches and marked 'unknown.'"[1]

By the time that November 1894 rolled around, Reed looked more prophetic than hyperbolic. The losses Democrats suffered in the House of Representatives remain to this day the worst in American history. The 53rd Congress, which sat during the first half of Cleveland's second term, had 218 Democrats in the lower chamber. Its successor, the 54th Congress, had only 93. In twenty-four states, Democrats did not win a single House seat; in six more, they took only one. Republicans also moved into the majority in the Senate, though the margins were close enough that the balance of power was held by the handful of Populists elected to the upper chamber (in addition to their own victories, the Populists had also denied Democrats seats in many contests by fusing with Republicans).[2]

The Democrats had been reduced to a southern rump party—and even there the GOP was making encroachments, picking up multiple seats in Kentucky, Maryland, Missouri, North Carolina, Tennessee, and Virginia. Champ Clark, the Missouri Democrat who would later serve as Speaker of the House for most of Woodrow Wilson's presidency, declared the results of the election "the greatest slaughter of innocents since the days of King Herod."[3] The outcome was not merely a temporary rebuke to a party presiding over economic torpor, but rather the beginning of a full-scale realignment. It would be eighteen years before Democrats gained back control of both houses of Congress, by which time the newly progressive party, headed by the incoming president Wilson, was unrecognizable as the one once helmed by Cleveland.

Like any leader who sees a realignment *away* from his party, Cleveland suffered his fair share of blame for the Democrats' prolonged descent into irrelevance. Some of it was surely deserved. Stubborn and self-assured, he was temperamentally and philosophically unfit to manage the internal divisions. Cleveland—of whom one Washington journalist wrote, "He did not know what conciliation meant and rubbed out sore spots with a brick"[4]—was not the most adroit negotiator, but even the most adroit negotiator would have had difficulty unifying Democratic factions whose views of public policy were irreconcilable.

Some of the fault, however, surely belonged to the institutional Democratic Party, which could hardly claim buyer's remorse over a man who had already served one term as president and whom they had given their presidential nomination for a *third* time. It was all well and good to complain that Cleveland was inflexible upon issues he regarded as matters of principle, but was this new information? The lineage of that criticism ran all the way back to his time as Erie County sheriff. Indeed, his nomination in 1892 had been predicated in large part on an act of defiance, his outspoken refusal to go along with the party's growing fetish for free silver. It was too late in the day to carp about the fact that Grover Cleveland meant what he said.

For his part, Cleveland did not necessarily interpret the electoral outcomes as a personal rebuke—at least not entirely. Rather, he thought Democrats were reaping the consequences of embracing the silver mania and failing to live up to their word on the tariff. Whether he truly believed this or was engaged in one of his trademark bouts of rationalization, the implications were the same: Grover Cleveland was not for turning. The next step in the economic crisis would make that all too clear—and essentially complete his alienation from the party.

While the rest of the country was focused on the election, a characteristically tunnel-visioned Cleveland spent November of 1894 consumed by the continued threat to the country's gold reserves. The bond issuance earlier that year had proved only a palliative, and by shortly after the midterms, the reserve had dwindled once again, now hitting $61 million. The president and Secretary of the Treasury Carlisle set to work on plans for another round of bonds, this one designed to address the shortcomings of its predecessor (Carlisle leaned on banks to prevent the withdrawal of gold to purchase bonds, in addition to threatening to publish the names of anyone who did so). The resulting issue—bought up entirely by a syndicate of bankers—pushed the reserves back up over the $100 million mark, but its success would prove evanescent. As the depression deepened in the winter, and as it became apparent that the popular sentiment toward silver was waxing rather than waning, anxious investors began withdrawing gold at a previously unseen pace. By January 31, less than three months after the second round of bonds, the gold reserve had declined to an alarming $45 million.[5] At one point, $20 million had been withdrawn in just nine days.

The Cleveland administration had never been so close to the abyss. Unless the underlying factors driving withdrawals were arrested, another round of bonds would likely repeat the same pattern: a brief stabilization, followed by a rapid drawdown of reserves. More ominously, the sense of panic that was pervading the economy—banks and corporations that had previously kept their wits about them had begun hoarding gold as well—suggested a level of confidence so low that another round of bonds could fail outright. The velocity with which gold was being snatched from the Treasury meant that the gold standard could be dethroned within a matter of weeks. If Washington couldn't find a sufficient number of bond buyers, the sense of dread would almost certainly become a contagion.

Adding to Cleveland's difficulties were the legal constraints on his power to remedy the situation. His authority for the bond issuances, derived from statutes passed long before his presidency, compelled higher interest rates and shorter maturities than he thought useful for the circumstances. Moreover, they stipulated payment to bondholders in "coin." Because investors could not be confident what metal that coin would be denominated in, the provision had the effect of reducing the value of the securities. Most important, to the president's mind, was that the Treasury was still obligated under law to return to circulation any paper currency turned in for gold, meaning that the same greenback could be used to call upon the reserves ad infinitum. The president begged Congress to remedy these defects.[6] The Congress, consisting mainly of Democrats who would be happy to see the gold standard fail and Republicans who would be happy to see Cleveland fail, remained unmoved.

If soldiers come to learn that there are no atheists in a foxhole, presidents likewise discover there are no ideologues in the midst of an economic crisis. In the same fashion that George W. Bush would declare over a century later that he had "abandoned free-market principles to save the free-market system," Cleveland's eventual solution to the gold problem was to violate one of his most deeply held beliefs: that the blending of government and corporate power was per se unacceptable. With the gold standard on the verge of collapse and the possibility that a failed bond issuance would only accelerate the slide into chaos, Cleveland and Carlisle desperately needed an alternative. They found it in the person of J. P. Morgan.

The Treasury Department, for which necessity had become the mother of invention, invited Morgan and his fellow financier Augustus Belmont Jr. to discuss the terms of a private sale, in which they would purchase $100 million worth of bonds with gold procured from Europe (so as to ensure no danger to the American supply). Cleveland was not exactly ecstatic about the arrangement, especially when the financial titans countered with an offer to purchase $50 million, get only half the gold from Europe, and ratchet up the interest rate. Once Congress officially rejected Cleveland's request to change the terms on which the administration could issue bonds, however, the die was cast. While the president was still angling for better terms with Morgan and Belmont, what little leverage he had was undermined during a February 8 White House meeting with the duo. Midway through the discussion, as a blizzard raged outside, a telephone call came in from the New York sub-treasury reporting that it had less than $9 million in gold coin left on hand. Morgan, whose knowledge of the financial terrain was unrivaled, noted that he was aware of an incoming withdrawal of $12 million, a fact that Carlisle confirmed.[7] The collapse could come before the end of their meeting. Cleveland took the deal.*

The final terms of the agreement were for $65 million worth of bonds, with half the gold brought in from Europe. More important,

---

*This was not to be the last time that J. P. Morgan propped up an ailing U.S. economy. Morgan would provide similar assistance during the Panic of 1907, a downturn that ultimately inspired the creation of the Federal Reserve System in 1913.

Morgan and Belmont pledged to use their combined market power to restrain the foreign exchange market, hampering the outflow of gold from the United States to abroad. There was no sign of gratitude from Congress. When Cleveland sent a message to Capitol Hill indicating that the federal government could save $16 million on the deal by simply stipulating that the bonds would be paid back in gold rather than "coin," the legislature refused to act. Too many members had either felt the sting that came with supporting Cleveland's economic policies or reaped the rewards of opposing them.

The Morgan Bonds, as they came to be known, did not fully stanch the bleeding, but they did mark an inflection point after which economic instability on the same scale was never again seen during the Cleveland administration. Morgan and Belmont's manipulation of the gold market successfully reduced the pace of the outflow, and Cleveland and Carlisle only had to resort to one further bond issuance, approximately a year later (thanks to the lack of volatility, they were able to do this via a public sale rather than another private arrangement). The gold reserve eventually stabilized, buttressed largely by the election of the pro-gold William McKinley as president alongside a sympathetic Congress.* By the time all was said and done, the Cleveland administration had issued $262 million worth of gold bonds, a total equal to $8.3 billion in 2020 dollars. The cost to the country was steep. The cost to Cleveland was political excommunication.

In his weaker moments, Cleveland had always had a penchant to imagine himself a martyr. On the gold issue, no imagination was necessary. For populist Democrats who already imagined the president a puppet of the eastern financial establishment, there could be no more explicit confirmation than a closed-door White House deal that put the fate of the country's economy in the hands of J. P. Morgan. Never mind that Congress had, by inaction, precluded any viable alternative. Never

---

*The silver issue would eventually lose its salience thanks in large part to an increase in the supply of gold at the end of the decade, driven in part by the Klondike Gold Rush. With more of the metal in circulation, the reliance on gold was no longer deflationary.

mind that Cleveland had made the deal only because he thought the very health of the economy was at stake. It was all evidence that the president had given himself up to the plutocracy. Not content to simply criticize the fact that Morgan and his associates had turned a handsome profit by reselling the bonds (though they did precisely that), the critics even alleged, without any evidence, that Cleveland and Carlisle had received kickbacks on the action. Rising to denounce the deal in the House, William Jennings Bryan first had the clerk read Shylock's bond from *The Merchant of Venice*.[8] Milford Howard, an irascible silverite Democrat from Alabama, would later draw up an impeachment resolution, though it went nowhere.[9]

For his part—could it be any other way?—Cleveland was defiant. In later years, he would write, "Without shame and without repentance, I confess my share of the guilt."[10] He would also deliver a biting riposte to the Bryanite critique of his collaboration with financiers like Morgan, saying "it never occurred to any of us to consult in this emergency farmers, doctors, lawyers, shoemakers, or even statesmen. We could not escape the belief that the prospect of obtaining what we needed might be somewhat improved by making application to those whose business and surroundings qualified them to intelligently respond."[11] If that seemed like gratuitous snark, it masked a deeper resentment: Cleveland still believed it was his disinterested classical liberalism, not Bryan's populism, that really protected the average American. In a letter to a group of Democratic New York editors a few months after the Morgan Bonds, he pronounced, "Our party is the party of the people not because it is wafted hither and thither by every sudden wave of popular excitement and misconception, but because, while it tests every proposition by the doctrines which underlie its organization, it insists that all interests should be defended in the administration of the government without especial favor or discrimination."[12] Those words were certainly true of Cleveland. By this point, however, he had no especially plausible claim to speak on behalf of the Democratic Party.

The trajectory of the party was now firmly toward free silver and populism, no matter the views emanating from the White House. Indeed, Cleveland came to be thought of as an utterly marginal figure. His assistant, Robert O'Brien, would later report that the president was in such low demand that "[h]is mail shrunk [until] it was less that than an ordinary businessman."[13] It didn't help matters any that events beyond his control were only deepening the perception that his administration was out of touch. The Supreme Court's decision to invalidate the income tax came only a few months after a ruling denying the federal government the ability to regulate manufacturing under the Sherman Antitrust Act.* Both opinions were authored by Chief Justice Melville Fuller, appointed by Cleveland in his first term, and both made the populists livid. John Altgeld, the Illinois governor with whom Cleveland had tangled over the Pullman Strike, declined an invitation to a Democratic dinner celebrating Thomas Jefferson's birthday with a bit of editorialization about the party's decline since the days of the third president: "Jefferson belonged to the American people; Cleveland to the men who devour widows' houses."[14] As state conventions gathered to choose delegates for the 1896 Democratic National Convention in Chicago (a compromise between the gold bugs' desire to meet in New York City and the silverite petition to convene in St. Louis), similar denunciations came from the grassroots. A delegate to the Ohio meeting referred to Cleveland as the "Benedict Arnold of the Democratic Party." The keynote speaker at the Illinois convention asked for God's forgiveness for Cleveland's nomination, lamenting that "[t]here must be a limit even to divine wrath, for we have since then been beaten as with a scourge of scorpions."[15]

For his part, the much-maligned president vacillated between de-

---

*The criticism of Cleveland as being indifferent to antitrust enforcement clung to him long after his presidency, though it is largely inaccurate. In his final annual message to Congress, the president called for greater state and federal antitrust efforts and argued that under the influence of the trusts "the farmer, the artisan, and the small trader is . . . relegated to the level of a mere appurtenance to a great machine, with little free will, with no duty but that of passive obedience, and with little hope or opportunity of rising in the scale of responsible and helpful citizenship."

spondency and obduracy. He never doubted he had pursued the correct course—but he was plagued by the fact that his party had refused to follow him. In a letter to his friend L. Clarke Davis, the president, noting cracks in his long-standing faith in the American people, confessed that "I have moments—only moments—sometimes of distressing misgivings. I am praying now that the prevalent infection may pass away, leaving life and hope of complete recovery. In the meantime, the brood of liars and fools must have their carnival."[16] To his former postmaster general, Donald Dickinson, Cleveland wrote, "I have never felt so keenly as now the unjust accusations of political antagonists and the hatred and vindictiveness of ingrates and traitors who wear the stolen livery of [the Democratic Party]."[17] In another note shortly thereafter, a fatigued Cleveland noted that there were "[t]wo things I am longing for—the adjournment of Congress and the 4th of March, 1897 [Inauguration Day]."[18]

Yet for all the venom, Cleveland remained unbowed. Sounding a note that would be echoed by many embattled presidents in the future, he told Dickinson, "I will patiently wait for the final verdict of my countrymen, which will certainly in due time be returned."[19] Told by his erstwhile congressional ally William L. Wilson (who, having lost his House seat in the 1894 bloodbath, had been absorbed into the administration as postmaster general) that history would judge him kindly, Cleveland playfully responded, "I am not concerning myself about what history will think, but contenting myself with the approval of a fellow named Cleveland whom I have found to be a pretty good sort of fellow."[20]

That reservoir of self-assurance would come in handy as the 1896 presidential election approached—and it became increasingly clear that the winner, regardless of party, would turn his back on the legacy of Grover Cleveland. In the run-up to the Democratic convention, Cleveland took one last, desperate stand against free silver, writing an open letter to Democratic voters in which he argued that the policy would "inflict a very great injury upon every interest of our country which it has been the mission of the Democracy to advance, and will result in lasting disaster to our party organization."[21] He even helped to organize a campaign aimed at keeping southern Democrats from falling under silver's sway (an effort motivated by the perception that their compatriots in the West were already too far gone to be saved).* None of it worked. There was a revolutionary mood brewing in the Democratic Party. The last person anyone was inclined to take guidance from was the head of the old regime. Only in elite precincts—among the eastern Democrats and some of the remaining Mugwumps—did he retain any purchase.

Despite his falling stock, there was still widespread speculation that Cleveland might pursue a third term—though the exhausted, isolated president never gave the prospect any serious consideration. Indeed, any sober observer realized the notion was utterly implausible.

The results of the 1896 national conventions set the country up for a stark choice in the general election. Meeting in St. Louis in June, the Republicans nominated McKinley (who had served as Ohio's governor after narrowly losing reelection to his House seat in the Democratic wave of 1890), with New Jersey politico Garret Hobart as his running mate. The GOP's decision to adopt a platform embracing the gold standard led to a walkout of silverite Republicans, adding a dash of political opportunism to the ideological fervor that Democrats already felt on the issue. By the time the party gathered in Chicago for their own convention a few weeks later, it was obvious that any attempt to keep Democrats in the embrace of Clevelandism was a rearguard action doomed to failure.†

The party platform denounced Cleveland across the board, not only in its calls for silver but in its condemnation of federal intervention in

---

*Cleveland didn't help matters any when he insulted the region in a speech at Carnegie Hall, warning that lawlessness and vice on the western frontier could lead to "badly regulated municipalities, corrupt and unsafe territories, and undesirable states."
†The silverite momentum was augmented by the disorganization of their opposition. Because Cleveland had never bothered to officially disclaim interest in a third term, there was no consensus candidate for pro-gold Democrats.

the Pullman Strike, its indictment of the administration for "trafficking with banking syndicates" in the bond issuances, and even its criticism of his tariff reforms as insufficient.[22] From the floor of the convention, North Carolina senator Ben Tillman hissed, "You ask us to endorse Cleveland's fidelity. In reply, I say he has been faithful until death—the death of the Democratic Party!"[23] It was a brutal attack, made worse by the fact that everyone knew Tillman was stabbing a political corpse.

Tillman's remarks may have been inflammatory, but they quickly receded from memory when William Jennings Bryan took to the stage later the same day. There was already a sense of religious fervor present in Chicago, a radical scent on the wind that led one Cleveland ally to declare, "For the first time I can understand the scenes of the French Revolution!"[24] All the convention needed was a candidate to channel that energy. By the time Bryan finished his address—a rhetorical masterpiece that so captivated the audience that they fell silent upon its conclusion before breaking into frenzied, almost manic applause—it was clear that the thirty-six-year-old former congressman from Nebraska was the vessel for which they had been looking. The speech, best known for its peroration—"Having behind us the producing masses of this nation and the world . . . we will answer their demand for a gold standard by saying to them: you shall not press down upon the brow of labor this crown of thorns, you shall not crucify mankind upon a cross of gold"—had sealed the matter: William Jennings Bryan was shortly thereafter nominated as the Democratic Party's candidate for president.* The era of Grover Cleveland—in fact, the entire philosophy of Grover Cleveland—was not just over; it was anathematized.

Cleveland was at Gray Gables during the convention, and his correspondence from the time reveals a man who, though technically still in office, was spiritually retired. In a letter to Olney, he washed his hands of the entire party: "Has it occurred to you that in view of the outcome

---

*Grover Cleveland was the last American president whose voice was never captured on an audio recording. In a cruel twist of fate, a widely circulated internet clip that purports to be of Cleveland is actually a recording of the "Cross of Gold" speech.

at Chicago no one can be fool enough to charge against this Administration the disasters that await the Democratic Party?"[25] In a more pugilistic mood, he wrote to his friend Don Dickinson, "If ever there was a penitentiary devoted to the incarceration of those who commit crimes against the Democratic Party, how easily it could be filled just at this time!"[26]

Grover Cleveland's argument that a Democratic Party that abandoned the principles of his administration was doomed to electoral failure may have been self-serving, but that didn't mean that it was wrong. Bryan's nomination immediately engendered a split in the party (though the nomination of a candidate from the Cleveland wing would surely have done the same). In September 1896, a group of breakaway gold Democrats, organized under the mantle of the "National Democratic Party," convened in Indianapolis to choose their own ticket, which paired John Palmer, a former Republican governor of Illinois and former Union general, with Simon Bolivar Buckner, a former Kentucky governor and former Confederate general. The Palmer/Buckner ticket never had a serious prospect of prevailing, nor was that its real purpose. The gold Democrats were simply spoilers, intended to throw the election to McKinley.

Cleveland's own correspondence at the time made clear that he, too, was hoping for a Republican victory, not only for the immediate good of the country but because of his hope that a loss would force Democrats to return to the true faith. Nevertheless, this presented two practical problems for the president: whether to speak out publicly on the race and how to handle members of his administration who pledged their support to Bryan.

On the first matter, Cleveland chose silence, realizing that "the Cleveland luck" had long since passed its expiration, and any words he spoke publicly were more likely to backfire than to effectively advance his cause. His only utterances would be elliptical. Delivering a speech ostensibly about the role of universities at Princeton's 150th anniversary shortly before the election, he told the assembled audience:

When popular discontent and passion are stimulated by the arts of designing partisans to a pitch perilously near to class hatred or sectional anger, I would have our universities and colleges sound the alarm in the name of American brotherhood and fraternal dependence. . . .

When selfish interest seeks undue private benefit through governmental aid, and public places are claimed as rewards of party service, I would have our universities and colleges persuade the people to a relinquishment of the demand for party spoils and exhort them to a disinterested and patriotic love of their government for its own sake, and because in its true adjustment and unperverted operation it secures to every citizen his just share of the safety and prosperity it holds in store for all.[27]

It was not a speech about the election. But it was also not *not* a speech about the election. Cleveland's meaning was clear enough for all those who cared to hear it.

Behind closed doors, he availed himself of no such subtleties. He chafed at administration appointees who threw in their lot with Bryan.[28] For the most part, he kept his powder dry, though not in the case of his cabinet. Secretary of the Interior Hoke Smith, a Georgian, asked for Cleveland's indulgence of his support for Bryan on the grounds that "the local situation is such in my own state that I consider the protection of person and property involved in the local Democratic success, which can only continue through Democratic organization."[29] Cleveland's response was icy: "The vital importance of the issues involved in the national campaign, and my failure to appreciate the inseparable relation between it and a state contest, prevent me from realizing the force of your reference to the 'local situation.' I suppose much was said about the 'local situation' in 1860."[30] Cleveland accepted Smith's resignation.*

---

*Despite his seeming bitterness, the president was able to separate personal and political disputes. Smith was invited back to the White House for a postelection cabinet dinner.

Election day was never going to bring Grover Cleveland vindication, but it did bring him relief. McKinley, dominating the Northeast and the upper Midwest while also grabbing California and Oregon, triumphed with 271 electoral votes. Bryan, who swept the South and swallowed up most of the Great Plains and the interior West, had 176. As much as the two men differed, Cleveland and Bryan shared the ability to shift blame when convenient, and the latter's diagnosis of his loss was straightforward: "I have borne the sins of Grover Cleveland."[31]

As Cleveland prepared to turn the White House over to McKinley, there was still one piece of official business to tend to. Since February 1895, the Spanish had faced a revolt in their colony of Cuba, a conflict that implicated the United States not only because of geographical proximity and commercial ties with the island but because much of the resistance had been fomented by Cuban expatriates in the United States and freelancing American expansionists. The conflict stirred the same jingoistic sentiments Cleveland had tried to suppress when it came to Hawaii—notions he told his friend Richard Watson Gilder amounted to "an epidemic of insanity."[32] And, as with Hawaii, Cleveland took it as his charge to keep them at bay. The president declared the United States' neutrality on the matter and imposed naval patrols to keep unauthorized Americans from making their way to the island.

Cleveland was not initially convinced that the rebellion would amount to anything—this was not the first time that Cuba had seen an attempted revolt against Spanish rule. By early 1896, however, with the rebellion still running strong, American public sentiment running in favor of the insurgents, and the disruptions to trade ongoing, the Republican Congress was pushing for action. While not acknowledging a legitimate right for the legislative branch to intervene in the matter, Cleveland and Olney nevertheless approached the Spanish government with an offer to provide America's good offices to help negotiate a modus vivendi that would keep Spain in control of the island and provide for greater Cuban autonomy. Madrid waved the offer away

Absent Spanish cooperation, Cleveland felt he had no reasonable policy levers at his disposal. He was skeptical of the idea of the United States buying the island, though he did not reject it out of hand. While he didn't believe Cuba could successfully be integrated into the United States, he also didn't believe that the United States could acquire the island and turn it over to the rebels, a notion he dismissed as "absurd."[33] In his final annual message, delivered to Congress during the lame-duck period in December 1896, Cleveland temporized, reminding the legislative branch that his conception of foreign policy relied on a constraint born out of moral considerations: "The United States has ... a character to maintain as a nation, which plainly dictates that right and not might should be the rule of its conduct." Nevertheless, he signaled that American patience would not last forever, that if Spain's "hopeless struggle [to reestablish sovereignty] has degenerated into a strife which means nothing more than the useless sacrifice of human life and the utter destruction of the very subject matter of the conflict, a situation will be presented in which our obligations to the sovereignty of Spain will be superseded by higher obligations, which we can hardly hesitate to recognize and discharge."[34]

The signal to Spain was clear enough: "Solve this problem before the United States has to solve it for you—which my successor is much more likely to do."* The Republican Congress, however, wasn't content to wait on McKinley. Frustrated that the annual message hadn't been more forceful, both houses began moving a resolution that would have compelled American recognition of Cuban independence—an act that would have been tantamount to an act of war against Spain. Given the composition of both chambers, the measure would have likely passed even over a Cleveland veto—presenting the daunting prospect that a lame-duck president would be dragged into military conflict against his will. A distressed Olney took his objections straight to the press, noting, "The power to recognize the so-called Republic of Cuba as an indepen-

---

*In February 1897 the Spanish did offer a package of governmental reforms, but they were refused by the Cuban rebels.

dent state rests exclusively with the executive."[35] Had the measure passed, the dying days of Grover Cleveland's second term would have been consumed by yet another crisis—and, doubtlessly, more economic turmoil as a result. Just this once, the cup passed from him. Congress backed down. Cuba—and everything else—would be William McKinley's problem now.*

By the time Inauguration Day came around on March 4, 1897, Grover Cleveland was exhausted, unpopular, and abandoned by his party. The figure who had come to Washington twelve years prior as the second-youngest president up to that time, who had risen from the Buffalo mayor's office to the White House in three short years seemingly on the basis of moral courage alone, was only a faint approximation of the man who stood next to McKinley as Melville Fuller issued the oath of office. He was now two weeks away from his sixtieth birthday, his hair lightening, his body never having regained the sturdiness it possessed before his surgery, the shadow of cancer always lingering just offstage. There was no more Cleveland luck. There were no more Mugwump hosannas. There was just a country that, in the view from the Capitol that day, looked like it had left him behind. His postmaster general William L. Wilson said of Inauguration Day, "I felt very much like I had been to a funeral."[36]

Cleveland had only two recorded observations of the day. He noted that McKinley was "an honest, sincere, and serious man." And he confessed that he envied the incoming president—because he was able to have his mother in attendance at his inauguration.[37]†

Free at last from his gilded prison, Grover Cleveland did precisely what anyone who had been paying attention for the dozen years that he'd been at the center of American politics would have predicted: he went hunting, spending three weeks traipsing around the South with

*The United States eventually declared war on Spain in April 1898.
†That Cleveland had not been given a similar opportunity always stung him. His subtle tribute to his mother at both of his inaugurations was to be sworn in on a Bible she had given him in his youth, a volume he kept in his desk throughout his presidency.

friends. There were longer-term plans, too. He and Frances, after initially considering a move to the New York City suburbs of Westchester County, settled instead on a retirement in Princeton, a town that had enchanted them both during his recent visit to the university campus. In that day before presidential pensions, he fretted about how to bring in an income, writing his de facto financial advisor E. C. Benedict for guidance and poignantly noting, "I am not afraid of the attempt [to make money] and I ask no quarter, but the fact that in the course of nature a young family may be left dependent on my present care and economy cannot, of course, be banished from my mind."[38]

To his friend Richard Watson Gilder, he wrote that "I have been so prodded by public duty for a number of years past that I have had no opportunity to look after the preservation of anything that might be useful in writing history. 'Things done are won, but joy's full soul lies in the doing,' has perforce been the motto over my mantel."[39] Besides, as he had told Gilder a few months earlier, there were already a number of worthy expositions of his presidency being written up. "The one I have heard the most of," he noted, "was when I last got sight of it running towards Prof. ____, the man who made the motion at Princeton. I've forgotten his name."[40]

The professor's name was Woodrow Wilson.

SIXTEEN

Paths Unknown

They had been friendly once, if not exactly friends. There were similarities between the two men: both the sons of Presbyterian ministers; both imbued, as a result, with a thoroughgoing moralism that often expressed itself as stubbornness. Early on, there was an ideological affinity as well: in the late nineteenth century Woodrow Wilson was still a conservative Democrat. He recoiled at the party's embrace of William Jennings Bryan, refusing to support him in 1896.[1] The following year, Wilson's *Atlantic Monthly* essay, "Mr. Cleveland as President," provided the single most insightful defense of the elder man's administration written by a contemporary. Elsewhere in his scholarship, Wilson would identify Cleveland as the only president to play "a leading and decisive part in the quiet drama of our national life" since Lincoln.[2]

There were differences as well—and in light of subsequent events they seem dispositive. Cleveland's education had ended at the age of sixteen; Wilson had a PhD from Johns Hopkins. Cleveland was a northerner who wanted to see the regional schisms of the Civil War left behind; Wilson, raised in Georgia and South Carolina, defended the Confederacy in his youth and, even in later years, never seemed to shake many of its racial prejudices.[3] Wilson derided the shortcomings of the Constitution in his scholarly work; Cleveland once explained to a friend that the reason a man of his limited education had been able to succeed as president was that "[t]he Constitution is so simple and so strong that all a man has to do is to obey it and do his best and he gets along." Wilson had visionary pretensions; Cleveland, in the words of the same friend above referenced, "was inclined to be afraid of grandiose plans to bring about in startling new ways a different sort of a world from the one we live in. The fact that he had done his duty in high places and in great crises, never suggested to him to try to remake society or recreate government."[4]

It is a remarkable twist of history that these two men—the only Democrats elected president in the seventy-two years that separated the election of Abraham Lincoln from that of Franklin D. Roosevelt— were, for more than a decade, neighbors and eventually colleagues in the then-still-quaint trappings of Princeton, New Jersey. It is even more remarkable that a growing antagonism between them in later years helped, in a roundabout way, to propel Wilson to the White House— and to permanently erase Clevelandism from the Democratic Party.

Though Cleveland withdrew his erstwhile objections to honorary degrees and accepted a doctor of laws from Princeton in 1897 (he winkingly reported to Olney that "the Latin investiture of the degree was to my certain knowledge faultless"),[5] he did not take on an official role with the university until 1899, when he began an annual lecture series, focusing each year on a different policy challenge faced by his administration.* Two years later, he accepted a seat on Princeton's board of trustees. When Wilson was installed as the university's president in 1902, it was Grover Cleveland presiding, delivering a speech in which he praised the incoming executive's "high character and acute moral sense."[6] The former commander in chief lent his support to Wilson's proposal to reorganize the administration and reduce the use of electives in the

---

*Cleveland's lectures—which covered the fight over the Tenure of Office Act, the Venezuela conflict, and the Pullman Strike—were later collated with a long essay he had written on the bond issuance controversies into a book titled *Presidential Problems*. The collection represents the only in-depth writing he ever produced about his time in office. It is a disappointing volume, insofar as Cleveland provides little behind-the-scenes perspective, relying mostly on a recapitulation of official documents. It is also incomplete: he abandoned plans for another lecture that would have covered the dispute over Hawaii.

curriculum. He also put his shoulder to the wheel in support of the new president's extraordinary fund-raising goals. (Wilson's plan called for raising an amount nearly twenty-five times greater than the university's annual budget.[7]) Cleveland helped convince Andrew Carnegie to fund the creation of an artificial lake that to this day is home to Princeton's crew program, and later implored the Scottish magnate to provide funds for the university's construction of a graduate school.[8] It was that latter project that would put Cleveland and Wilson at loggerheads— and shape the future not only of the school but of the nation.

Cleveland's closest friend and ally at Princeton was Andrew F. West, a classicist to whom the former president had taken such a shine that he christened his new house "Westland" in his honor. When, in 1900, the board of trustees approved plans to create a graduate school, West was chosen as the inaugural dean, though the actual inception of the program lay several years in the future. By 1906, a graduate campus had still not been constructed and the relationship between Wilson and West was fraying. The latter, having been offered the presidency of the Massachusetts Institute of Technology, threatened to leave the university. West was only persuaded to stay when the board's graduate school committee—chaired by Cleveland—pledged to break the logjam and get the new facilities built.[9] That process, however, touched off a round of bitter internecine warfare when Wilson insisted that the graduate school be located in the center of the existing campus, while West demanded that it be placed at a separate location, removed from undergraduate affairs. Though the stakes seemed small to outsiders (and even many board members), both men regarded the debate as central to the character of the university. Cleveland took West's side, occasioning repeated arguments between the former and future presidents of the United States, one of which concluded with Wilson icily responding to Cleveland's criticisms with a portentous "You will live to regret what you have said."[10]

Wilson was half-right. Cleveland surely would have regretted the ultimate consequences of the dispute—if he had lived to see them. The debate over the placement of the graduate campus rose to such high dudgeon that when West's vision finally won out in the spring of 1910, a dejected Wilson decided to leave Princeton behind for politics. Six months later, he was elected governor of New Jersey. Two years after that, he was elected the twenty-eighth president of the United States. Grover Cleveland was in his grave by the time of the 1912 election, but had he not been he surely would have marveled to see Professor Wilson, now an outspoken progressive, carrying the party standard. Even more improbably, the candidate who sounded most like a Cleveland Democrat was the doomed Republican incumbent, William Howard Taft. It was the beginning of a transformation in both parties after which the limited-government conservatism embodied by Cleveland would never again dominate among Democrats.

All things considered, it was probably for the best that Cleveland didn't live to see the change, which would have disturbed the otherwise redemptive arc of his retirement. When the former president first came to Princeton in March 1897, he felt a man alone, rejected by both his party and his country. In one oft-repeated anecdote, a dog belonging to a visitor to Westland managed to sneak into the living room and plop its head onto the ex-president's lap. When the embarrassed owner attempted to remove his pet, the former president waved him off: "No, let him stay. He at least likes me."[11]

For the next several years Cleveland would inveigh, by turns, against the false faith of the Bryan Democrats and the imperialist excesses of the McKinley Republicans. In his first speech after leaving office, he lit into the populists, whom he judged to be manipulating their followers into a false sense of victimization: "Those enlisted in this crusade of discontent and passion, proclaiming themselves the friends of the people, exclude from that list all their countrymen except those most unfortunate or unreasonable, and those whom they themselves have made the most discontented and credulous."[12] When Bryan received the party's presidential nomination again in 1900, many anxious Democrats wrote to Cleveland hoping for his permission to support the candidate, rationalizing that the campaign this time around was at least more focused on anti-imperialism than free silver. The former president, deeply resentful, would not budge. When Bryan lost a second time, and by bigger margins than he had in 1896, Cleveland—who had always augmented his principled argument with the contention that Bryanism was a sure political loser—felt vindicated.

His mirth at Bryan's defeat didn't translate into any special satisfaction with the prospect of a second term for President McKinley, however. Cleveland was grieved that the administration had allowed itself to be seduced by the imperialist bent of the Republicans in Congress. On the eve of the Cuban conflict's transformation into the Spanish-American War, he wrote to E. C. Benedict that "we face today a sad, afflictive war, that our own people will soon look upon as unprofitable and avoidable, and which, in the sight of contemporaneous judgment and history, may seem unjustifiable."[13] When Hawaii was annexed by the United States only a few months later, he wrote to Olney, "Hawaii is ours. As I look back upon the first steps in this miserable business, I am ashamed of the whole affair."[14] When the United States acquired the Philippines at the conclusion of the war, Cleveland announced it imperative "that our occupation and control of the islands shall only be for the purpose of leading the inhabitants to the establishment of their own government . . . and that when with our friendly aid such purpose is accomplished, our control and occupation of the islands shall cease. . . ."[15] (The Philippines would not be granted independence until 1946.)

Unlike with Bryan, however, Cleveland retained a personal respect and affection for McKinley. When the president was gunned down by an assassin in Buffalo in 1901, his predecessor delivered a heartfelt memoriam at Princeton, encouraging students to look to McKinley for proof of the principle that their character would ultimately do more than their intellect to determine their worth to society: "Here was a most distinguished man, a great man, a useful man—who became distinguished, great, and useful because he had, and retained unimpaired, qualities of heart which I fear university students sometimes feel like keeping in the background or abandoning."[16] He was solicitous of the young new president, too—a kindness that would not go forgotten. Theodore Roosevelt would later say that the kindest words he got from anyone upon assuming the White House came from Grover Cleveland. The actual sentiment is lost to history, but Roosevelt described it to Mrs. Cleveland as being "as if a senior had patted a freshman on the shoulder and assured him of his success."[17]

Ironically, the sentiment would grow widespread over the next few years that the ideal person to challenge Roosevelt in the 1904 election was . . . Grover Cleveland. The idea was implausible for at least two reasons: (1) Cleveland had a principled opposition to third terms* and (2) his health had declined to the point where he was no longer equal to public office. More salient, however, was one factor suddenly *not* obstructing his electoral prospects: his popularity. In the aftermath of Bryan's second defeat, both the Democratic Party and the country at large began reassessing their views of the man who seemed to have left Washington virtually friendless.

No moment represented the about-face as clearly as Cleveland's attendance in April 1903 at an event in St. Louis commemorating the hundredth anniversary of the Louisiana Purchase. He had largely abjured speechmaking in his post-presidency, disliking what he regarded as the torture of preparing his remarks and imagining himself a pariah even at Democratic events. He had certainly not spoken at any other mass gathering like this one. Yet when he took the stage in Missouri, his remarks coming right on the heels of Roosevelt's, something remarkable happened: Grover Cleveland, whom the nation couldn't wait to usher out of Washington six years earlier, inspired a round of sustained, thunderous applause that dwarfed that for the sitting president. The outpouring of affection was so dramatic that Roosevelt even felt compelled

---

*In 1940, Frances Cleveland refused to vote for Franklin Roosevelt, telling one of her children, "Your father never approved of a third term." She voted for FDR in 1944, however, saying, "Your father never said anything about a fourth term."

to mention it years later in a letter he wrote for Cleveland's memorial service. In the echoing of that applause a burden was lifted. The former president had imagined that he was doomed to a lifetime of public scorn. Frances would later testify, "From that moment, he was a different man."[18]

Even this burst of public approbation wasn't enough to make him seriously consider a fourth run for the White House, however. From virtually the moment chatter about a Cleveland campaign began he told friends and party operatives that he had no interest in the prospect. They encouraged him, however, to keep such pronouncements sotto voce, hoping to at least use him as a stalking horse for some other candidate of Clevelandite principles who could prevent the nomination of a populist (it was a testament to how much times had changed that Tammany Hall was among those on the former president's side of the party split).

Still, Cleveland seemed genuinely anxious that the whole thing was a ruse that would see him drafted into service at the last moment. In February 1904, he wrote to Dan Lamont, "I want to see the party succeed, but I hope there will be no idea of playing any kind of trick on me."[19] On the eve of the convention, nervous that he wouldn't be able to stop a draft movement from the remove of Gray Gables, he wrote to James Smith Jr., the chief power broker among New Jersey Democrats, insisting that he prevent his name from being put into nomination if such a stampede occurred.[20]

In the end, Grover Cleveland's wishes were heeded, though there was no question that the nomination could have been his for the taking.* Eight years after a Democratic convention that seemed to have been convened for the sole purpose of denigrating Cleveland's legacy, the

---

*Shortly after Cleveland avoided being drafted into the presidential race he was solicited to stand as the Democrats' candidate for governor of New Jersey, an offer he also declined. Had he succeeded in that pursuit he would have been one of only two people in American history to serve as the governor of two states. In the nineteenth century, Sam Houston was, by turns, the chief executive of both Tennessee and Texas.

1904 gathering in St. Louis included a moment where the mere mention of Cleveland's name generated "applause which lasted so long that the speaker had twice to take his seat before it subsided."[21] He was also paid the tribute of seeing the nomination go to an ideological kinsman, New York judge Alton B. Parker (Cleveland had hoped either Olney or former senator George Gray of Delaware would get the nod, but was satisfied with Parker's selection).

The satisfaction would prove short-lived, however. Contra Cleveland's predictions that a return to the true faith would also bring a return to power, Parker was utterly obliterated by Roosevelt in the fall, failing to win a single state outside of the South. A dumbfounded Cleveland began to wonder if he no longer understood the nation, writing to a friend "that sometimes, for a moment, the idea has entered my mind that a change in the character of our countrymen has taken place."[22] He would not live to see the 1908 convention and the third failed nomination of William Jennings Bryan, but the prospect was already on the horizon before his death. He openly talked of voting for a Republican in response, expressing a pronounced preference for Roosevelt's secretary of the Treasury, George Cortelyou—who had begun his career as Cleveland's private clerk in the second term.[23]

Cleveland's continued engagement with politics, though it occurred at the margins, was emblematic of a pathology typical to ex-presidents: he was restless. To Richard Watson Gilder he wrote, "I am not happy in the thought that sometimes crowds into my mind, leading to the fear that my working days are over . . . I am not sure that I am justified in *drifting* the rest of my life."[24] To another friend he noted that not having an outlet for his energies left him feeling "like a locomotive hitched to a boy's express wagon."[25] In an interview published posthumously in *American Magazine*, he confessed, "I am not sure I wasn't more unhappy out of office than in," adding, "I miss the strain, the spur of constant thinking, the consciousness of power, the knowledge I was acting for 70 million people."[26]

There were occasional projects to harness that excess energy. In addition to his responsibilities at Princeton, he would, from time to time, take on legal consulting work or write for publication, though he turned down offers to pen a regular column. Most of his written output was unremarkable, with the exception of an October 1905 piece in *Ladies' Home Journal* in which he opposed women's suffrage, arguing, "It is a mistake to suppose that any human reason or argument is needful or adequate to the assignment of the relative positions to be assumed by man and woman in working out the problems of civilization. This was done long ago by a higher intelligence than ours."[27] It sounds antediluvian to modern ears, but at the time it was representative of the views of significant swath of America—including Mrs. Cleveland, who would later become the vice president of the New Jersey Association Opposed to Women's Suffrage.

Cleveland's most notable post-presidential employment came in 1905, when he was asked to help rehabilitate the Equitable Life Assurance Society, a major insurance outfit under investigation for executive malfeasance. Though he had no previous experience in the insurance industry, it was the conviction of the firm's new controlling shareholder, Thomas Fortune Ryan, that Cleveland's distinctive value was his reputation for incorruptibility. Everything else he needed he could learn by study—as he always did. It was a good bet. The former president oversaw a reorganization of the firm's board that revived consumer faith in the industry to such an extent that he was subsequently asked to head a trade group for life insurance presidents, a part-time role he accepted only reluctantly and after his initial declination was refused.

The insurers weren't the only ones attempting to harness his reputation for probity—just the only ones who succeeded. He declined an offer from the Venezuelan government to sit on the commission that would arbitrate the boundary dispute, as well as one from President McKinley to be an arbitrator under the newly signed Hague Convention (an appointment he turned down in part because it came in the election year of 1900, and Cleveland thought it could be misinterpreted as a sign of partiality toward the incumbent president).[28] In 1902, he actually *volunteered* his services to Roosevelt when a major coal strike threatened to imperil the country's winter fuel supplies—a development that led to stirrings that TR might have to send in federal forces à la the Pullman Strike. Threatening to have troops work the mines while a Cleveland led-commission engaged in fact-finding, Roosevelt got both sides of the dispute to agree to arbitration—the preliminary negotiations for which resulted in the rejection of Cleveland as one of the mediators. This development irritated the former president—not because he wanted to be on the panel, but because he had never consented to be considered for it in the first place.*

There was one other task that Grover Cleveland could never be persuaded to take up, despite the importuning of many of his friends and admirers: writing a memoir. Early on in his retirement there were plenty of excuses. He argued that he hadn't kept his papers in order. He rationalized that "[w]hat I did is done and history must judge of its value, not I."[29] He reasoned that nothing he would write would sell anyway, since "No one wants to read anything from me in these days."[30] As time passed, however, he became more open to the idea. By 1905 he was writing to Gilder that he thought he might have something worthwhile to say—but that he feared nothing about it would be sensational enough to attract attention: ". . . I am by no means sure that it would be in tune with the vaudeville that attracts our people and wins their applause. Somehow, I don't want to appear wearing a fur coat in July."

In point of fact, an autobiographical project came tantalizingly close to reality. *McClure's Magazine* offered Cleveland an amount equal to about $300,000 in 2019 dollars for a twelve-part series of autobiographical essays. Cleveland rejected the offer but countered that he'd be willing to take on the project as an oral history if an interlocutor was provided. To the eternal frustration of future historians, *McClure's* de-

---

*He had only offered his services as an *investigator*, not a mediator, and he resented the fact that Roosevelt subsequently made the letter public, writing to Gilder that "there are some people in this country that need lessons in decency and good manners."

clined. For his part, the former president remained philosophical about the matter, softly noting to Gilder, "There is a circle of friends like you, who I hope will believe in me. I am happy in the conviction that they will continue in the faith whether an autobiography is written or not. I want my wife and children to love me now, and hereafter to proudly honor my memory. They will have my autobiography written on their hearts, where every day they may turn the pages and read it. In these days what else is there that is worthwhile to a man nearly 68 years old?"[31]

That delicacy and warmth of spirit was everywhere to be found in Cleveland's last years. A familiar pattern emerged in the tales from first-time visitors to Westland: most guests feared the acquaintance of a brusque, imperious malcontent. They found instead a gentle, shy host who preferred listening to talking, was more inclined toward a game of cribbage* than a discussion of matters of state, and, on the rare occasions when he mentioned his past station, always euphemized it as "when I was in Washington." Those who got to know him well were equally charmed by his dry wit and a kind of moral innocence that could express itself in moments of surprising poignance. In his remembrance of Cleveland, Andrew West, the Princeton dean with whom he had combatted Wilson, noted that the former president possessed a transcendentalist's reverence for nature:

A scene of sylvan beauty in the springtime, especially when the apple-blossoms were coming into flower amid the greenery and the songbirds were back again, moved him to deep silence. "I can't find a word for it," he said quietly on just such a day, after a

---

*Cleveland was a longtime cribbage player, but a truly shocking amount of his post-presidential correspondence is dedicated to the game. His favorite competitor was his old friend E. C. Benedict, the New York banker. In one especially spirited competition, Cleveland "won" from Benedict the *Oneida*—the yacht on which his cancer surgery had been performed in the second term. Because the former president was already free to use the vessel at his convenience, the change in ownership was purely pro forma.

flood of sunshine had burst through a light April shower. "What makes it so beautiful? There is no word good enough.'Ravishing' comes nearest, I think. Where does it come from? Do you know what I mean? It is too good for us. Do you understand me? It is something we don't deserve. . . ."

. . . One bright, still day in September he was fishing on a clear lake circled by hills covered with green forest, and only here and there were the leaves touched with crimson and gold. It was too much for him, and he stopped fishing. Then he gazed long and tranquilly at it all, as if spellbound. There was a look of joy in his face like that Fenimore Cooper gives in his novel to the old huntsman walking through the sunlit woods in calm communion with something beyond and back of what eyes could see. Long afterward he spoke of it, and with hesitation. He had felt it all.[32]

His other great vulnerability was children, a liability that only grew as the Cleveland household added two boys during his retirement: Richard, born in Princeton in 1897, and Francis, born at Gray Gables in 1903 (Cleveland was sixty-six at the time of his final child's birth). The former president was known to tear up watching his children playing in the yard. (He avoided the Christmas church services where children performed carols for the same reason.[33]) Frances later recalled a February evening when her husband overheard his young daughters mention that one little girl in their class had come up empty when the students received Valentines. The former president of the United States—the man who had sent federal troops to Chicago and whose signature move was a fist pounded into his desk—had his cheeks stained with tears at the idea of the child's heartbreak. A valentine bearing the name of Grover Cleveland was delivered to the little girl's home by messenger.[34]

For the first time in his turbulent life, Cleveland's retirement seemed to bring a measure of tranquility. Tragically, it would not hold. On January 2, 1904, Ruth Cleveland, the president's firstborn, was diagnosed with tonsillitis. As soon as the following day, she seemed to be showing signs of improvement. By the morning of January 6, however, she was diagnosed with diphtheria. Within twenty-four hours Ruth died, not quite thirteen years old. The January 8 diary entry in which the former president wrote simply, "We buried our daughter, Ruth, this morning" was scrawled in what one reader described as "a trembling, almost illegible hand."[35]

While Cleveland had never been a consistent churchgoer, the religious influence of his childhood, a consistent undercurrent of his adult life, only became more pronounced in his post-presidency. In the days following Ruth's death, however, he wrestled with his faith in a fashion he never otherwise expressed. On January 10, he recorded, "I had a season of great trouble in keeping out of my mind the idea that Ruth was in the cold, cheerless grave instead of in the arms of her Savior." The next day, he lamented, "It seems to me I mourn our darling Ruth's death more and more. So much of the time I can only think of her as dead, not joyfully living in heaven." In a demonstration of the resilience that had so often buoyed him throughout his life, by January 15 Cleveland would note, "God has come to my help and I am able to adjust my thought to dear Ruth's death with as much comfort as selfish humanity will permit." A few months later he would write to his sister, "We still miss dreadfully our dear Ruth; but I believe there has been given to both Frank and me such confident faith that it is well with her, and such a feeling that we are the only losers, as seems to be of very great comfort to us."[36]*

There were, however, limits to the president's capacity to cope—and one of the casualties was Gray Gables. In the early years of his retire-

---

*Despite her death at such a young age, Ruth proved to have the biggest cultural impact of all the Clevelands' children, albeit for a bizarre reason. The creators of the Baby Ruth candy bar claimed its name was inspired by Grover Cleveland's oldest child and the sensation caused upon her birth. That claim, however, has long been regarded with suspicion, given that the confection wasn't created until 1921. Skeptics of the official explanation have long argued that the supposed homage to Ruth was actually a cover story for the Curtiss Candy Company, the product's creator, to avoid having to compensate baseball great Babe Ruth, the likely inspiration for the name.

ment, which was littered with frequent fishing and hunting trips, the residence on Cape Cod—clearly the home to which Cleveland had the greatest emotional attachment over the course of his life—remained a sanctuary: the place where Grover Cleveland was allowed to be fully Grover Cleveland. Upon Ruth's death, however, the light went out of the place. Plans to build a canal near the property—along with Cleveland's sense that, in his advancing years, he might be better suited to recreation in the mountains—had already decreased the amount of time the family spent at Buzzards Bay. The first summer after Ruth's death, however, marked an inflection point. The ex-president wrote to his former cabinet member William Vilas that the Clevelands were headed to a cottage in the hills of New Hampshire so as not to subject the children "to any sad reminder of their sister's loss, which everything [at Gray Gables] would suggest."[37] The change proved to be permanent. He would eventually purchase a home, dubbed "Intermont," in Tamworth, New Hampshire, that would supplant the Massachusetts coast as his summer getaway. While he would occasionally sneak back to Gray Gables for a day or two of fishing, it never again played such a central role in his life.

A perusal of Cleveland's correspondence in his later years demonstrates a clear pattern, the tempo of which accelerated markedly toward the end of his life. Letters would issue from his desk at Princeton for most of the year. In the summer, they'd usually be dispatched from Gray Gables or, later on, Intermont. Sprinkled throughout the year would be dispatches from hunting trips, often in the South. Yet, once returned home, there were perennial complaints about his health. He'd often tell tales of gout that sidelined him for days and weeks. His digestion became so poor that he constantly kept a stomach pump at hand.[38] Eventually, the letters testify to hunting trips canceled because of his ailments. The periods of convalescence became longer (in one dispatch from September 1907 Cleveland describes having been incapacitated for thirteen weeks).[39] Richard Watson Gilder described him in the year

before his death as accompanied by a nurse and walking with the assistance of a cane.[40]

In early 1908, Cleveland repaired to Lakewood, New Jersey, a vacation spot he had frequented in the past, in an attempt to restore his
health, battered by a constellation of gout, gastrointestinal problems,
and ailments of the kidneys and heart. Though it is nowhere explicitly
acknowledged, the circumstances suggest that the former president, recently turned seventy-one years old, made peace with his mortality at
some point in the stay and decided to give up the fight. Stretched across
a mattress in the back of a private vehicle, he was transported back to
Princeton—the place, he had told E. C. Benedict a decade earlier, "where
I expect to live the remainder of my life, and at its end be laid to rest" [41]
—and never left again. Grover Cleveland died at home on the morning
of June 24, 1908. His last recorded words were "I have tried so hard to
do right."[42]

Two days later, the body of the twenty-second and twenty-fourth
president of the United States was interred at Princeton Cemetery, next
to the rose-strewn grave of his oldest daughter—and underneath a
gravestone that recorded no information apart from his name, his date
of birth, and his date of death. The Princeton-based playwright and
novelist Jesse Lynch Williams recorded that "his funeral, more private
than that of many an ordinary citizen, was so dramatically simple, indeed, that the representatives of foreign powers present could hardly
conceal their surprise."[43]

Cleveland's friend the journalist St. Claire McKelway reported that
the former president's courage stayed with him to the end. "As weakness
more encroached," he said, "he faced toward the inevitable with trust in
the Almighty and with good will to mankind. The intent look which
often came into his face was not due to apprehension."[44] At the time of
his death, the box next to Cleveland's bed contained a copy of the John
Greenleaf Whittier poem "At Last," a work that the president had cher-
ished ever since it was introduced to him by his friend and former secre-

tary of state Thomas Bayard, himself now a decade gone.[45] Its opening
stanza reads:

> When on my day of life the night is falling,
> And, in the winds from unsunned spaces blown,
> I hear far voices out of darkness calling
> My feet to paths unknown

"Someday, I'll Be Better Remembered"

There is no monument to Grover Cleveland in Washington—though he was, improbably, one of seventeen presidents selected for inclusion in a National Garden of American Heroes proposed by Donald Trump (plans for which were subsequently canceled by Joe Biden). There is no Grover Cleveland Museum, though an effort to that end—which would have appropriated a vacant library in Buffalo—was briefly undertaken in 2007. The only vestiges of Cleveland in the city he called home for over twenty-five years are a statue in front of Buffalo's City Hall (where it shares real estate with a likeness of the city's other president, Millard Fillmore) and an inconspicuous plaque marking the spot once occupied by his law offices.

There is no Cleveland estate that beckons visitors in the fashion of a Mount Vernon or Monticello. Most of the homes Cleveland lived in have long since been torn down. Gray Gables was converted into a hotel, which burned down in 1973; a private home inspired by Cleveland's was later built on the site. The "Westland" home in Princeton is in private hands, as is the "Intermont" property in New Hampshire. Apart from his grave, the only site that exists for those wishing to pay homage to the nation's twenty-second and twenty-fourth president is the modest

Caldwell, New Jersey, home where Grover Cleveland was born in 1837. It is hardly a tourist mecca. A representative local headline from 2019 read "That House You Drove by Across from Dunkin' Donuts? A President Was Born There."[1]

Grover Cleveland's lack of notoriety is, as an objective matter, inexplicable. Of the forty-five men who've served as president of the United States, Cleveland is one of only fourteen to have served eight full years; nearly all the rest are household names. He is one of only three presidents—Andrew Jackson and Franklin Roosevelt are the others—to win the popular vote three times. And he is, of course, the only president in American history to serve two nonconsecutive terms.

The Cleveland years did not lack for drama and the president himself did not lack for personality. All of the ingredients for a meaningful legacy are present. While there is no good case for Grover Cleveland to be on Mount Rushmore, there is likewise no good reason that he should be entirely absent from Americans' historical memory. Surely there is room for him in the ranks of presidents we regard as distinctive and significant even if they don't rise to the transcendent greatness of a Washington or a Lincoln.

That was certainly the verdict of many of his contemporaries. Mark Twain, a man not known for flattering politicians, declared Cleveland "the greatest and purest American citizen" and "a very great president, a man who not only properly appreciated the dignity of his high office but added to its dignity."*[2] In a commemoration of what would have been Cleveland's seventy-second birthday, the new president, William Howard Taft, said of his predecessor:

> He was a great president, not because he was a great lawyer, not because he was a brilliant orator, not because he was a statesman of profound learning, but because he was a patriot with

---

*Twain also compared Cleveland favorably to Theodore Roosevelt, the president at the time, declaring the difference between the two men "the contrast between an archangel and the Missing Link."

the highest sense of public duty; because he was a statesman of clear perceptions, of the utmost courage of his convictions, and of great plainness of speech; because he was a man of the highest character, a father and husband of the best type, and because throughout his political life he showed those rugged virtues of the public servant and citizen. . . .[3]

Taft was not the only member of the presidential fraternity whose admiration Cleveland earned. He elicited praise from Theodore Roosevelt and Woodrow Wilson, the latter of whom described him as "the sort of president the makers of the Constitution had vaguely in mind: more man than partisan; with an independent executive will of his own; hardly a colleague of the Houses so much as an individual servant of the country; exercising his powers like a chief magistrate rather than like a party leader."[4]

The praise wasn't limited to former presidents. So ubiquitous was the sense of his importance in the generations after his death that in Arthur Schlesinger's 1948 poll of historians, Grover Cleveland was ranked the eighth greatest president of all time, just behind Theodore Roosevelt and just ahead of John Adams.[5] When America's modern currency was designed in the 1920s, Cleveland was considered such a significant figure that Treasury Department staff suggested him for the $20 bill. (The then secretary Andrew Mellon instead placed him on the $1,000 bill, which had originally been intended for Andrew Jackson. The more valuable currency was mainly used for bank transfers and was discontinued in 1969.)[6]

Why did Grover Cleveland recede into relative anonymity? To some degree, it wasn't personal. The psychologist Henry L. Roediger III, who regularly tests how many presidents Americans can recall, has demonstrated that most of the men who helm the executive branch fade from memory in a fashion as predictable as it is quick. There are only three categories of presidents that Americans reliably remember: the first few, the most recent, and Abraham Lincoln. Even seemingly monumental figures like Andrew Jackson and Theodore Roosevelt come up with surprising infrequency. Upon releasing the 2014 iteration of his research, Roediger predicted, "By the year 2060, Americans will probably remember as much about the 39th and 40th presidents, Jimmy Carter and Ronald Reagan, as they now remember about our 13th president, Millard Fillmore."[7]

There are *degrees* of presidential obscurity, however, and Cleveland has surely sunk to unearned depths. A variety of factors explain this unjustified demotion. One element is surely chronology: the era Cleveland inhabited, between the tenures of Abraham Lincoln and Theodore Roosevelt, is one of the two great dead zones for presidential legacies, matched only by the period between Andrew Jackson and Lincoln. Both eras saw high turnover in the White House and a correspondingly strengthened Congress, leading popular tellings of American history to privilege *issues*—slavery in the case of the antebellum republic, economic change in the Gilded Age—over individuals in their recitation of events.

Another factor at work is that the Cleveland family conducted itself with the same modesty that distinguished its patriarch. Frances Cleveland remarried in 1913 (the only First Lady besides Jacqueline Kennedy to do so), wedding the Princeton archaeologist Thomas J. Preston Jr. She kept so low a profile that when she attended her final White House event in 1947, she was asked by General Dwight Eisenhower where she had lived during her time in Washington.[8]*

Each of the surviving Cleveland children moved away and kept at a remove from politics. Esther relocated to England, married a British soldier, and gave birth to a daughter whom the world would come to know as Philippa Foot, the famous philosopher who was a pioneer in the field of virtue ethics and invented the ethical dilemma popularly known as

---

*Frances Cleveland died in 1947 and was buried in Princeton (where she had continued to live), alongside her first husband and their deceased daughter, Ruth. It was a testimony to the age gap between spouses that Mr. Cleveland had been born shortly after Andrew Jackson left the White House while Mrs. Cleveland lived long enough to see a nuclear bomb dropped on Hiroshima.

"the trolley problem."* Marion, after a failed marriage to a journalist that took her to Colorado, returned to the East Coast, worked for the Girl Scouts of America, and married John Amen, a lawyer who would eventually serve as a prosecutor in the Nuremberg Trials. The president's oldest son, Richard, served as a Marine during World War I and later went on to a successful law practice in Baltimore, most notably serving as counsel for Whittaker Chambers in the Alger Hiss case (the younger Cleveland told Chambers's wife that his affection for her husband stemmed in part from the fact that he reminded him of his father).[9] The youngest of the Cleveland children, Francis, became an actor, appearing on Broadway in the original production of *Our Town* before permanently relocating to New Hampshire, where he started an acting troupe in the Clevelands' adopted hometown of Tamworth. None of them went into professional politics. None of them attempted to trade on the family name.

The paradox of the Cleveland legacy is that humility of this sort is both one of the reasons Grover Cleveland deserves recognition and one of the reasons he has not received it in adequate measure. No one bears more responsibility on this front than the president himself, whose failure to write an autobiography tended to privilege his critics' interpretation of his administrations.

The final factor, of course, is that Cleveland's conception of the role of the federal government—and, for that matter, the presidency—now seems so antiquated as to be unrecognizable to the average American. Indeed, there have been few presidents in American history so preoccupied with the notion that the government should show no special favor to any one group over another. This is compounded by the fact that many of the struggles Cleveland faced in office revolved around issues that seem antique to modern observers. Civil service protections in the federal government are now so widespread as to be unremarkable.

---

*It is not widely known that Philippa Foot was the granddaughter of an American president. Even less well known: her middle name was Ruth, a tribute to her late aunt.

Indeed, to the extent they're salient today it's often because of arguments that they have gone *too far*, limiting the executive branch's ability to dismiss underperforming employees. Since the adoption of the federal income tax, tariffs are no longer central to federal revenue; it's likewise hard to conceive of a time when military pensions had the budget ramifications of modern-day entitlement programs. The pressures on the presidency stemming from the Panic of 1893 are difficult to fathom in a world where the Federal Reserve has annexed responsibility for monetary policy. If Cleveland seems like an inaccessible figure, it's in large part because we don't understand the America he inhabited, a country somehow more alien to us than the more distant ones of the Civil War or the Founding Fathers. That is not Grover Cleveland's deficiency. It is ours.

It is not difficult to imagine a scenario that would have left Grover Cleveland with a legacy more intelligible to modern sensibilities. He could have been the president who acquired Hawaii and Cuba; he could have been the president who took America off the gold standard in order to counteract Gilded Age inequality; he could have even, had he not withdrawn the treaty he inherited from Chester Arthur, been the president responsible for finally building a canal connecting the Atlantic and the Pacific. What's more, each of those accomplishments would likely have redounded to his political benefit *in his own day*. Grover Cleveland didn't *miss* those opportunities because he was an inept president, however; he *refused* them because he thought they were *wrong*. Virtually everything worth saying about Grover Cleveland boils down to that one elemental fact: he possessed moral courage at almost superhuman levels. He was consistently motivated by conviction, even when he knew he'd suffer political harm as a result. As Woodrow Wilson observed, "His courses of action were incalculable to the mere politician, simply because they were not based upon calculation."[10]

This tenacious devotion to principle could be Cleveland's Achilles' heel just as often as it was his crowning virtue. His failure to unify and strengthen the Democratic Party—often the first count in the case against him—is a genuine demerit, though one that's often overstated. Cleveland's 1884 victory marked the first time Democrats had won the White House in twenty-eight years. It was perhaps inevitable that ideological divisions—usually more consequential when a party is in control—would spill out into the open after such a prolonged exile from power. Nor is it clear that there was any politically viable way for Cleveland to straddle the intraparty divide. Nevertheless, it's clearly the case that Grover Cleveland's stubbornness and high-handedness only exacerbated the existing tensions. What he perceived as high-minded devotion to principle many of his fellow Democrats regarded simply as sanctimony. There is ample reason that Mark Summers, the foremost historian of the Gilded Age presidency, titled his insightful lecture about Cleveland's presidency "A Good Man Is Hard to Take."

Indeed, many of Cleveland's shortcomings as president can arguably be traced to the fact that he was somewhat miscast in the role. Cleveland—not unlike Taft shortly thereafter—was a man of fundamentally judicial temperament. Rather than manipulating the factions inherent to democratic politics, he attempted to stand apart from them, to govern with a sort of Solomonic detachment that favored no man, including himself.

It is that disposition that makes Cleveland seem such a political anomaly. We are used to criticizing American presidents who possess the raw political skills needed to obtain office but lack the higher virtues needed to elevate them to the rank of statesmen. What makes Cleveland so peculiar is that he inverts the formula: he was a born statesman who never quite mastered the lower arts of politics. Moreover, it was an irremediable deficiency. There is no plausible scenario in which he could have behaved any other way, simply because Grover Cleveland met the definition of "genius" propounded by Thelonious Monk: "the one most like himself." His was a fully realized personality, for good and for ill.

Grover Cleveland deserves respect for his distinctive place in American history. He deserves tribute from those who share the classical liberal convictions that animated his career in politics. He also, however, deserves admiration even from those who regard him as ideologically anathema. The reason is simple: his career was a rebuke to political cynicism.

In the course of just three years, Grover Cleveland was elevated from the obscurity of a Buffalo law office to the presidency of the United States on the basis of one principle: integrity. The Cleveland philosophy was that the executive existed not to collaborate with the legislature but to do battle on behalf of otherwise voiceless citizens. Both the president's contemporaries and subsequent historians have been too quick to pronounce that conviction a kind of political naïveté. Yet Grover Cleveland knew exactly what he was doing. Late in life, when his friend Paul Van Dyke mentioned an opportunistic politician, the former president observed that "the trouble with that sort of fellow is that he is always ready to make the mistake of thinking there is no political force in a moral idea."[11] To Richard Watson Gilder, he once remarked, "This talk about the importance of 'playing politics'—look at the men who have played it. Have they got as far, after all, as I have?"[12]

It has become fashionable in recent years to imagine that character is a superfluous trait in our political leaders. In this purely instrumental view, it only matters what levers are being pulled, not whose hands are pulling them. The theory is not totally unfounded. Indeed, the American system was built to withstand mediocre leadership. No less a figure than James Madison was quick to note that "enlightened statesmen will not always be at the helm."[13] Yet it is an impoverished conception of America that imagines that the least we can tolerate is the most to which we can aspire. Many of the greatest moments in the history of the American presidency were moments of character: the restraint in Washington's decision to retire after two terms; the forbearance in Thomas Jefferson's proclamation, amid the first transfer of power between political parties in American history, that "We are all Republicans. We are all Federalists"; the mercy of Lincoln's second inaugural address, calling the nation to heal the wounds of the Civil War rather than succumb to the desire for vengeance. Grover Cleveland's two terms may never have yielded a moment of such high drama, but they displayed the same sense of republican virtue; the same conviction that a public man has duties that transcend self-interest or partisan gain.

Such men should be honored—if only so we may see their like again in the future.

Lonely the heart that listens to no voice
Save that of Duty; Lonely he how oft
When, turning from the smooth, advised path
He climbed the chill and solitary way;
Wondering that any wondered, when so clear
The light that led—the light of perfect faith
And passion for the right, that fire of heaven
Wherein self dies, and only truth lives on!
Lonely how oft when, with the statesman's art
He waited for the fullness of time,
And wrought the good he willed by slow degrees,
And in due order conquered wrong on wrong.
Lonely how oft when 'mid dark disesteem
He moved straightforward to a longed-for goal,
Doing each day the best he might, with vision
Firm fixt above, kept pure by pure intent.[14]

—Excerpt from a poem read by Richard Watson Gilder at the Grover Cleveland Memorial Meeting at Carnegie Hall, New York City, March 18, 1909

ACKNOWLEDGMENTS

The origins of this book trace back to a heroic act of parenting in the autumn of 1999. It was the first time I had ever visited the northeastern United States, and, of course, the item on the top of my agenda was precisely what you'd expect from a sixteen-year-old boy: a stop in Caldwell, New Jersey, to visit the birthplace of Grover Cleveland. There are many reasons my mother deserves more credit than these pages are adequate to convey, but foremost among them is that this request wasn't met with a call to a psychiatrist's office.

We made the stop but arrived too late: the site was closed for the day. My mother is far from the spoiling type, so I'm not sure what possessed her, but she placed a phone call to a number posted on the outside of the building ... and convinced the person on the other end of the line to open up the place just for us. I wish I remembered the name of that employee so that I could thank her for that act of kindness. And I wish I had words adequate to thank my mother for a lifetime of that kind of love.

Credit for the obsession that brought me to Caldwell is owed to my father, who inadvertently touched off my mania for American history with what seemed like an innocuous purchase at an Orange County, California, bookstore at some point in the early 1990s. My dad is a former teacher, and his principle was simple: you can have any book you want as long as you read it cover to cover before you ask for another one.

After I chose a volume on the American presidents featuring images from the National Portrait Gallery—I can't tell you why, although I distinctly recall being perplexed by Chester Arthur's sideburns—he probably would've killed for me to read *anything else*. He had to rebind that book three times. Without my father's encouragement to dig deep into whatever topic sparked my interest, that book would have remained on the shelf, and this one never would have been conceived of.

No one has endured more to make this project a reality than my wife, Veneta, who suffered through two years of her husband spending most of his free time with an obese, mustachioed nineteenth-century politician. That this process coincided with a global pandemic, a medical emergency that put me under the knife, and my cofounding a new and time-consuming business only compounded the burden placed upon her. Her patience for this work was more than any reasonable person could ask and her love is more than this author deserves.

Coming in a close second on the list of women whom no jury would have convicted for murdering me is my business partner, Vanessa Mendoza. She did not bat an eyelid when I told her that I had decided to take this project on simultaneous with us building a digital media company from scratch, which was an extraordinary and probably unreasonable gesture of support. For her graciousness she was rewarded with Monday morning recaps of the intricacies of the 1884 election, a reminder that no good deed goes unpunished.

The only reason this book exists is because of Matt Latimer and Keith Urbahn at Javelin, two men I'm proud to say were my friends long before they were my agents (and, for that matter, long before Javelin existed). My life has been punctuated by repeated instances of serendipity, but none quite as surreal as having them tell me during a purely social visit that there was a market for a new Grover Cleveland biography, neither of them realizing that they were sitting across the table from someone who had been nursing that very ambition for the better part of two decades.

My editor, Natasha Simons, has been a paragon of good judgment and professionalism throughout the writing of this book. There is a unique vulnerability that accompanies the first time you present work you've spent years on to someone else. Whatever anticipatory anxiety I felt was misbegotten. Not only has Natasha been endlessly supportive, but every word of the manuscript she has touched has been better for her intervention. That same excellence pervades the entire team at Threshold Editions, which has made my life easier at every step in the process.

A number of individuals provided valuable assistance on the research required to tell Grover Cleveland's story. Cynthia Van Ness, the director of library and archives at the Buffalo History Museum, helped me navigate materials from Cleveland's early years. Michelle Krowl at the Library of Congress went beyond the call of duty in guiding me through their Cleveland collection from a COVID-mandated distance. The University of Kentucky's Mark Summers was essential to navigating the ins and outs of the Halpin scandal. Brian Riedl, who has yet to meet an economic question he can't answer, was able to walk me through the complexities of inflation-adjusting figures from the nineteenth century. Terry Anderson provided valuable perspective on the Dawes Act and the economic dynamics facing Native Americans in Cleveland's era.

I owe a special debt to Jack Fowler, who, in a characteristic act of generosity, provided me with workspace to tackle this project in its earliest days. The only problem: sharing an office with Jack is too much fun . . . and productivity drops correspondingly. Still, I will never forget his kindness or the fact that *A Man of Iron*, though ultimately a product of Grover Cleveland's native New Jersey, had its origins in Milford, Connecticut.

The members of my immediate family—my stepfather George; my brother Travis, his wife, Abby, and their son Asher; my grandparents, Vern and Jerre; my uncle Marc and aunt Patty; and my stepmother, Karen, have all been immensely supportive of this project despite the fact that it meant lots of holidays when I was squirreled away in some back room trying to figure out exactly how over-the-top the *New York*

Times' coverage of Frances Cleveland's wardrobe had been. For their love and support I am eternally grateful.

Some of my closest friends have been hearing the dress rehearsal version of this book since long before it had any prospect of becoming a reality and are likely hoping its publication means we'll finally be able to talk about something else at dinner (suckers). Ashton Ellis, Ryan Burleson, and Tim Rice in particular have been with me every step of the way. I'm grateful to each of them for the kind of brotherhood that will last a lifetime. Fred Cole also belongs on that list but with the caveat that he'll still be talking about Grover Cleveland even after *I've* tired of the subject.

A number of colleagues, past and present, have been generous with their support throughout this endeavor. Foremost on that list are Tara-Marie Lynch, Michelle Arledge, and Leigh Harrington at Kite & Key, who've seamlessly adjusted not only to the pressures this book has placed on my schedule but also to the Zoom calls in which a Grover Cleveland bobblehead glowers at them from over my shoulder. Howard Husock and Brian Anderson were, as always, bottomless sources of good ideas. I'm certain Dale Thomas was the first person to uncork champagne once she heard about the book, though I am also reasonably confident that the bottle was open even before I called. The relentless positivity of Rafael Mangual, Tim Barkas, Dan and Jan Himebaugh, and Michael Barreiro kept me writing on days when the challenge would have otherwise felt insurmountable. Shannon Kelly likely doesn't remember that she was the one who first gave me the idea that this was a book, which is a perfect excuse to deny her the percentage of the royalties that are rightfully hers.

I would be remiss if I didn't acknowledge the individuals whose support has put me in the position to write this volume in the first place. Larry Hall, Vaughn May, and Bob Kaufman gave me tools without which this book couldn't have been written. Bill McGurn took a chance on an unknown twenty-four-year-old from an obscure corner of California and gave him one of the most consequential writing jobs in the country. Jeff Mazzella, Curtis Mack, Rob Long, Peter Robinson, Scott Immergut, Brian Calle, Chris Dauer, and Larry Mone all invested similar faith in me, which I hope I rewarded. And if I didn't . . . you still got your name in a book, which is not nothing.

In closing, I feel compelled to mention three men who touched my life—each of whom, in his own way, embodied the same principles that animated Grover Cleveland and each of whom died during the writing of this book.

Michael Uhlmann was a brilliant scholar, a dedicated public servant, and, quaint though the phrase may sound, a great American. His lifelong defense of the country's constitutional order represented a reverence for justice under law that echoed Cleveland's own convictions.

Former U.S. senator Tom Coburn embodied, more than any other figure in my lifetime, the kind of devotion to principle in public office that fueled Grover Cleveland's career. He carried himself with a decency and lack of pretense virtually unheard of in Washington, endearing him even to those who disagreed with him. His legacy proves, as did Cleveland's, that cynicism is not a prerequisite for success in American politics.

Bruce Herschensohn was perhaps the best man I've ever known, an award-winning filmmaker, a White House aide, a beloved broadcaster, but more than anything else a man who felt in his bones that to be an American was a moral proposition, demanding of us the vigilant defense of the values that formed the nation. We may think that men like Grover Cleveland, who regard statesmanship as a kind of monastic vocation, no longer exist. Bruce proved that proposition wrong. I owe him my entire career, but that is secondary to the debt incurred by his friendship.

To attempt a biography of Grover Cleveland is to gain a newfound appreciation for the nation's presidential libraries, dedicated as they are to preserving and curating the records of administrations long since passed. Because they did not exist prior to Franklin Roosevelt's far-sighted 1939 decision to donate his papers to the federal government—and didn't fully get rolling until Congress's passage of the Presidential Libraries Act in 1955—attempts to chronicle pre–World War II administrations can be devilishly complicated, particularly if the president in question is sufficiently obscure that no infrastructure has been created to bring his records together under one roof.

Grover Cleveland is especially vexing on this front, for several reasons.

Despite entertaining the prospect late in life, he never wrote a memoir. His only post-presidential attempt to chronicle his tenure in office was a series of lectures later collated and published under the title *Presidential Problems*. The collection suffers from an excess of formality and a lack of candor: its chapters are long on regurgitations of what appeared in official documents and short on insights into what happened behind closed doors.

By his own admission, Cleveland was careless in preserving his papers and didn't take any interest in the matter until it was too late to apply any remedial action. An additional difficulty until recently was that the papers that had survived were largely yet to be digitized.

Happily—and mercifully for the purposes of this book, written in the midst of a pandemic that closed most research facilities—the Library of Congress made digital copies of its Cleveland microfilm available in 2020, though even then significant difficulties remained. While documents in that collection have been digitally scanned, they have yet to be transcribed, so searching them remains a daunting and time-consuming proposition. My efforts to that end have been extensive but have still just scratched the surface. I am hopeful that the release of those documents will yield more insights into Cleveland's presidency as the years go by, but I issue a note of caution to any would-be researchers: contra his forbidding appearance, Grover Cleveland wrote in a script so delicate that his words are often illegible to any but the most sophisticated student of handwriting.

The research for this book has relied as much as possible on original sources and, when such sources were not available, on credible contemporaneous accounts. It has also called upon a handful of later works that explored with great rigor issues that were not adequately chronicled in their own time.

No serious work on this topic can fail to acknowledge its debt to Allan Nevins's Pulitzer Prize–winning 1932 biography, *Grover Cleveland: A Study in Courage*, which remains the most comprehensive account of the president's life and, because it drew heavily on accounts of the president's contemporaries, the single largest repository of information from primary sources found anywhere outside of Cleveland's own papers. Nevins also performed a valuable service to researchers by releasing a separate volume containing extensive transcripts of Cleveland's personal correspondence. While Nevins was at times excessively partisan in his admiration for the former president, that is a minor demerit relative to the treasure trove of information he made available to the public.

Cleveland's official state papers are also a tremendous resource, more so, in fact, than those of many other presidents. This is because Cleveland's lawyerly thoroughness meant that most of his official correspondence—letters to Congress, memos to members of the cabinet, etc.—took the form of lengthy, detailed analyses of whatever policy issue was under consideration at the time. Many of them read more like white papers churned out deep within the bowels of the bureaucracy than presidential pronouncements. This does not make for especially pleasurable reading, but it does provide a thorough understanding of the policy issues his administration faced and what he considered the relevant decision points. As for his speeches, they have been helpfully compiled in a volume from the University of California that spans his entire career.

A number of other volumes deserve mention both because they inform significant portions of this book and because they are valuable resources for readers pursuing a deeper understanding of Cleveland.

Of contemporaneous works, George F. Parker's *Recollections of Grover Cleveland* is the closest thing extant to an authorized biography. It is cursory on Cleveland's life through the first administration, but invaluable thereafter, when it covers the years in which Parker and Cleveland were in close contact. Robert McElroy's *Grover Cleveland: The Man and the Statesman* is commendably thorough, though in many places it simply reprints Cleveland's papers, often at distressing length. McElroy was a history professor at Princeton during Cleveland's time there and his work in many ways laid the groundwork for Nevins's, which followed about a decade later. Richard Watson Gilder's *Grover Cleveland: A Record of Friendship* is the only contemporaneous account that makes for enjoyable reading, as the book is heavily focused on Cleveland's private life from the second term forward and told through a series of brief, often humorous vignettes. William Dorsheimer and Charles Morris's *Life and Public Services of Grover Cleveland* originated as a campaign biography and thus should be given the appropriate discount, but it is nevertheless valuable as the earliest volume we have that attempts to provide a comprehensive account of his life and career.

The years before Cleveland entered the national spotlight are by far the least documented of his life and represent one of several sections of this book that have benefited from authors who have produced in-depth works on discrete parts of his career. Charles Armitage's *Grover Cleveland as Buffalo Knew Him*, produced as a project of the *Buffalo Evening News* in 1926, called on local sources and newspaper records to paint the most vivid picture we have of the president's early days. Mark Summers's *Rum, Romanism, and Rebellion: The Making of a President, 1884* is the definitive source on Cleveland's first presidential campaign. The University Press of Kansas's exceptional series on presidential elections includes two volumes—Charles Calhoun's *Minority Victory: Gilded Age Politics and the Front Porch Campaign of 1888* and R. Hal Williams's *Realigning America: McKinley, Bryan, and the Remarkable Election of 1896*—that were key to the chapters on those later races (reinforcing its reputation as one of the sleepier contests in American history, there is no book-length treatment of the 1892 presidential election). Richard Welch's *The Presidencies of Grover Cleveland*, part of another University Press of Kansas series, is the single best volume for understanding the public policy issues facing the Cleveland administrations.

Matthew Algeo's compulsively readable *The President Is a Sick Man* is a thorough treatment of Cleveland's cancer scare and the resulting surgery. The presentation of that issue here is deeply indebted not only to Algeo's careful reconstruction of events but also to the medical insights presented in his book. Nick Cleaver's *Grover Cleveland's New Foreign Policy: Arbitration, Neutrality, and the Dawn of Empire* is an exhaustive work of scholarship pulling together an incredibly wide range of resources to illuminate the struggles over Venezuela, Cuba, Samoa, and Hawaii. The third volume of Ralph Kuykendall's sprawling history, *The Hawaiian Kingdom*, was essential to the section of the book dealing with the annexation debate, as were the government-commissioned Blount Report and Morgan Report.

Other volumes provided key context for the individuals and issues that affected Cleveland's career. Hugh Kelly's *Honest John Kelly: Truth or Satire*; Gustavus Myers's *The History of Tammany Hall*; and Terry Golway's *Machine Made: Tammany Hall and the Creation of Modern American Politics* informed the sections on Cleveland's battles with political bosses. Milton Friedman's *A Monetary History of the United States, 1867–1960*, Douglas Irwin's *Clashing Over Commerce: A History of U.S. Trade Policy*, and John Cogan's *The High Cost of Good Intentions: A History of U.S. Federal Entitlement Programs* were key to the sections on monetary policy, tariffs, and pensions, respectively. Jack Kelly's *The Edge of Anarchy: The Railroad Barons, the Gilded Age, and the Greatest Labor Uprising in America* was a valuable resource on the Pullman Strike, as was the report commissioned by the federal government in its wake.

Finally, a few technical points: in multiple instances throughout this book, I provide inflation-adjusted numbers to provide context for dollar amounts from the nineteenth century. This is more art than science, as the data for the Consumer Price Index the federal government uses to calculate inflation adjustments only dates back to 1913. I have thus relied on a formula prescribed by the Bureau of Labor Statistics for making calculations from earlier eras, available on the website of the Federal Reserve Bank of Minneapolis. The resulting figures—calculated in 2019 dollars, the most recent year for which data was available at the time this book was written—are thus not necessarily precise to the decimal point, but provide credible, albeit rough, estimates.

At various points throughout the book, I have made minor alterations to the punctuation in quotations from Cleveland or others to conform with modern usage. In every instance this has been done only if it could increase clarity for the reader without materially altering the speaker's meaning. As is common with projects of this kind, many quotations have also been edited for clarity, with ellipses always present to inform the reader where original text has been omitted. Every effort has been made to ensure that none of these edits misrepresent the speaker or elide vital context, and readers are encouraged to follow the book's endnotes if they wish to read the original quotes in full.

Any substantive errors that appear in the text are mine and mine alone.

NOTES

---◆◆◆---

INTRODUCTION: A MAN OF IRON

1 "Franklin Delano Roosevelt: An Obituary," H. L. Mencken, *The American Mercury*, April 13, 1945

2 H. L. Mencken (gathered by Alistair Cooke), *The Vintage Mencken*, 114.

3 Melvin I. Urofsky (editor), *The American Presidents: Critical Essays*, 371.

4 *The Vintage Mencken*, 220–221

5 "Tracing the Quote: Everything That Can be Invented has been Invented," Dennis Crouch, Patentlyo.com, January 6, 2011.

6 Jeffrey Rosen, *William Howard Taft*, 104.

7 Jesse Lynch Williams, *Mr. Cleveland: A Personal Impression*, 6–7.

8 Allan Nevins, *Grover Cleveland: A Study in Courage* (1932), 318.

9 William C. Hudson, *Random Recollections of an Old Political Reporter*, 137.

10 "Vetoes, 1789 to Present," United States Senate, https://www.senate.gov/legislative/vetoes/vetoCounts.htm.

11 "Presidential Vetoes," American Presidency Project, https://www.presidency.ucsb.edu/statistics/data/presidential-vetoes.

12 "Interstate Commerce Act (1887)," Our Documents, https://www.ourdocuments.gov/doc.php?flash=false&doc=49.

13 "The Historic 54th Congress," U.S. House of Representatives Office of the Historian, https://history.house.gov/HistoricalHighlight/Detail/36702?current_search_qs=%3Fret%3DTrue%26PreviousSearch%3DSearch%252cAll%252cFalse%252cFalse%252cFalse%252cFalse%252cFalse%252c%252cmm%252fdd%252fyyyy%252cmm%252fdd%252fyyyy%252cTitle%26CurrentPage%3D33%26SortOrder%3DTitle%26Command%3D36.

CHAPTER 1: HE DID NOT SHINE

1 Alyn Brodsky, *Grover Cleveland: A Study in Character*, 19.

2 George Frederick Parker, *Recollections of Grover Cleveland*, 14.

3 Parker, 15.

4 "Obituary: Rev. Thomas G. Cleveland," *The Conway Daily Sun*, April 14, 2020.

5 *Pennsylvania Gazette*, August 18, 1757.

6 Brodsky, 14

7   Address at the Annual Banquet of the New England Society of Brooklyn, New York, December 21, 1891.
8   Nevins, 13.
9   Nevins, 12.
10 Brodsky, 15.

CHAPTER 2: BUFFALO GALS

1   Nevins, 22.
2   William Osborn Stoddard, *Grover Cleveland*, 63.
3   Stoddard, 27.
4   Christopher Maag, "Hints of Comeback for Nation's First Superhighway," *New York Times*, November 2, 2008.
5   Richard Dilworth, *Cities in American Political History*, 279.
6   Jeff Z. Klein, "Heritage Moments: Fugitive Slave Fights for a Family's Freedom," WBFO, November 23, 2015.
7   Nevins, 44.
8   Nevins, 49.
9   Nevins, 51.
10 Nevins, 52.

CHAPTER 3: THE HANGMAN

1   Michael Beebe and Robert J. McCarthy, "A Grand Day Out: When Sheriff Grover Cleveland Hanged a Man on the Downtown Buffalo Gallows, it was a Festive Spectacle that Drew Endless Public Fascination," *Buffalo News*, September 23, 1999.
2   Stoddard, 37.
3   Nevins, 51.
4   Nevins, 52, to *Buffalo Courier*.
5   Charles H. Armitage, *Grover Cleveland as Buffalo Knew Him*, 30.
6   Brodsky, 29.
7   Henry Perry Smith (editor), *History of the City of Buffalo and Erie County, Vol. 1*, 238.
8   Nevins, 58.
9   Nevins, 59.
10 Armitage, 55.
11 Brodsky, 32.
12 Armitage, 57.
13 Nevins, 76.
14 Ibid, 62.
15 Beebe and McCarthy, "A Grand Day Out."
16 Nevins, 63.
17 *Buffalo Courier*, July 24, 1875.
18 Nevins, 21.

19   Armitage, 28.
20   Nevins, 57.

CHAPTER 4: HIS OBSTINACY, GROVER OF BUFFALO

1   Stoddard, 71.
2   Armitage, 75–80.
3   Michael F. Rizzo, *Through the Mayors' Eyes: Buffalo, New York 1832–2005*.
4   Parker, 42.
5   Brodsky, 40.
6   Stoddard, 75.
7   Address before City Convention, Buffalo, NY, October 25, 1881.
8   Armitage, 102.
9   Stoddard, 79–80.
10   Stoddard, 81–82.
11   Inaugural Message as Mayor of Buffalo, January 2, 1882.
12   Stoddard, 80.
13   Stoddard, 94–95.
14   Armitage, 109.
15   Ibid.
16   Armitage, 105.
17   Nevins, 87.
18   Armitage, 114.
19   Stoddard, 87.
20   Nevins, 89.

CHAPTER 5: UGLY HONEST

1   Brodsky, 48.
2   U.S. Census, 1880.
3   Nevins, 99.
4   Nevins, 98.
5   Anne DiFabio, "Thomas Nast Takes Down Tammany: A Cartoonist's Crusade Against a Political Boss," Museum of the City of New York: New York Stories Blog, September 24, 2013.
6   Terry Golway, *Machine Made: Tammany Hall and the Creation of Modern American Politics*, 100.
7   Nevins, 99.
8   "Both New York Senators Resign," U.S. Senate Historical Office, https://www.senate.gov/artandhistory/history/minute/Both_New_York_Senators_Resign.htm.
9   DeAlva Stanword Alexander, *A Political History of the State of New York*, 493–94.
10   Denis Tilden Lynch, *Grover Cleveland: A Man Four Square*, 103.
11   Nevins, 103.
12   Stoddard, 113.

13   Cleveland letter to his brother, Rev. William N. Cleveland, November 7, 1882.
14   Stoddard, 127.
15   Candice Millard, *Destiny of the Republic*, 96.
16   Nevins, 109.
17   *Albany Evening Journal*, March 21, 1883.
18   Brodsky, 56.
19   Brodsky, 54.
20   *Albany Evening Journal*, April 10, 1883.
21   Parker, 60.
22   Brodsky, 52.
23   William C. Hudson, *Random Recollections of an Old Political Reporter*, 147–49.
24   Brodsky, 53.
25   Willaim Dorsheimer IV and Charles Morris, *Life and Public Services of Grover Cleveland*, 76–77.
26   Stoddard, 147.
27   Nevins, 143.
28   Annual message to Congress, December 6, 1887.
29   Hugh Kelly, *Honest John Kelly: Truth or Satire*, loc. 1845.
30   Ibid., loc. 4063.
31   Jon Knokey, *Theodore Roosevelt and the Making of American Leadership*.
32   Joseph Bucklin Bishop, *Notes and Anecdotes of Many Years*.
33   Nevins, 123.

CHAPTER 6: "RUM, ROMANISM, AND REBELLION"

1   Mark Summers, *Rum, Romanism, and Rebellion: The Making of a President, 1884*, 1.
2   Nevins, 66.
3   Cleveland to Charles S. Fairchild, March 17, 1884.
4   *Bicentennial Edition Historical Statistics of the United States, Colonial Times to 1970*; and Tax Policy Center briefing book 2019, "What Are the Sources of Revenue for the Federal Government?"
5   Dr. Howard Markel, "The Dirty, Painful Death of President James A. Garfield," PBS.org, September 16, 2016.
6   Summers, 126.
7   Jay Bellamy, "A Stalwart of Stalwarts: Garfield's Assassin Sees Deed as Special Duty," *Prologue Magazine*, Fall 2016.
8   Summers, 127.
9   Daniel DiSalvo, *Engines of Change*, 120.
10   Nevins, 146.
11   Summers, 141
12   Nevins, 146–67.
13   Summers, 147.
14   Letters and literary memorials of Samuel J. Tilden, vol. 2.

15   "Talks with Boss Kelly," *New York Times*, July 8, 1884.
16   Denis Tilden Lynch, *Grover Cleveland: A Man Four Square*, 171.
17   Ibid.
18   Cleveland letter to Daniel Manning, June 30, 1884.
19   Nevins, 153.
20   *Official Proceedings of the Democratic National Convention*, 1884, 176–77.
21   Hudson, 184.
22   Summers, 160.
23   Ibid.
24   Nevins, 154.
25   Lynch, 212.
26   Cleveland "Serenade speech" in Albany, July 11, 1884.
27   Lynch, 225.
28   "A Terrible Tale," *Evening Telegraph*, July 21, 1884.
29   Ibid.
30   "Old-Time Politics," *Cincinnati Enquirer*, August 11, 1884.
31   Cleveland telegram to Charles W. Goodyear, July 21, 1884.
32   Lynch, 220.
33   Lynch, 222.
34   Cleveland letter to Daniel N. Lockwood, July 31, 1884.
35   Cleveland letter to Wilson S. Bissell, September 11, 1884.
36   Nevins, 165.
37   *Buffalo Weekly Express*, June 19, 1884.
38   Summers, 180.
39   Summers, 184.
40   Summers, 186.
41   Dorsheimer, 100.
42   Hudson, 188–90.
43   Nevins, 161–62.
44   Summers, 207.
45   Lynch, 211.
46   Edmund Morris, *The Rise of Theodore Roosevelt*, 253.
47   Jeffers, 116–17.
48   Nevins, 170.
49   Brodsky, 82.
50   Summers, 211.
51   Brodsky, 85.
52   Summers, 224.
53   Summers, 84.
54   Summers, 235.
55   Rexford G. Tugwell, *Grover Cleveland*, 94.
56   Cleveland letter to Daniel S. Lamont, August 10, 1884.
57   Cleveland letter accepting nomination for president, August 18, 1884.

58 Cleveland address at Newark, New Jersey, October 26, 1884.

59 Cleveland letter accepting nomination for president, August 18, 1884.

60 Ibid.

61 Nevins, 173; Summers, 249.

62 Summers, 281.

63 *New York Times*, October 31, 1884.

64 *New York Tribune*, October 30, 1884.

65 *Chicago Tribune*, October 31, 1884.

66 Marie Solis, "How Many Presidents Have Been Accused of Sexual Assault? George H.W. Bush is the Latest," Newsweek.com, October 25, 2017.

67 Bruce E. Levin, "3 of the Biggest Misogynists to Reach the Oval Office Before Donald Trump Got There," Salon.com, July 8, 2017.

68 Susan Wise Bauer, "The Lessons of 1884," Theatlantic.com, June 7, 2020.

69 Charles Lachman, "Grover Cleveland's Sex Scandal: The Most Despicable in American Political History," thedailybeast.com, May 23, 2011.

70 Charles Lachman, *A Secret Life: The Lies and Scandals of President Grover Cleveland*, 431.

71 Charles Lachman, "Grover Cleveland's Sex Scandal: The Most Despicable in American Political History," thedailybeast.com, May 23, 2011.

72 *Detroit Free Press*, November 3, 1884.

73 Nevins, 281.

74 Summers, 282.

75 *Daily Morning Times*, November 8, 1884.

76 Cleveland telegram to Edward Murphy, November 6, 1884.

77 Nevins, 186.

78 Nevins, 187.

79 Summers, 300.

80 Nevins, 186.

81 Jeffers, 120.

82 Nevins, 183.

83 Cleveland to Shan Bissell, November 13, 1884.

84 *Albany Argus*, August 2, 1883.

CHAPTER 7: THE MEANEST MAN IN THE WORLD

1 Richard Welch, *The Presidencies of Grover Cleveland*, 227.

2 Brodsky, 111.

3 Cleveland letter to William J. Leader, November 27, 1884.

4 Nevins, 192.

5 McElroy, 100.

6 Zachary Karabell and Arthur M. Schlesinger Jr., "Chester Alan Arthur," 135.

7 Robert M. La Follette, *La Follette's Autobiography*, 53.

8 Karabell and Schlesinger, 159.

9   Stoddard, 235.

10   Brodsky, 158.

11   Nevins, 212.

12   McElroy, 112.

13   Nevins, 212.

14   Nevins, 206.

15   Welch, 66.

16   Nevins, 326.

17   Pension Act, July 14, 1862.

18   Dorsheimer, 257.

19   Welch, 62.

20   American Presidency Project, University of California, Santa Barbara, "Presidential Vetoes," https://www.presidency.ucsb.edu/statistics/data/presidential-vetoes.

21   Welch, 62.

22   Veto of the bill granting a pension to Elisabeth S. De Kraft, June 19, 1886.

23   Veto of the bill granting an increase of pension to John W. Farriers, June 21, 1886.

24   Veto of the bill granting a pension to John Hunter, June 19, 1886.

25   McElroy, 198.

26   Brodsky, 188.

27   Veto of the bill granting a pension to Elisabeth S. De Kraft, June 19, 1886.

28   Welch, 63.

29   McElroy, 202.

30   Veto of military pension legislation, February 11, 1887.

31   Nevins, 333.

32   Ibid.

33   Ibid., 338.

34   H. W. Brands, *The Man Who Saved the Union*, 543.

35   Cleveland letter to George W. Curtis, December 25, 1884.

36   Sean M. Theriault, "Patronage, the Pendleton Act, and the Power of the People," *Journal of Politics* 65, no. 1 (February 2003): 50–68.

37   Richard White, *The Republic for Which It Stands* (Oxford History of the United States), 467.

38   Welch, 61.

39   Library of Congress collection of Cleveland papers, mss16188, box VII:12; reel 162.

40   Ibid.

41   Letter to Charles W. Goodyear, August 6, 1885.

42   Nevins, 235.

43   Letter to Dorman B. Eaton, September 11, 1885.

44   Nevins, 207–8.

45   Nevins, 210.

46   McElroy, 132.
47   Nevins, 248.
48   Message relative to papers on file and other information touching suspensions from and appointments to office, March 1, 1886.
49   James Fallows, "The Passionless Presidency," *Atlantic Monthly*, May 1979.
50   Parker, 266.
51   Nevins, 232.
52   Annual report of the Secretary of the Navy, 1885.
53   Parker, 91–92.

CHAPTER 8: POINTS WEST

1   Cleveland first inaugural address, March 4, 1885.
2   Cleveland annual message to Congress, December 1885.
3   Cleveland annual message to Congress, December 1886.
4   Cleveland annual message to Congress, December 1888.
5   Veto of the bill to provide for the sale of certain New York Indian lands in Kansas, May 3, 1888.
6   Nevins, 230.
7   Ibid.
8   Robert M. Utley, *Geronimo*, 194.
9   Cleveland annual message to Congress, December 1885.
10   Helen Hunt Jackson letter to Grover Cleveland, August 8, 1885.
11   Cleveland annual message to Congress, December 1885.
12   McElroy, 227.
13   Cleveland letter to Secretary Hoke Smith, May 4, 1895.
14   Paul Stuart, "United States Indian Policy: From the Dawes Act to the American Indian Policy Review Commission," *Social Service Review* 51, no. 3 (September 1977): 451–63.
15   General Allotment Act, Section 5.
16   Terry Anderson, ed., *Unlocking the Wealth of Indian Nations*, 26.
17   Terry Anderson, *Sovereign Nations or Reservations? An Economic History of American Indians*, 117.
18   Ibid., 110.
19   Cleveland annual message to Congress, December 1885.
20   Nevins, 227.
21   Cleveland annual message to Congress, December 1888.
22   Welch, 76.
23   Grover Cleveland, *Fishing and Shooting Sketches*, 8.
24   Summers, 281.
25   Cleveland annual message to Congress, December 1885.
26   William Mulder, "Immigration and the 'Mormon Question': An International Episode," *Western Political Quarterly* 9, no. 2 (1956): 416–33.

27   Sarah Barringer Gordon, *The Mormon Question* (*Studies in Legal History*), 209.

28   M. Paul Holsinger, "Henry M. Teller and the Edmunds-Tucker Act," *Colorado Magazine* 48 (Winter 1971).

29   Utah State Constitution, Article III, Section I.

30   "The Chinese Exclusion Act," ourdocuments.gov.

31   Cleveland inaugural address, March 4, 1885.

32   Cleveland to Booker T. Washington, December 3, 1899.

33   Cleveland to the Reverend Charles Wood, November 2, 1902.

34   Cleveland address to Southern Educational Association, April 14, 1903.

35   T. A. Larson, *History of Wyoming*, 2nd ed., 1990, 141–44.

36   "To This We Dissented," statement of Chinese laborers of Rock Springs to the Chinese Consul at New York, 1885.

37   Tom Rea, "The Rock Springs Massacre," November 8, 2014, *Encyclopedia of Wyoming History* (Wyoming State Historical Society), https://www.wyohistory.org/encyclopedia/rock-springs-massacre.

38   Ibid.

39   Cleveland message relevant to Chinese treaty stipulation, March 1, 1886.

40   Ibid.

41   Cleveland annual message to Congress, December 1885.

42   Cleveland annual message to Congress, December 1886.

43   Cleveland message relating to the Chinese question, September 24, 1888.

44   Charles W. Calhoun, *Minority Victory: Gilded Age Politics and the Front Porch Campaign of 1888*, 81–82.

45   Cleveland annual message to Congress, December 7, 1896.

46   Veto of an act to amend the immigration laws of the United States, March 2, 1897.

47   Ibid.

48   Yasmin Sabina Khan, *Enlightening the World*.

49   Cleveland remarks accepting the Bartholdi statue of "Liberty Enlightening the World," October 26, 1886.

CHAPTER 9: GROVER, AT EASE

1   Patricia O'Toole, *The Five of Hearts: An Intimate Portrait of Henry Adams and His Friends, 1880–1918*, 149.

2   Grover Cleveland Papers: Series IX: Miscellany, -1906; Subseries C; Biographical material. -1906, 1743. Manuscript/Mixed Material. Retrieved from the Library of Congress, www.loc.gov/item/mss161880877/.

3   Annette Dunlap, *Frank: The Story of Frances Folsom Cleveland, America's Youngest First Lady*, 14.

4   "Lovely Frances," *Buffalo Evening News*, April 19, 1886

5   Grover Cleveland Papers: Series IX: Miscellany, -1906; Subseries C; Biographical

material. - 1906, 1743. Manuscript/Mixed Material. Retrieved from the Library of Congress, www.loc.gov/item/mss161880877/.

6   Dunlap, 7.
7   "Mrs. Grover Cleveland," *Atlanta Constitution*, November 25, 1888.
8   Dunlap, 23.
9   Nevins, 302.
10   "The Nation's First Lady," *New York Times*, June 3, 1886.
11   Ibid.
12   Dunlap, 11.
13   "The Nation's First Lady."
14   "Mrs. Grover Cleveland at Home," *New York Times*, December 25, 1887.
15   William H. Crook, *Memories of the White House: The Home Life of Our Presidents from Lincoln to Roosevelt*, loc 1565
16   "A Chapter on the Bustle," *Atlanta Constitution*, November 7, 1892.
17   Dunlap, 542.
18   Crook, loc 1668.
19   Dunlap, 42.
20   "In Honor of the Bride," *New York Times*, June 7, 1886.
21   Nevins, 306.
22   Nevins, 307.
23   Nevins, 309–10.
24   Brodsky, 175.
25   "Mrs. Cleveland at Home," *Washington Post*, June 26, 1886.
26   Dorsheimer, 202.
27   *New York World*, July 13, 1887.
28   Cleveland to Postmaster General Vilas, September 14, 1887.
29   Karabel, *Chester Arthur*, 208.
30   Dorsheimer, 232.
31   "In Memory of Henry Thomas Ellett," Memphis Bar, 1888.
32   Nevins, 319.
33   Dorsheimer, 233–34.
34   Dunlap, 580.
35   Nevins, 318.

CHAPTER 10: TURNED OUT

1   "Education," *New York Sun*, November 14, 1888.
2   Cleveland letter to the Honorable A. J. Warner and others, February 28, 1885.
3   Nevins, 202.
4   Cleveland letter to Samuel J. Randall, February 9, 1885.
5   Cleveland letter to the Honorable A. J. Warner and others, February 28, 1885.
6   Nevins, 203.
7   Nevins, 268.
8   Cleveland annual message to Congress, December 1885.

9   Cleveland annual message to Congress, December 1886.

10   Nevins, 270.

11   *New York Herald*, January 6, 1886.

12   Cleveland annual message to Congress, December 1885.

13   Nevins, 276.

14   Thomas L. Hungerford, "U.S. Federal Government Revenues: 1790 to the Present," Congressional Research Service, 2006.

15   Nevins, 280.

16   Douglas A. Irwin, *Clashing Over Commerce: A History of U.S. Trade Policy*, 311.

17   Irwin, 273.

18   *New York Herald*, June 17, 1886.

19   Irwin, 314.

20   Nevins, 376.

21   Lynch, 349.

22   McElroy, 271.

23   Ibid.

24   Jeffers, 202.

25   Lynch, 353.

26   Jeffers, 203.

27   *New York Tribune*, December 7, 1887.

28   Charles W. Calhoun, *Minority Victory* (American Presidential Elections), 148–49.

29   Ibid., 125.

30   Ibid., 98.

31   Nevins, 434.

32   Calhoun, 179.

33   Ibid., 182.

34   Brodsky, 226.

35   Calhoun, 173.

36   Nevins, 416.

37   Lynch, 363.

38   Irwin, 317.

39   Nevins, 423.

40   Lynch, 359.

41   Calhoun, 213.

42   Welch, 96.

43   Calhoun, 235.

44   Welch, 98.

45   McElroy, 298.

46   Calhoun, 230–31.

47   S. J. Ackerman, "The Vote That Failed," *Smithsonian*, November 1998.

48   Brodsky, 238–39.

49   Jeffers, 205.

50   Cleveland to Massachusetts Tariff Reform Association, December 24, 1888.

51   Cleveland annual message to Congress, December 3, 1888.
52   Cleveland to Shan Bissell, June 17, 1888.
53   William H. Crook, *Memories of the White House: The Home Life of Our Presidents from Lincoln to Roosevelt* (1911), loc 1688.

CHAPTER 11: INTERREGNUM
1   Cleveland letter to Shan Bissell, April 13, 1889.
2   McElroy, 305–6.
3   Cleveland letter to William F. Villas, May 20, 1889.
4   Gilder, 60.
5   Gilder, 60–61.
6   Gilder, 49.
7   Gilder, 50.
8   Cleveland address before the Medical Alumni Association of New York City, February 15, 1890.
9   Cleveland address on being received into fellowship by his neighbors at Sandwich, Massachusetts, July 25, 1891.
10   Cleveland letter to Shan Bissell, October 21, 1891.
11   Parker, 128.
12   Parker, 246–47.
13   John Cogan, *The High Cost of Good Intentions: A History of U.S. Federal Entitlement Programs*, 46.
14   Joanne R. Reittano, *The Tariff Question in the Gilded Age: The Great Debate of 1888*, 128.
15   Irwin, 323.
16   Benjamin Harrison annual message to Congress, December 1, 1890.
17   Cleveland letter to William F. Vilas, September 15, 1889.
18   Lynch, 384.
19   Cleveland letter to L. Clarke Davis, November 5, 1890.
20   Nevins, 466–67.
21   Parker, 151.
22   Gilder, 32–33.
23   Cleveland letter to Dan Lamont, September 13, 1890.
24   Cleveland letter to Shan Bissell, November 8, 1890.
25   Cleveland letter to Shan Bissell, December 12, 1891.
26   McElroy, 313.
27   Parker, 135–40.
28   *New York Tribune*, March 31, 1891.
29   Nevins, 483.
30   *New York World*, April 2, 1892.
31   Cleveland address at the University of Michigan, Ann Arbor, February 22, 1892.
32   Ibid.
33   Nevins, 491.

34   Henry Adams, *The Education of Henry Adams*, 232.

35   *The Campaign Textbook of the Democratic Party for the Presidential Election of 1892*, 17.

36   Cleveland address as chairman of the Democratic Ratification Meeting in the Cooper Union, October 9, 1891.

37   Cleveland address in Tremont Temple, October 31, 1891.

38   Cleveland letter to Abraham B. Tappan, June 30, 1890.

39   Cleveland letter to Shan Bissell, August 10, 1892.

40   Cleveland letter to Shan Bissell, September 4, 1892.

41   Nevins, 497.

42   McElroy, 348.

43   Populist Party Platform of 1892.

44   Lynch, 410–11.

45   Charles W. Calhoun and Arthur M. Schlesinger Jr., *Benjamin Harrison*, 296.

46   Nevins, 508–9.

CHAPTER 12: THE CRASH

1   *Chicago Tribune*, July 6, 1894.

2   Jack Kelly, *The Edge of Anarchy*, 188.

3   Gilder, 109.

4   Lynch, 418.

5   Cleveland letter to L. Clarke Davis, January 25, 1893.

6   Parker, 175.

7   Cleveland letter to the public, May 8, 1893.

8   Nevins, 519.

9   Nevins, 523.

10   Mark Zachary Taylor, *Ideas and Their Consequences: Benjamin Harrison and the Seeds of Economic Crisis, 1889–1893*.

11   Cleveland letter to Governor W. J. Northen, September 25, 1893.

12   Milton Friedman and Anna Jacobson Schwartz, *A Monetary History of the United States, 1867–1960* (National Bureau of Economic Research Publications), 200–201.

13   Nevins, 525.

14   Welch, 116.

15   Gary Richardson and Tim Sablik, "Banking Panics of the Gilded Age," federalreservehistory.org.

16   Nevins, 541.

17   William Jennings Bryan speech on the House floor, August 16, 1893.

18   Nevins, 540.

19   Welch, 126.

20   Douglas A. Irwin, "Higher Tariffs, Lower Revenues? Analyzing the Fiscal Aspects of 'The Great Tariff Debate of 1888,'" *Journal of Economic History* 58, no. 1 (March 1998).

21 Nevins, 574.
22 Ibid.
23 Ibid.
24 Cleveland letter to Everett P. Wheeler, April 16, 1894.
25 Cleveland letter to William L. Wilson, July 2, 1894.
26 "Mr. Gorman's Long Address," *New York Times*, July 24, 1894.
27 Welch, 135.
28 Cleveland letter to Representative Thomas C. Catchings, August 27, 1894.
29 Cleveland veto of Texas Seed Bill, February 16, 1887.
30 Kelly, 59.
31 Kelly, 101.
32 Report on the Chicago Strike of June–July 1894, United States Strike Commission, 32.
33 Ibid., 25.
34 Ibid., 36.
35 Cleveland message regarding U.S. labor force, April 22, 1886.
36 Kelly, 127.
37 Welch, 142.
38 *New York Times*, June 29, 1894.
39 Ibid., 123.
40 *Indianapolis News*, July 7, 1894.
41 Report on the Chicago Strike, 40.
42 Kelly, 142.
43 Nevins, 512.
44 Welch, 142.
45 Writ of Injunction, filed July 2, 1894; Civil Case File 23421, *United States of America v. Eugene V. Debs*, etc. U.S. Circuit Court, Northern District of Illinois, Eastern Division at Chicago.
46 Nevins, 620.
47 Paul Van Dyke, "My Neighbor, Grover Cleveland," *Scribner's Magazine* 81 (1927).
48 Report on the Chicago Strike, 15.
49 Nevins, 622–23.
50 Ibid., 628.
51 Ibid., 213.
52 Presidential proclamation, July 8, 1894.
53 Kelly, 230.
54 Report on the Chicago Strike, 23.
55 Ibid., 14.
56 Governor John P. Altgeld telegraph to Cleveland, July 5, 1894.
57 Cleveland telegraph to Governor John P. Altgeld, July 6, 1894.

CHAPTER 13: HOW WEAK THE STRONGEST MAN

1 Nevins, 522.
2 Ibid.
3 Matthew Algeo, *The President Is a Sick Man: Wherein the Supposedly Virtuous Grover Cleveland Survives a Secret Surgery at Sea and Vilifies the Courageous Newspaperman Who Dared Expose the Truth*, 15.
4 Geoffrey Blodgett, "Ethno-Cultural Realities in Presidential Patronage: Grover Cleveland's Choices," *New York History* 81, no. 2 (2000): 189–210.
5 William Williams Keen, *The Surgical Operations on President Cleveland in 1893*, 30.
6 Ibid., 31.
7 Ibid., 32.
8 Algeo, 71.
9 Keen, 29.
10 Algeo, 80.
11 Algeo, 84.
12 Keen, 33.
13 Keen, 35.
14 Algeo, 86.
15 Ibid., 74.
16 Nevins, 530.
17 Keen, 36.
18 Algeo, 89.
19 Algeo, 91.
20 Keen, 38.
21 Algeo, 94.
22 Keen, 40.
23 Algeo, 115.
24 Robert Lincoln O'Brien, "Grover Cleveland as Seen by His Stenographer: July, 1892–November, 1895," *Proceedings of the Massachusetts Historical Society* 70 (1950): 128–43.
25 Algeo, 105.
26 Ibid., 96
27 Quoted in Keen, 5.
28 Quoted in Keen, 10.
29 Nevins, 533.
30 Algeo, 127–28.
31 Algeo, 150.
32 Algeo, 167–70.
33 Keen, 42.
34 Nevins.
35 Algeo, 185.
36 O'Brien, 134.

37   Algeo, 95.
38   Ibid., 225.
39   Cleveland to Thomas Bayard, September 11, 1893.

CHAPTER 14: THE MORALIST ABROAD

1   Cleveland first inaugural address, March 4, 1885.
2   Nick Cleaver, *Grover Cleveland's New Foreign Policy: Arbitration, Neutrality, and the Dawn of American Empire*, 26.
3   Welch, 170.
4   Ralph S. Kuykendall, *The Hawaiian Kingdom, Vol. 3, 1874–1893*, 369–70.
5   Ibid., 586.
6   John L. Stevens to Secretary John W. Foster, February 1, 1893.
7   Kuykendall, 588.
8   Benjamin Harrison message to the Senate regarding Hawaiian annexation, February 15, 1893.
9   Kuykendall, 615.
10   Cleaver, 27–28.
11   Walter LaFeber, *The New Empire: An Interpretation of American Expansion*, 204.
12   Kuykendall, 623.
13   James H. Blount, *Foreign Relations of the United States, 1894: Affairs in Hawaii*.
14   Walter Q. Gresham, Memorandum, October 18, 1893.
15   Ambassador Willis telegram to Secretary Gresham, November 16, 1893.
16   Willis to Gresham, November 16, 1893.
17   Cleveland special message to Congress, December 18, 1893.
18   Thucydides, *History of the Peloponnesian War*, Chapter XVII.
19   Ibid.
20   "Cleveland and Annexation," *Rifle Reveille*, January 28, 1898.
21   Nevins, 633.
22   Cleaver, 129.
23   Olney to Ambassador Thomas F. Bayard, July 20, 1895.
24   Ibid.
25   Cleveland to Olney, March 3, 1901.
26   Grover Cleveland, *Presidential Problems*, 173.
27   Lord Salisbury to Sir Julian Pauncefote, November 26, 1895.
28   Ibid.
29   Cleveland special message to the Congress, December 17, 1895.
30   Secretary of State Gresham to Ambassador Bayard, July 13, 1894.
31   Parker, 200–201.
32   Olney to Bayard, July 20, 1895.
33   Cleveland, *Presidential Problems*, 205.
34   Parker, 191.
35   Nevins, 641.
36   Nevins, 639.

37   Cleaver, 132.
38   Gilder, 226.

CHAPTER 15: IN DUE TIME

1   Nevins, 650.
2   R. Hal Williams, *Realigning America: McKinley, Bryan, and the Remarkable Election of 1896*, 44.
3   "The Historic 54th Congress," U.S. House of Representatives, Office of the Historian, https://history.house.gov/Historical-Highlights/1851-1900/The-historic-54th-Congress/.
4   Williams, 39.
5   Nevins, 658.
6   Cleveland special message to Congress, January 28, 1895.
7   Nevins, 662.
8   Ibid., 665.
9   Stephen W. Stathis and David C. Huckabee, "Congressional Resolutions on Presidential Impeachment: A Historical Overview," Congressional Research Service, September 16, 1998.
10   Cleveland, *Presidential Problems*, 170.
11   Ibid., 147–48.
12   Cleveland to John S. Mason, May 20, 1895.
13   Nevins, 674.
14   Williams, 44.
15   Williams, 74.
16   Cleveland to L. Clarke Davis, May 14, 1896.
17   Cleveland to Don Dickinson, February 18, 1896.
18   Cleveland to Don Dickinson, March 19, 1896.
19   Cleveland to Don Dickinson, February 18, 1896.
20   Nevins, 698.
21   Cleveland letter to Democratic voters, June 16, 1896.
22   Williams, 80.
23   Ben Tillman address to 1896 Democratic National Convention, July 9, 1896.
24   Nevins, 700.
25   Cleveland to Richard Olney, July 13, 1896.
26   Nevins, 704.
27   Cleveland speech at Princeton's sesquicentennial celebration, October 23, 1896.
28   Cleveland to Senator William F. Vilas, September 5, 1896.
29   Hoke Smith to Cleveland, July 20, 1896.
30   Cleveland to Hoke Smith, August 4, 1896.
31   Williams, 154.
32   Gilder, 138.
33   Cleveland to Richard Olney, July 16, 1896.

34 Cleveland annual message to Congress, December 7, 1896.
35 *New York Times*, December 20, 1896.
36 *Cabinet Diary of William L. Wilson, 1896–1897*, March 4, 1897.
37 McElroy, vol. 2, 255.
38 Cleveland to E. C. Benedict, January 1, 1897.
39 Cleveland to Richard Watson Gilder, January 16, 1897.
40 Cleveland to Richard Watson Gilder, November 20, 1896.

CHAPTER 16: PATHS UNKNOWN

1   John Milton Cooper Jr., *Woodrow Wilson*, locs. 1540–1542.
2   Woodrow Wilson, *Constitutional Government in the United States*, "Ch. 3: The President of the United States."
3   Cooper Jr., locs. 470–471.
4   Paul Van Dyke, "My Neighbor Grover Cleveland," *Scribner's Magazine* 81 (January–June 1927): 350.
5   Cleveland to Richard Olney, June 19, 1897.
6   "Grover Cleveland's Address," *New York Times*, October 26, 1902.
7   "The Presidents of Princeton University—Woodrow Wilson," https://pr .princeton.edu/pub/presidents/wilson/.
8   Cleveland to Andrew Carnegie, January 18, 1908.
9   Nevins, 733–34.
10 Lucian Lamar Knight, *Woodrow Wilson: The Dreamer and the Dream*, 57.
11 McElroy, vol. 2, 259.
12 Cleveland address at the banquet of the Reform Club, New York, April 24, 1897.
13 Cleveland to E. C. Benedict, April 14, 1898.
14 Cleveland to Richard Olney, July 8, 1898.
15 Nevins, 746.
16 Cleveland address at the McKinley memorial services, Princeton, New Jersey, September 13, 1901.
17 Gilder, 181–82.
18 McElroy, vol. 2, 320.
19 Cleveland to Daniel S. Lamont, February 28, 1904.
20 Cleveland to James Smith Jr., June 26, 1904.
21 McElroy, vol. 2, 340.
22 Cleveland to A. B. Farquhar, December 12, 1904.
23 McElroy, vol. 2, 383.
24 Cleveland to Richard Watson Gilder, October 27, 1899.
25 McElroy, vol. 2, 269.
26 *American Magazine*, September 1908.
27 "Would Woman Suffrage Be Unwise?" *Ladies' Home Journal*, October 1905.
28 Cleveland to Wilson S. Bissell, September 16, 1900.
29 McElroy, vol. 2, 259.

30 Cleveland to Richard Watson Gilder, June 20, 1898.
31 Cleveland to Richard Watson Gilder, January 28, 1905.
32 Andrew F. West, "Grover Cleveland: A Princeton Memory," *Century Magazine*, January 1909.
33 Nevins, 741.
34 McElroy, vol. 2, 261.
35 Ibid., 327–28.
36 Nevins, 741.
37 Cleveland to William F. Vilas, June 24, 1904.
38 Nevins, 755.
39 Cleveland to E. C. Benedict, September 14, 1907.
40 Gilder, 230–31.
41 Cleveland to E. C. Benedict, November 27, 1896.
42 McElroy, vol. 2, 385.
43 Williams, 3.
44 McElroy, vol. 2, 385.
45 Nevins, 763–64.

AFTERWORD: "SOMEDAY, I'LL BE BETTER REMEMBERED"

1 Steve Strunsky, "That House You Drove by Across from Dunkin' Donuts? A President Was Born There," https://www.nj.com/essex/2019/09/that-house-you-drove-by-across-from-dunkin-donuts-a-president-was-born-there.html.
2 Mark Twain, *The Autobiography of Mark Twain*, vol. 3, 139, 238.
3 William Howard Taft speech at Grover Cleveland memorial, New York City, March 18, 1909.
4 Woodrow Wilson, "Mr. Cleveland as President," *Atlantic Monthly*, March 1897.
5 Schlesinger poll of Presidential Greatness, 1948.
6 Annie Linskey, "When Will Harriet Tubman Adorn the $20 Bill," *Washington Post*, June 3, 2021.
7 Roberto A. Ferdman, "The Presidents We Remember—And the Ones We've Almost Entirely Forgotten," *Washington Post*, December 1, 2014.
8 Dunlap. 162.
9 Whittaker Chambers, *Witness*, 728.
10 Wilson, "Mr. Cleveland as President."
11 Van Dyke, 352.
12 Gilder, 169.
13 James Madison, *The Federalist Papers No. 10*.
14 Gilder, vii.